FAULTLINES

FAULTLINES

Cultural Materialism
and the Politics of Dissident Reading

ALAN SINFIELD

CLARENDON PRESS • OXFORD

1992

This book has been printed digitally and produced in a standard design
in order to ensure its continuing availability

OXFORD
UNIVERSITY PRESS

Great Clarendon Street, Oxford OX2 6DP

Oxford University Press is a department of the University of Oxford.
It furthers the University's objective of excellence in research, scholarship,
and education by publishing worldwide in

Oxford New York

Athens Auckland Bangkok Bogotá Buenos Aires Cape Town
Chennai Dar es Salaam Delhi Florence Hong Kong Istanbul Karachi
Kolkata Kuala Lumpur Madrid Melbourne Mexico City Mumbai Nairobi
Paris São Paulo Shanghai Singapore Taipei Tokyo Toronto Warsaw
with associated companies in Berlin Ibadan

Oxford is a registered trade mark of Oxford University Press
in the UK and in certain other countries

Published in the United States
by Oxford University Press Inc., New York

© Alan Sinfield

The moral rights of the author have been asserted
Database right Oxford University Press (maker)

Reprinted 2001

ISBN 0-19-811995-X

Contents

	Illustrations	vii
	Preface	ix
ONE	Theaters of War: Caesar and the Vandals	1
TWO	Cultural Materialism, *Othello,* and the Politics of Plausibility	29
THREE	When Is a Character Not a Character? Desdemona, Olivia, Lady Macbeth, and Subjectivity	52
FOUR	Power and Ideology: An Outline Theory and Sidney's *Arcadia*	80
FIVE	*Macbeth:* History, Ideology, and Intellectuals	95
SIX	History and Ideology, Masculinity and Miscegenation: The Instance of *Henry V* *written with Jonathan Dollimore*	109
SEVEN	Protestantism: Questions of Subjectivity and Control	143
EIGHT	Sidney's *Defence* and the Collective-Farm Chairman: Puritan Humanism and the Cultural Apparatus	181
NINE	Tragedy, God, and Writing: Hamlet, Faustus, Tamburlaine	214
	A brief photo-essay on imperialism	252
TEN	Cultural Imperialism and the Primal Scene of U.S. Man	254
	Notes	303
	Index	353

Illustrations

1. "We helped protect the Globe in 1588"   xii

2. "You might be surprised by the theatres we play"
   (Reproduced by kind permission of Royal Ordnance,
   plc)   2

3. "Can you solve this problem faster than Shakespeare?"
   (Reproduced by kind permission of British Mensa Ltd)   27

4 and 5. "A Brief Photo-Essay on Imperialism"

   "Neptune Resigning the Empire of the Seas to
   Britannia," by William Dyce, 1847 (In Queen
   Victoria's Osborne House, Isle of Wight: reproduced
   by permission of English Heritage)   252

   "Thank God for U.S.," postcard on sale to tourists in
   Grenada, West Indies, 1984   253

Preface

Why does one find oneself lingering over prefaces and acknowledgments in literary-academic studies? Hoping, surely, for a handle to the book, a sneak preview of where it is coming from. For the main part of the text will almost certainly manifest high-gloss competence and completeness, and it will be written from the formal, mandarin writing stance required for professional respectability. In the preface and acknowledgments, readers may glimpse something of the activity—the labor, the vicissitudes, the diverse helping hands, the false turns and lucky breaks—through which the apparent facility of the book emerged. Also, though less than hitherto, the mandarin stance tends to smoothe away conflict, rendering alignments discreet and disputes polite; being too plain about what you are doing risks sounding clumsy. In the preface, the writer may expose his or her allegiances, even to the point of confiding selected nuggets of personal history. From such intimations of intimacy, readers may hope to glean something of the author as a fellow-person and, relatedly (for it is hard to be a professional academic today, or a corporate executive, without having your work pervade your life), something of his or her position in the current professional game. Indeed, the latter may well be followed more closely than the argument of the book, though it is not prudent to admit as much. We might term it the higher gossip.

Of course, the personal element in prefatory strategies has to coexist with professional routines—the initial mentor effusively thanked and subtly superseded, the big names dropped alongside the less-well-known associates, who doubtless contributed most; the journals where parts were published (enough of them to show that the work has been recognized, but not so many as to suggest that it is out of date); the grants that supported the work (a mark of establishment approval). Finally, there is the person without whom life would have been point-less (so *that's* who s/he has been seeing). Less often, these days, we have the ultimate solecism: thanking the wife for typing it all.

I hope it will be rapidly and continuously apparent where this book is coming from; and I cultivate personal reference in the text, from time to time, with the aim of disconcerting mandarin assumptions. However, to observe a structure is not necessarily to evade it (that is one thought that runs through this book). I must here record a debt to friends who have read and commented on parts of my work, all too often in not very cogent versions (but hey, what are friends for?): Janet Adelman, John Barrell, Catherine Belsey, Brian Cummings, Jonathan Dollimore, John Drakakis, Jonathan Goldberg, Christopher Highley, Peter Holland, Tony Inglis, Russell Jackson, Ann Rosalind Jones, David Norbrook, Stephen Orgel, David Rogers, Simon Shepherd, Lindsay Smith, Peter Stallybrass. I am grateful also to many colleagues and students at the University of Sussex for innumerable stimulating discussions along the way. Much of the book has been focused and refocused by invitations to speak in various places, where I have always been received with consideration, if not total appro-bation. The chapters that feature Anglo–U.S. professional relations are indebted particularly to invitations to stay at the University of California, Berkeley, to give the Mrs. William Beckman Lectures, and at the University of Alabama, Tuscaloosa, to give the Strode Seminars. I owe a special debt to people I worked and talked with at those places.

Two relatively short chapters (4 and 5) have been published pre-viously. Part of chapter 6, centering upon *Henry V*, has been published before, but the chapter now has a lengthy new section on "Masculinity and Miscegenation."[1] Other chapters are related to other published essays, or to my book *Literature in Protestant England, 1560–1660* (now out of print).[2] However, that work has all been totally rethought and rewritten in the light of recent scholarship and debates over cul-tural materialism, new historicism, the construction of the subject, reader relations, gender and sexualities, and cultural institutions. As-pects of early modern English writing that have preoccupied me for fifteen years or so seem to have arrived at a point of statement. A leading topic is the scope for dissident reading and culture (the term *dissidence* is proposed as preferable to *transgression* or *subversion*). I address this in relation to the legitimating and challenging of authority in the early modern period, considering especially the ideologies and institutions of gender and sexualities, ethnicity, the state, religion, and writing. In the opening chapter and in the longest, placed last, I discuss the cultural and institutional roles of Shakespeare in the United States, interactions between Britain and North America, and the structures of professional Englit.

What else? I have tried to quote from good, accessible, modernized texts; otherwise I have modernized. I am very grateful to Cedric Watts for helping with the proofs. The person-without-whom is Jonathan Dollimore. Oh, and I typed it myself.

We helped
protect
the Globe
in 1588.

Fig. 1. Advertisement for Royal Ordnance, plc (i).

1 Theaters of War: Caesar and the Vandals

April 6, 1974 was in France a national day of mourning for President Pompidou. Roland Barthes wrote:

> All day long, on the radio, "good music" (to my ears): Bach, Mozart, Brahms, Schubert. "Good music," then, is funereal music: an official metonymy unites death, spirituality, and the music of a certain class (on strike days, the radio plays only "bad music"). My neighbor, who ordinarily listens to pop music, doesn't turn on her radio today. Thus we are both excluded from the symbolics of State: she because she does not endure the signifier ("good music"), I because I do not endure the signified (Pompidou's death). Doesn't this double amputation make the music, thus manipulated, into an oppressive discourse?[1]

PLAYING THE GLOBE

"Soviet Gains in Armor/Antiarmor Shape US Master Plan"; "Services Adapt Airborne EW to Cope with Missile Threats"—these are titles of feature articles in the February 1989 issue of *Armed Forces Journal International*. In this context the armaments executive who wants his "news ahead of the pack" (the journal's target reader in its promotion) must have been surprised to see on page 73 a full-page picture purporting to represent the "Globe Theatre." It looks sepia, old, misty, low-tech (engraved), romantic, even sentimental; possibly the kind of print the executive might put on his office wall to show off his culture; a contrast with the business rather than a part of it.[2] However, the legend proclaims a connection: "We helped protect the Globe in 1588." Turning the page, the executive finds a more reassuring scene: a double spread showing a feast of modern weaponry, all very much in action.

1

You Might Be Surprised By The Theatres We Play.

Since Shakespeare's work played at the Globe Theatre in 1588, Royal Ordnance's products have been in action in every major event of Britain's military history.

Today, we serve every theater of military operations. In the air. On land. And at sea.

We design and manufacture a complete range of weapon systems and sub-systems; as well as the reliable munitions which made our reputation.

And we're using this comprehensive experience in cooperation with American companies to meet the demanding requirements of the U.S. Army, Navy, Air Force, and Marines.

We are involved in everything from ground attack weapons and air-combat missiles to infantry weapons, artillery systems, specialist combat vehicles, missile systems, torpedo warheads, and mines.

Current program work is as diverse as insensitive munitions, low signature and liquid propellants, mine clearing line charges, intercom systems, future mortar systems and their ammunition, low recoil force guns, reactive armors, and lightweight howitzer developments.

After 400 years, Royal Ordnance still plays the Globe. All of it. Thanks to partnerships born in tradition and designed for excellence.

Three panels in vivid color feature air, land, and sea operations; they are congested and overflow towards the right; the whole ensemble points towards the fourth panel and the headline that transforms catachresis into sense. Of course, it is a *theater of war*; as the headline says, "You might be surprised by the theaters we play." But the connection is specific: "Since Shakespeare's work played at the Globe Theatre in 1588, Royal Ordnance products have been in action in every major event of Britain's military history." This is true: the Royal Ordnance Company is a British weapons manufacturer deriving from the royal munitions factory and store of earlier centuries; in Queen Elizabeth I's time, it had quarters in the Tower of London, a store in the Minories nearby, and an artillery yard beyond Bishopsgate. Royal Ordnance did not help protect the Globe Theatre in 1588 because the Globe was not built until 1599, but it did help defend English interests worldwide (for that is part of the pun) from the Spanish Armada. Through the centuries of the British Empire, Royal Ordnance contributed to killing innumerable people around the globe.

Nowadays the empire is not what it was, and there are not so many opportunities for Britain to fight with ships and planes, other than as a U.S. satellite. Perhaps that is partly why the Thatcher government privatized Royal Ordnance in 1987: it is no longer credible for the British state to maintain an organization to supply it with a system of modern weaponry.[3] So, in February 1989, Royal Ordnance found itself exposed fully to the chilly blasts of private enterprise; and hence the advertisement. The profit these days is mostly in selling to dictatorial regimes that sustain themselves through repressing their citizenry and menacing their neighbors. In 1989, a year before the Iraqi invasion of Kuwait and despite an ostensible arms embargo, Ordnance was among the exhibitors at the Baghdad arms fair. In that year, and with encouragement from the British government's Department of Trade and Industry, Ordnance supplied strips of explosives retardant, necessary to help propel large rockets, to a middleman who sent them to Iraq.[4] In 1991 British Aerospace, now Ordnance's parent company, reported a 62 percent rise in profits from weaponry and declared itself in a strong position to take advantage of the "opportunities expected to emerge in the Middle East after the Gulf War."[5]

Despite such opportunities, the weapons business is an uncertain one for a British manufacturing base enfeebled by a decade of Thatcherism and subject to international developments over which it has no influence (on shipments to Iraq, the Trade and Industry minister advised that "if the political overtones of the Iraq/Iran conflict change, e.g. if the US becomes more supportive of one side than at present, then the current order may change").[6] Although the advertisement pictures ships and planes, the text indicates that Royal Ordnance is actually working on a sensibly unpretentious range of components, which it hopes to combine with the products of other firms. The special pitch in the advertisement is collaborations with U.S. companies. "Partners in Excellence," it says, with British and U.S. flags side by side. Ordnance may be a small company but it has tradition and excellence: "After 400 years, Royal Ordnance still plays the Globe. All of it. Thanks to partnerships born in tradition and designed for excellence." And the ultimate witness to those where Britain is concerned is Shakespeare. The Globe is indeed famous all round the globe; it is the part of English achievement that still flourishes; the best-known "royal" institution after the monarchy is the Royal Shakespeare Company. For U.S. entrepreneurs, it may yet recall the power that blasted out a worldwide empire, once including Iraq; once even North America.

So the military-industrial complex is not unrelated to cultural power, at least in the mind of a copywriter (who probably majored in English). Yet cultural and military-economic power are not simply aligned. In fact, the advertiser's strategy of surprise is quite risky; too much tradition is a dangerous thing. Knowledge of the Ordnance in Elizabethan times would certainly disturb the target reader of the advertisement. It was honeycombed with corruption—stores were improperly sold off, balances put to private uses, and kickbacks extracted from purveyors. An enquiry found losses from fraud totaling as much as £100,000; the Clerk of the Ordnance had to repay nearly £2,000. "The defeat of the Armada might have been even more conclusive," E. K. Chambers observes, "but for a shortage of ammunition in the English ships."[7] It was no better when the Earl of Essex became master in 1597—he saw the office merely as a chance to gain control of the military apparatus so that he could set up adventures like the disastrous search for the Spanish treasure fleet in the Azores. Such a tradition is dangerously close to the weapons procurement scandals reported today; not the kind of thing of which Royal Ordnance wants to remind, say, Lockheed or McDonnell Douglas.

However, the copywriter evidently intends to play upon a disequilibrium—*"you might be surprised* that we design and manufacture a complete range of weapon systems and sub-systems." Notice the spellings—"theater of military operations," but "Globe Theatre": that's tradition for you, they hang on to their quaint old way of writing (it has to be an English major)! It is a surprising strategy, for the link with Shakespeare and olden times does not suggest high-tech competence; it risks the thought that the British army might still be equipped with pikes and halberds, that British technology might be old-fashioned.

Furthermore, the kind of traditional excellence that is associated with Shakespeare is widely regarded as transcending physical conflict, technology, and politics. As John Fekete puts it, "The central problematic of the tradition is structured by questions of unity and equilibrium, of order and stability. From the beginning, but increasingly systematically, the tradition embraces the 'whole' and structures a totality without struggle and historical movement."[8] To many people, Shakespeare represents art and spiritual nobility, and they might well seem incompatible with the details of weapons procurement and killing all those people. This was not a problem of principle in Elizabethan times. William Painter was Clerk of the Ordnance from 1560 to 1594, and he was the compiler of *The Palace of Pleasure* (1566–67), a handy quarry of stories for English writers. For most of this period the Earl of Warwick was Master of the Ordnance, and he anticipated the revival of aristocratic patronage of music by employing Thomas Whythorne in 1556 (though they parted when the earl did not pay the promised annuity).[9] In 1585 Sir Philip Sidney became Joint Master with Warwick. High culture did not seem incompatible with weaponry (though in fact a piece of ordnance destroyed the Globe Theatre, which burned down after the firing of a cannon during a performance of *Henry VIII;* some of the smoldering wadding lodged in the thatched roof— probably after 375 years they have found ways of preventing that).

But today the Shakespeare connection is challenging. It could undermine, rather than validate, the ambitions of the weapons company. The potential gain from the advertiser's point of view, which makes this risk worthwhile, is *a legitimation of imperial enterprise.* For, as British cultural critics have shown, Shakespeare's achievement has been made to symbolize a supposed imperial English destiny to civilize the whole world. The Gulf, for instance; Thomas Carlyle declared: "Even in Arabia, as I compute, Mahomet will have exhausted himself and become obsolete, while this Shakespeare . . . may still be young;—while this Shakespeare may still pretend to be a Priest of Mankind, of Arabia as of other places, for unlimited periods to come!" At the time of the Falklands/Malvinas expedition, G. Wilson Knight reiterated his belief in "the Shakespearean vision" of "the British Empire as a precursor, or prototype, of world-order."[10] So Shakespeare's authority may be designed to work with distinctive subtlety in the mind of the company president—not at the point where he checks the figures on the most economical "low signature and liquid propellants" (perhaps for Iraqi rockets), but in that weakened moment of dawn waking when he wonders *what it is all for*. Then the slogan glimmers through his consciousness: "We helped protect the Globe in 1588" ... and later that morning he signs the contract with Royal Ordnance—in order to keep the world free for the performance of Shakespeare.

Royal Ordnance presents itself through Shakespeare and tradition because they are what Britain has left to sell. But even British priority in Shakespeare is doubtful—caught up in the long-term transfer of imperial power from the United Kingdom to the United States. Recent work, by Lawrence Levine, Don Wayne, and Michael Bristol in particular, has begun to trace how, through the nineteenth century and into the twentieth, North American commentators staked their own claim to Shakespeare—and hence to the civilization that seems to justify imperial domination (see chapter 10). Another concern in the present study is U.K.-U.S. relations; its writing derives partly from visits to North American universities (when Philip Sidney became Joint Master of the Ordnance, he straightaway used his credit to supply a "heroical design of invading and possessing America").[11] While Shakespeare remains important for Englishness, academic study of his work is dominated by U.S. scholars and critics. The United States is a giant economic and military power, and this puts resources into the university system and gives immense international kudos to the "American" way of doing things. J. Hillis Miller has made the point with respect to literary theory. "America has become the center of technological and economic 'power,' " Miller says. "Although literary theory may have its origin in Europe, we export it in a new form, along with other American 'products', all over the world—as we do many of our scientific and technological inventions," he adds cheerfully, "for example the atom bomb."[12]

Of course, U.S. weapons manufacture has its own tradition and excellence and scarcely needs Royal Ordnance, and U.S. scholarship and criticism also excel. In new historicism, recently, the retrieval of recondite historical materials, the subtlety and rigor of textual analysis, and the audacious scale of the overarching ideas must be seen as a major advance in modern intellectual possibilities. The present study is not a dispute with new historicism, which is not, anyway, a single approach but a bundle of preoccupations diversely elaborated (hence in part the crudeness of most attempted critiques). My strategy is to question, firm up, and develop certain tendencies in new historicism as they appear alongside and in interaction with a cultural-materialist project.

Apart from better resourcing, the reason for the quality of new historicists' work is that they really believe in literary research, whereas cultural materialists are beset by the question of what it is all for; to the latter, professional accomplishment is not enough. (Britons who believe in literary research for itself tend to be of the old Oxford-gentlemanly, dogged/dilettante schools.) Hence the attention cultural materialists give the institutions of culture, including the Englit business: it seems necessary to consider the general implications of intellectual work (whereas some prominent U.S. professors are happy to declare that there are none; see p. 289 below). For many British literary critics, including feminists and affiliates of ethnic and sexual minorities, the breakthrough of the late 1970s was less into theory and more away from formalism; in response to the disintegration of the postwar political consensus, it was into the possibility of relating English teaching and writing to left-wing political concerns. This has entailed violating the decorum of the Englit discourse, which, in both its gentlemanly/ladylike (British) mode and its professional-technical (U.S.) mode, has been constructed precisely in ways that make explicit political reference seem inappropriate, out of order, clumsy, improper. To politicized British critics, therefore, the very excellence achieved by North American academics may effect a kind of blinkering; sophistication, cleverness, abstruseness, difficulty, and professionalism screen out the wider culture. (However, we are now getting British graduate students who seem to manage the best of all worlds.)

While the professionalized U.S. discourse, pace William Bennett and E. D. Hirsch, Jr., can probably assimilate politicized criticism without much strain ["Cultural materialists? Don't we have one of those?—Hire one!"], in Britain, precisely because Englit is supposed to authorize so much more in the culture at large, incoherent frenzies are still aroused at the bad manners with which cultural materialists presume to intrude their impertinent concerns into the Shakespearean temple. During the summer in which this was written, the columns of the *London Review of Books* were clamorous with correspondence provoked by Terence Hawkes's remarking that new editions of Malcolm Evans's *Signifying Nothing* and Jonathan Dollimore's *Radical Tragedy* have appeared. James Wood writes to say that the work of cultural materialists is "predictable" and "sinister, in that it denies Shakespeare the freedom to dissent, to struggle with history." It is "standard," he says, for cultural materialists to regard Shakespeare's text as "merely the poor sponge that soaks up the various historical, ideological and social discourses of the day."[13] But Wood invents the enemy he wants to attack. It is pointed out in reply that, as Hawkes said, cultural materialism "sets out to judge *the degree to which* the drama *was or was not* complicit with the powers of the state"; that *Political Shakespeare* (edited by Dollimore and myself) has this as a running question; and that Dollimore's title, *Radical Tragedy* shows his investment in the argument that certain of Shakespeare's plays demystified and hence challenged state power.[14] But Wood cannot hear this reply; even the posing of questions about the politics of the Shakespeare business is sufficient to send him into a panic reassertion of the "freedom" of Shakespeare. For how can we market Royal Ordnance, not to speak of Stratford-upon-Avon, if Shakespeare is not maintained as a cultural token transcending political considerations?

It has become fashionable to begin by analyzing an obliquely relevant picture. Several of the preoccupations that have engaged me for a decade and more, and that run through this book, are broached in my opening. It is designed to epitomize a way of apprehending the strategic organizations of texts—both the modes by which they produce plausible stories and construct subjectivities, and the faultlines and breaking points through which they enable dissident reading. And it focuses institutions as well as texts, anticipating study of the cultural apparatuses that arrange writing and theater in early modern England and the modern world, and of their relations with other institutions (such as the church) that tend partly to legitimate state violence but may be bent partly to other purposes. The unstable juxtaposition of cultural and military-industrial discourses in my picture is typical of the uneven and changing relations between economic, political, military, and cultural power. It is the project of ideology to represent such relations as harmonious and coherent, so effacing contradiction and conflict; and the project of cultural materialists to draw attention to this. Much of the importance of Raymond Williams derives from the fact that at a time when Althusser and Foucault were being read in some quarters as establishing ideology and/or power in a necessarily unbreakable continuum, Williams argued the co-occurrence of subordinate, residual, emergent, alternative, and oppositional cultural forces alongside the dominant, in varying relations of incorporation, negotiation, and resistance.[15] Cultural materialism seeks to discern the scope for dissident politics of class, race, gender, and sexual orientation, both within texts and in their roles in cultures.

These are topics of some importance if "freedom" is to be detached from the ideologies that have appropriated it and to be more widely actualized in human societies. Of course, power resides with the collaborators and customers of Royal Ordnance, with their specialist combat vehicles and lightweight howitzer developments. Even so, weapons still depend on the authority to use them—the cannon in *Henry VIII* was not fired in battle but to add symbolic weight to the king's entrance. In many countries, at some time, the state and the military have had to yield when they have lost sufficient popular legitimation; conversely, in the "Western democracies," a major question is how right-wing governments get installed through the ballot. The conferral of cultural authority is a principal role of Shakespeare in our societies: he may be made to underwrite state bellicosity, or perhaps to say something different.

JULIUS CAESAR: ACTING PRECEDENTS

In summer 1988, thanks to the financial assistance of the National Endowment for the Humanities, which no doubt was looking for tradition and excellence, Dollimore and I were fortunate enough to be invited to the University of California at Santa Cruz to talk about Shakespeare. The condition was that we address the plays being performed in the theater there. I agreed to discuss *Julius Caesar*—it was a set text when I was a student, so I thought I would be all right. But coming back to the play, I found I didn't care for it much. I tried identifying with the characters in the way traditionally advised, but that hardly helped—senators and commanders, with their triumphs, victories, enterprises, and ensigns, sound unpleasantly like the brands of company cars supplied to Royal Ordnance middle management. Usually, in Shakespeare, the common humanity of such figures is supposed to shine through details of status, but I could not see it; and anyway, as a cultural materialist I don't believe in common humanity. However, as Catherine Belsey observes, *Julius Caesar* does stage political structures alternative to absolutism, raising questions of tyranny, sedition, and freedom that were difficult to handle in English history plays, so the play should offer some scope for political negotiation.[16] Like many Shakespearean plays, it is about gaining legitimation for the exercise of state violence. The wars initiated by powerful men—Pompey, Caesar, Brutus, Cassius, Antony, and Octavius—frame the action, but in between the issue is how people may be persuaded to accept rival authority claims.

Since the occasion was a theater festival, I went to the stage history. This confirmed what I had expected (funny how often that happens in literary study): that theater people through the centuries have got *Julius Caesar* to make sense for them by adjusting, often violently, what appears to be the tendency of the received text. Shakespeare is a powerful cultural token, such that what you want to say has more authority if it seems to come through him. That is how Shakespeare comes to speak to people at different times: the plays have been continuously reinterpreted in attempts to coopt the bard for this or that worldview. This is not surprising or illegitimate; it is a key practice through which cultural contest proceeds. In the eighteenth century, people experienced very reasonable anxieties about the blatantly unjust system of rule in Europe and North America, and *Julius Caesar* was understood as addressing despotism and the rule of the gentry through Parliament. Generally it was appropriated as a blast against autocracy, with Brutus as the hero of patrician oligarchy and Caesar as a ranting, strutting villain. Francis Gentleman believed in 1770 that the play inculcates "one of the noblest principles that actuates the human mind, the love of national liberty."[17] In fact, the text was cut, rewritten, and extended to produce this reading. The most awkward incidents were the killing of Cinna the Poet (3.3) and Octavius and Antony deciding who shall be murdered (4.1): they seem to present particularly discreditable consequences of the killing of Caesar, and hence were usually omitted.[18] And since it seemed unfair and superstitious that the noble and reasonable Brutus should be afflicted with Caesar's Ghost, they cut that as well. Productions in the American colonies shared the identification with the patricians—they thought they were as civilized as the classical Romans (well, they had Roman institutions like oligarchy and slavery). In the revolutionary period, *Julius Caesar* figured the struggle against English domination; in 1770 the play was advertised for the theater as "The noble struggles for liberty by that renowned patriot Marcus Brutus." Abigail Adams wrote to her husband John: "There is a tide in the affairs of men" and sometimes signed herself "Portia"; Thomas Jefferson's commonplace book begins with passages from the play. As president, George Washington is said to have staged an amateur production of *Julius Caesar* in the garret of his executive mansion in Philadelphia, with himself as Brutus.[19] Conversely, in England, although the play had been popular as alluding to British liberties, it was not performed at all from the time of the American Revolution, through the French Revolution, until well into the nineteenth century. The writer Mrs. Elizabeth Inchbald explained in 1808 that it had been not "advisable" to stage it:

> When men's thoughts are deeply engaged on public events, historical occurrences, of a similar kind, are only held proper for the contemplation of such minds as know how to distinguish, and to appreciate, the good and evil with which they abound. Such discriminating judges do not compose the whole audience of a playhouse; therefore, when the circumstances of certain periods make certain incidents of history most interesting, those are the very seasons to interdict their exhibition.[20]

Some of the less discriminating might have been inspired to stage their own revolution. Later, speeches from *Julius Caesar* were valued in the British Labor movement—the communist trades unionist Tom Mann was still roaring out in old age: "I had as lief not be as live to be / In awe of such a thing as I myself."[21]

For the centenary of U.S. independence in 1875–76, republican sentiments were combined with the nineteenth-century enthusiasm for spectacle. According to a contemporary record, the end of *Julius Caesar* was elaborated with the funeral pyre of Brutus:

> The lights of the distant city glitter on the hillside, and the army, marshalled in the foreground, looks strange and weird with its many torches and the reflected lights on helmets, shields, and spears. In the centre of the stage is the funeral-pyre, which is presently lighted; and then, amid music, a wild confusion of lights and mysterious shadows, warlike ranks with banners and glittering arms, and a leaping blaze in the centre, the curtain falls.[22]

As many as four hundred extras were used (almost on the scale of the battle scene in the Royal Ordnance advertisement; both reporters and airmen present at the initial, euphoric bombing of Baghdad in January 1991 said it was like fireworks on July 4). The idea may have been to recall the twelve-day funeral procession of Abraham Lincoln in 1865, some of it at night time "in the flare of torches and gaslights," with a guard of honor of prominent army officers and detachments from scores of regiments; in New York as the bells tolled midnight, "a German chorus of some seventy voices commenced suddenly to sing the *Integer vitae*." (At the rear in New York came a body of freed slaves, allowed to march after an appeal to the secretary of war, though it was feared they would provoke disorder.)[23] One opposition senator said it was all like "the crafty skill of Mark Anthony in displaying to the Roman people the bloody mantle of Caesar," but for many people Lincoln was the freedom-loving Brutus.[24] Or perhaps the idea was that Brutus's funeral would dispel other images of mass dedication to freedom: the demonstrations of farmers and workers in every part of the Union that marked the "red scare" of 1873–78. Strikers, the unemployed, socialists, and eight-hour campaigners, inspired by the Paris Commune and energized by economic recession, rallied in their thousands. In very many cases, they were brutally assaulted by militia and police.[25]

Modern productions of *Julius Caesar* usually take it to be about the personal qualities and dilemmas of the patricians. This liberal approach works by centralizing Brutus as the intellectual tempted out of his study, where he has maintained a noble integrity, and into the corrupting public world. It has an appeal for academics (we think of the colleague whom we urge to become dean of faculty so as to resist the autocratic college president, and how he or she becomes bewildered or autocratic in turn). For Orson Welles in 1937, the play was subtitled "Death of a Dictator": it was about "the eternal, impotent, ineffectual, fumbling liberal; the reformer who wants to do something about things but doesn't know how and gets it in the neck in the end." Rather gleefully, Welles saw Brutus as "the bourgeois intellectual, who, under a modern dictatorship would be the first to be put up against a wall and shot." The received text was thoroughly reorganized to produce this reading. In the drama of liberal anguish, the death of Cinna the Poet suddenly becomes crucial, for the danger from the populace seems as great as that from the dictator. Welles played Cinna's murder to big effect, augmenting it with lines from *Coriolanus*, believing that it is the crude, insensitive people that cause fascism—"the hoodlum element you find in any big city after a war, a mob that is without the stuff that makes them intelligently alive, a lynching mob, the kind of mob that gives you a Hitler or a Mussolini."[26] The theme of liberal impotence surfaced also in the 1953 film directed by Joseph L. Mankiewicz, with cautiously unobtrusive reference to the confusion of the well-intentioned in the face of the McCarthyite House Un-American Activities Committee. Mankiewicz had been elected president of the Screen Directors' Guild in 1950 on a platform of resistance to requiring members to swear that they were not communists. While Mankiewicz was absent in Europe, however, the right-wing Cecil B. deMille put through a mandatory oath and suggested that Mankiewicz was a "pinko," a "fellow traveller," an unreliable intellectual. After caucus meetings distinctly like those of the Brutus-Cassius conspiracy, Mankiewicz managed to preserve his position—but he felt it necessary to require the loyalty oaths anyway.[27]

Another liberal version was offered by Minos Volanakis in his London Old Vic production in 1962: Brutus is "the very embodiment of the ideals that fired the Renaissance and fostered modern liberalism," Volonakis said, asserting that the project of the play is "to examine and exhaust the possibility of salvation through politics."[28] Michael Kahn, director of the Shakespeare Theater, Ontario, produced a comparable version at the time of the Nixon-McGovern presidential election of 1972. Kahn says he wanted to do *Julius Caesar* then because he sympathized with McGovern but thought Nixon would make a stronger president; and that this was like Brutus and Caesar. Thinking of the slaughter in the Vietnam War and recent assassinations, Kahn asked himself, somewhat ambitiously, "Do you go out and bomb Hitler, do you kill Richard Nixon? . . . violence as a political act concerned me, and I continually faced my ambivalences about it."[29] Despite his respect for Caesar/Nixon, Kahn's "ambivalences" align him with his liberal Brutus; Kahn found politics "an almost insoluble problem to deal with," so in *Julius Caesar* "everybody was right and everybody was wrong" (p. 76). This is the dominant attitude among modern humanities intellectuals. At the same time, usually, the private individual is validated as against nasty public politics. Trevor Nunn, at the Royal Shakespeare Company in 1972, found in *Julius Caesar* "the theme of the disparity and friction between private and public. I mean private morality and public necessity." And again: the play is about "the requirements of a system of good government, of world politics as opposed to what it is that's rich and rare individually in people. Individuals are destroyed."[30] Arthur Humphreys in his Oxford edition of the play admires the BBC/Time-Life version (1978) which "went less for Romans or politicians than for human beings, caught in an impetuous action" (p. 71).

Such an interpretation plainly tends to discourage political engagement. To be sure, there is no system of government that will not require unremitting vigilance, and in many circumstances the cost of dissidence may be high. But it is not constructive to suggest that if you try to make the world better you will only sacrifice your integrity and probably make things worse. Nor is the individual outside politics. To the contrary, "the individual" is an ideological concept, and the whole idea of anything being outside politics is a political idea tending to inhibit understanding and action. *Julius Caesar* in fact raises these questions, in that Brutus is not, of course, a humanistic intellectual in any modern sense, but a senator, a senior member of the governing elite. Insofar as he is also a philosopher, that is because intellectual concerns were not believed to be incompatible with government at the time of either Brutus or Shakespeare (consider Cicero and Francis Bacon). It is characteristic of our cultures, not theirs, to validate art and philosophy by denying their connection with political power (such that Shakespeare and Royal Ordnance now constitute a provocative juxtaposition).

Although the received text of *Julius Caesar* encourages liberal attention to the personal qualities of the patricians, it also allows us to see other factors in the political process. The action is a feast for the new historicist idea of power as display:[31] set pieces alternate with sudden histrionic appeals, especially to the plebeians, for Caesar's success has problematized the prevailing conventions of authority in the Roman state. At the start, the tribunes Flavius and Marullus are persuading the people not to celebrate Caesar's triumph; they remove his trophies from statues. "Leave no ceremony out," Caesar says (1.2.11), perhaps thinking to stage his coronation. He is the arch performer in the theater of power—the people "clap him and hiss him, according as he pleas'd and displeas'd them, as they use to do the players in the theatre" (1.2.255–58). Brutus has a similarly theatrical notion of political activity: "Let not our looks put on our purposes," he tells his fellow conspirators, "But bear it as our Roman actors do" (2.1.225–26). He assumes that popular support must be won by suitable representation, and he wants to manage the killing of Caesar such that "appearing to the common eyes, / We shall be call'd purgers, not murderers" (2.1.179–80). Legitimacy in Rome depends on theatrical flare in public relations. The first move after the assassination must be to "Run hence, proclaim, cry it about the streets" (3.1.79); hence the importance of the rival speeches of Brutus and Antony in the forum. The battle at Philippi is determined by the loyalties of the armies and the patricians' apprehensions about them. Octavius (a great patron of the arts) is to alter this pattern by suppressing popular rights and instituting an even more elaborate apparatus of theatrical representation, posing as a god in an imperial cult of personality. Such a sequence has occurred in many countries.

These aspects of the play enable us to glimpse a *Julius Caesar* with a different politics to those so far discussed, one that would center upon the relations between the people and those who scheme to gain their allegiance. The problem is how to bring it out, given that the received text seems mainly concerned with the patricians, with but slight, and slighting, role for the plebeians. One indication of the extent to which Shakespearean interpretation is not a quest for the true reading but a historically located cultural convention, or rather bundle of conventions, is the wider freedom that theater directors are customarily allowed. Since my talk at Santa Cruz was to accompany a theater festival, I thought I might commandeer some of the director's larger license, releasing myself from the demand of literary criticism that lines that seem to resist your reading must somehow be incorporated or explained away. Inspired by the diverse renderings of *Julius Caesar* on the stage, I felt emboldened to devise a reworking of my own—hoping to find a new enthusiasm for the play, and thereby to counter the fear of Boris Ford, in the *London Review of Books* correspondence (July 12, 1990), that cultural materialists rarely read one of Shakespeare's plays "because they find them profoundly moving, or spiritually restoring, or simply strangely enjoyable."

An obvious strategy would be to undermine the status of the patricians by making them appear analogous to stupid and corrupt modern politicians. We might make the theatrical Caesar resemble Ronald Reagan—who, after all, was identified by Gore Vidal as the "acting president" and by Michael Rogin as *"Ronald Reagan," The Movie*. Both leaders have perplexed commentators by combining star-wars fantasies of omnipotence with bumbling, forgetfulness, and superstition that might or might not be strategic.[32] It would be important not to suggest that others of the ruling elite are more honest or capable than Caesar (that is the liberal move); they are parts of the same gang (they all turn out to be superstitious). However, one drawback with such a comparison between *Julius Caesar* and the modern political situation lurks in the region of U.S.–U.K. power relations. For if imperial Rome is the United States then Britain, as in Roman times, is a remote outpost of empire; and hence a candidate, like Shakespearean Egypt, for a tourist theme park where the imperial power can fantasize an exotic other (for Alexandria read, say, Stratford). Gruesomely, this gives us an equivalent to Cleopatra—one held in awe by all for her daunting presence but fatal, as Antony finds, if her policies are followed: Margaret Thatcher.[33]

CREATIVE VANDALISM

The other drawback with such a version of *Julius Caesar* is that ridiculing the governing elite, which of course has often been done, maintains its centrality; in the modern equivalent, it maintains the

media fiction that Washington infighting is the necessary and adequate
site of political activity. To represent the potential of other forces in
the state, it will be necessary to engineer a radical shift in perspective.
Given the license of the theater director, I would move the plebeians
to the center, challenging directly the tendency of criticism to see
them as the eternal mob and the tribunes as rabble-rousers (even
Annabel Patterson, who argues for a positive representation of the
citizens in *Coriolanus*, sees them in this way).[34] The received text
certainly licenses such a view. Casca finds Cassius persuasive when he
blames the people for Caesar's dominance:

> And why should Caesar be a tyrant then?
> Poor man! I know he would not be a wolf,
> But that he sees the Romans are but sheep;
> He were no lion, were not Romans hinds.
> Those that with haste will make a mighty fire
> Begin it with weak straws. What trash is Rome,
> What rubbish, and what offal, when it serves
> For the base matter to illuminate
> So vile a thing as Caesar!
>
> (1.3.103–11)

Upper-class rule is necessary, it is suggested, because the people are
likely to endorse tyranny. But "the mob" is not an adequate concept
with which to handle the roles of the plebeians, even in the received
text. To be sure, some of them perpetrate unreasonable violence, but
to a tiny extent in comparison with the patricians in their battles. The
play in fact allows us to see that at other times the people are lively,
independent, shrewd, and sensible.

The key figures are the tribunes, Marullus and Flavius. An attractive
reading is to see the plebeians in the opening scene as unruly Bakh-
tinian revelers, the possessors of a traditional popular wisdom that is
put down by the tribunes. Richard Wilson considers the tribunes'
ordering the plebeians back to work in the light of Christopher Hill's
thesis that puritans attacked popular festivities in order to control the
emerging work force.[35] However, it is a mistake to abstract carnival
from historical conditions, to regard it as an absolute political quality.
As Wilson shows, it was not a single, unitary discourse, "but a symbolic system over which continuous struggle to wrest its meaning was
waged by competing ideologies"; the ceremonies are made to feed
into Caesar's coronation and the carnivalesque "becomes a model of
authoritarian populism" (pp. 42, 36). With this in mind, I would
activate a fact that is widely overlooked, and that admittedly, is

scarcely registered in the Shakespearean play—namely, that the tribunes, historically, were not "ruling-class" spokesmen, but the chosen leaders of the plebeians.[36] Their election by open popular ballot was, at least in potential, a democratic feature of the republican polity, a major constitutional check upon patrician power. In 81 B.C. the dictator Sulla undermined the role of the tribunes when they "revived the dormant sovranty of the People"; Pompey restored their rights in 70 B.C.[37] So in the opening scene of *Julius Caesar*, Marullus and Flavius are understandably dismayed by their constituents' enthusiasm for Caesar and remind them of their erstwhile support for Pompey. The subversive vitality of the Cobbler is very well, but if popular rights are to be defended, it has to be blended with analysis, organization, and strategy; party discipline has to be maintained. Machiavelli argues the need for plebeian leaders: as an "excited crowd," the populace may become "cowardly and weak," he says, so "it should at once make one of its members a leader so that he may correct this defect, keep the populace united, and look to its defence; as did the Roman plebs, when, after the death of Virginia they quitted Rome and for safety's sake appointed twenty of their members as tribunes." Machiavelli adds that in hundreds of years, the Roman populace "did not make four elections of which it had to repent."[38]

In *Julius Caesar*, the tribunes' political program is vastly superior to that generated among the ruling elite, for instead of plotting to murder Caesar, they exhort the people to act openly, constitutionally, and collectively against the alterations to the constitution proposed by Caesar's party. They urge them to display signs of their crafts, for class solidarity, and to organize a counter-demonstration against Caesar's triumph:

> Go, go, good countrymen, and for this fault
> Assemble all the poor men of your sort;
> Draw them to Tiber banks, and weep your tears
> Into the channel, till the lowest stream
> Do kiss the most exalted shores of all.
>
> (1.1.56–60)

That concluding image, of the popular demonstration flooding the political system, such that the "lowest" people achieve a significant voice, proves optimistic, but the people do, in fact, exercise their influence against Caesar's undermining of traditional rights. Even through the snobbish and disdainful (funny) speech of Casca, it is clear that the plebeians cheer Caesar when he reluctantly *refuses* the crown offered him by Antony:

He put it the third time by; and still as he refus'd it, the rabblement hooted, and clapp'd their chopt hands, and threw up their sweaty night-caps, and uttered such a deal of stinking breath because Caesar refus'd the crown, that it had, almost, choked Caesar; for he swounded, and fell down at it.

(1.2.239–45)

Contrary to the idea implicit in some new historicist writing, the people are not easily fooled by the theater of state that the patricians clumsily improvise. Caesar is forced into improvisation and offers his throat for the cutting, perceiving that "the common herd was glad he refus'd the crown" (1.2.260–64). Mark Hunter's assertion in his 1900 edition of the play that the plebeians are "thoroughly monarchical in sentiment" is presumably owing to political blindness; strangely, Arthur Humphreys endorses it in his recent Oxford edition (p. 97). It is the senators who want to make Caesar king (1.3.85–88, 2.2.93–94).

However, we hear shortly, "Marullus and Flavius, for pulling scarfs off Caesar's images, are put to silence" (1.2.282–83). This is a move against the political power of the people—in North's Plutarch we read that in accusing "the tribunes of the people," Caesar "spake also against the people, and called them Bruti and Cumani, to wit, beasts and fools."[39] Hereafter, the substance of the play, in my version, is the destruction of plebeian political institutions and consciousness. Deprived of their leaders, the people gradually become pawns and victims in the power struggle of the ruling elite. In the forum scene, they plan responsibly, at the start, to evaluate the speeches of Brutus and Antony:

FIRST PLEBEIAN: I will hear Brutus speak.

SECOND PLEBEIAN: I will hear Cassius, and compare their reasons, When severally we hear them rendered.

(3.2.8–10)

But they get manipulated. Not allowing the people a serious stake in the system turns a few of them into the louts who murder Cinna. The moral for us is that lower-class and other dissident political groupings should be strengthened to resist the encroachments of the governing elite. Most of the play therefore, in my version, is the agon of the tribunes: they suffer as the people are exploited. I would represent this by having Flavius and Marullus taken, when they are arrested, one to each side of the stage. There they would be detained for the rest of the action, being tortured by the patricians' officers—all, of course, in the usual

Royal Shakespeare Company kinky black PVC, chains, and construction-site helmets. At moments of special frustration in the political process, the tormenters would intensify their activity so that the tribunes shriek out in pain. They are tortured, figuratively, by the destruction of plebeian institutions and consciousness.

Strangely enough, retaining Flavius and Marullus to the side of the stage as significant spectators is not altogether unhistorical. Thomas Kyd's *Spanish Tragedy* has Don Andrea similarly placed, watching and suffering as the action of the play threatens the people he loves. Revenge assures him that it will all work out: "Here sit we down to see the mystery, / And serve for Chorus in this tragedy."[40] They sit throughout between the audience and the action:

> Be still, Andrea; ere we go from hence,
> I'll turn their friendship into fell despite,
> Their love to mortal hate, their day to night,
> Their hope into despair, their peace to war,
> Their joys to pain, their bliss to misery.
>
> (1.5.5–10)

This prophetic frame structures the audience's perspective; it guarantees that the most bizarre twists and turns of court intrigue are governed by a higher power. Revenge may sleep (as Andrea complains), but his continuous presence shows "What 'tis to be subject to destiny" (3.15.27). So with my placing of Flavius and Marullus: it keeps before the audience a point of view that might otherwise be forgotten.

Even so, reorienting the action so as to produce such a political slant will require some violence to the received text. I call it the New Reductionism. But then in *The Wars of the Roses,* done for the Royal Shakespeare Company in 1963, John Barton made three plays out of just over half the lines of *Richard III* and the three parts of *Henry VI,* together with 1,400 lines of his own.[41] My *Julius Caesar* could be accomplished by the commoner and more discreet tactics usual in the theater—namely, cutting patrician scenes (admittedly heavily) so as to make prominent the incidents where the people feature, and supplying "business." Reported events involving the plebeians would be performed in mime, the battle scenes would show, not the anguished integrity of the leaders, but the plight of the ordinary soldiers (according to Plutarch thousands were slain), and the final spectacle would be, not the funeral of Brutus, but Octavius and Antony establishing authoritarian power in Rome. My ultimate precedent, of course, is Shakespeare's political license with his sources. Plutarch,

the principal source for *Julius Caesar,* presents the plebeians and tribunes much more respectfully, particularly in their rejection of Caesar's
monarchical aspirations; Shakespeare has slanted his representation,
producing a certain political effect. In *2 Henry VI,* comparably, the
revolutionary leader, Jack Cade, is changed from the "young man of
goodly stature and pregnant wit," a "subtle captain," "sober in communication" and "wise in disputing," described by Edward Hall, the
Tudor apologist (Cade must have had some competence, after all, for
he captures London). In Shakespeare's version Cade is cruel and stupid, admitting his own dishonesty, viewed skeptically even by his
followers.[42] By thus altering his sources, Shakespeare produces one
story about disruptive lower-class people. My version of *Julius Caesar*
attempts to substitute an alternative.

My aim is simply this: to check the tendency of *Julius Caesar* to
add Shakespearean authority to reactionary discourses. Shakespearean
plays are powerful cultural tokens, places where meaning is established
and where it may be contested. The received text collaborates with
Caesar's dictatorial tendency by removing the tribunes from the action, so allowing members of an audience to forget the principles that
they may represent. The tribunes are not quite Pierre Macherey's "not-
said," since they have appeared. But the putting of Marullus and
Flavius to silence constitutes them as a point at which the text falls
silent, and a point, therefore, at which its ideological project may be
apprehended. All stories comprise within themselves the ghosts of the
alternative stories they are trying to repress.[43] Holding the tribunes
at each side of the stage holds them and their political significance in
view. It is comparable to the way the received text keeps the idea of
Caesar before the audience by making his ghost appear.

Conservative criticism has generally deployed three ways of making
literature politically agreeable: selecting the canon to feature suitable
texts, interpreting these texts strenuously so that awkward aspects are
explained away, and insinuating political implications as alleged formal properties (such as irony and balance).[44] As a consequence of the
long-term practice of these three strategies, the received literary canon
and discourses of criticism are, of course, resistant to progressive readings. Even so, the three strategies are available also to dissident critics,
who may offer their own texts, re-read canonical texts so as to produce
acceptable political tendencies, and propose that formal properties
inscribe a progressive politics (social realism, for instance, or internal
distanciation). So dissident critics may join and perhaps take over the
Englit game.

There is a fourth way: placing a text in its contexts. This strategy repudiates the supposed transcendence of literature, seeking rather to understand it as a cultural intervention produced initially within a specific set of practices and tending to render persuasive a view of reality; and seeing it also as re-produced subsequently in other historical conditions in the service of various views of reality, through other practices, including those of modern literary study. In the instance of *Julius Caesar*, one might consider how the play drew upon and contributed to notions of legitimacy and tyranny in 1599, and how it has done that subsequently (I attempted the latter in the second section of this chapter). Through such consideration, the processes by which textual reading is transformed into cultural significance may become manifest. And the (perhaps reactionary) values stated or implied in a text lose some of their power, since it is no longer assumed that they are simply to be endorsed as the insights of genius, transcending historical contexts. Canonical texts may then be respected as serious attempts to comprehend and intervene in the world, and we may quarrel with them as questionable constructions made by other people in other circumstances. This is a rough program for cultural materialism, and it is the dominant method of this book.

My re-handling of *Julius Caesar* suggests a fifth way: blatantly re-working the authoritative text so that it is forced to yield, against the grain, explicitly oppositional kinds of understanding. This strategy confronts both the attitudes and the status that have accrued to the canon. It is a strategy scarcely available in the established discourse of literary criticism. It seems out of order there (which is why my present effort has to appear humorous, something of a jeu d'esprit). But blatant reworking is used freely in other kinds of writing, for instance in plays such as Arnold Wesker's *Shylock* (formerly called *The Merchant*), Charles Marowitz's *Measure for Measure,* and Edward Bond's *Lear.* It is what Dollimore, with reference to Howard Barker's rewriting of Thomas Middleton's *Women Beware Women,* calls creative vandalism.[45]

Even with the boldest dramatic and fictive reworkings, it is often insisted that the authentic Shakespeare is being retrieved. In Charles Marowitz's *Collage Hamlet,* "the play was spliced-up into a collage with lines juxtaposed, sequences rearranged, characters dropped or blended, and the entire thing played out in short, discontinuous fragments which appeared like subliminal flashes out of Hamlet's life and, in every case, used Shakespeare's words, though radically rearranged."[46] And all this, Marowitz asserted, brought us closer to Shakespeare: "One has direct access to the play's ambiances" and "contact with what is essential in *Hamlet*."[47] Through such a claim, the creative vandal is protected against people who think it impertinent to interfere with Shakespeare, and may appropriate at least some of the authority of Shakespeare for the new work. This is the approach of most theater directors of versions of the received Shakespearean texts. For if they did not claim respectfully to be presenting the authentic bard, what status would they have? Would the school parties come? Most professional stage presentations are, in fact, cunning manipulations of the texts, together with conventionally permitted stage business, aiming at what the director hopes will be a relevant, vibrant (etc.) effect for the tourists. Otherwise few would understand the plays or find them interesting. But this cannot be admitted—that modern presentations produce their own Shakespeares—because that would spoil the game. And certainly it cannot be allowed that such efforts might excel Shakespeare, *particularly in values,* for the authority of the whole enterprise depends on that being impossible. So Peter Hall declared that *The Wars of the Roses* retrieved important Shakespearean values that were embedded in the first tetralogy, and Barton spoke of his changes as bringing out *the* historical and thematic point. Actually, as I tried to show in *Political Shakespeare,* Hall and Barton were creating a fashionable combination of E. M. W. Tillyard, Jan Kott, and Konrad Lorentz. In 1978 (at the RSC), Michael Bogdanov did marvelously to produce *The Taming of the Shrew* in a highly inventive version that foregrounded the brutality of Petruchio and the system within which he was operating. But Bogdanov had to assert that this was how the text was meant to be played, that Shakespeare was "a feminist." Jonathan Miller, conversely, thinks it wrong "to make that play into a feminist tract"; he has his own idea of the real Shakespeare, believing that patriarchal attitudes in the *Shrew* relate to Elizabethan Puritan belief in the sacramental nature of marriage. However, in his television production for the BBC/Time-Life series (1980), Miller also did not rely upon the received text to secure his reading. He added the singing of a psalm at the end, celebrating the orderliness and beauty of the family. Like Bogdanov, he declares that such innovation is only bringing out "what Shakespeare had in mind," the "spirit" of the play.[48]

The drawback, from a dissident point of view, of asserting that your production is really Shakespeare—and the same applies to literary-

critical interpretations—is that it does not challenge the bardic ac-
cumulation of cultural authority. Insinuating dissident work through
"privileged institutions," as Raymond Williams remarks, still leaves
as the longer-term, large-scale effect "the slow building of *authority*,"
with the inclusion of "minority elements of dissent or opposition"
contributing to that authority. The apparent capacity of Shakespearean
texts to speak from so many positions is assimilated happily to their
mysterious protean power (Humphreys, after surveying the diversity
in stage productions of *Julius Caesar*, concludes: "Still, Shakespeare
himself takes no sides, or all sides").[49] Blatant reworkings of Shakespearean texts may offer a more ambitious challenge to cultural power.
After the *Collage Hamlet*, with reworkings of *The Taming of the Shrew*,
Measure for Measure, and *The Merchant of Venice*, Marowitz decided
that his goal was "a head-on confrontation with the intellectual sub-
structure of the plays, an attempt to test or challenge, revoke or destroy
the intellectual foundation which makes a classic the formidable thing
it has become." Wesker in *Shylock* plainly intends to correct the political emphasis of Shakespeare's play.[50] Instead of trying to share the
cultural authority of the bard, it is possible to confront it. My *Julius
Caesar* is, self-consciously, an impudent anti-reading; a creative vandalism that might even restore some of the lively atmosphere of Shakespeare's theater before the Shakespeareans got to it.

THE DREAM OF CINNA THE POET

Reorienting *Julius Caesar* by bringing minor characters into the foreground and suppressing the principals might be attempted also with
the women. Robert Miola believes the "Roman" demand that Portia
and Calphurnia conduct themselves like heroic men indicates a culture
that is "strange, unnatural, inhuman, and doomed." The turning of
Caesar from Calphurnia, Miola says, and "of Portia from herself and
her womanhood, implicitly denies sexual identity, the fundamental
principle of procreation and healthy family life."[51] For those of us
who want to deny those things, the play might be reoriented to indicate the opposite: the indeterminacy of sexual identities and the
cultural organization of gender roles. Suppose some of the senators
were women?

The other figure who might be centralized is Cinna the Poet who,
after all, is a far more plausible ancestor of the modern humanities
intellectual than Brutus. "I am Cinna the poet, I am Cinna the Poet,"
he says, "not Cinna the conspirator" (3.3.29, 31)—hoping to save

himself by invoking just such a demarcation as characterizes present-day assumptions about aesthetics and politics. But there is no safety in withdrawal, Cinna gets caught in the crossfire. His brief appearance and early death may seem to spoil my idea of making him a central character; but that would not have stopped G. Wilson Knight. Luckily there is a second poet in the text. He comes on in the quarrel scene (4.3) and tells Brutus and Cassius to make friends; they mock him, not welcoming the intrusion of the Globe Theatre upon their theater of war. And there is Cicero, who surely means to encourage creative vandalism in his only two cogent lines: "But men may construe things, after their fashion, / Clean from the purpose of the things themselves" (1.3.34–35). To centralize humanities intellectuals I obviously have to amalgamate these characters, so that the idea of them dominates the action; and to do that I have to make the whole production surreal, dreamlike. Luckily again, Cinna says he has this ominous dream:

> I dreamt to-night that I did feast with Caesar,
> And things unluckily charge my fantasy.
> I have no will to wander forth of doors
> Yet something leads me forth.
> (3.3.1–4)

This is the dream and the nightmare of modern intellectuals: that they are invited to feast with Caesar, to become significant in government. That is why they imagine themselves as Brutus (and, indeed, as Hamlet). But the dream is fraught with anxiety about the consequences of commitment. The second poet sustains the fantasy that he might contribute a transcendent insight to the generals' quarrel. Appealing to an ancient heroic culture in which poets were the keepers of the communal lore, he quotes Nestor's lines from the *Iliad:* "Love, and be friends, as two such men should be; / For I have seen more years, I'm sure, than ye" (4.3.130–31). But Cassius and Brutus thrust him out.

In my version, *Julius Caesar* is the fantasy of Cinna as well as the agon of Flavius and Marullus. In fact the whole play is Cinna's dream, his tormented vision of a political reality that constructs, entices, and destroys him. It is the anxious fantasy of the Shakespearean intellectual, despised by the military-industrial complex and scapegoated by the people.[52] So, explicitly, I would have Cinna on stage at the start, he would fall asleep and dream *Julius Caesar.* "I dreamt to-night that

I did feast with Caesar," he would say, "And things unluckily charge my fantasy." And these things would be the play, Cinna's play. This device is not altogether un-Shakespearean. Dreams of power inform the framing induction to *The Taming of the Shrew:* Christopher Sly, the tinker, is quite ready to cultivate the notion that he is a great lord, and the Lord, fresh from hunting, is happy to sponsor a fantasy of male power (the Petruchio-Katherina play). Indeed, it has been suggested that almost the whole performance is Sly's dream of a more powerful position in the social order.[53] I propose Cinna as such a creative dreamer—after all, he is a poet.

Such centering of Cinna's self-destructive ambitions may seem to be leading back towards the liberal notion, which I have rejected, that no productive political engagement is feasible for intellectuals. However, if Cinna dreams *Julius Caesar,* then at least, so to speak, he writes the play (if he does not figure very well in it, that is because he has timorously deferred to those senators and generals). Cultural producers, this suggests, cannot jump out of ideology, but they do have a certain distinctive power—an ideological power—to write some of the scripts. And that includes dramatists, copywriters, and literary critics. In the *Shrew,* the First Huntsman reassures the Lord that identity is socially constructed and within his control:

> My Lord, I warrant you we will play our part
> As he shall think by our true diligence
> He is no less than what we say he is.
> (Induction, 1.74)

I argue in the next chapter particularly that meaning is produced culturally, and that humanities intellectuals contribute to the contest to make some stories, some representations, more plausible than others. Our sense of who we are is of a piece with the ideas we have of proper authority and of the potential for dissidence. Brutus and Cassius kill themselves rather than be led in triumph through the streets of Rome (5.1.108–13); such a spectacle would contribute to the legitimacy of Antony and Octavius. As Walter Benjamin remarked, "cultural treasures" are usually a principal feature of triumphal processions; it is our task to resist this parading, to prevent such "documents of civilization" being coopted to enhance the plausibility of oppressive stories. What we make of Shakespeare is important politically because it affects what he makes of us. It is, we may say, a theater of war. My *Julius Caesar* follows Benjamin's recommendation that

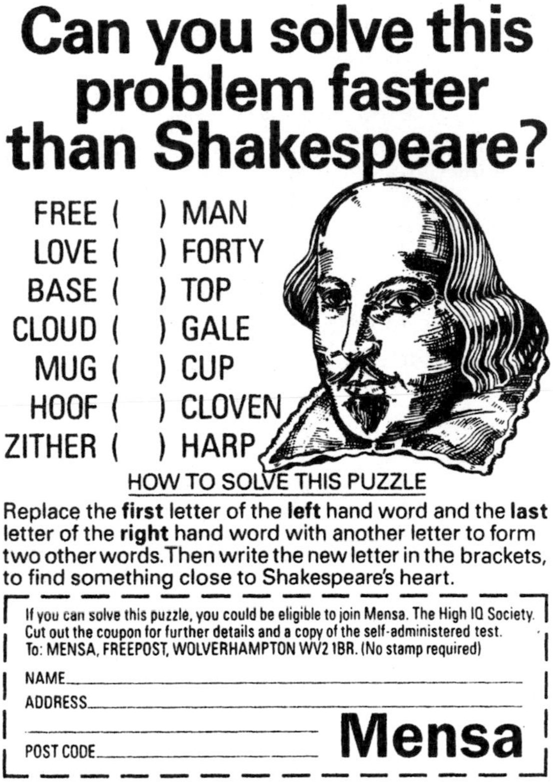

Can you solve this problem faster than Shakespeare?

Fig. 3. Advertisement for Mensa, the high-IQ society.[54]

we regard cultural treasures with cautious detachment, brushing history "against the grain."[55]

The career of Cinna the Poet raises these issues; in my version he would manifest authorial power. So he would look like—well, you've guessed, he would look like "Shakespeare," the enigmatic bust with the noble forehead (though probably Shakespeare did not wander forth of doors during the Essex rebellion, and so lived to tell the tale). Yet also Cinna would merge, ultimately, with Caesar himself; their deaths are the same death, for there are cultural empires as well as geographical. And the backdrop would be "the Globe Theatre," romantic in appearance and still powerful after 400 years (thanks, it would say in the program, to sponsorship from Royal Ordnance). Shakespeare, as our cultures have produced him, has dreamt us; for centuries he has been a key imperial site where ideology is produced. As Cassius warns,

> How many ages hence
> Shall this our lofty scene be acted over,
> In states unborn and accents yet unknown!
> (3.1.111–13)

But in the long term, the emperors could not keep out the Vandals. We may challenge, perhaps in uncouth accents, the stories that Shakespeare is usually made to tell; we too may intervene among the contested scripts of our societies.

2 Cultural Materialism, *Othello*, and the Politics of Plausibility

" 'TIS APT AND OF GREAT CREDIT"

Cassio, in Shakespeare's *Othello*, is discovered in a drunken brawl. He laments: "Reputation, reputation, I ha' lost my reputation!" (2.3.254).[1] Iago replies, "You have lost no reputation at all, unless you repute yourself such a loser" (2.3.261–63), but this assertion is absurd (though attractive), since reputation is by definition a social construct, concerned entirely with one's standing in the eyes of others. In fact, language and reality are always interactive, dependent upon social recognition; reputation is only a specially explicit instance. Meaning, communication, language work only because they are shared. If you invent your own language, no one else will understand you; if you persist, you will be thought mad. Iago is telling Cassio to disregard the social basis of language, to make up his own meanings for words; it is the more perverse because Iago is the great manipulator of the prevailing stories of his society.

Stephen Greenblatt has remarked how Othello's identity depends upon a constant performance of his "story";[2] when in difficulty, his immediate move is to rehearse his nobility and service to the state. Actually, all the characters in *Othello* are telling stories, and to convince others even more than themselves. At the start, Iago and Roderigo are concocting a story—a sexist and racist story about how Desdemona is in "the gross clasps of a lascivious Moor" (1.1.126). Brabantio believes this story and repeats it to the Senate, but Othello contests it with his "tale":

> I will a round unvarnish'd tale deliver,
> Of my whole course of love.
>
> (1.3.90–91)

29

The tale is—that Othello told a story. Brabantio "Still question'd me the story of my life" (1.3.129), and this story attracted Desdemona. She asked to hear it through, observing,

> if I had a friend that lov'd her,
> I should but teach him how to tell my story,
> And that would woo her.
>
> (1.3.163–65)

So the action advances through a contest of stories, and *the conditions of plausibility* are therefore crucial—they determine which stories will be believed. Brabantio's case is that Othello must have enchanted Desdemona—anything else is implausible:

> She is abus'd, stol'n from me and corrupted,
> By spells and medicines, bought of mountebanks,
> For nature so preposterously to err,
> (Being not deficient, blind, or lame of sense,)
> Sans witchcraft could not.
>
> (1.3.60–64)

To Brabantio, for Desdemona to love Othello would be preposterous, an error of nature. To make this case, he depends on the plausibility, to the Senate, of the notion that Blacks are inferior outsiders. This, evidently, is a good move. Even characters who want to support Othello's story accept that he is superficially inappropriate as a husband for Desdemona. She says as much herself when she declares, "I saw Othello's visage in his mind" (1.3.252): this means, he may look like a black man but really he is very nice. And the Duke finally tells Brabantio: "Your son-in-law is far more fair than black" (1.3.290)—meaning, Othello doesn't have many of those unpleasant characteristics that we all know belong to Blacks, he is really quite like a white man.

With the conditions of plausibility so stacked against him, two main strategies are available to Othello, and he uses both. One is to appear very calm and responsible—as the Venetians imagine themselves to be. But also, and shrewdly, he uses the racist idea of himself as exotic: he says he has experienced "hair-breadth scapes," redemption from slavery, hills "whose heads touch heaven," cannibals, anthropophagi, "and men whose heads / Do grow beneath their shoulders" (1.3.129–45). These adventures are of course implausible—but not when attributed to an exotic. Othello has little credit by normal upper-class Venetian criteria, but when he plays on his strangeness, the Venetians tolerate him, for he is granting, in more benign form, part of Brabantio's case.

Partly, perhaps, because the senators need Othello to fight the Turks for them, they allow his story to prevail. However, this is not, of course, the end of the story. Iago repeats his racist and sexist tale to Othello, and persuades him of its credibility:

> I know our country disposition well . . .
> She did deceive her father, marrying you . . .
> Not to affect many proposed matches,
> Of her own clime, complexion, and degree,
> Whereto we see in all things nature tends . . .
> (3.3.205, 210, 233–35)

Othello is persuaded of his inferiority and of Desdemona's inconstancy, and he proceeds to act as if they were true. "Haply, for I am black," he muses (3.3.267), and begins to take the role of the "erring barbarian" (1.3.356–57) that he is alleged to be. As Ania Loomba puts it, "Othello moves from being a colonised subject existing on the terms of white Venetian society and trying to internalise its ideology, towards being marginalised, outcast and alienated from it in every way, until he occupies his 'true' position as its other."[3] It is very difficult not to be influenced by a story, even about yourself, when everyone else is insisting upon it. So in the last lines of the play, when he wants to reassert himself, Othello "recognizes" himself as what Venetian culture has really believed him to be: an ignorant, barbaric outsider—like, he says, the "base Indian" who threw away a pearl. Virtually, this is what Althusser means by "interpellation": Venice hails Othello as a barbarian, and he acknowledges that it is he they mean.[4]

Iago remarks that the notion that Desdemona loves Cassio is "apt and of great credit" (2.1.282); and that his advice to Cassio to press Desdemona for his reinstatement is "Probal to thinking" (2.3.329). Iago's stories work because they are plausible—to Roderigo, Brabantio, the Senate, even to Othello himself. As Peter Stallybrass has observed, Iago is convincing not because he is "superhumanly ingenious but, to the contrary, because his is the voice of 'common sense', the ceaseless repetition of the always-already 'known', the culturally 'given'."[5] The racism and sexism in the play should not be traced just to Iago's character, therefore, or to his arbitrary devilishness, but to the Venetian culture that sets the conditions of plausibility.

THE PRODUCTION OF IDEOLOGY

I have spoken of stories because I want an inclusive term that will key in my theory to the continuous and familiar discourses of everyday life. But in effect I have been addressing the production of ideology. Societies need to produce materially to continue—they need food, shelter, warmth; goods to exchange with other societies; a transport and information infrastructure to carry those processes. Also, they have to produce ideologically (Althusser makes this argument at the start of his essay on ideological state apparatuses).[6] They need knowledges to keep material production going—diverse technical skills and wisdoms in agriculture, industry, science, medicine, economics, law, geography, languages, politics, and so on. And they need understandings, intuitive and explicit, of a system of social relationships within which the whole process can take place more or less evenly. Ideology produces, makes plausible, concepts and systems to explain who we are, who the others are, how the world works.

The strength of ideology derives from the way it gets to be common sense; it "goes without saying." For its production is not an external process, stories are not outside ourselves, something we just hear or read about. Ideology makes sense for us—of us—because it is already proceeding when we arrive in the world, and we come to consciousness in its terms. As the world shapes itself around and through us, certain interpretations of experience strike us as plausible: they fit with what we have experienced already, and are confirmed by others around us. So we complete what Colin Sumner calls a "circle of social reality": "understanding produces its own social reality at the same time as social reality produces its own understanding."[7] This is apparent when we observe how people in other cultures than our own make good sense of the world in ways that seem strange to us: their outlook is supported by their social context. For them, those frameworks of perception, maps of meaning, work.

The conditions of plausibility are therefore crucial. They govern our understandings of the world and how to live in it, thereby seeming to define the scope of feasible political change. Most societies retain their current shape, not because dissidents are penalized or incorporated, though they are, but because many people believe that things have to take more or less their present form—that improvement is not feasible, at least through the methods to hand. That is why one recognizes a dominant ideology: were there not such a powerful (plausible) discourse, people would not acquiesce in the injustice and humiliation that they experience. To insist on ideological construction is not to deny individual agency (though it makes individual agency less interesting). Rather, the same structure informs individuals and the society. Anthony Giddens compares the utterance of a grammatical sentence, which is governed by the lexicon and syntactical rules that constitute the language, but is individual and, through its utterance, may both confirm and slightly modify the language.[8]

Ideology is produced everywhere and all the time in the social order, but some institutions—by definition, those that usually corroborate the prevailing power arrangements—are vastly more powerful than others. The stories they endorse are more difficult to challenge, even to disbelieve. Such institutions, and the people in them, are also constituted in ideology; they are figures in its stories. At the same time, I would not want to lose a traditional sense of the power elite in the state exercising authority, through the ideological framework it both inhabits and maintains, over subordinate groups. This process may be observed in Shakespearean plays, where the most effective stories are given specific scope and direction by powerful men. They authorize scripts, we may say, that the other characters resist only with difficulty. Very often this does not require any remarkable intervention, or seems to involve only a "restoration of order," for the preferences of the ruling elite are already attuned to the system as it is already running. Conversely, scripting from below by lower-order characters immediately appears subversive; consider Shylock, Malvolio, Don John, Iago, Edmund, Macbeth, Caliban. Women may disturb the system (I return to this shortly), and in early comedies they are allowed to script, sometimes even in violation of parental wishes, but their scripts lead to the surrender of their power in the larger story of marriage. Elsewhere, women who script men are bad—Goneril and Regan, Lady Macbeth, the Queen in *Cymbeline*. Generally, the scripting of women by men is presented as good for them. Miranda's marriage in *The Tempest* seems to be all that Prospero has designed it to be. In *Measure for Measure,* Isabella is given by the Duke the script she ought to want—all the men in the play have conspired to draw her away from an independent life in the convent. To be sure, these are not the scripts of men only. As Stephen Orgel remarks, the plays must have appealed to the women in the audience as well: these were the fantasies of a whole culture.[9] But insofar as they show the powerful dominating the modes in which ideology is realized, these plays record an insight into ideology and power.

The state is the most powerful scriptor; it is best placed to enforce its story. In *Othello*, the Duke offers Brabantio, for use against Desdemona's alleged enchanter, "the bloody book of law" (1.3.67–70):

the ruling elite have written this, and they decree who shall apply it. At the end of the play, Othello tries to control the story that will survive him—"When you shall these unlucky deeds relate, / Speak of them as they are . . ." (5.2.342–43). However, the very last lines are spoken by Lodovico, the Venetian nobleman and representative of the Senate: "Myself will straight aboard, and to the state / This heavy act with heavy heart relate." The state and the ruling elite will tell Othello's story in the way they choose. They will try to control Iago's story as well, torturing him until he speaks what they want to hear: the state falls back on direct coercion when its domination of the conditions of plausibility falters. Through violence against Iago, the state means to make manifest his violence while legitimating its own.

The relation between violence and the ideological power of the state may be glimpsed in the way Othello justifies himself, in his last speech, as a good Venetian: he boasts of killing someone. Not Desdemona—that, he now agrees, was bad—but "a malignant and a turban'd Turk," who "Beat a Venetian, and traduc'd the state." Othello says he "took by the throat the circumcised dog, / And smote him thus" (5.2.352–57). And so, upon this recollection, Othello stabs himself, recognizing himself, for the last time, as an outsider, a discredit to the social order he has been persuaded to respect. Innumerable critics discuss Othello's suicide, but I haven't noticed them worrying about the murdered Turk. Being malignant, circumcised, and wearing a turban into the bargain, he seems not to require the sensitive attention of literary critics in Britain and North America. The character critic might take this reported murder as a last-minute revelation of Othello's long-standing propensity to desperate violence when people say things he doesn't like. But the violence here is not Othello's alone, any more than Venetian racism and sexism are particular to individuals. Othello's murder of the Turk is the kind of thing the Venetian state likes—or so we must assume, since Othello is in good standing in Venice as a state servant, and presents the story to enhance his credit. "He was great of heart," Cassio enthuses (5.2.362), pleased that he has found something to retrieve his respect for Othello. In respect of murdering state enemies, at least, he was a good citizen.

It is a definition of the state, almost, that it claims a monopoly of legitimate violence, and the exercise of that violence is justified through stories about the barbarity of those who are constituted as its demonized others. For the Venetians, as for the Elizabethans, the

Turks were among the barbarians.[10] In actuality, in most states that we know of, the civilized and the barbaric are not very different from each other; that is why maintaining the distinction is such a constant ideological task. It is not altogether Othello's personal achievement, or his personal failure, therefore, when he kills himself declaring, with respect to the Turk, that he "smote him thus." Othello becomes a good subject once more by accepting within himself the state's distinction between civilized and barbaric. This "explains" how he has come to murder Desdemona: it was the barbarian beneath, or rather in, the skin. And when he kills himself it is even better, because he eradicates the intolerable confusion of finding both the citizen and the alien in the same body. Othello's particular circumstances bring into visibility, for those who want to see, the violence upon which the state and its civilization rest.

STRUCTURE AND INDIVIDUALS

My argument has reached the point where I have to address the scope for dissidence within ideological construction. "The class which is the ruling material force is, at the same time, its ruling intellectual force. The class which has the means of material production at its disposal, has control at the same time over the means of mental production," Marx and Engels declare in *The German Ideology*.[11] The point is surely only sensible: groups with material power will dominate the institutions that deal with ideas. That is why people can be persuaded to believe things that are neither just, humane, nor to their advantage. The issue is pressed harder in modern cultural theory. In work deriving from Althusser and Foucault, distinct as those two sources are, ideological constructedness, not just of our ideas but of our subjectivities, seems to control the scope for dissident thought and expression. This is a key question: if we come to consciousness within a language that is continuous with the power structures that sustain the social order, how can we conceive, let alone organize, resistance?

The issue has been raised sharply by feminist critics, in particular Lynda E. Boose and Carol Thomas Neely. They accuse both new historicism and cultural materialism of theorizing power as an unbreakable system of containment, a system that positions subordinate groups as effects of the dominant, so that female identity, for instance, appears to be something fathered upon women by patriarchy.[12] How, it is asked, can women produce a dissident perspective from such a complicit ideological base? And so with other subordinated groups:

if the conditions of plausibility persuade black or gay people to assume subjectivities that suit the maintenance of the social order, how is a radical black or gay consciousness to arise?

Kathleen McLuskie's argument that *Measure for Measure* and *King Lear* are organized from a male point of view has received particular attention. There is no way, McLuskie says, to find feminist heroines in Regan and Goneril, the wicked women, or in the good woman, Cordelia. Feminist criticism "is restricted to exposing its own exclusion from the text."[13] The alternative feminist position, which we may term a humanist or essentialist feminism, is stated by Carolyn Ruth Swift Lenz, Gayle Greene, and Carol Thomas Neely in their ground-breaking collection of essays, *The Woman's Part*. They believe feminist critics should, typically, be finding that Shakespeare's women characters are *not* male constructions—not "the saints, monsters, or whores their critics have often perceived them to be." Rather, "like the male characters the women are complex and flawed, like them capable of passion and pain, growth and decay."[14] This perspective is evidently at odds with the approach I am presenting. In my view, when traditional critics perceive Shakespearean women characters in terms of stereotypes, they are often more or less right (I argue this further in the next chapter). Such critics recognize in the plays the ideological structures that our cultures have been producing. My dispute with them begins when they admire the patterns they find and collaborate in rendering them plausible, instead of offering a critique of them. As McLuskie says, we should attend to "the narrative, poetic and theatrical strategies which construct the plays' meanings and position the audience to understand their events from a particular point of view."[15]

There are in fact two issues here. One is whether there is (for women or men) any such fullness of personhood as Lenz, Greene, and Neely propose, or whether subjectivity is, as I have been arguing, an effect of cultural production. The other is the authority of Shakespeare: can we reasonably assume that he anticipated a progressive modern sexual politics? As McLuskie points out, he was working within "an entertainment industry which, as far as we know, had no women shareholders, actors, writers, or stage hands" (p. 92). Ultimately these issues converge: the idea that Shakespearean texts tune into an essential humanity, transcending cultural production, is aligned with the idea that individual characters do that. As Lynda Boose says, the question is whether the human being is conceived as inscribing "at least something universal that transcends history, or as an entity completely produced by its historical culture." Boose credits McLuskie with "unblinkered honesty," but complains that one has "to renounce completely one's pleasure in Shakespeare and embrace instead the rigorous comforts of ideological correctness."[16] Maybe one does (try listening again to the words of most Christmas carols); but pleasure in Shakespeare is a complex phenomenon, and it may not be altogether incompatible with a critical attitude to ideology in the plays.

The essentialist-humanist approach to literature and sexual politics depends upon the belief that the individual is the probable, indeed necessary, source of truth and meaning. Literary significance and personal significance seem to derive from and speak to individual consciousnesses. But thinking of ourselves as essentially individual tends to efface processes of cultural production and, in the same movement, leads us to imagine ourselves to be autonomous, self-determining. It is not individuals but power structures that produce the system within which we live and think, and focusing upon the individual makes it hard to discern those structures; and if we discern them, hard to do much about them, since that would require collective action. To adopt the instance offered by Richard Ohmann in his book *English in America,* each of us buys an automobile because we need it to get around, and none of us, individually, does much damage to the environment or other people. But from that position it is hard to get to address, much less do anything about, whether we should be living in an automobile culture at all.[17]

I believe feminist anxiety about derogation of the individual in cultural materialism is misplaced, since personal subjectivity and agency are, anyway, unlikely sources of dissident identity and action. Political awareness does not arise out of an essential, individual, self-consciousness of class, race, nation, gender, or sexual orientation; but from involvement in *a milieu, a subculture.* "In acquiring one's conception of the world one belongs to a particular grouping which is that of all the social elements which share the same mode of thinking and acting," Gramsci observes.[18] It is through such sharing that one may learn to inhabit plausible oppositional preoccupations and forms—ways of relating to others—and hence develop a plausible oppositional selfhood. That is how successful movements have worked (I return to this thought towards the end of chapter 10).

These issues have been most thoroughly considered by recent theorists of lesbian identity. Judith Butler argues against a universalist concept, "woman," not only on the ground that it effaces diversities of time and place, but also because it is oppressive: it necessarily involves "the exclusion of those who fail to conform to unspoken normative requirements of the subject."[19] Butler asks if "unity" is indeed necessary for effective political action, pointing out that "the articulation of an identity within available cultural terms instates a definition that forecloses in advance the emergence of new identity concepts in and through politically engaged actions" (p. 15). For agency to operate, Butler points out, a "doer" does not have to be in place first; rather, she or he is constructed through the deed. Identity develops, precisely, in the process of signification: "identity is always already signified, and yet continues to signify as it circulates within various interlocking discourses" (pp. 142–43). So "construction is not opposed to agency; it is the necessary scene of agency, the very terms in which agency is articulated and becomes culturally intelligible" (p. 147). Identity is not that which produces culture, nor even that which is produced as a static entity by culture: rather, the two are the same process.

If these arguments are correct, then it is not necessary to envisage, as Neely does, "some area of 'femaleness' that is part biological, part psychical, part experiential, part cultural and that is not utterly inscribed by and in thrall to patriarchal ideology and that makes possible female discourse."[20] "Female discourse" will be the discourse that women work out together at a historical conjuncture, and it will be rendered plausible by social interaction, especially among women. Desdemona gets closest to seeing what is going on when she talks with Emilia (what she needs is a refuge for battered wives); Othello gets it wrong because he has no reliable friends with whom to check out his perceptions. Subcultures constitute consciousness, in principle, in the same way that dominant ideologies do—but in partly dissident forms. In that bit of the world where the subculture runs, you can feel confident, as we used to say, that Black is beautiful, gay is good: there, those stories work, they build their own kinds of interactive plausibility. Validating the individual may seem attractive because it appears to empower him or her, but actually it undervalues potential resources of collective understanding and resistance.

ENTRAPMENT AND FAULTLINES

While the ideology of individualism is associated mainly with traditional modes of literary criticism, the poststructuralist vein in recent cultural work, including new historicism, has also helped to obscure the importance of collectivities and social location. A principal theoretical task in such work has been to reassess the earlier Marxist base/

superstructure model, whereby culture was seen as a one-way effect of economic organization. (In apparent ignorance of this work, much of which has been conducted in Europe, J. Hillis Miller supposes that people of "the so-called left" hold "an unexamined ideology of the material base.)"[21] It was necessary to abandon that model, but in the process, as Peter Nicholls has pointed out, the tendency in new historicism has been "to replace a model of mechanical causality with one of structural homology." And this works to "*dis*place the concepts of production and class which would initiate a thematics of historical change." Homology discovers synchronic structural connectedness without determination, sometimes without pressure or tension. Hence "the problem of ideology becomes a purely superstructural one."[22] The agency that has sunk from view, following Nicholls's argument, is that, not of individuals, but of classes, class fractions, and groups. Yet Marx was surely right to envisage such collectivities as the feasible agents of historical change.

New historicism has been drawn to what I call the "entrapment model" of ideology and power, whereby even, or especially, maneuvers that seem designed to challenge the system help to maintain it. Don E. Wayne says new historicism has often shown "how different kinds of discourse intersect, contradict, destabilize, cancel, or modify each other . . . seek[ing] to demonstrate how a dominant ideology will give a certain rein to alternative discourses, ultimately appropriating their vitality and containing their oppositional force."[23] The issue informs the ambiguous title of *Renaissance Self-Fashioning:* Stephen Greenblatt's central figures aspired to fashion themselves, but he finds that their selves were fashioned for them. So Wyatt "cannot fashion himself in opposition to power and the conventions power deploys; on the contrary, those conventions are precisely what constitute Wyatt's self-fashioning."[24] Hence Carolyn Porter's complaint that the subordinate seems a mere discursive effect of the dominant in new historicism.[25]

Of course, not all work generally dubbed "new historicist" takes such a line (not that of Louis Adrian Montrose). Nor is entrapment only here at issue—it arises generally in functionalism, structuralism, and Althusserian Marxism. Greenblatt has recently denied proposing that resistance is always coopted, and he is in my view right to say that his "Invisible Bullets" essay has often been misinterpreted.[26] I associate the entrapment model with new historicism nevertheless, because its treatment there has been distinctively subtle, powerful, and pressured, and because it is, of course, not by chance that this aspect of new historicism has been emphasized. The notion that dissidence is characteristically contained has caught the imagination of the profession. Therefore, even while acknowledging the diversity and specificity of actual writing (which I draw upon frequently in the pages that follow), it is the aspect of new-historicist thought that has to be addressed.

An instance that confronts the entrapment model at its heart is the risk that the legally constituted ruler might not be able to control the military apparatus. Valuable new-historicist analyses, considering the interaction of the monarch and the court, have tended to discover "power" moving in an apparently unbreakable circle—proceeding from and returning to the monarch (see pp. 80–81 below). But although absolutist ideology represents the ruler as the necessary and sufficient source of national unity, the early modern state depended in the last analysis, like other states, upon military force. The obvious instance is the Earl of Essex's rebellion in 1601. With the queen aging and military success in Cádiz to his credit, it was easy for the charismatic earl to suppose that he should not remain subordinate. Ideological and military power threaten to split apart; it is a faultline in the political structure. Indeed, army coups against legitimate but militarily dependent political leaders still occur all the time. In the United States, during the Korean War, General Douglas MacArthur believed he could override the authority of President Harry S Truman.

In *Macbeth*, Duncan has the legitimacy but Macbeth is the best fighter. Duncan cannot but delegate power to subordinates, who may turn it back upon him—the initial rebellion is that of the Thane of Cawdor, in whom Duncan says he "built / An absolute trust."[27] If the thought of revolt can enter the mind of Cawdor, then it will occur to Macbeth, and others; its source is not just personal (Macbeth's ambition). Of course, it is crucial to the ideology of absolutism to deny that the state suffers such a structural flaw. Hence the projection of the whole issue onto a supernatural backdrop of good and evil, and the implication that disruption must derive, or be crucially reinforced, from outside (by the Weird Sisters and the distinctively demonic Lady Macbeth). Macbeth's mistake, arguably, is that he falls for Duncan's ideology and loses his nerve. However, this does not mean that absolutist ideology was inevitably successful—when Charles I tried to insist upon it there was a revolution.

Henry V offers a magical resolution of this faultline by presenting the legitimate king as the triumphant war leader. The pressure of aspiration and anxiety around the matter may be gauged from the reference to Essex by the Chorus of act 5. In the most specific contemporary allusion in any Shakespeare play, Henry V's return from France is compared first to Caesar's return as conqueror to Rome and then to Essex's anticipated return from Ireland:

> As, by a lower but by loving likelihood,
> Were now the general of our gracious empress,
> As in good time he may, from Ireland coming,
> Bringing rebellion broached on his sword,
> How many would the peaceful city quit
> To welcome him! much more, and much more cause,
> Did they this Harry.[28]

Notice the prudent qualification that this is "a lower . . . likelihood" insofar as Essex is but "the general of our gracious empress"; Harry would be welcomed "much more, and much more cause." The text strives to envisage a leader whose power, unlike that of the queen, would be uncontestable, but yet at the same time that of the queen. Promoting Elizabeth to empress (of Ireland) seems to give her a further edge over her commander. Even so the comparisons refuse to stabilize, for Henry V himself has just been likened to a caesar, and Julius Caesar threatened the government after his triumphal entry into Rome. And Elizabeth becomes empress only through Essex's military success, and that very success would enhance his potential for revolt. With the city specified as "peaceful," it seems only thoughtful to wonder whether it would remain so. However, faultlines are by definition resistant to the fantasies that would erase them. The epilogue to *Henry V* has to record that the absolutist pyramid collapsed with the accession of Henry VI, who, precisely, was not the strongest military leader. And Essex failed to mobilize sufficient support to bring Elizabeth within his power.

My argument is that dissident potential derives ultimately not from essential qualities in individuals (though they have qualities) but from conflict and contradiction that the social order inevitably produces within itself, even as it attempts to sustain itself. Despite their power, dominant ideological formations are always, in practice, under pressure, striving to substantiate their claim to superior plausibility in the face of diverse disturbances. Hence Raymond Williams's observation that ideology has always to be *produced*: "Social orders and cultural orders must be seen as being actively made: actively and continuously, or they may quite quickly break down."[29] Conflict and contradiction stem from the very strategies through which ideologies strive to contain the expectations that they need to generate. This is where failure—inability or refusal—to identify one's interests with the dominant may occur, and hence where dissidence may arise. In this argument the dominant and subordinate are structurally linked, but not in the way criticized by Carolyn Porter when she says that although "masterless men" (her instance) may ultimately have been controlled, "their subversive resistance cannot [therefore] be understood simply as the product of the dominant culture's power."[30] It was the Elizabethan social structure that produced unemployed laborers, and military leaders, but it could not then prevent such figures conceiving and enacting dissident practices, especially if they were able to constitute milieux within which dissidence might be rendered plausible.

DESDEMONA'S DEFIANCE

Another key point at which to confront the entrapment model concerns the scope of women. *Othello,* like many contemporary texts, betrays an obsessive concern with disorder; the ideology and power of the ruling elite are reasserted at the end of the play, but equilibrium is not, by any means, easily regained. The specific disruption stems from Desdemona's marital choice.[31] At her first entrance, her father asks her: "Do you perceive in all this noble company, / Where most you owe obedience?" She replies that she sees "a divided duty"—to her father and her husband:

> I am hitherto your daughter: but here's my husband:
> And so much duty as my mother show'd
> To you, preferring you before her father,
> So much I challenge, that I may profess,
> Due to the Moor my Lord.
>
> (1.3.179–89)

And to justify the latter allegiance, she declares: "I did love the Moor, to live with him" (1.2.248).

This is a paradigm instance. For, in her use of the idea of a divided duty to justify elopement with an inappropriate man, Desdemona has not discovered a distinctive, radical insight (any more than Cordelia does when she uses it). She is offering a straightforward elaboration of official doctrine, which said that a woman should obey the male head of her family, who should be first her father (or failing that a brother or uncle), then her husband. Before marriage, the former; afterwards, the latter. Ideally, from the point of view of the social order, it would all be straightforward. The woman's transition from daughter to wife—from one set of duties to another—would be accomplished smoothly, with the agreement of all parties. But things could go wrong here; it was an insecure moment in patriarchy. The danger derived from a fundamental complication in the ideology of gender relations. Marriage was the institution through which property arrangements were made and inheritance secured, but it was supposed also to be a fulfilling personal relationship. It was held that the people being married should act in obedience to their parents, but also that they should love each other.[32] The "divided duty" was not especially Desdemona's problem, therefore; it is how the world was set up for her.

The Reformation intensified the issue by shifting both the status and the nature of marriage. The Catholic church held that the three reasons for matrimony were, first, to beget children; second, to avoid carnal sin; and third, for mutual help and comfort. Protestants stressed the third objective, often promoting it to first place; the homily "Of the State of Matrimony" says: "it is instituted of God, to the intent that man and woman should live lawfully in a perpetual friendly fellowship, to bring forth fruit, and to avoid fornication."[33] Thus protestants defined marriage more positively, as a mutual, fulfilling, reciprocal relationship. However, they were not prepared to abandon patriarchal authority; it was too important to the system. In *Arcadia*, Philip Sidney presents an ideal marriage of reciprocity and mutual love, that of Argalus and Parthenia: "A happy couple: he joying in her, she joying in herself, but in herself, because she enjoyed him: both increasing their riches by giving to each other; each making one life double, because they made a double life one." However, the passage concludes: "he ruling, because she would obey, or rather because she would obey, she therein ruling."[34] Does this mean that Parthenia was fulfilled in her subordinate role; or that by appearing submissive she managed to insinuate her own way? Neither seems ideal. In *The Anatomy of Melancholy*, Robert Burton displays a protestant enthusiasm: "You know marriage is honourable, a blessed calling, appointed by God himself in paradise; it breeds true peace, tranquillity, content and happiness." But the elaboration is tricky: "The husband rules her as head, but she again commands his heart, he is her servant, she his only joy and content."[35] The alternation of head and heart sounds reciprocal but is not, for we know that the head should rule the heart. Then the strong phrasing of "servant" reverses altogether the initial priority, introducing language more appropriate to romantic love; and finally "only joy and content" seems to privilege the wife but also places upon her an obligation to please. Coercion and liberty jostle together unresolved, and this is characteristic of protestant attitudes.

In fact, protestantism actually strengthened patriarchal authority. The removal of the mediatory priest threw upon the head of household responsibility for the spiritual life and devout conduct of the family. Also, there was a decline in the significance of great magnates who might stand between subject and monarch. From these developments, protestants devised a comprehensive doctrine of social control, with a double chain of authority running from God to the husband to the individual, and from God to the monarch to the subject. The homily "Against Disobedience and Wilful Rebellion" derives earthly rule from God and parallels the responsibilities of the monarch and the head of household.[36] Indeed, the latter could be said to have the more important role. "A master in his family hath all the offices of Christ, for he must rule, and teach, and pray; rule like a king, and teach like a prophet, and pray like a priest," Henry Smith declared in "A Preparative to Marriage" (1591). This leaves little space for independence for offspring, or anyone else in the household. Smith says parents must control marital choice because, after all, they have the property: "If children may not make other contracts without [parents'] good will, shall they contract marriage, which have nothing to maintain it after, unless they return to beg of them whom they scorned before?"[37] As with other business deals, it is wrong to enter into marriage unless you can sustain the costs. This was one extreme; at the other, only radicals like the Digger Gerrard Winstanley proposed that "every man and woman shall have the free liberty to marry whom they love."[38] In between, most commentators fudged the question, suggesting that children might exercise a right of refusal, or that even if they didn't like their spouses at first, they would learn to get on. "A couple is that whereby two persons standing in mutual relation to each other are combined together, as it were, into one. And of these two the one is always higher and beareth rule: the other is lower and yieldeth subjection," William Perkins declared.[39] The boundaries are plainly unclear, and conflict is therefore likely. Hence the awkward bullying and wheedling in the disagreements between Portia and Bassanio, Caesar and Portia, Othello and Desdemona, Macbeth and Lady Macbeth, Leontes and Hermione. Lawrence Stone says dutiful children experienced "an impossible conflict of role models. They had to try to reconcile the often incompatible demands for obedience to parental wishes on the one hand and expectations of affection in marriage on the other."[40] At this point, the dominant ideology had not quite got its act together.

Parental influence over marriage in early modern England is nowadays often regarded simply as an instance of the oppressiveness of patriarchy, but that is not quite all. The ambiguity of official doctrine afforded one distinct point at which a woman such as Desdemona could produce a crisis in the patriarchal story. "Despite the economic and social mechanisms that reinforced parental authority, it was in marriage that parents were most often defied," Dympna Callaghan observes.[41] All too often, such defiance provoked physical and mental violence; at the least it must have felt very unpleasant. That is how it is when you disturb the system—the tendency of ideology is, precisely, to produce good subjects who feel uncomfortable when they transgress. But contradictions in the ideology of marriage produced, nevertheless, an opportunity for dissidence, and even before the appearance of Othello, we are told, Desdemona was exploiting it—refusing "The wealthy curled darlings of our nation" (1.2.68). Her more extreme action—marrying without parental permission, outside the ruling oligarchy, and outside the race—is so disruptive that the chief (male) council of the state delays its business. "For if such actions may have passage free," Brabantio says, "Bond-slaves, and pagans, shall our statesmen be" (1.2.98). Desdemona throws the system into disarray—and just when the men are busy with one of their wars—killing people because of their honor and their property—proving their masculinity to each other.

To be sure, Desdemona was claiming only what Louis Montrose calls "the limited privilege of giving herself,"[42] and her moment of power ends once the men have accepted her marriage. But then dissident opportunities always are limited—otherwise we would not be living as we do. Revolutionary change is rare and usually dependent upon a prior buildup of small breaks; often there are great personal costs. The point of principle is that scope for dissident understanding and action occurs not because women characters, Shakespeare, and feminist readers have a privileged vantage point outside the dominant, but because the social order *cannot but produce* faultlines through which its own criteria of plausibility fall into contest and disarray. This has been theorized by Stuart Hall and his colleagues at the Centre for Contemporary Cultural Studies at the University of Birmingham:

> the dominant culture of a complex society is never a homogeneous structure. It is layered, reflecting different interests within the dominant class (e.g. an aristocratic versus a bourgeois outlook), containing different traces from the past (e.g. religious ideas within a largely secular culture), as well as emergent elements in the present. Subor-

dinate cultures will not always be in open conflict with it. They may, for long periods, coexist with it, negotiate the spaces and gaps in it, make inroads into it, "warrenning [*sic*] it from within."[43]

Observe that this account does not offer to decide whether or not dissidence will be contained; it may not even be actualized, but may lie dormant, becoming disruptive only at certain conjunctures. But if ideology is so intricately "layered," with so many potential modes of relation to it, it cannot but allow awareness of its own operations. In *Othello*, Emilia takes notable steps towards a dissident perception:

> But I do think it is their husbands' faults
> If wives do fall: say, that they slack their duties,
> And pour our treasures into foreign laps;
> Or else break out in peevish jealousies,
> Throwing restraint upon us; or say they strike us . . .
> (4.3.86–90)

Emilia has heard the doctrine of mutual fulfillment in marriage, and from the gap between it and her experience, she is well able to mount a critique of the double standard. At faultlines, such as I am proposing here, a dissident perspective may be discovered and articulated.

The crisis over marital choice illustrates how stories work in culture. It appears again and again—in *A Midsummer Night's Dream, The Merchant of Venice, The Taming of the Shrew, Romeo and Juliet, Measure for Measure, King Lear, The Winter's Tale, The Tempest*. Roughly speaking, in comedies parents are eventually reconciled to children's wishes; in tragedies (as in *Othello*), precipitate actions without parental authority lead to disaster. And in writing, on through the ensuing centuries until the late nineteenth century, the arranged- versus the love-match is a recurring theme in literature. This is how culture elaborates itself. In these texts, through diverse genres and institutions, people were talking to each other about an aspect of their life that they found hard to handle. When a part of our worldview threatens disruption by manifestly failing to cohere with the rest, then we reorganize and retell its story, trying to get it into shape—back into the old shape if we are conservative-minded, or into a new shape if we are more adventurous. The question of the arranged- versus the love-match died out in fiction in the late nineteenth century because then, for most people in Britain, it was resolved in favor of children's preferences, and therefore became uninteresting (but not, however, for British families deriving recently from Asia). The other great point at which the woman could disturb the system was by loving a man not her husband, and that is why adultery is such a prominent theme in literature. It upsets the husband's honor, his masculinity, and (through the bearing of illegitimate children) his property. Even the rumor of Desdemona's adultery is enough to send powerful men in the state into another anxiety.

This is why it is not unpromising to seek in literature our preoccupations with class, race, gender, and sexual orientation: it is likely that literary texts will address just such controversial aspects of our ideological formation. Those faultline stories are the ones that require most assiduous and continuous reworking; they address the awkward, unresolved issues, the ones in which the conditions of plausibility are in dispute. For authors and readers, after all, want writing to be interesting. The task for a political criticism, then, is to observe how stories negotiate the faultlines that distress the prevailing conditions of plausibility.

READING DISSIDENCE

The reason why textual analysis can so readily demonstrate dissidence being incorporated is that dissidence operates, necessarily, with reference to dominant structures. It has to invoke those structures to oppose them, and therefore can always, ipso facto, be discovered reinscribing that which it proposes to critique. "Power relations are always two-way; that is to say, however subordinate an actor may be in a social relationship, the very fact of involvement in that relationship gives him or her a certain amount of power over the other," Anthony Giddens observes.[44] The inter-involvement of resistance and control is systemic: it derives from the way language and culture get articulated. Any utterance is bounded by the other utterances that the language makes possible. Its shape is the correlative of theirs: as with the duck/rabbit drawing, when you see the duck the rabbit lurks round its edges, constituting an alternative that may spring into visibility. Any position supposes its intrinsic *op*-position. All stories comprise within themselves the ghosts of the alternative stories they are trying to exclude.

It does not follow, therefore, that the outcome of the interinvolvement of resistance and control must be the incorporation of the subordinate. Indeed, Foucault says the same, though he is often taken as the theorist of entrapment. In *The History of Sexuality: An Introduction,* he says there is no "great Refusal," but envisages "a plurality of resistances . . . spread over time and space at varying densities, at times mobilising groups or individuals in a definitive way." He *denies* that these must be "only a reaction or rebound, forming with respect to the basic domination an underside that is in the end always passive, doomed to perpetual defeat."[45] In fact, a dissident text may derive its leverage, its purchase, precisely from its partial implication with the dominant. It may embarrass the dominant by appropriating its concepts and imagery. For instance, it seems clear that nineteenth-century legal, medical, and sexological discourses on homosexuality made possible new forms of control; but, at the same time, they also made possible what Foucault terms "a 'reverse' discourse," whereby "homosexuality began to speak in its own behalf, to demand that its legitimacy or 'naturality' be acknowledged, often in the same vocabulary, using the same categories by which it was medically disqualified."[46] Deviancy returns from abjection by deploying just those terms that relegated it there in the first place. A dominant discourse cannot prevent "abuse" of its resources. Even a text that aspires to contain a subordinate perspective must first bring it into visibility; even to misrepresent, one must present. And once that has happened, there can be no guarantee that the subordinate will stay safely in its prescribed place. Readers do not have to respect closures—we do not, for instance, have to accept that the independent women characters in Shakespearean comedies find their proper destinies in the marriage deals at the ends of those plays. We can insist on our sense that the middle of such a text arouses expectations that exceed the closure.

Conversely, a text that aspires to dissidence cannot control meaning either. It is bound to slide into disabling nuances that it fails to anticipate, and it cannot prevent the drawing of reactionary inferences by readers who want to do that. (Among other things, this might serve as a case against ultra-leftism, by which I mean the complacency of finding everyone else to be ideologically suspect.) There can be no security in textuality: no scriptor can control the reading of his or her text. And when, in any instance, either incorporation or resistance turns out to be the more successful, that is not in the nature of things. It is because of *their relative strengths in that situation*. So it is not quite as Jonathan Goldberg has recently put it, turning the entrapment model inside out, that "dominant discourses allow their own subversion precisely because hegemonic control is an impossible dream, a self-deluding fantasy."[47] Either outcome depends on the specific balance of historical forces. Essex's rebellion failed because he could not muster adequate support on the day. It is the same with competence. Williams remarks that the development of writing reinforced cultural divisions, but also that "there was no way to teach a man to read the Bible . . . which did not also enable him to read the radical press." Keith Thomas observes that "the uneven social distribution of literacy skills greatly widened the gulf between the classes"; but he illustrates also the fear that "if the poor learned to read and write they would become seditious, atheistical, and discontented with their humble position."[48] Both may occur, in varying degrees; it was, and is, all to play for.

It is to circumvent the entrapment model that I have generally used the term *dissident* rather than *subversive,* since the latter may seem to imply achievement—that something *was subverted*—and hence (since mostly the government did not fall, patriarchy did not crumble) that containment must have occurred. "Dissidence" I take to imply refusal of an aspect of the dominant, without prejudging an outcome. This may sound like a weaker claim, but I believe it is actually stronger insofar as it posits a field necessarily open to continuing contest, in which at some conjunctures the dominant will lose ground while at others the subordinate will scarcely maintain its position. As Jonathan Dollimore has said, dissidence may provoke brutal repression, and that shows not that it was all a ruse of power to consolidate itself, but that "the challenge really *was* unsettling."[49]

The implications of these arguments for literary criticism are substantial, for it follows that formal textual analysis cannot determine whether a text is subversive or contained. The historical conditions in which it is being deployed are decisive. "Nothing can be intrinsically or essentially subversive in the sense that prior to the event subversiveness can be more than potential; in other words it cannot be guaranteed a priori, independent of articulation, context and reception," Dollimore observes.[50] Nor, independently of context, can anything be said to be safely contained. This prospect scandalizes literary criticism, because it means that meaning is not adequately deducible from the text-on-the-page. The text is always a site of cultural contest, but it is never a self-sufficient site.

It is a key proposition of cultural materialism that the specific historical conditions in which institutions and formations organize and are organized by textualities must be addressed. That is what Raymond Williams was showing us for thirty years. The entrapment model is suspiciously convenient for literary criticism, because it means that little would be gained by investigating the specific historical effectivity of texts. And, indeed, Don Wayne very shrewdly suggests that the success of prominent new historicists may derive in large part from their skills in close reading—admittedly of a far wider range of texts—

which satisfy entirely traditional criteria of performativity in academic criticism.[51] Cultural materialism calls for modes of knowledge that literary criticism scarcely possesses, or even knows how to discover— modes, indeed, that hitherto have been cultivated distinctively within that alien other of essentialist humanism, Marxism. These knowledges are in part the provinces of history and other social sciences—and, of course, they bring in their train questions of historiography and epistemology that require theory more complex than the tidy post-structuralist formula that everything, after all, is a text (or that every-thing is theater). This prospect is valuable in direct proportion to its difficulty for, as Foucault maintains, the boundaries of disciplines effect a policing of discourses, and their erosion may, in itself, help to "detach the power of truth from the forms of hegemony (social, economic and cultural) within which it operates at the present time" in order to constitute "a new politics of truth."[52]

Shakespearean plays are themselves powerful stories. They contrib-ute to the perpetual contest of stories that constitutes culture: its representations, and our critical accounts of them, reinforce or chal-lenge prevailing notions of what the world is like, of how it might be. "The detailed and substantial *performance of a known model* of 'people like this, relations like this', is in fact the real achievement of most serious novels and plays," Raymond Williams observes;[53] by appealing to the reader's sense of how the world *is*, the text affirms the validity of the model it invokes. Among other things, *Othello* invites *recognition* that this is how people are, how the world goes. That is why the criteria of plausibility are political. This effect is not countered, as essentialist-humanists have long supposed, by literary quality; the more persuasive the writing, the greater its potential for political intervention.

The quintessential traditional critical activity was always interpre-tive, getting the text to make sense. Hence the speculation about character motivation, image patterns, thematic integration, structure: the task always was *to help the text into coherence*. And the discovery of coherence was taken as the demonstration of quality. However, such practice may feed into a reactionary politics. The easiest way to make *Othello* plausible in Britain is to rely on the lurking racism, sexism, and superstition in British culture. Why does Othello, who has considerable experience of people, fall so conveniently for Iago's stories? We can make his gullibility plausible by suggesting that black people are generally of a rather simple disposition. To explain why Desdemona elopes with Othello and then becomes so submissive, we might appeal to a supposedly fundamental silliness and passivity of women. Baffled in the attempt to find motive for Iago's malignancy, we can resort to the devil, or the consequence of skepticism towards conventional morality, or homosexuality. Such interpretations might be plausible; might "work," as theater people say; but only because they activate regressive aspects of our cultural formation.

Actually, coherence is a chimera, as my earlier arguments should suggest. No story can contain all the possibilities it brings into play; coherence is always selection. And the range of feasible readings depends not only on the text but on the conceptual framework within which we address it. Literary criticism tells its own stories. It is, in effect, a subculture, asserting its own distinctive criteria of plausibility. Education has taken as its brief the socialization of students into these criteria, while masking this project as the achievement by talented individuals (for it is in the program that most should fail) of a just and true reading of texts that are just and true. A cultural materialist practice will review the institutions that retell the Shakespeare stories, and will attempt also a self-consciousness about its own situation within those institutions. We need not just to produce different readings but to shift the criteria of plausibility.

3 When Is a Character Not a Character? Desdemona, Olivia, Lady Macbeth, and Subjectivity

Why, in the Peking Opera, are women's roles played by men?
... Because only a man knows how a woman is supposed to act.
David Henry Hwang, *M. Butterfly*

Nothing so true as what you once let fall,
"Most Women have no Characters at all."
Alexander Pope, "To a Lady"

THE DISCONTINUITY OF DESDEMONA

Desdemona is not usually regarded as a problem.[1] Traditionally, she has been celebrated as one of Shakespeare's great women characters—celebrated mainly, of course, by men, since they have dominated the discourses of criticism. But surely there is a great mystery. On her first appearance, Desdemona is spectacularly confident, bold, and unconventional. Summoned to the Senate to explain her elopement with Othello, she justifies herself coolly and coherently, confessing without a blush that she was "half the wooer" (1.3.176).[2] Further, she speaks up uninvited, and on the outrageous theme of women's sexual desire, demanding to go with her husband to Cyprus so that they may consummate the marriage:

> if I be left behind,
> A moth of peace, and he go to the war,
> The rites of love for which I love him are bereft me.
> (1.3.255–57)

Despite such extraordinarily spirited behavior, Desdemona becomes the most conventional spouse. Mainly we see her wheedling for the restoration of Cassio, in the sad posture of the wife trying to manage her husband:

> my lord shall never rest,
> I'll watch him tame, and talk him out of patience;
> His bed shall seem a school, his board a shrift.
>
> (3.3.22–24)

Even this she does ineptly: despite her earlier intuition on how to address the Senate, she is now stupidly blind to the effect she is having. When Othello starts to abuse her, she is abjectly fearful and consequently dishonest, making matters worse. In her denials, even, she is strangely acquiescent:

> those that do teach young babes
> Do it with gentle means, and easy tasks;
> He might ha' chid me so, for, in good faith,
> I am a child at chiding.
>
> (4.2.113–60)

She allows herself to be killed with slight protest (5.2.23–85).

Now, I don't think it implausible, in principle, that Desdemona could be so disheartened by Othello's attitude that she might eventually lose all her original spirit and intelligence. How this happens might be elaborated through action, dialogue, and soliloquy. It may not be easy, but Shakespeare is reckoned to be good at this sort of thing—in Othello's case, we may observe his changing attitudes in considerable detail. Desdemona is a disjointed sequence of positions that women are conventionally supposed to occupy. The bold Desdemona of the opening romantic initiative is one possible position—we see it also in Rosalind in *As You Like It*, Jessica in *The Merchant of Venice*, Perdita in *The Winter's Tale*. The nagging spouse is another. Linda Woodbridge wants to believe that early modern authors created full, lively characters, rather than following their own stultifying theories of womanhood, but in this respect she is uneasy nonetheless: "Although Desdemona is no domineering shrew, her behaviour at one point comes dangerously close to stereotype."[3] The final Desdemona, who submits to Othello's abuse and violence, takes the posture of other abused women in texts of the period—sitting like Patience on a monument, as Viola puts it in *Twelfth Night*.[4] It is almost as if the Wife of Bath were reincarnated as Griselda. If most critics have not noticed this discontinuity in Desdemona, it is because each of her appearances is plausible in itself, insofar as it corresponds to one of the models for "woman" that prevail in our cultures; and because, as Catherine Belsey observes, "discontinuity of being" can be read as the "inconstancy" that is supposed to be typically "feminine."[5]

Desdemona has no character of her own; she is a convenience in the story of Othello, Iago, and Venice. Othello asks, "Was this fair paper, this most goodly book, / Made to write 'whore' upon?" (4.2.73–74). The writing is done by Othello, Iago, Roderigo, Brabantio, the Duke, and Lodovico—they take Desdemona as a blank page for the versions of her that they want. She is written into a script that is organized through the perceptions and needs of male dominance in heterosexuality and patriarchal relations.[6]

Janet Adelman has identified a similar pattern in the presentation of Cressida. Despite her argument elsewhere that we should "respond to Shakespeare's characters as whole psychological entities," Adelman finds that "characters may not always permit us to respond to them in this way."[7] The early scenes of *Troilus and Cressida,* she shows, "establish not only some sense of Cressida but also the expectation that we will be allowed to know her as a full character, that she will maintain her relationship with us" (p. 122). But from the time when she arrives in the Greek camp, she appears as "a mere character type, a person with no conflict or inwardness at all." There are several ways, Adelman says, in which we might imagine motivations for Cressida, but the text affords "no enlightenment." Thus the play seems to enact the fantasy that Cressida becomes radically unknowable, irreducibly other, at the moment of her separation from Troilus (pp. 127–28). Adelman's argument as to why this should be is complex and psychoanalytic; ultimately, she says, "the necessities of Troilus' character, rather than of Cressida's require her betrayal of him. . . . she becomes a whore to keep him pure" (pp. 137–38). And this suits not only Troilus, of course: Adelman could easily have shown how Cressida's behavior has seemed, to many critics, no more than we should expect. Like Desdemona, Cressida is organized to suit her role in the story of the men. A character is not a character when she or he is needed to shore up a patriarchal representation.

FREUD ON LADY MACBETH

Freud's comments on Lady Macbeth do not produce a distinctive psychoanalytic insight, but his readiness not to accept common sense at face value leads him to ask a question that we have not often heard. Freud is struck by Lady Macbeth's initial determination: "Here is no hesitation, no sign of any internal conflict in her"—just "one faint stirring of reluctance" when she says she would have killed Duncan herself, "Had he not resembled / My father as he slept" (2.2.12–13). But after the banqueting scene (3.4), Freud observes, "she disappears from view" until the sleepwalking in act 5 scene 1. Now "she who had seemed so remorseless seems to have been borne down by remorse."[8] Freud finds this change to need explanation:

> And now we ask ourselves what it was that broke this character which had seemed forged from the toughest metal? Is it only disillusionment—the different aspect shown by the accomplished deed—and are we to infer that even in Lady Macbeth an originally gentle and womanly nature had been worked up to a concentration and high tension which could not endure for long, or ought we to seek for signs of a deeper motivation which will make this collapse more humanly intelligible to us? It seems to me impossible to come to any decision.
>
> (pp. 319–20)

Note that Freud is *not* satisfied with the idea that Lady Macbeth had "an originally gentle and womanly nature" and collapsed from the strain of violating that nature; for him this is not the way to make her "humanly intelligible."

Freud's suggestion is that childlessness is at the back of it all. He points out that Queen Elizabeth was obliged to recognize James VI of Scotland as her heir because she, like Lady Macbeth, produced no direct heirs, and that James was the son of Mary Stuart, whose execution Elizabeth had ordered. So "the accession of James I was like a demonstration of the curse of unfruitfulness and the blessings of continuous generation. And the action of Shakespeare's *Macbeth* is based on this same contrast" (p. 320). Hence the importance of Lady Macbeth's children: Macbeth is excited when he expects her to "Bring forth men-children only" (1.7.73), seeks to destroy Banquo's line (and indeed Macduff's and Siward's), and is marked as crucially disabled by Macduff's comment, "He has no children!" (4.3.216). On this premise, Freud suggests, Lady Macbeth's collapse could be explained as a reaction to her childlessness, which tells her "that it is through her own fault if her crime has been robbed of the better part of its fruits" (p. 322). The problem, of course, is that the play does not seem to allow long enough for the childlessness of the Macbeths to become an issue. In Holinshed's *Chronicles,* ten years pass, and there, as Freud thinks, failure to produce offspring might explain Macbeth's eventual transformation into a bloodthirsty tyrant. I have my own explanation for the compression of action in *Macbeth:* it is that Macbeth (like Richard III) cannot be seen to be settled as a de facto monarch because that would make his overthrow problematic. Jamesian ideology held that no established ruler should be challenged; out of respect for this, it is made to seem that Macbeth has hardly become king—significant thanes do not swear allegiance at his coronation and his attempt to hold a state banquet is a fiasco; his removal occurs within a phase of general uncertainty and instability (see chapter 5).

Baulked by the time scheme of the childlessness explanation, Freud returns to expressions of bafflement: "We must, I think, give up any hope of penetrating the triple layer of obscurity into which the bad preservation of the text, the unknown intention of the dramatist, and the hidden purport of the legend have become condensed" (p. 323). Reluctant, still, "to dismiss a problem like that of *Macbeth* as insoluble," he suggests that Lady Macbeth and Macbeth may be two parts of a single split personality, in which case "it would of course be pointless to regard her as an independent character and seek to discover the motives for her change, without considering the Macbeth who completes her" (p. 323). The character of Lady Macbeth is explicable only when she is not a character.

Other commentators have not experienced the difficulty that Freud does, and almost universally this is because they accept the interpretation of Lady Macbeth that he rejects: that she had "an originally gentle and womanly nature" that might be "worked up to a concentration and high tension" but "could not endure for long" such violence upon itself (p. 320). This case depends upon the notion of an essential gentleness—deriving of course from womanliness—that Lady Macbeth must *really, naturally,* have instantiated. This may be violated but yet, being as fundamental as her gender, it will return to possess her imagination. In this way, virtually the same pattern is presumed for Lady Macbeth as for Desdemona: initial bold behavior is succeeded eventually by a reversion to "feminine" passivity, with an episode of nagging the husband in between. Again, because this sequence seems plausible in our cultures, it seems satisfactory as character analysis, but in fact it is a story about the supposed nature of women. Strength and determination in women, it is believed, can be developed only at a cost, and their eventual failure is at once inevitable, natural, a punishment, and a warning. Lady Macbeth is a fantasy arrangement of elements that are taken to typify the acceptable and unacceptable faces of woman, and the relations between them. And this is what strikes critics as realistic.[9]

CHARACTER, SUBJECTIVITY, AND POSTSTRUCTURALISM

Of course, the character as category of analysis, in the manner of A. C. Bradley, has been repudiated often enough. In the 1930s, G. Wilson

Knight set it aside because he believed that each play was "a visionary whole, close-knit in personification, atmospheric suggestion, and direct poetic-symbolism."[10] This was a symbolist-modernist poetic; Knight's *Wheel of Fire* opened with a preface by T. S. Eliot. L. C. Knights was not quite so "visionary," but his disqualification of the naive question, "How many children had Lady Macbeth?" came from a similar belief in a poetic whole of which character might be quite a trivial part.[11] Also in the 1930s, character criticism was repudiated by historical scholars like Muriel Bradbrook and Lily B. Campbell, who insisted on the dependence of the plays upon conventions of story and stagecraft current when Shakespeare was writing. Campbell argued that Shakespeare was not using modern ideas of personality, but "the prevailing ideas of [sixteenth-century] humanists in regard to passion." Bradbrook denied that the characters are transcriptions from life, arguing rather that they depend on three main conventional principles: the superhuman nature of heroes, decorum, and the theory of humors.[12] Bradbrook remarked a disjunction between "the very simple and rigid moral framework of the plays" and "the system of rigidly defined types, of stock motivation and fixed plot." This, she held, produced a "kind of double personality" (pp. 61, 67–69). However, unlike cultural materialists and many feminists, Bradbrook did not go on to observe that such conventions relate to the organization of power relations in their society.

Despite these interventions, character criticism has remained the dominant mode; it has the advantage of opening the plays, relatively, to the ways nonprofessional audiences and readers think and live. Some scholar-critics also still rely on it. Recently Barbara Everett, of Oxford University, has suggested that changes in "the Macbeths" may be understood as married couples tending to grow like each other; this not only regards them as actual people but imagines a time scale far beyond the supposed time of the play.[13] Everett has evidently observed the discontinuity that Freud remarked, but seeks to explain it by a speculation about supposed personal development. John Bayley, also at Oxford, declared in 1981 that the distinctive quality of *Macbeth* derives from the feeling that we enter the consciousness of the protagonist: "mind and consciousness take over from tragic action, creating their own intimacies with us alongside and in defiance of it."[14] As for Bradley, these are people like us (though doubtless of a more refined quality). Even what appear to be new modes of analysis may rely upon a similar assumption. Some feminist critics have believed that they should defend the fullness and reality of female characters.[15] Linda Woodbridge argues that although Shakespeare and his contemporaries made "stuffy pronouncements on women" based on "the orthodox theory, . . . the lively women they created showed that their hearts were very impressed with (and often quite fond of) exuberant English Woman exactly as they found her."[16]

At another extreme, poststructuralist theory threatens to make character an altogether inappropriate category of analysis. Jonathan Goldberg calls upon critics to give up "notions of character as self-same, owned, capable of autonomy and change." He disputes that the voices of women characters are typically silenced, since *no* character has an autonomous voice anyway. We are in error when we attribute speech to individuals—"Do I speak or does something speak in me, something no smaller than the entire culture with all its multiple capacities?"[17] Goldberg develops his case especially in relation to Portia in *The Merchant of Venice,* where disguise indeed unsettles any expectations as to stability of personality. He says Portia "moves through the text, affirming the meeting of, the suspension of, difference." Her voice "plays on the unconscious of the text, reveals what is repressed when the law acts as if it were univocal" (p. 125). Catherine Belsey has argued similarly in relation to Viola in *Twelfth Night:* when she speaks as Cesario, she is "neither Viola nor Cesario, but a speaker who at this moment occupies a place which is not precisely masculine or feminine, where the notion of identity itself is disrupted to display a difference within subjectivity, and the singularity which resides in *this* difference." Drawing upon Julia Kristeva's essay "Women's Time," Belsey repudiates the liberal feminist idea of a "specifically feminine identity": "In the post-structuralist analysis subjectivity is not a single, unified presence but the point of intersection of a range of discourses, produced and re-produced as the subject occupies a series of places in the signifying system, takes on the multiplicity of meanings language offers."[18]

I agree with Goldberg and Belsey that what is recognized in our cultures as "character" in a play must be an effect of "the entire culture" and a "point of intersection of a range of discourses." However, Shakespearean plays have plainly given character critics a good deal to chew upon for a couple of centuries, and this I suspect is because they are written so as to produce, in some degree, what are interpreted (by those possessing the appropriate decoding knowledges) as character effects. This is Joel Fineman's view. He holds that in Shakespeare's sonnets the tradition of Petrarchan idealizing poetry is sensed as old-fashioned, so opening up a space for subjective introspection.

"The subject of Shakespeare's sonnets experiences himself *as* his difference from himself," Fineman asserts, and this accounts for "the deep personal interiority of the sonnets' poetic persona." From this point "a literature of deep subjective affect" is inaugurated, such that "even Shakespeare's most thinly developed dramatic characters, his Hermias and Helenas, have always been seen to participate in, and to accommodate themselves to, a theatre organised by a logic of personality—a theatre of psycho-logic as opposed to an Aristotelean theater of logical action—whose subjective intelligibility and authority have been uniformly remarked by the entire tradition of Shakespeare criticism, and not only by romantic critics of character." This, Fineman insists, is not a matter of intuiting the truth of human nature, but "a determinate literary effect," inducing "the literary effect of a subject."[19]

A persuasive account of how dramatis personae may be written so as to produce character effects is offered by William Nigel Dodd. He holds that in such dramatic texts "the audience demands and receives 'information about' something conventionally agreed to be 'happening', coincidentally with this information, here and now on the stage." The actors are, in fact, transmitting messages to the audience, but they are scripted to behave as if they are transmitting messages to each other. By thus appearing to recognize and respond to each other, they "simulate the conditions of social exchange" and hence appear as *selves*. For such exchange permits the dramatis persona "not only to reify himself (or other) as *sender/receiver,* but also to attribute *intentionality/non-intentionality* to self or other, thus creating the prerequisites for the representation of *decision* which, as Peter Szondi has shown, is the nucleus of intersubjective drama."[20] Further indicators of subjectivity might be self-reference and self-questioning (including soliloquy), indecision, lying. To be sure, such features do not amount to a modern conception of character. Rather, Dodd suggests, this semantic strategy is the means through which "authors operating in the period when the modern conception of the individual person was only just beginning to acquire its present contours (roughly from the mid-16th century on in England) were, and still are in many cases, able to communicate this sense of depth in spite of the fact that the formal psychology upon which they often drew (typically that of the 'humours') offers an inadequate account of man's inner nature (even by Renaissance standards)" (p. 146). So some early modern texts produce a sufficient impression of interaction between simulated selves to enable modern character criticism. This could be coincidence (the signals encoded in an alien culture affording an alternative pattern of significance to modern readers); more likely it is because there is a sufficient continuity—by no means an identity—between early modern ideas of subjectivity and what later critics apprehend as character.

For, as Belsey has demonstrated, it is in the Elizabethan theater distinctively that the development of modern indicators of subjectivity may be observed. She defines the modern sense of character as "locating agency and meaning in the unified human subject" and finds it fully in place in the Restoration. But Belsey shows some modern markers of subjectivity to be present already in early modern plays. The examples she adduces are all ambivalent, never quite separating the speaking "I" that is a subject for him- or herself from the representative figures of fifteenth-century drama. Gloucester in *3 Henry VI* may seem to be "defining an emerging interiority, an independent realm of consciousness," but he is also—in Belsey's reading *rather*— "declaring a total and unified commitment to evil."[21] In my view, Belsey is slightly too insistent on banishing agency and meaning from the dramatis personae of early modern plays. To be sure, when the Duchess of Malfi says, "I am Duchess of Malfi still" (4.2.147), she is not observing one of the customary markers of modern ideas of subjectivity—namely, a distinction between public and private identities. But this is in a context where the duchess has violated the public requirements of such a personage by conceiving an inappropriate private passion (inappropriate in the view of Antonio, Bosola, and Cariola as well as Ferdinand); in such a context, "I am Duchess of Malfi still" is *reasserting* a continuity of public and private that the action thus far has drawn into question.

In another important analysis, Francis Barker also takes the question of subjectivity historically, arguing that "*Hamlet* is a contradictory, transitional text" in this respect—that it is still defining its subjects largely in terms of their place in the social plenum. For although, in the speech where Hamlet says "I have that within that passes show" (1.2.85), a separation opens up between the inner reality of the subject and an inauthentic exterior, and "an interior subjectivity begins to speak," this interiority remains, Barker says, "gestural."[22] Critics have striven "to recuperate [Hamlet] to a conception of essential subjectivity *fully realised*," but "rather than the plenitude of an individual presence, the text dramatises its impossibility." At the center of the mystery of Hamlet, Barker memorably declares, there is "nothing" (pp. 36–38). But, as with Belsey, I find Barker too ready to discount interiority in these plays. It should be possible to probe further into the relations between subjectivity and character, between traditional and poststructuralist criticism. Simon Shepherd acknowledges rather reluctantly that "the Elizabethan theatre did develop towards the portrayal of apparently more unitary subjects," but finds this to be not an even "progress," as traditional criticism has supposed.[23] He demonstrates that crucial boundaries—self and not-self, private and public, natural law and individuality—were under contest from Anglican, Machiavellian, and puritan conceptions of the self. In the first of these, people were said to be governed by reason, a natural faculty; in the second, to be moved primarily by individual self-preservation; and in the third, they might speak disruptively out of a confident possession of the word of God. Such contest obviously does not allow for any straightforward establishment of the individual as a single, unified presence, but it does point towards an enhancement of subjectivity. Shepherd quotes *De la vérité de la religion chrestienne* by Philippe de Mornay (in the translation attributed to Philip Sidney): "There is in man a double speech; the one in the mind, which they call the inward speech, which we conceive afore we utter it; and the other the sounding image thereof, which is uttered by our mouth and is termed the speech of the voice; either of both the which we perceive at every word that we intend to pronounce" (p. 79). This does not suppose a unitary "I," but it indicates a complex awareness of interiority.

What has partly moved recent commentators, in my view rightly, is awareness that character as it has been envisaged in our cultures involves essentialist humanism. This conception of "Man," basically a development of the Enlightenment, Jonathan Dollimore summarizes as "an ideology of a transhistorical human nature and an autonomous subjectivity, the second being an instantiation of the first; in short, a metaphysics of identity [that] occludes historical and social process. A critique of essentialism is about making history visible both within the subjectivity it informs, and beyond subjectivity, by, as it were, restoring individuals to history."[24] One objection to essentialist humanism is that it is anachronistic. Dollimore argues that human identity was understood in the early modern period as constituted as well as constitutive; Machiavelli, Montaigne, and Bacon anticipate a materialist perspective by suggesting that it is constituted socially, but even those who believed that Man is informed by God allow that such constitution occurs and, further, that it correlates with the requirements of the social order (which were supposed to be the requirements of God). Dollimore takes Descartes's *cogito ergo sum* (1637) as marking a crucial stage in the history of metaphysics, a point at which "the metaphysically derivative soul gives way to the autonomous, individuated essence, the self-affirming consciousness" (p. 254). The second objection to essentialist humanism is that it imagines the self as autonomous, self-constituting, and self-sufficient, and as the uniquely valid source of meaning and truth. Thus Bradley's statement, which he intended not just as a description of a certain kind of drama but a truth about life: "The centre of tragedy, therefore, may be said with equal truth to lie in action issuing from character, or in character issuing in action."[25] This effaces the mechanisms of cultural production and their implication in power structures.

None of the opponents of character criticism I have been invoking disputes altogether that dramatis personae in Shakespearean plays are written, at least some of the time, in ways that suggest that they have subjectivities. The objection is to jumping from that point to a Bradleyan or essentialist-humanist conception of character. My contention is that some Shakespearean dramatis personae are written so as to suggest, not just an intermittent, gestural, and problematic subjectity, but a continuous or developing interiority or consciousness; and that we should seek a way of talking about this that does not slide back into character criticism or essentialist humanism. This way of talking would not suppose that performances attempted an unbroken illusionistic frame; or that this continuous interiority is self-constituted and independent of the discursive practices of the culture; or that it manifests an essential unity. The key features in this redefined conception of character are two: an impression of subjectivity, interiority, or consciousness, and a sense that these maintain a sufficient continuity or development through the scenes of the play. The impression of subjectivity I have explored already, using William Dodd's model of how dialogue simulates the conditions of social exchange. A sense of continuity or development is crucial also: it involves the indicators of subjectivity appearing sufficiently connected for the audience to regard the character as a single person throughout. The evidence that many early modern people were at least beginning to experience themselves approximately and partly in such a manner is in my judgment abundant (I argue in chapter 7 that one attraction of protestantism was as a self-consciousness-producing agent). It is to be observed neither in explicit pronouncements nor especially in moments of disjunctive awareness, but in the unselfconscious texture of such day-to-day intercourse as survives for us to inspect. These people were very different from us, but not totally different.

So when critics believe they find a continuous consciousness in Desdemona and Lady Macbeth, they are responding to cues planted in the text for the initial audiences. My contention earlier in this chapter that those cues do not work out in the way traditional character critics assert—that Desdemona and Lady Macbeth seem for a while to have continuous consciousnesses but collapse back into stereotypical notions of woman—does not mean that the cues are not there or that the codes for reading them are wrong. It means that the project ran into difficulty (later in this chapter I say more of how that works). In principle, Goldberg and Belsey are right: continuous interiority in a dramatis persona can only be an effect of culture and its multiple discourses, and those can never be held to a determinate meaning. There is no stability in textuality, as poststructuralist critics have been able to show. Nevertheless, this does not mean that there is some kind of free play of discourse or textuality; nor is it a reason for dispensing altogether with character—as I have redefined it. To the contrary, it is one of the major discursive formations active in these texts, and it needs to be addressed if we are to explore how subjectivities are constituted. For in our cultures, character is a major category through which we conceptualize. Jacqueline Rose writes of "that myth of linguistic cohesion and sexual identity which we must live by."[26] There is no essential woman or man, but there are ideas of women and men and their consciousnesses, and these appear in representations.

The character of Macbeth, then, is not a mysterious natural essence. Rather, he is situated at the intersection of discourses and historical forces that are competing, we might say, to fill up his subjectivity. At the start, he is acting out the dominant story—killing traitors to the current regime. This story, we hear, has the support of nature and God, but even so Duncan (judging by the revolts he is suffering) is having trouble getting it to stick. The culture represented in the play offers an alternative scenario—one that Macbeth's experience of Scottish politics, the Witches, his wife, and his own importance in the state suggest to him—namely that he might overthrow Duncan and replace him. Even so, Macbeth does not easily free himself from Duncan's story and the construction of selfhood it is supplying. In the soliloquy at the start of act 1 scene 7, he cannot find it in himself to discard the religious, natural, and social sanctions that legitimate Duncan's authority. His sense of himself is bound up with recognition of his place in the current order:

> He hath honour'd me of late; and I have bought
> Golden opinions from all sorts of people,
> Which would be worn now in their newest gloss,
> Not cast aside so soon.
>
> (1.7.32–35)

However, Lady Macbeth says it will be easy to make the alternative story work, and she reinforces her case with an appeal to manliness. Significantly, manliness comes from within the orthodox idea of what a thane should be like—he is supposed to be bold and virile to maintain and justify his superior status. This is a good instance of how disruption derives from contradiction within the dominant: the masculine ethos that generally secures the conditions for Duncan's rule cannot altogether be controlled, and may be mobilized to facilitate his overthrow. So Macbeth finds the alternative story persuasive, and persuades himself that others will be persuaded also: "Will it not be receiv'd / . . . That they have done't?" Lady Macbeth's rejoinder is more circumspect: "Who dares receive it other . . . ?" (1.7.75–80). She does not shrink from acknowledging that compulsion may help an uncertain story to prevail.

I have given a rather schematic account, but it may serve to show how Macbeth's subjectivity is not his unique, ineluctable possession but constituted from rival stories that are current, though not equally authorized, in his society. His dissidence arises not from a confident subjectivity choosing to reorient itself—though this is the story Macbeth aspires to—but from a radically insecure subjectivity, one swaying between divergent possible selves and vulnerable to manipulation. Personal consistency, like stability of language and referent, is a myth. Nevertheless, Macbeth's subjectivity appears adequately continuous, unlike that of Lady Macbeth; though many ideological complexities may be observed in his representation, he does not have to fall silent (Othello and Desdemona form a similar contrast). Insofar as the concept of character is active in the play, Macbeth is compatible with it. But insofar as this concept is suggested in respect of Lady Macbeth, as it is initially, it cannot be carried through. In fact, she is sacrificed to keep Macbeth's story going. Correspondingly, he appears to have the fuller subjectivity (he is scripted so as to produce more of what our cultures customarily interpret as psychological density). The key to this effect seems to be that Macbeth entertains more than one discourse at a time, and interiority is projected by an audience or reader as the place where discourses intersect. He appears to choose between competing discourses, and hence to stand as a subject, independently of either. The audience observes Macbeth continuing to believe in the dominant story even after he has chosen to defy it (and as a consequence becoming the tyrant that that story says he must become). Lady Macbeth, conversely, cannot articulate complexity. Initially she is committed to the murder; when she changes, it is a sudden switch and is explored in neither soliloquy nor dialogue. Her character breaks down when it has to change.[27]

In my redefinition of character as continuous consciousness, I have not posited metaphysical coherence or "unity." For my argument, it is necessary only that the character manifest adequate continuity; as Dodd suggests, the reader will fill this in as psychological density if she or he wishes. Unity is expected in essentialist humanism, and generally it is discovered through consideration of the characters of Shakespearean plays. However, in my view this is a delusion: the effect attributed to unity derives from something else. That is why character critics only occasionally express disappointment: though full realization of unified psychological density can only be a chimera, they do not experience it like that. The reason is that the subjectivities that are admired in the plays do not actually depend upon the achievement of unity, coherence, and full presence. Character criticism depends in actuality not on unity but on superfluity—on the *thwarting* of the aspiration to realize unity in the face of material resistance. That is why "stereotypical" characters, who do have a certain unity, are thought unsatisfactory, and why when characters gain an appearance of unity through closure at the end of a text they become suddenly uninteresting. And it is why there are so many essays on the characters of Hamlet and Macbeth: they resist any convenient coherence. Francis Barker, I have noted, finds Hamlet's interiority merely "gestural," not offering "the plenitude of an individual presence," having "nothing" at the center. In my view that is not quite right: I see Hamlet producing subjectivity effects all the time in his dialogue, but some of them are provocatively discontinuous, one with another. They construct a sequence of loosely linked interiorities, not a coherent identity. That is why, as Barker observes, Hamlet tantalizes traditional critics: they cannot quite get him to add up without surplus. But this is not because there is insufficient subjectivity in the text for them to work on, but because there is too much. The text overloads the interpretive system.

What poststructuralist theory has not explained is the complacency of essentialist-humanist critics, who have generally found Shakespearean characters very rewarding to speculate about. Character criticism is not disappointed by superfluity because the condition for its practice is an incoherence that challenges interpretation; the text produces too much meaning for a unitary account, and at that point provokes (like the introspecting self) the stabilizing intervention of interpretation. Each reading is attributed to an original unity, as essentialist ideology requires, and the occurrence of multiple and incompatible readings is attributed to the fertility of Shakespeare's genius. So interpretation disavows that which incites it. The essentialist critical project is, of course, never achieved, but that deferral allows its continuance (there must always be more readings). And that is why poststructuralist analysis can show those readings to be inadequate to texts that are compounded of divergent, incompatible, and contradictory discourses, and yet not apparently disable traditional practice (though it does tell it something it has been trying not to notice).

WHAT OLIVIA WANTS

I am going to take Olivia in *Twelfth Night* as a further test of my contention that Shakespearean plays produce dramatis personae that are like characters—to the extent that they are presented in ways that invite an expectation of an adequately continuous interiority. Once more, the expectation is eventually frustrated, Olivia falls silent, representation breaks down. Finally she proves to be not a continuous consciousness (let alone an autonomous essence), but a strand in a far wider cultural argument. Also, I shall again show how critics write as if they respect the individuality of Olivia as a character, but actually subordinate their account of her to their need to cover over the point at which the impression of continuous consciousness breaks down. Whatever her subjective preferences have seemed to be, Olivia must be discovered to want what the play's closure needs her to have; and the effect, again, is a regressive gender politics.

Important recent work on previously "unthinkable" topics, cross-dressing and homosexuality, helps us to take seriously the relationship of Antonio and Sebastian in *Twelfth Night*—which is mutual, emotional, and substantially presented.[28] Stephen Orgel has argued that Shakespeare's culture was *not* morbidly fearful of male homosexuality—because this was not perceived, generally, as an impediment to heterosexuality and marriage. Hence the genial deployment of cross-dressing in these comedies. Rather, it was women and heterosexuality that generated the stronger anxiety for men—they threatened the profoundest potential disruptions to the male psyche and the social order. Louis Montrose has powerfully analyzed the idea of the Amazon in *A Midsummer Night's Dream,* observing that such mythology "seems symbolically to embody and to control a collective anxiety about the power of the female not only to dominate or reject the male but to create and destroy him."[29]

But what about Olivia's passion for Cesario, the disguised Viola? In his essay "Fiction and Friction," Stephen Greenblatt evokes the "scandalous shadow story" that "the gross impropriety of a homosexual coupling" may be at issue there. However, Sebastian is set up to substitute for Cesario, and so Olivia's love was, after all, a happy swerving from nature's bias—at least, that is how Sebastian thinks of it (5.1.258).[30] But is it right to read Olivia's passion as *really* for Viola, and hence as lesbian? Olivia does not think of herself as experiencing lesbian attraction—she believes she is in love with the young man Cesario. Taking the real issue as a lesbianism of which Olivia is unaware allows critics to discount her apparent wishes: Greenblatt says: "Only by not getting what she wants has Olivia been able to get what she wants and, more important, to want what she gets" (p. 71). But what does Olivia want? A leading tactic for controlling the desires of women in our cultures is refusing to believe them when they say what they want. Nor is this specially the mode of male commentators—feminist psychoanalytic critics also have assumed that Olivia has at some level made a homosexual object choice.[31]

I shall try to take seriously what Olivia says—which is that she wants neither a lesbian relationship nor marriage with a man like Orsino. She wants to marry a man like Cesario. In exploring this, I shall be treating Olivia, initially, as if she were a person with continuous consciousness. This is surely what the text invites us to do, for it is widely agreed that Olivia's scenes with Cesario/Viola produce distinctively intricate impressions of interaction between simulated selves—giving rise to self-reference and self-questioning, soliloquy, indecision, and lying. And there is continuity:

> Give me leave, beseech you. I did send,
> After the last enchantment you did here,
> A ring in chase of you. So did I abuse
> Myself, my servant, and, I fear me, you.
> Under your hard construction must I sit,
> To force that on you in a shameful cunning
> Which you knew none of yours. What might you think?
> (3.1.113–19)

Olivia interrupts Cesario, reminds him of earlier interactions, interprets not just her own behavior and feelings but those of others, and asks for Cesario's interpretation. And Viola/Cesario remembers, understands, and responds. The scene is written so as to lead an audience to infer a continuous interiority in Olivia.

What, then, does Olivia want? She is reported as being in mourning: the Captain says she is

> A virtuous maid, the daughter of a count
> That died some twelvemonth since; then leaving her
> In the protection of his son, her brother,
> Who shortly also died; for whose dear love
> (They say) she hath abjur'd the company
> And sight of men.
>
> (1.2.36–41)

Critics have generally assumed that Olivia is preoccupied with her brother,[32] but the Captain's report introduces a hesitation ("(They say)"), and we have in the next scene a different account of her motivation from Sir Toby:

> She'll none o' the' Count; she'll not match above her degree, neither in estate, years, nor wit; I have heard her swear't.
>
> (1.3.106–8)

This, surely, is why Olivia falls for Cesario. He seems the son of a gentleman (whereas she is the daughter of a count) and is younger than she. He seems intelligent enough, but is readily dominated by her—he backs off as she advances. Olivia wants a man who is not too masculine. The deaths of her male kin have left her in the rare situation of being an independent woman,[33] and from this privileged position she has decided that she would prefer not to marry a man who will dominate her. She has not seen Orsino, notice—she dislikes the very idea of him. To Cesario she does not plead her mourning, but repeats, directly, "I cannot love him" (1.5.261, 266, 284). She pauses when she fears that Cesario may be other than he appears—not a woman, the fear that critics presume—but Orsino: "Not too fast: soft! soft! / Unless the master were the man" (1.5.297–98). Olivia wants *the man* without *the master*.

Orsino's expressed attitudes towards women are quite unpleasant; they allow us to see that Olivia's intuition about him is well-founded. He says Cesario should marry a woman younger than himself because men are inconstant and abandon women when they lose their "fair flower"; therefore, he says, the best way of keeping a marriage going is for the wife to start with the advantage of relative youth, so that her physical attractions will last longer (2.4.29–39). Viola agrees—

unlike Olivia, she is thoroughly self-oppressed. Actually, Orsino himself doesn't appear very masculine, but this, I suggest, is because he is courting Olivia. Men were—indeed are—supposed to adopt a submissive, pleading posture during the period of courtship; upon marriage, conventionally, they revert to a "masculine" stance. Commentators assume that it is in Orsino's character to be "effeminate,"[34] but Linda Woodbridge recognizes it as a role: "Male characters under the influence of Petrarchanism wept, sighed, complained, exchanged their manly freedom for abject slavery to feminine whim."[35] Olivia credits Orsino with the masculine virtues customary for a man of his class—

> In voices well divulg'd, free, learn'd, and valiant,
> And in dimension, and the shape of nature,
> A gracious person.
>
> (1.5.264–66)

Indeed, he plays his subordinate, courtship role with little conviction; his inclination, evidently, is to be peremptory and domineering. His idea of love is male domination—he begins by declaring how marvelous it will be when Olivia devotes herself to him such that the "sovereign thrones" of her passions, thoughts, and emotions, and her "sweet perfections," will all be supplied and filled "with one self king." And that king will be Orsino (1.1.35–40). He despises women:

> Alas, their love may be call'd appetite,
> No motion of the liver, but the palate,
> That suffers surfeit, cloyment, and revolt.
>
> (2.4.98–100)

This is hardly ever true of women in Shakespeare's writing; even the "false" Cressida is so under duress. At the start of act 5, Orsino impatiently accosts Olivia, imperiously upbraids her and violently threatens her and Cesario (5.1.110–29). The "lover" gives way to masculine and class assertiveness. Orsino, in fact, is like Oberon in Montrose's description: he wants to "gain possession . . . of the woman's desire and obedience; he must master his own dependency upon his wife."[36] Olivia is surely right to think that Orsino is not the kind of man she would like.

Olivia's independent position makes her sole head of the household. According to Sebastian, she manages it well—it is a sign of her sanity, without which

> She could not sway her house, command her followers,
> Take and give back affairs and their despatch,
> With such a smooth, discreet, and stable bearing
> As I perceive she does.
>
> (4.3.17–20)

Even so, Olivia has trouble with Sir Toby, who is inclined to masculine roistering; as a dependent relative, he should be subject to the discipline of the head of household, but he does not accord Olivia the authority of a man. Indeed, if Sir Toby could get her to marry Sir Andrew, he would control her through him. The Malvolio disturbance stems from the same source (all these matters are far more tightly interconnected than can be appreciated by critics who see the question of marriage in the play as individual and psychological). He is the senior male and some responsibilities of the head of household devolve upon him—in particular, Olivia tells him to turn Sir Toby out of doors (2.3.73–75). The obvious literary comparison is with *The Duchess of Malfi*. There a woman is almost free of domineering male kin and tries to take Olivia's stance. Antonio, like Malvolio, is the steward, with a similar commitment to an orderly household—he admires the way the king of France "quits first his royal palace / Of flatt'ring sycophants, of dissolute / And infamous persons."[37] The Duchess finds that Antonio has taken her cares upon him (1.1.295) and proposes to him, observing: "The misery of us that are born great— / We are forc'd to woo because none dare woo us" (1.2.363–64). It is not quite so surprising, therefore, that Malvolio imagines himself having greatness thrust upon him in the form of marriage with Olivia: the idea is produced by his structural position as well as by Maria's plot. Olivia's refusal to commit her affairs to the management of a strong male troubles the system.

The outcome is like that we have seen with Lady Macbeth and Desdemona: the woman who tries to pursue her own line is discovered trying to manipulate men and is prevented. It is a profoundly conservative scenario—and, of course, one that many critics have embraced—usually in the guise of an expectation that Olivia should make a "natural," psychologically "mature" match. This was C. L. Barber's position, in a strangely admired book—admired by heterosexuals presumably, since Barber imagines that all readers and audiences will experience as "wish-fulfilment" the idea that "playful reversal of sexual roles can renew the meaning of the normal relation."[38] Even Barber is disconcerted by the tidy way Sebastian is substituted for Cesario, but he is prepared to put up with anything so long as masculinity triumphs: "The particular implausibility that there should be an identical man to take Viola's place with Olivia is submerged in the general, beneficent realisation that there is such a thing as a man" (p. 246). To Barber, Sebastian's "manly reflex is delightful" when he fights Sir Andrew: it shows that "Sebastian is not likely to be dominated" (p. 246). He thinks this is as it should be—Sebastian will sort out "this spoiled and dominating young heiress" (p. 245). Alternatively, we may ponder how coercive is the demand to join the heterosexual majority—characteristic as it is of most accounts of comedy.

My complaint is not that Barber is wrong about *Twelfth Night,* but that he is pleased about it; in fact he comes nearer than most commentators to seeing how precisely Olivia is frustrated. For, of course, the play depends on Sebastian not being *altogether* identical with Viola: not only is he a man, he is just such a man as Olivia does not want. Even at the point of marriage, she believes she is marrying an unmasculine man, for Sebastian backs off, like Cesario, until the last moment:

> OLIVIA: Nay, come, I prithee; would thou'dst be rul'd by me!
> SEBASTIAN: Madam, I will.
> OLIVIA: O, say so, and so be.
>
> (4.1.63–64)

Sebastian is hesitant because he hasn't met Olivia before; she cannot know that his compliance in such circumstances must indicate a bold—manly—kind of person. The action confirms this: Sebastian has already beaten Sir Andrew and proceeds at once to fight with and subdue Sir Toby, so his capacity to rule Olivia's household is clear enough. This is *not* what Olivia wanted. The Duke's reassurance makes it worse: "Be not amaz'd, right noble is his blood" (5.1.262). Cesario implied that he was a gentleman, but Sebastian turns out to be at least as statusful as Olivia. Furthermore (unsurprisingly, along with his fighting), Sebastian also has a complacent, conventional attitude to gender relations: "So comes it, lady, you have been mistook. / But nature to her bias drew in that" (5.1.257–58).

At this most crucial point, like Desdemona and Lady Macbeth, Olivia collapses as a character—insofar as that means the representation of a personage of continuous interiority. Just when all her desires have been systematically frustrated, she has virtually nothing to say. She has no lines at all to help us envisage the impact of it all on her subjectivity. Only a moment before, she has been typically independent—urging Cesario to assert their love and defy Orsino:

Fear not, Cesario, take thy fortunes up,
. Be that thou know'st thou art, and then thou art
As great as that thou fear'st.

(5.1.146–48)

But from the appearance of Sebastian alongside Cesario, at the point where it would be most interesting to see how Olivia will respond, she says only "Most wonderful!" (5.1.223). And to the "reassurances" of Orsino and Sebastian, which I have just quoted, she says nothing whatsoever. She could and should call for an annulment—get back to her initial position—she has the money to do that. But she reenters the dialogue only to handle, with her usual efficiency, the release of Malvolio (5.1.276–314, 327–78; in this respect her character is allowed to continue). In the middle of that, while they are fetching Malvolio, she has just one comment on her marriage:

My lord, so please you, these things further thought on,
To think me as well a sister, as a wife,
One day shall crown th'alliance on't, so please you,
Here at my house, and at my proper cost.

(5.1.315–18)

Orsino as brother is virtually as bad as Orsino as husband, of course, for he becomes a senior male kinsman alongside Sebastian, entitled to interfere in her affairs—already he is telling her what to think about her marriage. But she makes no complaint; on the contrary, she offers to pay for the weddings.

Like Desdemona and Lady Macbeth, Olivia capitulates; and the break in presentation is negotiated by silence and, all too often, the assumption that Olivia's subjection to a "real man" is only right and proper. The critical record indicates how well it has worked. But the contradiction in the ideology of gender relations has been smoothed over at the expense of Olivia as a simulated person with continuous interiority. To be sure, finding herself married to Sebastian might lead her to experience some new, complex change; she might stop being bold and independent and become timid and acquiescent. But if she is to remain a character, we need to know what she feels, how she registers it in her consciousness. Olivia cannot be allowed to say anything about any of it, because anything she could say would disrupt the play's closure. She becomes another character who is not a character. And this occurs not because Olivia cannot be allowed a lesbian relationship—which she has not contemplated—but because she cannot be allowed to have a man who will not dominate her. For heterosexual men in patriarchy, Olivia's preference may well be more

subversive than lesbianism—which mainly triggers the male heterosexual anxiety that women have a secret, intimate area closed to men.
It is through the supposed demand of women that men be "masculine" that heterosexual men justify their dominance. Olivia's preference for an unmasculine man challenges this ethos.

Meanwhile—and this too confirms Orgel's argument about where
the anxiety resides—Orsino gets what he wants when he marries Viola:
a woman who believes in the conventional patterns of gender relations
(often she uses her male disguise to insist on her underlying femininity), a woman happy to be a favored, but junior, servant. And I
see no reason why Antonio should appear at the end as the defeated
and melancholy outsider that critics have assumed. Leslie Fiedler, who
gives Antonio more thoughtful attention than most, capitulates to
the modern stereotype and declares that "hatred and distrust of self
are Antonio's chief motivations."[39] To be sure, Antonio experiences
the most vivid suffering in the play, when he believes that Sebastian
does not care for him (3.4.356–79; 5.1.74–90). But this appears so
only because of the intervention of Cesario; actually Sebastian has not
forsaken his friend—he has him in mind even as he ponders Olivia's
proposal (4.3.4–8). When the disguises are removed, Antonio is
strongly reassured:

> SEBASTIAN: Antonio! O my dear Antonio,
> How many hours rack'd and tortur'd me,
> Since I have lost thee!
>
> ANTONIO: Sebastian are you?
>
> SEBASTIAN: Fear'st thou that, Antonio?
> (5.1.216–19)

Only Antonio has not been deluded about Sebastian; he is the man
Antonio thought he was. There is no significant confusion in their
relationship, and no reason why marriage to a stranger heiress should
change it. If I were directing the play, I would show Antonio delighted
with the way it all turns out.

BREAKING POINTS

The female characters, in the instances I have discussed, fall silent at
the moments when their speech could only undermine the play's
attempt at ideological coherence. We may think of such moments as
manifesting a strategic deployment of perfunctory closure: like the
law-and-order finale of the cops-and-robbers movie, they are conventionally required but scarcely detract from the illicit excitement of the

bulk of the text. They are the price that has to be paid for the more adventurous representation, and because an audience knows this, it may discount them. The marriages of some Shakespearean heroines may be of this kind, for some audiences at least; Olivia perhaps, and Isabella in *Measure for Measure*—she is the bold woman silenced most spectacularly when marriage is proposed. Alternatively, as Dympna Callaghan suggests, we may relate the disallowing of women's voices in these plays to Pierre Macherey's analytical model, wherein the point at which the text falls silent is recognized as the point at which its ideological project is disclosed. What may be discerned there is both necessary and necessarily absent; it may be figured as the "unconscious" of the text.[40] In this view, the gaps in character continuity I have been considering represent not only the silencing of particular female characters; they also manifest breaking points of the text, moments at which its ideological project is under special strain.

Either way, gaps in ideological coherence are in principle bound to occur. No text, literary or otherwise, can contain within its ideological project all of the potential significance that it must release in pursuance of that project. The complexity of the social formation combines with the multiaccentuality of language[41] to produce an inevitable excess of meaning, as implications that arise coherently enough at one point cannot altogether be accommodated at another. The whole tendency of ideology, as Nicos Poulantzas explains, is to reconstitute contradictions "on an imaginary level" within "a relatively coherent discourse."[42] But it is a condition of representation that such a project will incorporate the ground of its own ultimate failure. The customary notions of woman in our cultures are contradictory and indeterminate. When such a key concept is structurally unstable, it produces endless textual work. The awkward issue has continually to be revisited, reworked, rediscovered, reaffirmed. And because closure is tantalizingly elusive, texts are often to be found pushing representation to a breaking point where contradiction comes to the surface. Some commentators will then seek to help the text into coherence—in the present instances, supplying characters with feasible thoughts and motives to smooth over the difficulty. This has been the virtual raison d'être of traditional criticism. Other commentators may take the opportunity to address the ideological scope of the text—how its closures provoke collusion or questioning.

Sometimes a text will so stretch the ideological suppositions upon which it relies that even traditional critics admit a difficulty. *Measure for Measure* was dubbed a "problem play" by W. W. Lawrence and

E. M. W. Tillyard because they could not get its elements to cohere (however, the quest for coherence continued—F. R. Leavis found the ending "a consummately right and satisfying fulfilment of the essential design").[43] There is a recalcitrant factor in the presentation of Desdemona that I have not so far considered. It is usually agreed that she is a good woman—excellent, in fact, and quite unjustly maligned. But two incidents have disturbed that story. One is her genial sexual banter with Iago when Othello is in danger on the sea in act 2 scene 1; the second is her sudden thought that "Lodovico is a proper man" as she prepares for bed on her final night (4.2.35). Critics (for example, M. R. Ridley in the New Arden edition, pp. 54, 166) are troubled: is Desdemona exhibiting in these incidents a hint of the lust and treachery of which Othello—falsely . . . but then is it quite?—accuses her. What we are seeing here is a common tendency in the deployment of stereotype. The excellent Desdemona is, of course, the madonna in the customary madonna/whore binary, but the two elements in such binaries are always collapsing into each other.[44] Partly because her excellence is an unstable compound of beauty and purity, the more innocent the woman appears, the more dangerous she may actually be—that is the fear that besets Othello. Our cultures need to think of Desdemona as innocent because they fear that if she is not, she may be whorish. Where women are concerned, it is believed, there is no smoke without fire; that is why judges in rape cases assume that women invite assault upon themselves. The effect of Desdemona's strangely sexual remarks is as Lisa Jardine says: they allow "the shadow of sexual frailty" to hover over Desdemona, despite her technical innocence.[45]

Richard P. Wheeler offers a comparable argument about the innocent Isabella in *Measure for Measure.* Pondering why the Duke makes her go through the presumably traumatic parade of declaring publicly that she has had sexual intercourse with Angelo, Wheeler concludes that it makes Isabella assume traces of the whore and that thus, in the organization of the play, she becomes an acceptable bride for the Duke.[46] In *Measure for Measure,* the whorish alternative for female sexuality is defined by the prostitutes (establishing what Dympna Callaghan calls a "dynamic of the polarised feminine," within whose terms the heroine is framed).[47] In *Othello,* this role is taken by Bianca—

> A housewife that by selling her desires
> Buys herself bread and clothes: it is a creature
> That dotes on Cassio: as 'tis the strumpet's plague

To beguile many, and be beguil'd by one.
He, when he hears of her, cannot refrain
From the excess of laughter.

(4.1.94–97)

At first sight, Bianca is Desdemona's opposite. But here again the whore intrudes upon the madonna, for the ambiguity of "housewife" (=courtesan/manager of household affairs) links Bianca to both extremes of supposed female behavior. Furthermore, since she is condemned and mocked for her loyalty to Cassio as much as for her alleged promiscuity, where does this leave Desdemona's commitment to Othello? Edward A. Snow draws attention to an exchange shortly before the murder.[48] To Othello's injunction, "Think on thy sins," Desdemona replies, "They are loves I bear to you." Othello comments, "And for that thou diest" (5.2.40–41). In other words, Othello finds himself acknowledging that Desdemona's offense resides in her *legitimately expressed* sexuality.

Thomas Rymer thought Desdemona was being punished by and for her aberrant desire—he quotes the moral from Cinthio's story— "a caution to all Maidens of Quality how, without their parents' consent, they run away with Blackamoors."[49] Marrying a black man seemed a convincing instance of the danger of allowing women to do what they want. Most people, where I come from, think this nasty and racist or merely stupid—though John Quincy Adams, the sixth president of the United States, proposed a similar reading, and it has been offered in our time by Allan Bloom.[50]

To others, however, Desdemona may appear *subliminally* lustful, and this is sufficient to admit the thought that even best of women may be whorish underneath, or anyway in potential. So with Olivia and Lady Macbeth: female desires are disruptive. Ultimately this seems to justify the general subordination of women. Nonetheless, it doesn't quite work in *Othello*. For however attractive the notion may be to some people, Desdemona cannot, reasonably, be thought to deserve her fate; and that is why the banter with Iago and thought of Lodovico have been found problematic. This, I hold, is because deployment of the feminine stereotype is taken too far here. Alongside the ideal of the innocent woman who submits and suffers, the text offers, as well, the bad woman who asks for trouble. It is this strain, I suggest, that produces the notorious dual time scheme of the play. Critics note that there seems scarcely time for Desdemona to consummate the marriage with Othello, yet he can believe she has been unfaithful with Cassio a thousand times (5.2.213). She must appear either virginal or whorish; even her husband—especially this husband—would be a violation. But the two ideas cannot be contained within the one time scheme. In this respect also, the contradiction in the presentation of Desdemona is so blatant that it becomes implausible. The stereotype that aspires to define and control "woman" overreaches itself and, to the thoughtful, betrays itself.

As I have suggested in respect of *Hamlet,* traditional cruces in Shakespearean texts—those perplexing moments where textual insecurity seems to combine with plot and character indeterminacy—often manifest not a lack of meaning, as might be supposed, but a superfluity. Too much meaning is being offered, to the point where it cannot all be made to cohere. And this may indicate anxiety and excessive ideological work such as I have been discussing. Strain deriving from overambitious deployment of supposed female attributes is evident again in the famous question about whether Lady Macbeth has children: this is by no means trivial, given that *Macbeth* is so concerned with lineage. The play needs Lady Macbeth to have "given suck" so that she can signal her shockingly "unfeminine" determination by declaring that she would have dashed the baby's brains out if she had sworn and reneged as Macbeth has done (1.7.54–59). However, the play is not content with this: later on, Lady Macbeth has to be childless so that nature can be shown getting its own back on her. Typically, in such circumstances, criticism looks for ways of talking the text back into sense. Perhaps the line "He has no children" (4.3.216) refers to Malcolm. Or perhaps Lady Macbeth has had children and they died. But these devices do not answer to the weight of the imagery, and only the more literally minded have embraced them. The dominant reading is as Peter Stallybrass suggests: we are "asked to accept a logical contradiction for the sake of a symbolic unity: Lady Macbeth is *both* an unnatural mother *and* sterile."[51]

The other famous crux in *Macbeth* concerns why Lady Macbeth faints when their story about the grooms killing Duncan is received with incredulity (2.3.118). Is this one more sign of her fiendish presence of mind, or is it the first sign of the reemergence of her womanly nature? Within the gender assumptions that produce Lady Macbeth, the two readings are equally feasible; indeed, within the notions about character and femininity that modern critics have attempted to deploy, it is quite impossible to choose between them. But if she is a character with a continuous consciousness, she must be manifesting *either* presence of mind *or* panic. In a way, this episode might be regarded as the pivot of the play: on one side of it, Lady Macbeth is "unnaturally" cool and collected, on the other "appropriately" conscience-stricken. But we never see how she gets from one to the other; as I have argued, she is not constructed so as to *entertain* contradictory attitudes; she can figure only as the site upon which they are displayed. The fainting/feinting incident gives us the "impossible" point at which the two contradictory features of the stereotype coincide as equally plausible. However, since they cannot coexist, but only collide, they allow an audience or reader to see, if we will, that Lady Macbeth is compounded of contradictory stereotypes—a character who is not a character.

HUMAN NATURE AND CONTEST

I have been trying to exemplify a way of reading in which speech and action in a fictional text may be attributed to characters—understood not as essential unities, but as simulated personages apparently possessing adequately continuous or developing subjectivities. But, beyond that, the presentation of the dramatis personae must be traced to a textual organization in which character is a strategy, and very likely one that will be abandoned when it interferes with other desiderata. To observe this is important, not just as a principle of literary criticism, but because it correlates with a repudiation of the assumption that reality, in plays or in the world, is adequately explained by reference to a fixed, autonomous, and self-determining core of individual being. Rather, subjectivity is itself produced, in all its complexity, within a linguistic and social structure.

But, you may ask, is there not a loss? Does not character criticism attend to individuals, and thereby sustain a generous openness to the diversity of human experience? I think not, for the counterpart of the individual is the universal; so while characters are supposed to be essentially themselves, they end up reduced to an essential human nature—to *man*. Further, when the individual and the universal come into focus, the social, the historical, and the political become blurred or fade from view. And they are the frameworks within which we might observe the operations of power and envisage alternative scope for human lives.

Key maneuvers in most character interpretation involve the surface/depths binary. Through this model, one side of an opposition is credited with the authority of profundity, while the other is relegated to the superficial. In traditional criticism, of course, the individual and the universal are profound, whereas social and political considerations are superficial. This pattern operates also in the processes claimed for critical appreciation, with full revelation of character achieved only in the last scene, yet understood to have been deeply present all along. Typically, illusion is said to yield, slowly but surely, to the reality that was always-already there; the individual, in learning from experience to reconcile himself or herself to the world, becomes fully the person he or she always was. The ultimate profundity is alleged to appear in tragedy, where the truth about Man is said to emerge from the depths of the individual. And this usually, in modern times, is the truth of our atavistic nature—the savage Othello underlies the noble one (he may be savage and noble at once, but still the savagery seems more fundamental). This is the most disabling of essentialist myths.[52] Of course people behave in extreme ways in extreme conditions, but this does not demonstrate an underlying Man. Rather, people react diversely in diverse circumstances in diverse cultures. None of these reactions is necessarily more profound than the others; they are all ways people behave. The person who betrays his or her comrades under torture, who eats them to survive an aeroplane disaster, who kills them under intolerable stress, is no more "real" than the caring and cooperative person we see in more congenial circumstances. It is essentialist humanism, not cultural materialism, that has the narrow view of human potential.

4 Power and Ideology:
An Outline Theory and
Sidney's *Arcadia*

In 1579 John Stubbe wrote a tract: *The Discoverie of a gaping gulf whereinto England is like to be swallowed by another French mariage, if the Lord forbid not the banes by letting her majestie see the sin and punishment thereof.* But the sin and the punishment were to be Stubbe's and his publisher's; they were sentenced to have their right hands chopped off.

> "I can remember," wrote Stow the chronicler, who was present, "standing by John Stubbe [and] so soon as his right hand was off, [he] put off his hat with his left, and cried aloud 'God save the queen.' The people round stood mute, whether stricken with fear at the first sight of this kind of punishment, or for commiseration of the man whom they reputed honest."[1]

A theory of power and ideology should enable us to account for Stubbe's critique of royal policy (we might say his attempt to subvert it), and also for what we might consider his perverse loyalty. Philip Sidney also wrote criticizing the French marriage, taking arguments and phrases from Stubbe.[2] In this chapter, I discuss the roles of the *Arcadia* and of a person such as Sidney in Elizabethan political structures, hoping to arrive at a general theory of intellectual dissidence in early modern England.

In chapter 2, I broached the entrapment model of ideology. In his book *Renaissance Self-Fashioning*, Stephen Greenblatt looks for "subversion," but finds, often brilliantly, that it is constructed within the discourse of power. So he presents Marlowe's rebels and skeptics as "embedded within this orthodoxy: they simply reverse the paradigms and embrace what the society brands as evil."[3] In an essay entitled "Invisible Bullets," Greenblatt carries the argument further, treating subversion, in many cases, not as something that power has to contain but as a strategic maneuver by which power is perpetuated. So an ideal image like that of the reformed Prince Hal "involves as its positive condition the constant production of its own radical subversion and the powerful containment of that subversion."[4] Thus the power/subversion dialectic develops the structure of a circle labeled "containment," and any prospect of significant dissent and change is not just headed off but strategically placed before it can even be thought.

Jonathan Goldberg brings a sophisticated analysis of the working of language to his investigation of the relations of power in *James I and the Politics of Literature*. But despite his earlier criticism of Greenblatt's "totalistic urge," he arrives at a similar sense of containment. His belief that "political reality, ordinary events, and staged ones are all matters of representation" makes it difficult for him to distinguish propaganda from actuality—strategies of containment from the political pressures they might be trying to manage or conceal. Goldberg sees language as equivocal and contradictory, but also as the vehicle, solely, of a royal power that has always already incorporated all possibilities: "Employing royal language, poets turned the tables on the monarch, appropriating power against power by engaging the most radical potential that resides in language, its own multivalent, self-contradictory nature. This does not make the King's poets subversives or revolutionaries; on the contrary, royalists all, they followed the King's prescriptions, pursuing his sustaining contradictions."[5] Power = representation produces the same outcome as power/subversion: an unbreakable circle of power, proceeding from and returning to the monarch.

The assumption that supports the entrapment model—sometimes explicit and at other times the only inference we can draw—is that Elizabethan and Jacobean England was an absolutist state, and that propaganda that centered on the monarch was directly expressing and sustaining power relations in their actual configuration (e.g. "We need in effect a poetics of Elizabethan power. Testing, recording, and explaining are elements in this poetics that is inseparably bound up with the figure of Queen Elizabeth"; in the "theatrical/political situation in the time of James I . . . James was God's lieutenant; he stood in his place; re-placed him, represented him, and doubled his power."[6] But the insistence in representations upon unity in a simple hierarchy does not mean that that is how the state actually worked, only that this is the way major parts of the ruling fraction represented it as working.

Any direct association between the imagery of monarchy and the actual structure of the state is open to three objections: (1) it mistakenly supposes that England was a fully absolutist state; (2) it overestimates the centralization and concentration of power in an absolutist state; and (3) it oversimplifies the relationship between power and ideology. I shall take each point in turn.

The structure of the absolutist state is complex and disputed, but substantial agreement allows me to take my first point rapidly: "In England," writes Nicos Poulantzas, "because of its different concrete situation, the transition from the feudal to the capitalist state seems to be both more tardy and more direct, allowing only a precarious existence to the absolutist state."[7] Perry Anderson agrees: "Before it could reach the age of maturity, English Absolutism was cut off by a bourgeois revolution";[8] and V. G. Kiernan writes of "the limited growth of absolutism in England."[9]

Insofar, then, as the absolutist state centralized and concentrated power in and through the figure of the monarch, we might expect England to be an incomplete instance. But, second, "power relations do not constitute a simple expressive totality, any more than structures or practices do; but they are complex and dislocated relations, determined in the last instance by economic power. Political or ideological power is not the simple expression of economic power. Numerous examples of a class which is economically but not politically dominant, ideologically but not economically or politically dominant, etc., can be cited" (Poulantzas, pp. 113–14).

This critique of a unitary conception of power certainly applies to the absolutist state. Historians dispute the precise relations of power, but it is plain that the political power of the feudal nobility continued (in Anderson's view, this was the fundamental determination) alongside the developing economic power of the urban bourgeoisie (in Poulantzas's view, early modern England was in major respects a capitalist state, but one in which political and economic power were not yet aligned); and a further complication, which will concern us later, was the development of a bureaucracy. Anderson remarks that "the very term 'Absolutism' was a misnomer":

> No Absolutist State could ever dispose at will of the liberty or
> landed property of the nobility itself, or the bourgeoisie, in the fash-
> ion of the Asian tyrannies coeval with them. Nor did they ever
> achieve any complete administrative centralisation or juridical unifica-

tion; corporative particularisms and regional heterogeneities inherited from the medieval epoch marked the Ancien Régimes down to their ultimate overthrow.

(pp. 49, 51)

Such repudiation of the idea of the concentration and centralization of power in the monarch does not derive only from Marxist historians. W. T. MacCaffrey believes that during Elizabeth's reign "the long-run trends moved against the monarchy, limiting its initiative, throwing it upon the defensive at the very time that the aristocracy was casting its political conviction into concrete policies and learning how to use the instrument by which it might enforce its collective will upon its old master."[10] Ernest William Talbert, citing Sir Thomas Smith, Richard Hooker, John Ponet, and city pageants, assembles extensive evidence that current political theory insisted upon the role of Parliament and upon legal limits to the power of the Crown. He quotes Smith's *De republica Anglorum* (1583):

> But as such absolute administration in time of war when all is in arms, and when laws hold their peace because they cannot be heard, is most necessary: so in time of peace, the same is very dangerous, as well to him that doth use it, and much more to the people upon whom it is used: whereof the cause is the frailty of man's nature, which (as Plato saith) cannot abide or bear long that absolute and uncontrolled authority, without swelling into too much pride and insolency.[11]

In the absolutist state, power did not simply radiate from the monarch; even the idea that Louis XIV was an absolute monarch has been effectively challenged.[12]

My third point is the complexity of the relations between power and ideology. We must be prepared to envisage "a whole series of dislocations between the dominant ideology and the politically hegemonic class or fraction" (Poulantzas, p. 203), including, as we shall see, those deriving from the specific autonomy of the fractions and institutions involved in the production of ideology. For ideology, by definition, does not directly express the actual power structure—that is what it is designed to obscure: "Ideology has the precise function of hiding the real contradictions and of *reconstituting* on an imaginary level a relatively coherent discourse" (Poulantzas, p. 207). Any text stands in a complex relation to the power structure. The focus on the monarch in the court masque, for instance, must not be taken as a direct expression of power relations in that society. So MacCaffrey observes: "All the conventions of a highly formalized court asserted the unique and lofty authority of the monarch and the submissive role of the subject. Yet these conventions barely served to veil the unceasing and often bitter struggle between royal and conciliar wills."[13] He stresses the extent to which the Crown had to be "sensitive to every nuance of public feeling, every tremor of discontent, within the limited range of the politically active classes." This need governed the dispensing of patronage.[14]

We should bear in mind just this about the Stuart court masque: the monarch is always a monarch *with courtiers*.[15] The royal figure is frozen into a representation of sheer "power," but this power can be exercised only through the courtiers, whose devotion to the person of the monarch only lightly masks a competition for the possession of a part of his or her authority. The lines of perspective that focus upon the king's chair, and that correspond to the hierarchy of the court audience, not only privilege the king's position, they also hold him trapped—that is why the court representatives at Oxford in 1605 complained because the king's chair was not raised and the audience would not be able to see him.[16] It is thus the knights who act in Spenser's *Faerie Queene,* while the monarch is static with the weight of ideological significance. And even in Sidney's *Lady of May,* where, as Louis Montrose has shown, the queen is invited to choose between two lines of policy, they are policies espoused by competing factions within the continuing hegemony of the nobility.[17]

The challenges of Sidney and Stubbe over the French marriage exemplify the dislocated relations of power and ideology. An over-simple notion of these relations within absolutism would suppose that the state religion worked merely to secure royal power, but protestantism was the site of the monarch's initial defeat in 1559 and of continual maneuvering among the unevenly disposed forces of the Crown, Privy Council, bishops, and Parliament.[18] As Sidney put it in his letter to Elizabeth, her subjects were "divided into two mighty factions, and factions bound upon the never ending knot of religion" (*Miscellaneous Prose,* p. 47). The vicious punishment that Stubbe received reflects his having called into public question divisions the governing class preferred to obscure behind the unitary image of the monarch. His exclamation—"God save the queen!"—shows him either mystified by the power game upon which he had so unwisely intruded or capable of extraordinary strategic presence of mind at such a desperate moment. If the queen was angered by Sidney's letter, as has been thought, it may be because he, too, drew unwelcome attention to the real conditions of her power: with the protestant faction, he told the queen, "by the continuance of time, by the multitude of them, by the principal offices and strengths they hold, and lastly, by your dealings both at home and abroad against the adverse party, your state is so enwrapped, as it were impossible for you, without excessive trouble, to pull yourself out of the party so long maintained" (*Miscellaneous Prose,* p. 47). Sidney perceived the state religion not just as a way of securing popular subjection—though it surely was that—but also as an agency of coherence among the nobility and gentry through which they imposed limitations upon Elizabeth's power.

LOCATING SIDNEY

Sidney's preoccupation with issues of political control and ideological strategy appears throughout both his career as a courtier and his literary work. It may be related to his complex position in the power structure of his society. Louis Montrose discerns in *The Lady of May* Sidney's determination "to explore the foundations and limits of royal power, and to promote the rights and interests of men of his own status vis-à-vis the Crown and the peerage" (Montrose, p. 22). The letter on the French marriage contrasts her French suitor Alençon's "ambitious hopes" with those of the queen, who has been "taught what you should hope" (*Miscellaneous Prose,* p. 52). Fulke Greville glossed this as a fear that "our moderate form of monarchy" would be transformed into "a precipitate absoluteness."[19] Sidney's emphasis in the *Arcadia* on the need to limit royal power has long been recognized, and we may understand this text as a continuation of his concern with the rights of the nobility and gentry as against any absolutist tendency. In 1931–32, William Dinsmore Briggs demonstrated the harmony between Sidney's thought and that of radical protestants like Philippe du Plessis Mornay, François Hotman, and Hubert Languet.[20] In 1962, in *The Problem of Order,* Talbert refocused the picture by arguing that Sidney's outlook was indeed as Briggs suggested, but that it was not exclusive to radical protestants.

There are at least six ways in which the *Arcadia* manifests, in effect, a critique of absolutist tendencies. First, it is primarily about the deeds of subaltern figures. Second, the failures of monarchs are emphasized and attributed to refusals to heed wise advisers. Third, Amphialus's revolt is treated with respect and is said to be based on true arguments about the responsibilities of "subaltern magistrates and officers of the crown," though in a wrong cause.[21] Fourth, in three instances (two in Phrygia and one in Pontus), monarchs are shown being deposed for tyrannical behavior and constitutional restraints are enforced (*Ar-*

cadia, ed. Evans, pp. 269–73). Fifth, when Basilius seems to be dead, the confusion of the people is said to result from their lack of experience in government (p. 766), and Euarchus is chosen as judge by the estates, within "the laws, customs and liberties of Arcadia" (p. 787). And sixth, Philisides's song, "As I my little flock on Ister bank," attributed to Languet, is a fable against absolutism (pp. 704–9).

An incident that demands attention is the tournament of the Queen of Iberia, which Frances Yates and Roy Strong have shown to be related to Elizabeth's Accession Day Tilts.[22] By emphasizing the narrator's praise of the Queen of Corinth and associating her with Queen Elizabeth, commentators have managed to see this episode as an endorsement of a supposed Elizabethan state focused upon the rule of the monarch. But the Queen of Corinth's success is achieved not through absolutism but through tactful negotiation with her aristocracy (pp. 351–52); and the tournament is actually arranged on behalf of another monarch altogether, the Queen of Iberia. She is tyrannically domineering and manipulative and the victim of ungovernable adulterous desire (pp. 346–51), and the tournament is by no means a successful celebration of her rule. Some of the combatants are performing under constraint, and the tilt becomes the occasion of their escape, helped by the queen's son; she causes his death, kills herself, and dies cursing (pp. 353–57). Surely neither of these queens has an exclusive relation to Elizabeth. The Queen of Corinth uses tilting to perfect her nobles in fighting without going to war; the Queen of Iberia uses it to "proclaim to the world how dear she was to that people" (pp. 351–52). Both motives are manifest in Elizabethan practice. We may see Elizabeth, here, as split between the two queens, the object of a divided perception, which Sidney could perhaps not present to himself in any more direct way.

Of equal interest is the speech with which Pyrocles defuses the Arcadian rebellion. There is no appeal to the ideology of absolutism; on the contrary, it is acknowledged that "your own prince, after thirty years' government, dare not show his face unto his faithful people" (p. 384), that their fury has not been overmastered "with the holy name of your natural prince" (p. 385). The arguments for according respect to Basilius are pragmatic ("What choice of choice find you, if you had lost Basilius?" [p. 385]), and they assume a contract theory of rule: "O what would your forefathers say if they lived at this time, and saw their offspring defacing such an excellent principality, which they with much labour and blood so wisely have established?" (p. 385).

It may seem, then, that Sidney is presenting through these incidents, and in the *Arcadia* generally, the claims of the aristocracy to a share in rule and the disabilities of absolutist tendencies. But the issue seems more fundamental than that. Throughout the book, there is a repudiation of the customary images of social harmony. Only the shepherds have satisfactory ways of resolving social conflict. The beasts in Philisides's fable were happy until they appointed a king: each contributes its particular quality to the monarch, but the outcome is, not a harmonious pyramidal society with at its apex the complete creature whose superiority is imaged in his comprising the best parts of all his subjects, but a tyranny that sets the beasts against each other for its own ends (pp. 704–6). When Pyrocles is defusing the rebellion, he does not cite ideas of social equilibrium; he sets the rebels at odds among themselves, engendering division and weakness (pp. 383–84). The obvious comparison is Menenius Agrippa's handling of the mutinous citizens of Rome, instanced by Sidney in *The Defence of Poetry:* he appealed to the cooperation of the parts of the body and "upon reasonable conditions a perfect reconcilement ensued" (*Miscellaneous Prose,* p. 93). Pyrocles enacts the disintegration of this image when he spectacularly strikes off the parts of the body that most pertain to the occupations and expectations of the rebels (pp. 380–81). The same kind of confusion occurs among the higher orders upon the supposed death of Basilius: "altogether like a falling steeple, the parts whereof—as windows, stones, and pinnacles—were well, but the whole mass ruinous . . . the great men looking to make themselves strong by factions; the gentlemen, some bending to them, some standing upon themselves, some desirous to overthrow those few which they thought were over them" (pp. 766–67).

Sidney seems to have little confidence in either the rhetoric or the practice of the state as he could envisage it. In the letter on the French marriage, he writes of "this body politic, whereof you are the only head," but the figure is completed by the queen's subjects, her "inward force," and they are "divided into two mighty factions" (*Miscellaneous Prose,* p. 47). The standard image of harmony in the state is denied its usual conclusion.

This reluctance to endorse customary imagery of social equilibrium leads us to question whether the *Arcadia* is committed to the hegemony of *any* class or class fraction—whether Sidney is prepared to envisage any satisfactory mode of rule and order within the configuration of power as he perceived it. There is even a vein of criticism of Pyrocles and Musidorus. It is not necessary to take sides in the continuing debate about how far we are to endorse the charges laid against them in the concluding trial: that such a dispute is possible establishes the case for an uneasiness in the text about the roles and assumptions of these young princes. Other members of the aristocracy are definitely destructive—Amphialus despite and even because of his good qualities, and Timautus ("a man of middle age but of extreme ambition, as one that had placed his uttermost good in greatness" [p. 768]). Even when Pyrocles and Musidorus are doing manifestly good things, they are peculiarly marginal. Although one may posit an analogy between them and "subaltern magistrates and officers of the crown," they are not in their own country and do not have the normal responsibilities of such men. Amphialus, who uses of himself the phrase just quoted, is, if anyone is, the figure in the *Arcadia* whose structural position approximates that of the Elizabethan aristocracy. When Pyrocles addresses the rebels, he begins by referring to his strange status: "An unused thing it is, and I think not heretofore seen, O Arcadians, that a woman should give public counsel to men, a stranger to the country people, and that lastly in such a presence, by a private person the regal throne should be possessed" (p. 384). All this is not precisely accurate—Pyrocles is not a woman or a private person—but awareness of this only emphasizes in a reader's mind the extent of Pyrocles's displacement from any customary role.

In brief, Sidney is prepared to endorse none of the sociopolitical groups who claim to bring order to the society of the *Arcadia:* he may come close to doing that with Pyrocles and Musidorus, but we cannot interpret them, even indirectly, as a force in the Elizabethan state. Pamela and Philoclea are credited with many noble virtues, but are seen governing only themselves. We require a more elaborate model of the potential for dissent in the Elizabethan state, a model that will enable us to theorize Sidney's relative independence of thought about the power structure of his society and the competing groups within it. We shall have to look more precisely at his position in the social order.

We may assume that Sidney identified himself and his class in Pyrocles and Musidorus, but this is not necessarily so, and his actual position was far more problematic. He had hopes of being Leicester's heir, and in his "Defence of the Earl of Leicester" gave most attention to the charge that Leicester "hath not ancient nobility" (*Miscellaneous Prose,* p. 124). When the earl fathered a child, Sidney had the device on his tilting shield, *speravi,* dashed through. But the connection with Leicester was through Sidney's mother; his father, though he held high office, was very much a functionary, and that is how Elizabeth treated him. When Sidney challenged the Earl of Oxford to a duel, the queen reminded him that he was only a gentleman. Sidney's political stance in the *Arcadia* may be traced in part to confusions of class allegiance.

The question of Sidney's class location is complicated by the fact that, with the decline in the traditional roles of the feudal aristocracy (Sidney's death in battle was most untypical in the period), the nobility and gentry were redefining their importance to society in terms of public service. At the same time, the developing Tudor bureaucracy was recruiting relatively lower-class men of talent who were thus gaining preferment to the higher gentry and the aristocracy.[23] So there was an uneven and mobile overlap of classes, roles, and aspirations, and within this Sidney's family was placed quite ambivalently: he was at a point of structural confusion. Moreover, his enthusiastic commitment to the ideal of public service was bound up with his earnest protestantism (a person was required to labor in his or her calling) and hence with policies that the queen opposed as rash, expensive, and radical. Thus, at this level also, Sidney was caught in a contradiction: the ground of his commitment hindered him in the exercise of it. At best he was engaged in a service whose policies he could not altogether trust. "If her Majesty were the fountain I would fear considering what I daily find that we should wax dry, but she is a means whom God useth," he wrote from the Netherlands.[24] And at worst he was not allowed to serve, and was left to complain: "To what purpose should our thoughts be directed to various kinds of knowledge, unless room be afforded for putting it into practice, so that public advantage may be the result, which in a corrupt age we cannot hope for?"[25]

Sidney's complex and unsatisfactory positioning is perhaps behind the extreme dislocation of social identity manifested by Philisides in the *Arcadia*. At the Iberian tilt, he is said to be a shepherd who has become a knight: his equipment is "dressed over with wool, so enriched with jewels artificially placed that one would have thought it a marriage between the lowest and the highest," and his *impresa* is "Spotted to be known" (p. 353). He appears in the third eclogue as a foreign shepherd—he commutes more readily than any other character between the social worlds of the book but is at home in none of them. He is said to suffer love melancholy, but it is easy to give his characterization a stronger significance—a stranger in the country and "a stranger . . . to himself" (p. 700), reluctant "to discover unto them his estate" (p. 704). It is from this stance that he sings the fable "As I my little flock on Ister bank," concluding with the ambiguous but potentially revolutionary couplet: "And you poor beasts in patience bide your hell, / Or know your strengths, and then you shall do well" (p. 708). Love melancholy issues in a political critique, and this may justify associating Philisides's general restlessness with Sidney's complex class position.

The other character we should consider is Philanax, public servant and king-lover. His role in the state has distinct similarities with Sidney's and his father's. Initially he is the wise counselor who writes Basilius a letter of sound advice (like Sidney's letter on the French marriage). He seems the ideal public servant: "There lives no man whose excellent wit more simply embraceth integrity, beside his unfeigned love to his master, wherein never yet any could make question saving whether he loved Basilius or the prince better" (pp. 79–80). But this utter devotion—which, of course, is part of the ideology of absolutism—is not endorsed by Sidney: it proves to be the source of Philanax's corruption. It commits him to putting down a revolt that would not have occurred if his advice had been followed, and finally unbalances his judgment: he prosecutes the princes with "the uttermost of his malice" and suppresses the princesses' letters, seeing this as "his last service to his faithfully beloved master" (pp. 822, 829, 816). At the same time, because of his authority in the state, Philanax is used by Amphialus as a pretext for the revolt and attacked as "a man neither in birth comparable to many, nor for his corrupt, proud, and partial dealing, liked of any" (p. 453); and when Basilius is thought dead, his "care of the state's establishment" (p. 783) is interpreted by the ambitious nobleman Timautus as personal ambition (pp. 768–70, 783–86).

Sidney's critique of the likely involvement of the state servant in absolutist tendencies and his recognition that such a man is likely to find himself at odds with the aristocracy indicate his concern with the unsatisfactory and difficult role of the bureaucrat. Even this position in the power structure is not identified positively in the *Arcadia*. Nevertheless, it is from such a position—bureaucrat—that aspects of Sidney's relatively independent political stance (including his critique of the bureaucrat's position) can be derived. The role of state servant, because of its structural specificity, may promote a distinctive political awareness. It is one of the positions from which the Elizabethan state might be criticized, if not subverted.

Bureaucrats, like intellectuals—these are the two social ensembles Poulantzas instances as *social categories* (p. 84)—occupy a special position in terms of their class affiliations and relations with state power.

The class from which they originate is not necessarily the same as the hegemonic class they serve; and even when it is (as is in part Sidney's case), their political power is

> not always directly determined by . . . class affiliation: it passes through the intermediary of the state. The characteristics of unity and cohesion peculiar to the bureaucracy as a specific category . . . depend on the bureaucracy's specific relation with the state and on the fact that it belongs to the state apparatus. It is precisely this which allows it to function politically with relative autonomy vis-à-vis the hegemonic class . . . whose power it exercises.
>
> (Poulantzas, pp. 336–37)

The disjunctions in the roles and affiliations of the bureaucracy that, in Poulantzas's account, help it to develop a degree of political autonomy may also give rise to a degree of independent political thought, such as I have been discovering in Sidney's instance. He attends precisely to the diverse allegiances of the state servant and the uneven relations between him and the state and the aristocracy—and he regards them, quite steadily, with the divided perception of the bureaucrat.

There is ample evidence of the independent political stances of members of the Tudor and Stuart bureaucracy. Perez Zagorin identifies them as "court" rather than "country," but remarks the uncertainty of their allegiance.[26] Under Elizabeth, bureaucratic independence was particularly a matter of the radical protestantism of privy councilors such as Leicester, Warwick, Huntingdon, Walsingham, Mildmay, and Knollys. They incited opposition to state policy in Parliament and the church, and they encouraged Sidney to write the letter on the French marriage. In general, MacCaffrey believes, the Crown "depended more and more on the good will of its servants and upon the degree of their sympathy with its policies" ("The Crown and the New Aristocracy," p. 61). When they were unsuccessful, they complained bitterly: "How unpleasant it is to be employed in so unfortunate a service I leave to your Lordship's good judgement," Walsingham wrote to Burghley.[27]

The identification of state servants as a category who might express a specific political stance in literary work is open to some further extension. It is, in effect, Lucien Goldmann's theory about the Jansenism of *officiers* of the ancien régime.[28] Of course, an independent stance is not the only possibility—a determined identification with one element in the situation (with the class of origin, the state, or the hegemonic class) is one way of handling the disjunction. My concern is to establish in principle the possibility of a structural position from which state ideology might be perceived critically. If we consider the writing of Spenser, Raleigh, and Fulke Greville, we may discern a range of negotiations within the complex positioning of the state servant.

THE RELATIVE AUTONOMY OF WRITERS

Comparable to bureaucracy in its offering of a distinctive perspective, and of even wider significance, is the social category of *intellectuals.* A principal factor that should inhibit any proposal to read off ideology directly in respect of state or class power is the relative autonomy both of intellectuals as a category and of the cultural institutions through which they work. Pierre Bourdieu insists "that ideologies are always *doubly determined,* that they owe their most specific characteristics not only to the classes or class fractions which they express . . . but also to the specific interests of those who produce them and to the specific logic of the field of production."[29] Thus schoolbooks and sermons will represent interests specific to educators and churchmen as well as the ideologies of class and state. And writing, even when it is purposefully in the service of an ideology, will very often manifest a slant towards the interests of the writer *as writer.* This is discernible even in the Stuart court masque (hence the dispute arising from the rival aspirations of Jones and Jonson); and consider the eventual emergence in the *Faerie Queene* of Colin Clout as the agent of a higher insight than Calidore's.

The relative autonomy of writers will not necessarily be disruptive—it may involve only an attention to writing itself, perhaps expressed through imagery of writing or a self-conscious style. But in a society where writing is taken seriously as an ideological agency (where there is censorship and the direct promotion of writing as an instrument of prestige and manipulation) and where the role of writer is undergoing rapid development (in terms of professionalization and the beginnings of a market economy), the writer is well placed to gain a distinctive perspective on the relations of power in the society. We would expect this particularly to involve the nexus of ideology and power, for this is where the writer, as writer, is vitally engaged. It might not amount to subversion in Greenblatt's definition ("a challenge to the principles upon which authority was based" ["Invisible Bullets," p. 41]), but it may open the workings of power and ideology to scrutiny and contest.

Of course, the category "writer" (which I have perhaps incautiously developed out of "intellectuals") should be broken down—we may distinguish the different structural positions of humanists, courtiers, preachers, professionals seeking patronage, professionals in the market, writers in the theater.[30] And the specific configuration will depend on the writer's class of origin and his or her relation to the state, the aristocracy, and the bourgeoisie, and on the characteristics of the institutions of cultural production in which he or she is involved. But, in principle, we see that a critique of power relations might be conceived from the position of writer. Sidney's position might seem less disjunctive than most, but he was less constrained than most by the need to please patron or public.

In the *Arcadia,* we find a highly self-conscious style (in syntax, figures, point of view, narrative construction) together with a preoccupation with the manipulative power of language. Much of the story is narrated by characters who are not totally disinterested, and a series of set debates and speeches manifests devices of enticement, evasion, special pleading, suppression of evidence, and metaphorical coloring, often conducted in bad faith (Philanax's initial letter to Basilius is a striking exception). Much of this manipulation is directly political. We have considered the strategy of Pyrocles's speech defusing the rebellion; Amphialus's revolt is sustained by a propaganda campaign: "He caused a justification of this his action to be written, whereof were sowed abroad many copies which, with some glosses of probability, might hide indeed the foulness of his treason, and from true common-places fetch down most false applications. . . . To this effect, amplified with arguments and examples, and painted with rhetorical colours, did he sow abroad many discourses" (pp. 452, 454).

Both those who would defend and those who would disturb the state issue manipulative pronouncements. Timautus inveighs against Philanax, "drawing everything to the most malicious interpretation." Philanax replies: "Who hath an evil tongue can call severity cruelty, and faithful diligence diligent ambition" (pp. 769–70). Especially pertinent, in view of the emphasis on theatricality in the transmission of Elizabethan ideology, is Sidney's awareness of dramatic effects. The rebels are persuaded by "the action Zelmane [i.e., Pyrocles] used, being beautified by nature and apparelled with skill" (p. 386). When Philanax wipes his eyes, the narrator remarks that they "either wept, or he would at that time have them seem to weep" (p. 817). Clinias's political effectiveness is attributed to his having acted in tragedies "where he had learned (besides a slidingness of language) acquaintance with many passions and to frame his face to bear the figure of them" (p. 387). For Sidney, as for tragedians later, courtly elaboration of language overlies political power.

The position of writer, like that of state servant, afforded access to a critical perception of power relations. Sidney's determined exposure of the means by which ideology is promoted is not exactly subversion, but it might certainly contribute to an understanding of the mechanisms of power and how they might be challenged—the kind of understanding that might have warned poor John Stubbe not to place too much trust in the queen's oft-proclaimed concern for the welfare of such as himself.

I have argued that the complexities of the power structure make it possible to envisage the literary text, not necessarily as subversive or contained, but as a site of contest; and that the distinctive location of the state servant might produce a critical perspective. Finally, the role of the writer as writer is likely to stimulate awareness of the importance of ideological production in the sustaining, negotiating, and contesting of power in the state.

Since I have offered this essay as an outline theory, I should admit that one half of the topic has not been discussed. I have tried to theorize ideological disruption of the *Arcadia* from the point of view of its inception—of how a person in Sidney's position might develop a critical analysis. But this shows little of its reception—of what its actual political impact might have been. Hermeneutically, it is convenient and perhaps not unreasonable to assume that those like-minded with Sidney read the *Arcadia* approximately as he meant it, but others may have read it differently (Leonard Tennenhouse has shown how this happened to Raleigh's *History of the World*).[31] We may assume in principle that any text that achieves wide acceptibility is, in fact, being read in diverse ways, producing diverse patterns of confirmation, negotiation, and perhaps even subversion. These concerns have threaded their way through this book and receive further development in succeeding chapters. As John Fiske and John Hartley remark of television programs, "the same message can be decoded according to different codes, corresponding to the social experience of the decoder, and yet remain meaningful for all groups."[32] *Arcadia* has at least this in common with a television program, and the analysis of its reception will require a no less complex model of the relations of power and ideology.

5 *Macbeth:*
History, Ideology,
and Intellectuals

It is often said that *Macbeth* is about "evil," but we might draw a more careful distinction: between the violence the state considers legitimate and that which it does not. Macbeth, we may agree, is a dreadful murderer when he kills Duncan. But when he kills Macdonwald—"a rebel" (1.2.10)—he has Duncan's approval:

> For brave Macbeth (well he deserves that name),
> Disdaining Fortune, with his brandish'd steel,
> Which smok'd with bloody execution,
> Like Valour's minion, carv'd out his passage,
> Till he fac'd the slave;
> which ne'er shook hands, nor bade farewell to him,
> Till he unseam'd him from the nave to th' chops,
> And fix'd his head upon our battlements.
> DUNCAN. O valiant cousin! worthy gentleman!
> (1.2.16–24)[1]

Violence is good, in this view, when it is in the service of the prevailing dispositions of power; when it disrupts them, it is evil. A claim to a monopoly of legitimate violence is fundamental in the development of the modern state; when that claim is successful, most citizens learn to regard state violence as qualitatively different from other violence, and perhaps they don't think of state violence as violence at all (consider the actions of police, army, and judiciary as opposed to those of pickets, protesters, criminals, and terrorists). *Macbeth* focuses major strategies by which the state asserted its claim at one conjuncture.

Generally in Europe in the sixteenth century, the development was from feudalism to the absolutist state.[2] Under feudalism, the king held authority among his peers, his equals, and his power was often little more than nominal; authority was distributed also among overlapping non-national institutions such as the church, estates, assemblies, regions, and towns. In the absolutist state, power became centralized in the figure of the monarch, the exclusive source of legitimacy. The movement from one to the other was, of course, contested, not only by the aristocracy and the peasantry, whose traditional rights were threatened, but also by the gentry and urban bourgeoisie, who found new space for power and influence within more elaborate economic and governmental structures. The absolutist state, I have argued, was never fully established in England. Probably the peak of the monarch's personal power was reached by Henry VIII; the attempt of Charles I to reassert that power led to the English Civil War. In between, Elizabeth and James I, and those who believed their interests to lie in the same direction, sought to sustain royal power and to suppress dissidents. The latter category was broad; it comprised aristocrats like the Earls of Northumberland and Westmorland, who led the Northern Rising of 1569, and the Duke of Norfolk, who plotted to replace Elizabeth with Mary Queen of Scots in 1571; clergy who refused the state religion; gentry who supported them and who tried to raise awkward matters in Parliament; writers and printers who published criticism of state policy; the populace when it complained about food prices, enclosures, or anything. The exercise of state violence against such dissidents depended upon the achievement of a degree of legitimation, and hence the ideology of absolutism, which represented the English state as a pyramid, any disturbance of which would produce general disaster, and which insisted increasingly on the "divine right" of the monarch. This system was said to be "natural" and ordained by "God"; it was "good," and disruptions of it were "evil." This is what some Shakespeareans have celebrated as a just and harmonious "world picture." Compare Perry Anderson's summary: "Absolutism was essentially just this: *a redeployed and recharged apparatus of feudal domination,* designed to clamp the peasant masses back into their traditional social position."[3]

The reason why the state needed violence and propaganda was that the system was subject to persistent structural difficulties. *Macbeth,* like very many plays of the period, handles anxieties about the violence exercised under the aegis of absolutist ideology. Two main issues come into focus. The first is the threat of a split between legitimacy and actual power—when the monarch is not the strongest person in the state. Shakespeare's Richard II warns Northumberland, the king-maker, that Northumberland is bound, structurally, to disturb the rule of Bolingbroke:

> thou shalt think,
> Though he [Bolingbroke] divide the realm and give thee half,
> It is too little, helping him to all.[4]

Jonathan Dollimore and I have argued that the potency of the myth of Henry V in Shakespeare's play, written at the time of Essex's ascendancy, derives from the striking combination in that monarch of legitimacy and actual power.[5] At the start of *Macbeth*, the manifest dependency of Duncan's state upon its best fighter sets up a dangerous instability (this is explicit in the sources). In the opening soliloquy of act 1 scene 7, Macbeth freely accords Duncan entire legitimacy: he is Duncan's kinsman, subject, and host, the king has been "clear in his great office," and the idea of his deposition evokes religious imagery of angels, damnation, and cherubim. But that is all the power the king has that does not depend upon Macbeth; against it is ranged "vaulting ambition," Macbeth's impetus to convert his actual power into full regal authority.

LAWFUL GOOD KING / USURPING TYRANT

The split between legitimacy and actual power was always a potential malfunction in the developing absolutist state. A second problem was less dramatic but more persistent. It was this: what is the difference between absolutism and tyranny?—having in mind contemporary state violence such as the Massacre of St. Bartholomew's Day in France in 1572, the arrest of more than a hundred witches and the torturing and killing of many of them in Scotland in 1590–91, and the suppression of the Irish by English armies. The immediate reference for questions of legitimate violence in relation to *Macbeth* is the Gunpowder Plot of 1605. This attempted violence against the state followed upon many years of state violence against Roman Catholics: the absolutist state sought to draw religious institutions entirely within its control, and Catholics who actively refused were subjected to fines, imprisonment, torture, and execution. Consider the sentence passed upon Jane Wiseman in 1598:

> The sentence is that the said Jane Wiseman shall be led to the prison of the Marshalsea of the Queen's Bench, and there naked, except for

a linen cloth about the lower part of her body, be laid upon the ground, lying directly on her back: and a hollow shall be made under her head and her head placed in the same; and upon her body in every part let there be placed as much of stones and iron as she can bear and more; and as long as she shall live, she shall have of the worst bread and water of the prison next her; and on the day she eats, she shall not drink, and on the day she drinks she shall not eat, so living until she die.[6]

This was for "receiving, comforting, helping, and maintaining priests," refusing to reveal, under torture, who else was doing the same thing, and refusing to plead. There is nothing abstract or theoretical about the state violence to which the present essay refers. Putting the issue succinctly in relation to Shakespeare's play, what is the difference between Macbeth's rule and that of contemporary European monarchs?

In *Basilikon Doron* (1599), King James tried to protect the absolutist state from such pertinent questions by asserting an utter distinction between "a lawful good King" and "an usurping Tyran":

The one acknowledgeth himself ordained for his people, having received from God a burthen of government, whereof he must be countable: the other thinketh his people ordained for him, a prey to his passions and inordinate appetites, as the fruits of his magnanimity: And therefore, as their ends are directly contrary, so are their whole actions, as means whereby they press to attain to their ends.[7]

Evidently James means to deny that the absolutist monarch has anything significant in common with someone like Macbeth. Three aspects of James's strategy in this passage are particularly revealing. First, he depends upon an utter polarization between the two kinds of ruler. Such antitheses are characteristic of the ideology of absolutism: they were called upon to tidy the uneven apparatus of feudal power into a far neater structure of the monarch versus the rest, and protestantism tended to see "spiritual" identities in similarly polarized terms. James himself explained the function of demons like this: "Since the Devil is the very contrary opposite to God, there can be no better way to know God, than by the contrary."[8] So it is with the two kinds of rulers: the badness of one seems to guarantee the goodness of the other. Second, by defining the lawful good king against the usurping tyrant, James refuses to admit the possibility that a ruler who has *not* usurped will be tyrannical. Thus he seems to cope with potential splits between legitimacy and actual power by insisting on the unique status of the lawful good king, and to head off questions about the violence committed by such a ruler by suggesting that all his actions will be uniquely legitimate. Third, we may notice that the whole distinction, as James develops it, is cast in terms, not of the *behavior* of the lawful good king and the usurping tyrant, respectively, but of their *motives*. This seems to render vain any assessment of the actual manner of rule of the absolute monarch. On these arguments, any disturbance of the current structure of power relations is against God and the people, and consequently any violence in the interest of the status quo is acceptable. Hence the legitimate killing of Jane Wiseman. (In fact, the distinction between lawful and tyrannical rule eventually breaks down even in James's analysis, as his commitment to the state leads him to justify even tyrannical behavior by established monarchs.)[9]

It is often assumed that *Macbeth* is engaged in the same project as King James: attempting to render coherent and persuasive the ideology of the absolutist state. The grounds for a Jamesian reading are plain enough—to the point where it is often claimed that the play was designed specially for the king. At every opportunity, Macbeth is disqualified ideologically and his opponents are ratified. An entire antithetical apparatus of nature and supernature—the concepts through which a dominant ideology most commonly seeks to establish itself—is called upon to witness against him as usurping tyrant. The whole strategy is epitomized in the account of Edward's alleged curing of "the Evil"—actually scrofula—"A most miraculous work in this good King"(4.3.146–47). James himself knew that this was a superstitious practice, and he refused to undertake it until his advisers persuaded him that it would strengthen his claim to the throne in the public eye.[10] As Francis Bacon observed, notions of the supernatural help to keep people acquiescent (e.g. the man in pursuit of power will do well to attribute his success "rather to divine Providence and felicity, than to his own virtue or policy").[11] *Macbeth* draws upon such notions more than any other play by Shakespeare. It all suggests that Macbeth is an extraordinary eruption in a good state—obscuring the thought that there might be any proneness to structural malfunctioning in the system. It suggests that Macbeth's violence is wholly bad, whereas state violence committed by legitimate monarchs is quite different.

Such maneuvers are even more necessary to a Jamesian reading of the play in respect of the deposition and killing of Macbeth. Absolutist ideology declared that even tyrannical monarchs must not be resisted, yet Macbeth could hardly be allowed to triumph. Here the play offers two moves. First, the fall of Macbeth seems to result more from (super)natural than human agency: it seems like an effect of the opposition of good and evil ("Macbeth / Is ripe for shaking, and the Powers above / Put on their instruments" [4.3.237–39]). Most cunningly, although there are material explanations for the moving of Birnam Wood and the unusual birth of Macduff, the audience is allowed to believe, at the same time, that these are (super)natural effects (thus the play works upon us almost as the Witches work upon Macbeth). Second, insofar as Macbeth's fall is accomplished by human agency, the play is careful to suggest that he is hardly in office before he is overthrown. The years of successful rule specified in the chronicles are erased, and, as Henry Paul points out, neither Macduff nor Malcolm has tendered any allegiance to Macbeth.[12] The action rushes along, he is swept away as if he had never truly been king. *Even so,* the contradiction can hardly vanish altogether. For the Jamesian reading, it is necessary for Macbeth to be a complete usurping tyrant in order that he shall set off the lawful good king, and also, at the same time, for him not to be a ruler at all in order that he may properly be deposed and killed. Macbeth kills two people at the start of the play: a rebel and the king, and these are apparently utterly different acts of violence. That is the ideology of absolutism. Macduff also, killing Macbeth, is killing both a rebel and a king, but now the two are apparently the same person. The ultimate intractability of this kind of contradiction disturbs the Jamesian reading of the play.

Criticism has often supposed, all too easily, that the Jamesian reading of *Macbeth* is necessary on historical grounds—that other views of state ideology were impossible for Shakespeare and his contemporaries. But this was far from being so: there was a well-developed theory allowing for resistance by the nobility,[13] and the Gunpowder Plotters were manifestly unconvinced by the king's arguments. Even more pertinent is the theory of the Scotsman George Buchanan, as we may deduce from the fact that James tried to suppress Buchanan's writings in 1584 after his assumption of personal rule; in *Basilikon Doron,* James advises his son to "use the Law upon the keepers" of "such infamous invectives" (p. 40). With any case so strenuously overstated and manipulative as James's, we should ask what alternative position it is trying to put down. Arguments in favor of absolutism constitute one part of *Macbeth's* ideological field—the range of ideas and attitudes brought into play by the text; another main part may be represented by Buchanan's *De jure regni* (1579) and *History of*

Scotland (1582). In Buchanan's view, sovereignty derives from and remains with the people; the king who exercises power against their will is a tyrant and should be deposed.[14] The problem in Scotland is not unruly subjects, but unruly monarchs: "Rebellions there spring less from the people than from the rulers, when they try to reduce a kingdom which from earliest times had always been ruled by law to an absolute and lawless despotism."[15] Buchanan's theory is the virtual antithesis of James's; it was used eventually to justify the deposition of James's son.

Buchanan's *History of Scotland* is usually reckoned to be one of the sources of *Macbeth*. It was written to illustrate his theory of sovereignty and to justify the overthrow of Mary Queen of Scots in 1567. In it the dichotomy of true, lawful king and usurping tyrant collapses, for Mary is the lawful ruler *and* the tyrant, and her deposers are usurpers *and yet* lawful also. To her are attributed many of the traits of Macbeth: she is said to hate integrity in others, to appeal to the predictions of witches, to use foreign mercenaries, to place spies in the households of opponents, and to threaten the lives of the nobility; after her surrender, she is humiliated in the streets of Edinburgh as Macbeth fears to be. It is alleged that she would not have shrunk from the murder of her son if she could have reached him.[16] This account of Mary as arch-tyrant embarrassed James, and that is perhaps why just eight kings are shown to Macbeth by the Witches (4.1.119). Nevertheless, it was well established in protestant propaganda and in Spenser's *Faerie Queene,* and the Gunpowder Plot would tend to revivify it. Any recollection of the alleged tyranny of Mary, the lawful ruler, prompts awareness of the contradictions in absolutist ideology, disturbing the customary interpretation of *Macbeth*. Once we are alert to this disturbance, the Jamesian reading of the play begins to leak at every joint.

One set of difficulties is associated with the theology of good, evil, and divine ordination that purports to discriminate Macbeth's violence from that legitimately deployed by the state. I write later of the distinctive attempt of Reformation Christianity to cope with the paradoxical conjunction in one deity of total power and goodness.[17] There is also a sequence of political awkwardnesses. These are sometimes regarded as incidental, but they amount to an undertow of circumstances militating against James's binary. Duncan's status and authority are in doubt, he is imperceptive, and his state is in chaos well before Macbeth's violence against it (G. K. Hunter in the introduction to his Penguin edition [1967] registers unease at the "violence and bloodthirstiness" of Macbeth's killing of Macdonwald [pp. 9–10]). Nor is Malcolm's title altogether clear, since Duncan's declaration of him as "Prince of Cumberland" (1.4.35–42) suggests what the chronicles indicate—namely that the succession was not necessarily hereditary. Macbeth seems to be elected by the thanes (2.4.29–32). Although *Macbeth* may be read as working to justify the overthrow of the usurping tyrant, the *awkwardness* of the issue is brought to the surface by the uncertain behavior of Banquo. In the sources, he collaborates with Macbeth, but to allow that in the play would taint King James's line and blur the idea of the one monstrous eruption. Shakespeare compromises and makes Banquo do nothing at all. He fears Macbeth played "most foully for't" (3.1.3) but does not even communicate his knowledge of the Witches' prophecies. Instead, he wonders if they may "set me up in hope" (3.1.10). If it is right for Malcolm and Macduff, eventually, to overthrow Macbeth, then it would surely be right for Banquo to take a clearer line.

Furthermore, the final position of Macduff appears quite disconcerting, once we read it with Buchanan's more realistic, political analysis in mind: Macduff at the end stands in the same relation to Malcolm as Macbeth did to Duncan in the beginning. He is now the kingmaker on whom the legitimate monarch depends, and the recurrence of the whole sequence may be anticipated (in production this might be suggested by a final meeting of Macduff and the Witches).[18] The Jamesian reading requires that Macbeth be a distinctively "evil" eruption in a "good" system; awareness of the role of Macduff in Malcolm's state alerts us to the fundamental instability of power relations during the transition to absolutism, and consequently to the uncertain validity of the claim of the state to the legitimate use of violence. Certainly Macbeth is a murderer and an oppressive ruler, but he is one version of the absolutist ruler, not the polar opposite.

Malcolm himself raises very relevant issues in the conversation in which he tests Macduff: specifically tyrannical qualities are invoked. At one point, according to Buchanan, the Scottish lords "give the benefit of the doubt" to Mary and her husband, following the thought that "more secret faults" may be tolerated "so long as these do not involve a threat to the welfare of the state" (*Tyrannous Reign*, p. 88). Macduff is prepared to accept considerable threats to the welfare of Scotland:

> Boundless intemperance
> In nature is a tyranny; it hath been
> Th' untimely emptying of the happy throne,

And fall of many kings. But fear not yet
To take upon you what is yours: you may
Convey your pleasures in a spacious plenty,
And yet seem cold—the time you may so hoodwink:
We have willing dames enough; there cannot be
That vulture in you, to devour so many
As will to greatness dedicate themselves,
Finding it so inclin'd.

(4.3.66–76)

Tyranny in nature means disturbance in the metaphorical kingdom of a person's nature but, in the present context, one is likely to think of the effects of the monarch's intemperance on the literal kingdom. Macduff suggests that such behavior has caused the fall not just of usurpers but of kings, occupants of "the happy throne." Despite this danger, he encourages Malcolm to "take upon you what is yours"— a sinister way of putting it, implying either Malcolm's title to the state in general or his rights over the women he wants to seduce or assault. Fortunately, the latter will not be necessary, there are "willing dames enough": Macduff is ready to mortgage both the bodies and (within the ideology invoked in the play) the souls of women to the monster envisaged as lawful good king. It will be all right, apparently, because people can be hoodwinked: Macduff allows us to see that the virtues James tries to identify with the absolutist monarch are an ideological strategy, and that the illusion of them will probably be sufficient to keep the system going.

Nor is this the worst: Malcolm claims more faults, and according to Macduff "avarice / Sticks deeper" (lines 84–85): Malcolm may corrupt not merely people but also property relations. Yet this too is to be condoned. Of course, Malcolm is not actually like this, but the point is that he could well be, as Macduff says many kings have been, and that would all be acceptable. And even Malcolm's eventual protestation of innocence cannot get round the fact that he has been lying. He says "my first false speaking / Was this upon myself" (lines 130–31) and that may indeed be true, but it nevertheless indicates the circumspection that will prove useful to the lawful good king, as much as to the tyrant. In Holinshed the culminating vice claimed by Malcolm is lying, but Shakespeare replaces it with a general and rather desperate evocation of utter tyranny (lines 91–100); was the original self-accusation perhaps too pointed? The whole conversation takes off from the specific and incomparable tyranny of Macbeth, but in the process succeeds in suggesting that there may be considerable overlap between the qualities of the tyrant and the true king.

READING DISTURBANCE

Macbeth allows space for two quite different interpretive organizations: against a Jamesian illustration of the virtues of absolutism, we may produce a disturbance of that reading, illuminated by Buchanan. This latter makes visible the way religion is used to underpin state ideology, and undermines notions that established monarchs must not be challenged or removed and that state violence is utterly distinctive and legitimate. It is commonly assumed that the function of criticism is to resolve such questions of interpretation—to go through the text with an eye to sources, other plays, theatrical convention, historical context, and so on, deciding on which side the play comes down and explaining away contrary evidence. However, this is neither an adequate program nor an adequate account of what generally happens.

Let us suppose, to keep the argument moving along, that the Jamesian reading fits better with *Macbeth* and its Jacobean context, as we understand them at present. Two questions then offer themselves: what is the status of the disturbance of that reading, which I have produced by bringing Buchanan into view? And what are the consequences of customary critical insistence upon the Jamesian reading?

On the first question, I would make three points. First, the Buchanan disturbance *is in the play,* and inevitably so. Even if we believe that Shakespeare was trying to smooth over difficulties in absolutist ideology, to do this significantly, he must deal with the issues that resist convenient inclusion. Those issues must be brought into visibility in order to be handled, and once exposed, they are available for the reader or audience to seize and focus upon, as an alternative to the more complacent reading. Even James's writings are vulnerable to such analysis—for instance, when he brings up the awkward fact that the prophet Samuel urgently warns the people of Israel against choosing a king, because he will tyrannize over them. This prominent biblical example could hardly be ignored, so James cites it and says that Samuel was preparing the Israelites to be obedient and patient.[19] Yet once James has brought Samuel's pronouncement into visibility, the reader is at liberty to doubt the king's tendentious interpretation of it. It is hardly possible to deny the reader this scope: even the most strenuous closure can be repudiated as inadequate.

Second, the Buchanan disturbance has been activated, in the present essay, as a consequence of the writer's skepticism about Jamesian ideological strategies and his concern with current political issues. It is conceivable that many readers of *Macbeth* will come to share this outlook. Whether this happens or not, the theoretical implication may be taken: if such a situation should come about, the terms in which *Macbeth* is customarily discussed would shift, and eventually the Buchanan disturbance would come to seem an obvious, natural way to consider the play. That is how notions of appropriate approaches to a text get established. We may observe the process, briefly, in the career of the Witches. For many members of Jacobean audiences, witches were a social and spiritual reality: they were as real as Edward the Confessor, perhaps more so. As belief in the physical manifestation of supernatural powers, and especially demonic powers, weakened, the Witches were turned into an operatic display, with new scenes, singing and dancing, fine costumes, and flying machines. In an adaptation by Sir William Davenant, this was the only stage form of the play from 1674 to 1744, and even after Davenant's version was abandoned, the Witches' divertissements were staged, until 1888.[20] Latterly we have adopted other ways with the Witches—being still unable, of course, to contemplate them, as most of Shakespeare's audience probably did, as phenomena one might encounter on a heath. Kenneth Muir comments: "With the fading of belief in the objective existence of devils, they and their operations can yet symbolize the workings of evil in the hearts of men" (New Arden *Macbeth*, p. lxx). Recent critical accounts and theatrical productions have developed all kinds of strategies to make the Witches "work" for our time. These successive accommodations of one aspect of the play to prevailing attitudes are blatant, but they illustrate the extent to which critical orthodoxy is not the mere response to the text it claims to be: it is *remaking* it within currently acceptable parameters. The Buchanan disturbance may not always remain a marginal gloss to the Jamesian reading.

Third, we may assume that the Buchanan disturbance was part of the response of some among the play's initial audiences. It is in the nature of the matter that it is impossible to assess how many people inclined towards Buchanan's analysis of royal power. That there were such may be supposed from the multifarious challenges to state authority—culminating, of course, in the Civil War. *Macbeth* was almost certainly read against James by some Jacobeans. This destroys the claim to privilege of the Jamesian reading on the ground that it is historically valid: we must envisage diverse original audiences, activating diverse implications in the text.

With these considerations about the status of the Buchanan disturbance in mind, the question about the customary insistence on the

Jamesian reading appears as a question about the politics of criticism. Like other kinds of cultural production, literary criticism helps to influence the way people think about the world; that is why the present study seeks to make space for an oppositional understanding of the text and the state. It is plain that most criticism has not only reproduced but also endorsed Jamesian ideology, so discouraging scrutiny, which *Macbeth* may promote, of the legitimacy of state violence. That we are dealing with live issues is shown by the almost uncanny resemblances between the Gunpowder Plot and the bombing in 1984 by the Irish Republican Army of the Brighton hotel where leading members of the British government were staying, and in the comparable questions about state and other violence that they raise. My concluding thoughts are about the politics of the prevailing readings of *Macbeth*. I distinguish conservative and liberal positions; both tend to dignify their accounts with the honorific term *tragedy*.

The conservative position insists that the play is about "evil." Kenneth Muir offers a string of quotations to this effect: it is Shakespeare's "most profound and mature vision of evil"; "the whole play may be writ down as a wrestling of destruction with creation"; it is "a statement of evil"; "it is a picture of a special battle in a universal war"; and it "contains the decisive orientation of Shakespearean good and evil."[21] This is little more than Jamesian ideology writ large: killing Macdonwald is "good" and killing Duncan is "evil," and the hierarchical society envisaged in absolutist ideology is identified with the requirements of nature, supernature, and the "human condition." Often this view is elaborated as a sociopolitical program, allegedly expounded by Shakespeare, implicitly endorsed by the critic. So Muir writes of "an orderly and close-knit society, in contrast to the disorder consequent upon Macbeth's initial crime [i.e., killing Duncan, not Macdonwald]. The naturalness of that order, and the unnaturalness of its violation by Macbeth, is emphasized" (New Arden *Macbeth*, p. li). Irving Ribner says Fleance, Banquo's son, is "symbolic of a future rooted in the acceptance of natural law, which inevitably must return to reassert God's harmonious order when evil has worked itself out."[22]

This conservative endorsement of Jamesian ideology is not intended to ratify the modern state. Rather, like much twentieth-century literary criticism, it is backward-looking, appealing to an imagined earlier condition of society. Roger Scruton comments: "If a conservative is also a restorationist, this is because he lives close to society, and feels in himself the sickness which infects the common order. How, then, can he fail to direct his eyes towards that state of health from which things have declined?"[23] This quotation is close to the terms in which many critics write of *Macbeth,* and their evocation of the Jamesian order allegedly restored at the end of the play constitutes a wistful gesture towards what they would regard as a happy ending for our troubled society. However, because this conservative approach is based on an inadequate analysis of political and social process, it gains no purchase on the main determinants of state power.

A liberal position hesitates to endorse any state power so directly, finding some saving virtue in Macbeth: "To the end he never totally loses our sympathy"; "we must still not lose our sympathy for the criminal."[24] In this view there is a flaw in the state; it fails to accommodate the particular consciousness of the refined individual. Macbeth's imagination is set against the blandness of normative convention, and for all his transgressions, perhaps because of them, he transcends the laws he breaks. In John Bayley's version: "His superiority consists in a passionate sense for ordinary life, its seasons and priorities, a sense which his fellows in the play ignore in themselves or take for granted. Through the deed which tragedy requires of him he comes to know not only himself, but what life is all about."[25] I call this view "liberal" because it is anxious about a state, absolutist or modern, that can hardly take cognizance of the individual sensibility, and it is prepared to validate to some degree the recalcitrant individual. But it will not undertake the political analysis that would press the case. Hence there is always in such criticism a reservation about Macbeth's revolt and a sense of relief that it ends in defeat: nothing could have been done anyway; it was all inevitable, written in the human condition. This retreat from the possibility of political analysis and action leaves the state virtually unquestioned, almost as fully as the conservative interpretation.

Shakespeare, notoriously, has a way of anticipating all possibilities. The idea of literary intellectuals identifying their own deepest intuitions of the universe in the experience of the "great" tragic hero who defies the limits of the human condition is surely a little absurd; we may sense delusions of grandeur. *Macbeth* includes much more likely models for its conservative and liberal critics in the characters of the two doctors. The English Doctor has just four and a half lines (4.3.141–45), in which he says that King Edward is coming and that sick people whose malady conquers the greatest efforts of medical skill await him, expecting a heavenly cure for "evil." Malcolm, the king to be, says, "I thank you, Doctor." This doctor is the equivalent of conservative intellectuals who encourage respect for mystificatory images of ideal hierarchy that have served the state in the past, and who invoke "evil," "tragedy," and "the human condition" to produce, in effect, acquiescence in state power.

The Scottish Doctor, in act 5 scenes 1 and 3, is actually invited to cure the sickness of the rulers and by implication the state: "If thou couldst, Doctor, cast / The water of my land, find her disease" (5.3.50–51). But this doctor, like the liberal intellectual, hesitates to press an analysis. He says: "This disease is beyond my practice" (5.1.56); "I think, but dare not speak" (5.1.76); "Therein the patient / Must minister to himself" (5.3.45–46); "Were I from Dunsinane away and clear, / Profit again should hardly draw me here" (5.3.61–62). He wrings his hands at the evidence of state violence and protects his conscience with asides. This is like the liberal intellectual who knows there is something wrong at the heart of the system but will not envisage a radical alternative and, to ratify this attitude, discovers in Shakespeare's plays "tragedy" and "the human condition" as explanations of the supposedly inevitable defeat of the person who steps out of line.

By conventional standards, this chapter is perverse. But an oppositional criticism is bound to appear thus: its task is to work across the grain of customary assumptions and, if necessary, across the grain of the text, as it is customarily perceived. Of course, literary intellectuals don't have much influence over state violence; their therapeutic power is very limited. Nevertheless, writing, teaching, and other modes of communicating all contribute to the steady, long-term formation of opinion, to the establishment of legitimacy. This contribution King James himself did not neglect.

6 History and Ideology, Masculinity and Miscegenation: The Instance of *Henry V*

WRITTEN WITH JONATHAN DOLLIMORE

WARRING IDEOLOGIES

> Behind the disorder of history Shakespeare assumed some kind of order or degree on earth having its counterpart in heaven. Further, . . . in so assuming he was using the thought-idiom of his age and could have avoided doing so only by not thinking at all.[1]

The objections are familiar enough: the "Elizabethan World Picture" simplifies the Elizabethans and, still more, Shakespeare. Yet if we look again at what Tillyard was opposing, his historicism seems less objectionable—assertions, for example, that Shakespeare does not "seem to call for explanations beyond those which a whole heart and a free mind abundantly supply"; that "he betrays no bias in affairs of church or state"; that "no period of English literature has less to do with politics than that during which English letters reached their zenith."[2] All these quotations are taken by Lily B. Campbell from critics influential between the wars. She and Tillyard demonstrate unquestionably that there was an ideological position, something like "the Elizabethan World Picture," and that it is a significant presence in Shakespeare's plays. Unfortunately, inadequacies in their theorizing of ideology have set the agenda for most subsequent work. We shall argue initially that even criticism that has sought to oppose the idea that Shakespeare believed in and expresses a political hierarchy whose rightness is guaranteed by its reflection of a divine hierarchy is trapped nevertheless in a problematic of order, one which stems from a long tradition of idealist philosophy.

Tillyard makes little of the fact that the writers he discusses were members of the class fraction of which the government of the country

109

was constituted, or were sponsored by the government, or aspired to be. He seems not to notice that the *Homily against Disobedience and Wilful Rebellion* is designed to preserve an oppressive regime—he admires the "dramatic touch" at the start, "a splendid picture of original obedience and order in the Garden of Eden." His skills of critical analysis do not show him that the projection of an alleged human order onto an alleged divine order affords, in effect even if not in intention, a mystifying confirmation of the status quo. On the contrary, he claims to show that Shakespeare was "the voice of his own age first and only through being that, the voice of humanity."[3] In similar fashion, Campbell speaks of "the political philosophy of [Shakespeare's] age" as "universal truth." "If, however, he is not merely a poet but a great poet, the particulars of his experience are linked in meaning to the universal of which they are a representative part . . . a passion for universal truth . . . takes his hatred and his love out of the realm of the petty and into the realm of the significant," she observes.[4]

Of course, much critical energy has been spent opposing Tillyard and Campbell; they were writing during World War II, and the idea that the great English writer propounded attitudes that tended to encourage acquiescence in government policy has come to seem less attractive subsequently. One alternative point of view argues that Shakespeare saw through the Tudor Myth and, with it, through all human aspirations, and especially political aspirations. Shakespeare's plays are thus made to speak an absurdist or nihilist idea of the "human condition"—a precise reversal of the divinely guaranteed harmony proclaimed by Tillyard. Another point of view also argues the limitations of the Tudor Myth and the futility of politics, asserting instead the possibility of individual integrity. This even more effectively inhibits specific consideration of how power works and how it may be challenged, since integrity may be exercised within—or, even better, over and against—any sociopolitical arrangements.

Anguish at the failure of the idea of order is represented most importantly by Jan Kott's *Shakespeare Our Contemporary* (1967). Kott sees that the Tudor Myth was always a political device, and he argues that the history plays disclose this. He sees also that the legitimacy or illegitimacy, the goodness or badness of the monarch, is not the real issue: "There are no bad kings, or good kings; kings are only kings. Or let us put it in modern terms: there is only the king's situation, and the system." Kott has here the basis for a materialist analysis of power and ideology, but then takes the argument towards an inevitable, all-encompassing inversion of cosmic order: "The implacable roller of history crushes everybody and everything. Man is determined by his situation, by the step of the grand staircase on which he happens to find himself."[5] There seems to be no play in such a system—no scope for intervention, subversion, negotiation; analysis of specific historical process, with the enabling as well as the limiting possibilities within an ideological conjuncture, seems futile—the point being, precisely, that everything is pointless.

Kott does little more than invert the Elizabethan World Picture: the terms of the debate are not changed. As Jacques Derrida insists, a metaphysic of order is not radically undermined by invoking disorder; the two terms are necessary to each other within the one problematic.[6] Order is predicated on the undesirability of disorder, and vice versa. "Theatre of the Absurd," which Kott invokes in his chapter comparing *King Lear* to Samuel Beckett's *Endgame,* takes its whole structure from the absence of God, and therefore cannot but affirm the importance and desirability of God. Kott's approach has been influential, especially in the theater, for it has chimed in with attention to modernist and existentialist writings that offer as profound studies of the human condition a critique of progressive ideals and an invocation of "spiritual alienation."[7]

The limitations of the Tudor Myth are pressed also by Wilbur Sanders in *The Dramatist and the Received Idea* (1968). Here the switch is not towards the futility of existence generally but towards the priority of personal integrity. Like Kott, Sanders sees the plays as showing political action to be essentially futile, and that there is an inevitability in historical process before which "even the best type of conservatism is ultimately powerless." However, his next move is not into the absurd, but into a countervailing ideal order of individual integrity: the issue is how far any character "has been able to find a mature, responsible, fully human way of preserving his integrity in face of the threatening realities of political life."[8] The selfish and inconsequential nature of this project, especially insofar as it is assigned to those who actually exercise power over others in their society, seems not to strike Sanders. Moreover, by refusing to discuss the political conditions within which integrity is to be exercised, he deprives his characters of knowledge they would need to make meaningful choices; for instance, the decision York has to make between Richard II and Bolingbroke is structured by contradictions in the concept of monarchy and the position of regent, and York's integrity cannot be analyzed sensibly without discussing those contradictions.[9]

Sanders's position approaches the point where historical sequence, with all its injustice and suffering, may be regarded merely as a testing ground for the individual to mature upon. He seeks to fend off such anarchistic implications by declaring that "in Shakespeare's imagination the ideal social order, the mutuality of fulfilled human society, is inseparably bound up with the sacredness of the individual" (p. 332). Literary critics have tended to place much stress on the sacredness, the redemptive power of the individual, especially in discussions of the tragedies. G. K. Hunter summarizes what he calls the "modern" view of *King Lear:* it "is seen as the greatest of tragedies because it not only strips and reduces and assaults human dignity, but because it also shows . . . the process of restoration by which humanity can recover from degradation. . . . [Lear's] retreat into the isolated darkness of his own mind is also a descent into the seed-bed of a new life; for the individual mind is seen here as a place from which a man's most important qualities and relationships draw the whole of their potential."[10] Sanders's recourse to the individual is less confident than this; in fact in places he remains poised uneasily between Kott and Tillyard, unable entirely to admit or to repudiate the position of either. The characters he considers prove "seriously defective," and he is driven to acknowledge the possibility that Shakespeare is expressing "tragic cynicism" (p. 185). Thus he veers towards Kott. To protect himself from this, and to posit some final ground for the integrity he demands, he swerves back towards something very like Tillyard's Christian humanism, wondering even "whether we can receive [the Elizabethans'] humane wisdom without their belief in absolutes" (p. 333). The entrapment of the Shakespearean characters is thus reproduced for the modern reader, who is required similarly to quest for an elusive wholeness within conditions whose determinants are to be neither comprehended nor challenged.

Perhaps the most fundamental error in all these accounts of the role of ideology is falsely to unify history and/or the individual human subject. In one, history is unified by a teleological principle conferring meaningful order (Tillyard), in another by the inverse of this—Kott's "implacable roller." And Sanders's emphasis on moral or subjective integrity implies a different, though related, notion of unity: an experience of subjective autonomy, of an essential self uncontaminated by the corruption of worldly process; "individual integrity" implies in the etymology of both words an ideal unity: the undivided, the integral.

Theories of the ultimate unity of both history and the human subject derive, of course, from a Western philosophical tradition where, moreover, they have usually implied each other: the universal being seen as manifested through essences that in turn presuppose universals. Often unawares, idealist literary criticism has worked within or in the shadow of this tradition, as can be seen for example in its insistence that the universal truths of great literature are embodied in coherent and consistent "characters."

The alternative to this is not to become fixated on its negation—chaos and subjective fragmentation—but rather to understand history and the human subject in terms of social and political process. Ideology is composed of those beliefs, practices, and institutions that work to legitimate the social order—especially by the process of representing sectional or class interests as universal ones.[11] This process presupposes that there are other, subordinate cultures that, far from sharing the interests of the dominant one, are in fact being exploited by it. This is one reason why the dominant tend not only to "speak for" the subordinate but actively to repress it as well. This repression operates coercively but also ideologically (the two are in practice inseparable). So, for example, at the same time that the Elizabethan ruling fraction claimed to lead and speak for all, it not only persecuted those who did not fit in, but even blamed them for social instability that originated in its own policies. This is an instance of a process of displacement crucial then (and since) in the formation of dominant identities—class, cultural, racial, and sexual.

Ideology is not just a set of ideas; it is material practice, woven into the fabric of everyday life. At the same time, the dominant ideology is realized specifically through the institutions of education, the family, the law, religion, journalism, and culture. In the Elizabethan state, all these institutions worked to achieve ideological unity—not always successfully, for conflicts and contradictions remained visible at all levels, even within the dominant class fraction and its institutions. The theater was monitored closely by the state—both companies and plays had to be licensed—and yet its institutional position was complex. On the one hand, it was sometimes summoned to perform at Court and as such may seem a direct extension of royal power;[12] on the other hand, it was the mode of cultural production in which market forces were strongest, and as such it was especially exposed to the influence of subordinate and emergent classes. We should not, therefore, expect any straightforward relationship between plays and ideology: on the contrary, it is even likely that the topics that engaged writers and audiences alike were those where ideology was under strain. We shall take as an instance for study *Henry V*, and it will appear that even in this play, which is often assumed to be the one where Shakespeare is closest to state propaganda, the construction of ideology is complex—even as it consolidates, it betrays inherent instability.

The principal strategy of ideology is to legitimate inequality and exploitation by representing the social order that perpetuates these things as immutable and unalterable—as decreed by God or simply natural. Since the Elizabethan period, the ideological appeal to God has tended to give way to the equally powerful appeal to the natural. But in the earlier period, both were crucial: the laws of degree and order inferred from nature were further construed as having been put there by God. One religious vision represented ultimate reality in terms of unity and stasis: human endeavor, governed by the laws of change and occupying the material domain, is ever thwarted in its aspirations, ever haunted by its loss of an absolute that can only be regained in transcendence, the move through death to eternal rest, to an ultimate unity inseparable from a full stasis, "when no more *Change* shall be" and "all shall rest eternally" (Spenser, *Faerie Queene* 7.2). The metaphysical vision has its political uses, especially when aiding the process of subjection by encouraging renunciation of the material world and a disregard of its social aspects such that oppression is experienced as a fate rather than an alterable condition. Protestantism tended to encourage engagement in the world rather than withdrawal from it; most of the *Faerie Queene* is about the urgent questing of knights and ladies. The theological underpinning of this activist religion was the doctrine of callings: "God bestows his gifts upon us . . . that they might be employed in his service and to his glory, and that in this life."[13] This doctrine legitimated the expansive assertiveness of a social order that was bringing much of Britain under centralized control, colonizing parts of the New World and trading vigorously with most of the Old, and that was to experience revolutionary changes. At the same time, acquiescence in an unjust social order (like that encouraged by a fatalistic metaphysic of stasis) seemed to be effected, though less securely, by an insistence that "whatsoever any man enterpriseth or doth, either in word or deed, he must do it by virtue of his calling, and he must keep himself within the compass, limits or precincts thereof."[14] This ideology was none the less metaphysical.

Such an activist ideology is obviously appropriate for the legitimation of warfare. It is offered by the Archbishop of Canterbury in *Henry V,* and as the Earl of Essex set off for Ireland in 1599, Lancelot Andrewes assured the queen in a sermon that it was "a war sanctified."[15] In the honeybees speech in *Henry V,* human endeavor is not denigrated but harnessed in an imaginary unity quite different from that afforded by stasis: "So may a thousand actions, once afoot / End in one purpose."[16] Like so many political ideologies, this one shares something essential with the overtly religious metaphysic it appears to replace—namely a teleological explanation of its own image of legitimate power, based on the assertion that such power derives from an inherent natural and human order encoded by God. Thus the "one purpose" derives from an order rooted in "a rule of nature" (1.2.188), itself a manifestation of "heavenly" creation, God's regulative structuring of the universe. What this inherent structure guarantees above all is, predictably, obedience:

> Therefore doth heaven divide
> The state of man in divers functions,
> Setting endeavour in continual motion;
> To which is fixed, as an aim or butt,
> Obedience.
> (1.2.183–87)

And what in turn underpins obedience is the idea of one's job or calling—in effect one's beelike *function*—as following naturally from a God-given identity: soldiers,

> armed in their stings,
> Make boot upon the summer's velvet buds;
> Which pillage they with merry march bring home
> To the tent-royal of their emperor.
> (1.2.193–96)

The activist ideology thus displaces the emphasis on stasis yet remains thoroughly metaphysical nonetheless. More generally, in this period, perhaps more than any since, we can see a secular appropriation of theological categories to the extent that it may be argued that Reformation theology actually contributed to secularization;[17] nevertheless, it was an appropriation that depended upon continuities, the most important of which, in ideological legitimation, is this appeal to teleology.

Not only the justification of the war but, more specifically, the heroic representation of Henry works in such terms. His is a power rooted in nature—blood, lineage, and breeding: "The blood and courage that renowned them / Runs in your veins" (1.2.118)—but also deriving ultimately from God's law as it is encoded in nature and, by extension, society: France belongs to him "by gift of heaven, / By law of nature and of nations" (2.4.79). Conversely, the French king's power is construed in terms of "borrowed glories," "custom" and "mettle . . . bred out" (2.4.79, 83; 2.5.29). With this theory of legitimate versus illegitimate power, the responsibility for aggression is displaced onto its victims. Thus does war find its rationale, injustice its justification.

There are two levels of disturbance in the state and the ideology that legitimates it: contradiction and conflict.[18] Contradiction is the more fundamental, in the sense of being intrinsic to the social process as a whole—when for example the dominant order negates what it needs or, more generally, in perpetuating itself produces also its own negation. Thus, for example, in the seventeenth century, monarchy legitimated itself in terms of religious attitudes that themselves came to afford a justification for opposition to monarchy. We shall be observing contradiction mainly as it manifests itself in the attempts of ideology to contain it. Conflict occurs between opposed interests, either as a state of disequilibrium or as active struggle; it occurs along the structural faultlines produced by contradictions. Moreover, ideology is destabilized not only from below but by antagonisms within and among the dominant class or class fraction (high, as opposed to popular, literature will often manifest this kind of destabilization).

Ideologies that represent society as a spurious unity must of necessity also efface conflict and contradiction. How successful they are in achieving this depends on a range of complex and interrelated factors, only a few of which we have space to identify here. One such will be the relative strength of emergent, subordinate, and oppositional elements within society.[19] The endless process of contest and negotiation between these elements and the dominant culture is often overlooked in the use of some structuralist perspectives within cultural analysis. A further factor militating against the success of ideological misrepresentation involves a contradiction fundamental to ideology itself (and this will prove especially relevant to *Henry V*): the more ideology (necessarily) engages with the conflict and contradiction that it is its raison d'être to occlude, the more it becomes susceptible to incorporating them within itself. It faces the contradictory situation whereby to silence dissent, one must first give it a voice; to misrepresent it, one must first present it.

These factors make for an inconsistency and indeterminacy in the representation of ideological harmony in writing: the divergencies have to be included if the insistence on unity is to have any purchase, yet at the same time their inclusion invites skeptical interrogation of the ideological appearance of unity, of the effacements of actual conflict. There may be no way of resolving whether one, or which one, of these tendencies (unity versus divergencies) overrides the other in a particular play, but in a sense it does not matter: there is here an indeterminacy which alerts us to the complex but always significant process of theatrical representation and, through that, of political and social process.

AESTHETIC COLONIZATIONS

It is easy for us to assume, reading *Henry V,* that foreign war was a straightforward ground upon which to establish and celebrate national unity. In one sense this is so, and it is the basic concern of the play. But in practice foreign war was the site of competing interests, material and ideological, and the assumption that the nation must unite against a common foe was shot through with conflict and contradiction. Such competition occurred equally in the hegemonic class fraction, though it was they who needed, urgently, to deny divisions and insist that everyone's purpose was the same. Queen Elizabeth feared foreign war because it was risky and expensive and threatened to disturb the fragile balance on which her power was founded. Members of the Privy Council favored it—in some cases because it would strengthen their faction (puritans continually urged military support for continental protestants), in other cases because it would enhance their personal, military, and hence political, power. The church resented the fact that it was expected to help finance foreign wars; but in 1588 Archbishop John Whitgift encouraged his colleagues to contribute generously towards resistance to the Armada on the grounds—just as in *Henry V*—that it would head off criticism of the church's wealth.[20]

For the lower orders, war meant increased taxation, which caused both hardship and resentment, as Francis Bacon testified in Parliament in 1593. On the other hand, war profited some people, though in ways that hardly inspired national unity. Some officers took money in return for discharging mustered men and enlisting others instead—Essex complained in Star Chamber in 1596 that "the liege and free people of this realm are sold like cattle in a market."[21] In 1589 Sir

John Smith overheard two gentlemen joking that the recent military expedition against Spain "would be worth unto one of them above a thousand marks and to the other above £400 . . . by the death of so many of their tenants that died in the journey: that the new fines for other lives would be worth that or more." War, in these aspects, must have tended to discredit ideas of shared national purpose. Indeed, there are a number of reports of mutinous individuals asserting that poor people would do better under the king of Spain.[22] This desperate or perverse inversion, whereby the demonized other of state propaganda was perceived as preferable, indicates both the failure of that propaganda and its success. For the perceived alternative was only another version of the existing power structure—the Spanish monarchy, of course, behaved broadly like the English one.

In fact, *Henry V* only in one sense is "about" national unity: its obsessive preoccupation is insurrection. The king is faced with actual or threatened insurrection from almost every quarter: the church, "treacherous" fractions within the ruling class, slanderous subjects, and soldiers who undermine the war effort, either by exploiting it or by skeptically interrogating the king's motives. All these areas of possible resistance in the play had their counterparts in Elizabethan England, and the play seems, in one aspect, committed to the aesthetic colonization of such elements in Elizabethan culture; systematically, antagonism is reworked as subordination or supportive alignment. It is not so much that these antagonisms are openly defeated but rather that they are represented as inherently submissive. Thus the Irish, Welsh, and Scottish soldiers manifest, not their countries' centrifugal relationship to England, but an ideal subservience of margin to center. Others in the play are seen to renounce resistance in favor of submission. Perhaps the most interesting instance of this is the full and public repentance of the traitors, Cambridge, Grey, and Scrope. Personal confession becomes simultaneously a public acknowledgment of the rightness of that which was challenged. It is, of course, one of the most authoritative ideological legitimations available to the powerful: to be sincerely validated by former opponents—especially when their confessional self-abasement is in excess of what might be expected from the terms of their defeat.

Nevertheless, we should not assume inevitable success for such strategies of containment; otherwise how could there have been Catholic recusants, the Essex rebellion, enclosure riots? *Henry V* belongs to a period in which the ideological dimension of authority—that which helps effect the internalization rather than simply the coercion of obedience—is recognized as imperative and yet, by that selfsame recognition, rendered vulnerable to demystification. For example, the very thought that the actual purpose of the war might be to distract attention from troubles at home would tend to undermine the purposed effect. The thought is voiced twice in 2 Henry IV: it is part of the advice given to Hal by his father (4.5.212–15) and John of Lancaster envisages it in the final speech. It is suppressed in Henry V— yet it twice surfaces obliquely (2.1.90–92; 4.1.228–29).

At the height of his own program of self-legitimation, Henry "privately" declares his awareness of the ideological role of "ceremony" (4.1.242–45). In the same soliloquy, Henry speaks his fear of deceptive obedience—masking actual antagonism. It is a problem of rule that the play represses and resolves and yet reintroduces here in a half-rationalized form, as the "hard condition, / Twin born with greatness" is presented initially as the sheer burden of responsibility carried by the ruler, the loneliness of office, but then as a particular kind of fear. As the soliloquy develops, its subtext comes to the fore, and it is the same subtext as that in the confrontation with Bates and Williams: the possibility, the danger of subjects who disobey. What really torments Henry is his inability to ensure obedience. His "greatness" is "subject to the breath / Of every fool," "instead of homage sweet," he experiences "poisoned flattery," and although he can coerce the beggar's knee he cannot fully control it (4.1.240–41, 256–57). Not surprisingly, he has bad dreams. The implication is that subjects are to be envied not because, as Henry suggests, they are more happy in fearing than (like him) being feared, but almost the reverse: because, as subjects, they cannot suffer the king's fear of being disobeyed and opposed. Henry indicates a paradox of power, only to misrecognize its force by mystifying both kingship and subjection. His problem is structural, since the same ceremony and role-playing that constitute kingship are the means by which real antagonisms can masquerade as obedience—"poisoned flattery." Hence, perhaps, the slippage at the end of the speech from relatively cool analysis of the situation of the laboring person (referred to initially as "private men," lines 243–44) into an attack on him or her as "wretched slave . . . vacant mind . . . like a lackey" (274–79), and finally "slave" of "gross brain" (287–88).

The play circles obsessively around the inseparable issues of unity and division, inclusion and exclusion. Before Agincourt, the idea of idle and implicitly disaffected people at home is raised (4.3.16–18), but this is converted into a pretext for the king to insist upon his army as a "band of brothers" (4.3.60). Conversely, unity of purpose may be alleged and then undercut. The act 3 Chorus asks:

> For who is he, whose chin is but enrich'd
> With one appearing hair, that will not follow
> These cull'd and choice-drawn cavaliers to France?
>
> (lines 22–24)

But within fifty lines Nym, the Boy, and Pistol are wishing they were in London.

However, the threat of disunity did not involve only the common people. That the king and the aristocracy have more interest in foreign wars and in the area of "England" produced by them than do the common people is easy enough for us to see now. But such a straightforward polarization does not yield an adequate account of the divergent discourses informing *Henry V;* on the contrary, it accepts uncritically a principal proposition of Elizabethan state ideology—namely that the ruling class was coherent and unified in its purposes, a proposition necessary to the idea that the state could be relied upon to secure the peace of all its subjects. Evidence to the contrary was dangerous, helping to provoke the thought that most violence stemmed from the imposition of "order."

In practice, while the aristocracy helped to sponsor the ideology of the monarch's supreme authority, it actually retained considerable power itself, and the power of the Crown probably decreased during Elizabeth's reign.[23] Elizabeth could maintain her position only through political adroitness, patronage, and force—and all these, the latter especially, could be exercised only by and through the aristocracy itself. Elizabeth could oppose the Earl of Leicester if supported by Burghley, or vice versa, but she could not for long oppose them both. After the death of Leicester in 1589, the power struggle was not so symmetrical. The rise of the youthful, charismatic, and militarily impressive Earl of Essex introduced a new element: he rivaled the queen herself, as Burghley and Leicester never did. The more service, especially military, Essex performed, the more he established a rival power base, and Elizabeth did not care for it.[24] The Irish expedition was make or break for both; Essex would be away from court and vulnerable to schemes against him, but were he to return with spectacular success he would be unstoppable. In the event he was not successful, and thus found himself pushed into a corner where he could see no alternative but direct revolt. The exuberance of *Henry*

V leads most commentators to link it with the early stages of the Irish expedition, when a successful return could be anticipated; the Chorus of act 5 (lines 29–35) actually compares Henry's return to England with it, and there are indeed parallels between Henry and Essex. Both left dangers at home when they went to war, besieged Rouen, sacked foreign towns, were taken to represent a revival of chivalry and national purpose; Essex was already associated with Bolingbroke.[25] The crucial difference, of course, is that Essex was not the monarch. That is why Henry must be welcomed "Much more, and much more cause." Henry is both general and ruler, and therefore the structural problem of the over-mighty subject—the repeated theme of other plays—does not present itself.

Henry V was a powerful Elizabethan fantasy simply because nothing is allowed to compete with the authority of the king. The noblemen are so lacking in distinctive qualities that they are commonly reorganized or cut in production. And the point where the issue might have presented itself—the plot of Cambridge, Scrope, and Grey—is hardly allowed its actual historical significance. Holinshed makes it plain that Cambridge's purpose in conspiring against Henry was to exalt to the crown Edmund Mortimer, and after that himself and his family; that he did not confess this because he did not want to incriminate Mortimer and cut off this possibility; that Cambridge's son was to claim the crown in the time of Henry VI, and that this Yorkist claim was eventually successful.[26] Cambridge makes only an oblique reference to this structural fault in the state (2.2.151–53). The main impression we receive is that the conspirators were motivated by greed and incomprehensible evil—according to Henry, like "Another fall of man" (line 142). Such arbitrary and general "human" failings obscure the kind of instability in the ruling fraction to which the concurrent career of Essex bore witness.

That the idea of a single source of power in the state was, if not a fantasy, a rare and precarious achievement is admitted in the Epilogue. The infant Henry VI succeeded, "Whose state so many had the managing / That they lost France and made his England bleed" (lines 11–12). Many managers disperse power, and unity falls apart.

The aristocracy is the most briskly handled of the various agents of disruption. Whether this is because it was the least or the most problematic is a fascinating question, but one upon which we can only speculate. *Henry V* far more readily admits of problems in the role of the church, though the main effect of this is again to concentrate power, now spiritual as well as secular, in the king. The archbishop's readiness to use the claim to France to protect the church's interests tends to discredit him and the church, but this allows the king to appropriate their spiritual authority. Thus power, which in actuality was distributed unevenly across an unstable fraction of the hegemonic class, is drawn into the person of the monarch; he becomes its sole source of expression, the site and guarantee of ideological unity. This is a crucial effect of a process already identified—namely a complex, secular appropriation of the religious metaphysic in the legitimation of war:

> his wildness, mortified in him,
> Seem'd to die too; yea, at that very moment,
> Consideration like an angel came,
> And whipp'd th'offending Adam out of him.
> (1.1.26–29)

The language is that of the Prayer Book service of baptism: Henry takes over from the church sacramental imagery that seems to transcend all worldly authority. Thus he is simultaneously protected from any imputation of irreligion that might seem to arise from his preparedness to seize church property and becomes the representative of personal piety, which adhered only doubtfully to the bishops. In him, contradictions are resolved or transcended. This presumably is why the clerics are not needed after act 1. From the beginning, and increasingly, Henry's appeals to God, culminating in the insistence that "God fought for us" (4.8.118), enact the priestly role as Andrewes identified it in his sermon on the Essex expedition, where he observed that in successful Old Testament wars "a captain and a Prophet sorted together." The two roles are drawn into the single figure of Henry V.[27]

On the eve of Agincourt, Henry gives spiritual counsel to his soldiers:

> Every subject's duty is the king's; but every subject's soul is his own.
> Therefore should every soldier in the wars do as every sick man in
> his bed, wash every mote out of his conscience; and dying so, death
> is to him advantage; or not dying, the time was blessedly lost
> wherein such preparation was gained.
> (4.1.182–89)

It is the high point of Henry's priestly function, the point at which the legitimation religion could afford to the state is most fully incorporated into a single ideological effect. Yet Henry is defensive and troubled by the exchange, and Williams is not satisfied. What has happened, surely, is that the concentration of ideological power upon Henry seems to amount also to a concentration of responsibility:

> Upon the king! let us our lives, our souls,
> Our debts, our careful wives,
> Our children, and our sins, lay on the king!
> (4.1.236–38)

In the play the drive for ideological coherence has systematically displaced the roles of church and aristocracy, and nothing seems to stand between the king and the souls of his subjects who are to die in battle.

Henry handles the issue in two main ways. First, he reduces it to the question of soldiers who have committed serious crimes, for which Henry can then refuse responsibility; initial questions about widows and orphans (4.1.141–43) slip out of sight. Second, the distinction between him and his subjects is effaced by his insistence that "the King is but a man" (4.1.101–2) and that he himself gains nothing, indeed loses, from the power structure:

> O ceremony, show me but thy worth!
> What is thy soul of adoration?
> Art thou aught else but place, degree, and form,
> Creating awe and fear in other men?
> Wherein thou art less happy, being fear'd,
> Than they in fearing.
> (4.1.250–55)

Here the king himself is collapsed, syntactically, into the mere shows of ceremony: "thou" in the third line quoted refers to "ceremony," in the fifth to Henry, and he slips from one to the other without the customary formal signals.[28] The effect, if we credit it, is to leave "place, degree, and form," "awe and fear" standing without the apparent support of human agency: Henry engrosses in himself the ideological coherence of the state and then, asked to take responsibility for the likely defeat at Agincourt, claims to be an effect of the structure he seemed to guarantee.

The act 2 Chorus wants to proclaim unity: "honour's thought / Reigns solely in the breast of every man"—but is rapidly obliged to admit treachery: "O England . . . Were all thy children kind and natural" (lines 3–4, 16, 19). The following scene is not, however, about Cambridge, Scrope, and Grey, but about Nym, Bardolph, and Pistol. This disputatious faction proves much more difficult to incorporate than the rebel nobility. Increasingly, since 2 *Henry IV,* sympathy for these characters has been withdrawn; from this point on there seems to be nothing positive about them. It is here that Fluellen enters, offering an alternative to Falstaff among the lesser gentry and an issue—the control of England over the British Isles—easier to cope with. Fluellen may be funny, old-fashioned, and pedantic, but he is totally committed to the king and his purposes, as the king recognizes (4.1.83–84). The low characters are condemned not only to death but also to exclusion from national unity; it is as if they have had their chance and squandered it. Gower describes Pistol as "a gull, a fool, a rogue, that now and then goes to the wars, to grace himself at his return into London under the form of a soldier" (3.6.68–70), and Bardolph endorses the identification:

> Well, bawd I'll turn,
> And something lean to cut-purse of quick hand.
> To England will I steal, and there I'll steal:
> And patches will I get unto these cudgell'd scars,
> And swear I got them in the Gallia wars.
>   (5.1.89–93)

This group, disbanded soldiers, was a persistent danger and worry in Elizabethan society; William Hunt suggests that "embittered veterans and deserters brought back from the Low Countries the incendiary myth of an army of avengers." Two proclamations were issued in 1589 against "the great outrages that have been, and are daily committed by soldiers, mariners and others that pretend to have served as soldiers, upon her Highness' good and loving subjects"; martial law was instituted to hang offenders.[29] The Elizabethan state was prepared to exclude such persons from its tender care, perhaps exemplifying the principle whereby dominant groups identify themselves by excluding or expelling others; not only are the virtues necessary for membership identified by contrast with the vices of the excluded but, often, the vices of the dominant are displaced onto the excluded. That Pistol has this degree of significance is suggested by the play's reluctance to let him go. He is made to discredit himself once more at Agincourt (4.4), and in his final confrontation with Fluellen he is clumsily humiliated (5.1).

Despite the thorough dismissal of Bardolph, Nym, and Pistol, *Henry V* does not leave the issue of lower-class disaffection. If those characters must be abandoned because unworthy or incapable of being incorporated into the unified nation, others must be introduced who will prove more tractable.

The issue of the English domination of Wales, Scotland, and Ireland appears in the play to be more containable, though over the centuries it may have caused more suffering and injustice than the subjection of the lower classes. The scene of the four captains (3.3) seems to effect an effortless incorporation, one in which, as Philip Edwards has pointed out, the Irish Macmorris is even made to protest that he does not belong to a distinct nation.[30] The English captain, of course, is more sensible than the others. Most attention is given to Fluellen—Wales must have seemed the most tractable issue, for it had been annexed in 1536, and the English church and legal system had been imposed; Henry V and the Tudors could indeed claim to be Welsh. The jokes about the way Fluellen pronounces the English language have, apparently, for Elizabethan audiences and many since, been an adequate way of handling the repression of Welsh language and culture; the annexation of 1536 permitted only English speakers to hold administrative office in Wales.[31]

Ireland was the great problem—the one Essex was supposed to resolve. The population was overwhelmingly Catholic and liable to support a continental invader, and resistance to English rule proved irrepressible, despite or, more probably, because of the many atrocities committed against the people—such as the slaughter of all the six hundred inhabitants of Rathlin Island by John Norris and Francis Drake in 1575. The assumption that the Irish were a barbarous and inferior people was so ingrained in Elizabethan England that it seemed no more than a natural duty to subdue them and destroy their culture. Indeed, at one level, their ideological containment was continuous with the handling of the disaffected lower-class outgroup (a proclamation of 1594 dealt together with vagabonds who begged "upon pretense of service in the wars without relief" and "men of Ireland that have these late years unnaturally served as rebels against her majesty's forces beyond the seas").[32] But much more was at stake in the persistent Irish challenge to the power of the Elizabethan state, and it should be related to the most strenuous challenge to English unity in Henry V: like Philip Edwards, we see the attempt to conquer France and the union in peace at the end of the play as a re-presentation of the attempt to conquer Ireland and the hoped-for unity of Britain.[33] The play offers a displaced, imaginary resolution of one of the state's most intractable problems.

Indeed, the play is fascinating precisely to the extent that it is implicated in and can be read to disclose both the struggles of its own historical moment and their representations. To see the play in such

terms is not at all to conclude that it is merely a deluded and mystifying ideological fantasy. We have observed that the king finally has
difficulty, on the eve of Agincourt, in sustaining the responsibility
that seems to belong with the ideological power that he has engrossed
to himself: thus the fantasy of establishing ideological unity in the
sole figure of the monarch arrives at an impasse that it can handle
only with difficulty. As we have argued, strategies of containment
presuppose centrifugal tendencies, and how far any particular instance
carries conviction cannot be resolved by literary criticism. If we attend
to the play's different levels of signification rather than its implied
containments, it becomes apparent that the question of conviction is
finally a question about the diverse conditions of reception. How far
the king's argument is to be credited is a standard question for conventional criticism, but a materialist analysis takes several steps back
and reads real historical conflict in and through his ambiguities. Relative to such conflict, the question of Henry's integrity becomes less
interesting.

[From the preceding two paragraphs as originally published, Richard Levin has drawn the assertion that "according to Jonathan Dollimore and Alan Sinfield, the project of *Henry V* is the 'establishing
[of the] ideological unity' of the state and its class system and the
'ideological containment' of threats to it."[34] The words in quotation
marks have indeed just appeared; the reader may judge whether in
context they mean what Levin says they mean.]

If *Henry V* represents the fantasy of a successful Irish campaign, it
also offers, from the very perspective of that project, a disquietingly
excessive evocation of suffering and violence:

> If not, why, in a moment look to see
> The blind and bloody soldier with foul hand
> Defile the locks of your shrill-shrieking daughters;
> Your fathers taken by the silver beards,
> And their most reverend heads dash'd to the walls;
> Your naked infants spitted upon pikes,
> Whiles the mad mothers with their howls confus'd
> Do break the clouds, as did the wives of Jewry
> At Herod's bloody hunting slaughtermen.
>   (3.3.33–41)

This reversal of Henry's special claim to Christian imagery—now he
is Herod against the Innocents—is not actualized in the play (contrary
to the sources, in which Harfleur is sacked), but its rhetoric is powerful, and at Agincourt the prisoners are killed (4.6.37). Here and

elsewhere, the play dwells upon imagery of slaughter to a degree that disrupts the harmonious unity towards which ideology strives. So it was with Ireland: even those who, like the poet Edmund Spenser, defended torture and murder expressed compunction at the effects of English policy: "[The Irish] were brought to such wretchedness, as that any stony heart would have rued the same. Out of every corner of the woods and glens they came creeping forth upon their hands, for their legs would not bear them. . . . They did eat of the dead carions."[35]

The human cost of imperial ambition protruded through even its ideological justifications, and the government felt obliged to proclaim that its intention was not "an utter extirpation and rooting out of that nation."[36] The claim of the English state to be the necessary agent of peace and justice was manifestly contradicted. Ireland was, and remains, its bad conscience.

Henry V can be read to reveal not only the rulers' strategies of power, but also the anxieties informing both them and their ideological representation. In the Elizabethan theater, to foreground and even to promote such representations was not to foreclose on their interrogation. We might conclude from this that Shakespeare was indeed wonderfully impartial on the question of politics (as the quotations in our opening paragraph claim); alternatively, we might conclude that the ideology that saturates his texts, and their location in history, are the most interesting things about them.

MASCULINITY

Sexualities and genders constitute a further ground of disturbance in the England of *Henry V*, overlapping the preceding discussion at virtually every point. Of course, critics have discovered ideal unities here also. To old historicists, the marriage of Henry to Princess Katharine is the key embodiment of the harmony supposedly attained at the play's closure. This attitude is still active; for George L. Geckle, Henry's wooing of Katharine is "a microcosmic reflection of the macrocosmic conflict between the two nations of England and France with the English representing masculine aggressiveness and the French representing feminine passivity." Fortunately the princess, as her "bawdy English lesson" proves, "is a normal young woman in her private life and worthy of England's finest." So the king manifests "a truly integrated personality" and brings "political order out of disorder and sexual unity out of an aggressive courtship."[37] The feminist challenge to such genial complacency has sometimes taken a psychoanalytic perspective that regards sexuality as mainly an individual matter. Linda Bamber believes that "by refusing the simple code of manliness [Hal/Henry] becomes more of a man than he would by accepting it"; Peter Erickson holds that "the ending of *Henry V* proposes to round out the king's character by providing him with a woman, but this proposal cannot be enacted because his character is too entrenched in a narrow masculinity. All emotional depth is concentrated in male relations."[38] Both these psychoanalytic readings depend on a binary composed of the individual psyche and a normative curve of maturation that the individual is supposed to achieve. Thus they reconstitute a metaphysic of teleological integration comparable to that supposed in earlier criticism; they relocate it for literary intellectuals of our time, for whom notions like God and national unity are problematic, in the individual psyche.

Rather, sexualities, genders, and the norms proposed for them are principal constructs through which ideologies are organized, diversely in diverse cultures but always with reference to power structures that are far wider than individuals and their psyches. They are major sites of ideological production upon which meanings of very diverse kinds are established and contested. That the ideological maneuverings already addressed in *Henry V* are continuous in scope and relevance with sexualities and genders is evident from the way they present similar patterns: potentially insubordinate features are expelled after being demonized, or incorporated after being represented as inherently submissive. Even so, again, state orthodoxy proves unable entirely to banish the specter of revolt. This is not to say that sexuality produces some pure, unmediated revolt of the body against ideology, in the manner suggested by some followers of Bakhtin.[39] But genders and sexualities, like other ideological formations, cannot but allow skeptical interrogation as well as acquiescence. Even the marriage of Henry and Katharine, which has often seemed a triumphant achievement of state and individual integration, proves in its historical context to hold a specific residuum of anxiety.

It is often said that women have little place in the history plays because the men there define themselves against other men.[40] In a way, this is true, but the men do this through constant reference to ideas of the feminine and the female (once again, the matter is not adequately addressed at the level of individuality alone). At the start of the play, the feminine and the female are invoked only to be set aside as the state gears itself for war: "Silken dalliance in the wardrobe lies," the Chorus says at the start of act 2; and Mistress Quickly is brought in to marry Pistol so that, like the wives of Hotspur and Mortimer in *1 Henry IV,* she can be abandoned for war (2.3). This is the pattern we have observed with other disorderly elements: genders and sexualities are among the potential disruptions that Henry must incorporate or expel in order to appear the undivided leader of an undivided kingdom. However, as it transpires, this exclusion of sexual disruption has to be repeated all through the play: banishment of the feminine and the female, even as these are conceived of by the masculine and the patriarchal, cannot easily be achieved. One reason is that Henry's title to the lands of France depends on Edward III's mother—Isabella, daughter of Philip IV of France. The French declare that their Salic law bars such succession through the female line: "they would hold up this Salic law / To bar your highness claiming from the female."[41] The archbishop counters that Salic law is not properly applied to the lands of France (1.2.32–64), and that diverse claims through the female line have already been asserted there. However, this latter argument contributes to the play's nervousness about the female, for the claims of Pepin, Hugh Capet, and Lewis X through the female line seem, in the archbishop's presentation, to have involved continuous quarreling and uncertainty (1.2.64–95).

In fact, this dependence upon female influence over inheritance, legitimacy, and the state produces so much anxiety that the English can hardly bring themselves to name it. The crucial fact that Isabella was daughter of Philip IV and mother of Edward III is not actually stated by the archbishop. Gary Taylor suggests in his Oxford edition of the play that "Shakespeare assumes his audience's familiarity with this fact, as Canterbury assumes Henry's" (p. 102). Perhaps. But Henry's *male* lineage, which was certainly more familiar, is repeatedly reasserted. The archbishop, enthusiastic as he is about Henry's pedigree, does not invite him to dwell upon Isabella, his great-great-grandmother:

> Look back into your mighty ancestors:
> Go, my dread lord, to your great-grandsire's tomb,
> From whom you claim; invoke his warlike spirit,
> And your great-uncle's, Edward the Black Prince . . .
> (1.2.102–5)

The more important the female influence, the more the masculinity of the English must be stressed. This is perhaps why the archbishop's speech has so often been found problematic in the theater, and may even be played for laughs as the foolish jargon of a legalistic mind: the speech is unfocused because it cannot admit its central concern. Even the pedigree Exeter presents to the French shows Henry "evenly deriv'd / From his most fam'd of famous ancestors, / Edward the Third" (2.4.911–13), apparently not mentioning the source of the claim, the maternal lineage of Edward himself. Phyllis Rackin has shown how this topic informs *King John:* "The son's name and entitlement and legitimacy all derived from the father, and only the father was included in the historiographic text. But only the mother could guarantee that legitimacy. As bearers of the life that names, titles, and historical records could never fully represent, the women were keepers of the unspoken and unspeakable reality that always threatened to belie the words that pretended to describe it."[42]

In *Henry V*, the superior manliness of the English is so insisted upon that it comes to appear the main validation of their title: because they are more manly than the French, they are more fit to rule anywhere. Before Harfleur, the king exhorts his army in these terms:

> On, on, you noblest English!
> Whose blood is fet from fathers of war-proof;
> Fathers that, like so many Alexanders,
> Have in these parts from morn till even fought,
> And sheath'd their swords for lack of argument.
> Dishonour not your mothers; now attest
> That those whom you call'd fathers did beget you.
> (3.1.17–23)

The danger Henry disavows is that his men might not be truly descended from their warlike fathers; their mothers' contribution is envisaged as either facilitating the transmission of English male qualities or impeding them by cuckolding their husbands. Hence Henry's ready threatening of the citizens of Harfleur, three times in his speech before the town, with rape: "What is't to me," he asks, "If your pure maidens fall into the hand / Of hot and forcing violation?" (3.3.20–21). On the one hand, this shows that Henry is too much of a man to worry if the lads go a bit too far; in fact, his scopophilic anticipation is disconcertingly fulsome. On the other, the speech exhibits an uneasy identification with the fear he attributes to the men of Harfleur, that women's sexuality is a likely ground of male humiliation.

The most persistent alarm is not that women will intrude upon the state and its wars, but that the men will prove inadequate. The "feminine" and the "effeminate" appear alongside the female, fatally

tainted by it, and as attributes applicable to men. The opposition is
starkly presented in *1 Henry IV* through Hotspur's dismissal of the
"popinjay" who upset him after the real men had been having one of
their battles by being "perfumed like a milliner" and talking "like a
waiting-gentlewoman."[43] But suppose "effeminacy" gets into the
mainstream of the state?—already the popinjay positions the Court as
effete center versus manly margin. At the margins of the city, Bolingbroke complains at the end of *Richard II*, the Prince of Wales is
in the taverns with "unrestrained loose companions":

> he, young wanton, and effeminate boy,
> Takes on the point of honour to support
> So dissolute a crew.[44]

"Effeminacy" in early modern England included virtually everything
that was not claimed as distinctively masculine. In *Richard III*, the
king is credited (falsely) with "gentle, kind, effeminate remorse" in
being reluctant to depose his brother's son—it is implied that he will
have to overcome it for the good of the commonwealth. Too much
devotion to women produces effeminacy (I cease the quotation marks,
but it should be remembered that this is a coercive construct, not a
natural category). Romeo, distressed at his failure to defend Mercutio,
complains that Juliet's beauty "hath made me effeminate."[45] Effeminacy is any male falling away from the proper totality of masculine
essence. Hence the banishment of Falstaff in *2 Henry IV* and, more
decisively, his death in *Henry V*. Falstaff represents in part effeminate
devotion to women (though there is far more talk of that than action),
and in part male bonding with the "wrong" person (interpreted lately
as homosexuality, since that has become the most prominent kind of
"wrong" male bonding). The relation between these two aspects of
effeminacy will appear shortly. But above all, with his drinking, eating,
jesting, and fatness, Falstaff embodies unmasculine *relaxation*—loos-
ening, softening, languishing, letting go. He is "fat-witted with drinking of old sack, and unbuttoning thee after supper, and sleeping upon
benches after noon"; if his girdle breaks, his guts will fall about his
knees. Bolingbroke defined the prince's effeminacy as consorting with
"unrestrained loose companions."[46] The masculine, conversely, is represented as *taut*, often with phallic connotation: "Stiffen the sinews,"
Henry urges before Harfleur, "Now set the teeth and stretch the nostril
wide, / Hold hard the breath, and bend up every spirit / To his full
height! ... I see you stand like greyhounds in the slips, / Straining
upon the start" (3.1.7, 15–17, 31–32). Rachel Blau DuPlessis, in her

essay "For the Etruscans," quotes Frances Jaffer on gendering in the customary language of criticism: " 'lean, dry, terse, powerful, strong, spare, linear, focused, explosive'—god forbid it should be 'limp'!! But—'soft, moist, blurred, padded, irregular, going round in circles,' and other descriptions of *our* bodies—the very *abyss* of aesthetic judgment."[47] "Screw your courage to the sticking-place," Lady Macbeth says, wanting her husband to be a man; he says he will "bend up / Each corporal agent" (1.7.61, 80–81). Prince Hal worries his father because effeminate behavior means a general failure to remain lean and taut for active male responsibility—though in fact the king is nearer the truth when he describes the prince as having his feminine qualities under proper restriction:

> He hath a tear for pity, and a hand
> Open as day for melting charity:
> Yet notwithstanding, being incens'd, he's flint.

The dominance of the latter quality in the reign of Henry V is demonstrated when Mistress Quickly and Doll Tearsheet are taken to be whipped as accessories to manslaughter ("for the woman is dead that you and Pistol beat"). Prostitution and motherhood—ultimate marks of male dependence upon the female—coincide in Doll's fake or real pregnancy; and the beadles are said to be notably thin.[48]

Both the English and French men figure their countries as women requiring masculine control. In the French view, Henry's effeminacy renders him an unlikely challenger for the female French body:

> there's nought in France
> That can be with a nimble galliard won;
> You cannot revel into dukedoms there.
> (1.2.251–53)

The effeminate virtues of courtship are irrelevant, France has to be taken by force—and, indeed, we do not see Henry trying to win the hearts of French citizens. Nor is it only that the monarch would need masculine vigor. As Jean Howard observes, "the legitimacy of the monarch is always a question in the history play, and the impression of legitimacy depends in part both on the monarch's production of gender difference and on the powerful subordination of the feminine to masculine authority."[49] The Dauphin believes Henry has not the male charisma to dominate France—England

> is so idly king'd
> Her sceptre so fantastically borne

By a vain, giddy, shallow, humorous youth,
That fear attends her not.

(2.4.26-29)

In fact the charge of effeminacy is made by both sides—by the French against the English and by the play against the French. The latter seek to establish their superiority by bragging continually of their manly strength. "My horse is my mistress," declares the Dauphin, "I once writ a sonnet in his praise" (3.7.41–42, 45). A series of misogynist puns follows. However, the French overdo it and appear florid and effete; the Dauphin's horse is referred to as a "palfrey," suggesting a lady's mount.[50] At Agincourt, the French are wearing "gay new coats" while the English have "not a piece of feather in our host" (4.3.112, 118). The English are the real men, and this masculinity seems to legitimate their war effort. When the French realize this, they apprehend it at once in terms of power over women:

Our madams mock at us, and plainly say
Our mettle is bred out; and they will give
Their bodies to the lust of English youth
To new-store France with bastard warriors.

(3.5.28-31)

These attitudes run through the English too: Nym and Pistol dispute over Mistress Quickly (2.1), and even the deferential Fluellen has to prove his manhood against Macmorris and Pistol (3.2.132–35; 3.6.84–86; 5.1). There seems nothing else to talk about. However, Henry's manhood is supposed to be effortless—when he finds himself boasting of English superiority, he quickly attributes such vaunting to the air of France (3.6.155–58).

In all this, women are the losers, as Henry readily acknowledges when throwing back the French challenge: "many a thousand widows / Shall this his mock mock out of their dear husbands; / Mock mothers from their sons" (1.2.284–86). The terms get even more unpleasant when defeat is likely. Bourbon says of the Frenchman who will not return with him to the field at Agincourt,

Let him go hence, and with his cap in hand,
Like a base pandar, hold the chamber-door
Whilst by a slave, no gentler than my dog,
His fairest daughter is contaminated.

(4.5.13-16)

The price of male failure is greater oppression of women. The other losers are men who do not relish such adventures. The Chorus at the start of act 3 says England is left

> Guarded with grandsires, babies, and old women,
> Either past or not arriv'd to pith and puissance:
> For who is he, whose chin is but enrich'd
> With one appearing hair, that will not follow
> These cull'd and choice-drawn cavaliers to France?
> (lines 20–24)

Who indeed? There may be such men, but they are obviously under considerable coercion to conform. The king at Agincourt says those not present may "hold their manhoods cheap whiles any speak / That fought with us upon Saint Crispin's day" (4.3.66–67). No space is left for a kind of manhood that would not be fighting. Of course, all strongly held convictions tend to place pressure upon those who disagree, but assertive masculinity is oppressive in principle, for it justifies itself by its success in intimidating others.

Plainly we are on the territory of the homosocial, as Eve Sedgwick has identified it: "the status of women, and the whole question of arrangements between genders, is deeply and inescapably inscribed in the structure even of relationships that seem to exclude women—even in male homosocial/homosexual relationships." The English and French men fight over the bodies of France and French women, giving great attention to their standing with each other and precious little to the welfare of their peoples. However, the cement of their homosocial rivalry is not, in this version, hostility towards homosexuality, as Sedgwick finds it to be in our modern cultures. As she and others have shown, the place of same-sex love was not the same in early modern England as now, and hence "the structure of homosocial continuums [must be] culturally contingent, not an innate feature of either 'maleness' or 'femaleness.' "[51] In *Henry V,* I see no sign that homosexuality is distinctly apprehended as a category. Effeminacy, as constructed in the play, is not specifically linked to same-sex physical passion; its stigma is, more directly, associated with regression towards the female. This is compatible with a major strand in early modern gender theory, which has been shown to derive from Galen and Aristotle. In brief, it was held that women and men were not essentially different biologically; rather, women were taken to be incomplete versions of men, falling short of the highest kind of creation.[52] Conversely, the danger for the male was effeminacy—the disastrous slide back into the female; and same-sex passion was relatively unimportant. Masculine qualities in a female might be even admired, at least in some circumstances, as an upward movement. England did well in a manly way when previously her menfolk were fighting in France:

When all her chivalry hath been in France
And she a mourning widow of her nobles,
She hath herself not only well defended,
But taken and impounded as a stray
The King of Scots.

(1.2.157–61)

Queen Elizabeth at the time of the Armada might declare, "I know I have the body of a weak and feeble woman, but I have the heart and stomach of a king."[53] But the idea of the male regressing to the female always made for anxiety. Patroclus warns Achilles in *Troilus and Cressida,* in respect of Achilles' devotion to Hector's sister, Polyxena,

A woman impudent and mannish grown
Is not more loath'd than an effeminate man
In time of action.

Those are the priorities; and the relationship between Achilles and Patroclus is not in question, because it does not undermine warrior values—Patroclus, although he has "little stomach to the war," is urging Achilles to fight. Stephen Orgel summarizes: "The fear of effeminization is a central element in all discussions of what constitutes a 'real man' in the period, and the fantasy of the reversal of the natural transition from woman to man underlies it."[54] How precarious, and how cultural, masculinity might be is illustrated by an instance offered in Spenser's *View of the Present State of Ireland:*

Then when Cyrus had overcome the Lydians that were a warlike nation, and devised to bring them to a more peacable life, he changed their apparel and music, and instead of their short warlike coats, clothed them in long garments like wives, and instead of their warlike music, appointed to them certain lascivious lays and loose gigs, by which in short space their minds were so mollified and abated that they forgot their former fierceness and became most tender and effeminate.[55]

The most surprising passage in *Henry V*—one that, because it is hard to handle in our cultures, has attracted little comment—is the love-death of Suffolk and York at Agincourt:

Suffolk first died; and York, all haggled over,
Comes to him, where in gore he lay insteep'd,
And takes him by the beard, kisses the gashes
That bloodily did yawn upon his face;
And cries aloud, "Tarry, my cousin Suffolk!
My soul shall thine keep company to heaven;

> Tarry, sweet soul, for mine, then fly abreast,
> As in this glorious and well-foughten field
> We kept together in our chivalry!"
> Upon these words I came and cheer'd him up;
> He smil'd me in the face, raught me his hand,
> And, with a feeble gripe, says, "Dear my lord,
> Commend my service to my sovereign."
> So did he turn, and over Suffolk's neck
> He threw his wounded arm, and kiss'd his lips;
> And so espous'd to death, with blood he seal'd
> A testament of noble-ending love.
> The pretty and sweet manner of it forc'd
> These waters from me which I would have stopp'd;
> But I had not so much of man in me,
> And all my mother came into mine eyes
> And gave me up to tears.
>
> (4.6.11–32)

York kisses Suffolk twice, on the gashes on his face and on the lips; Gary Taylor notes uneasily that "Shakespeare's contemporaries were less squeamish than we about men kissing men" (p. 241), but that hardly addresses the emotional weight of the scene. Suffolk is called "sweet soul," embraced, "espous'd" (I think—the referent is uncertain). Their "testament of noble-ending love" is called "pretty and sweet." And Exeter's response is to weep, to lose manly control, to surrender himself to the feminine response inherited from his mother. In this play, no behavior could be more highly charged, and the episode is placed at the point where the battle is still in question, where its particular emotions may be most finely apprehended. What is apparent is that same-sex passion, when sufficiently committed to masculine warrior values, is admired, even at the point where it slides towards the feminine. "In this glorious and well-foughten field / We kept together in our chivalry! . . . Commend my service to my sovereign." In such a context of devotion to the state, its fighting and its command structure, there is no damaging effeminacy in same-sex passion; it is women and popinjays that are the danger (the same considerations apply to Coriolanus and Aufidius). Intense emotion between men, so long as it is associated with something manly like trying to kill people, is not a drawback; on the contrary, it is the implicit goal and ultimate expression of their efforts.[56] There is a deal of this in the rage against the treacherous noblemen in act 2 scene 2. Over Suffolk and York, Henry finds himself moved to "mistful eyes," but only for a moment: news that the French have reinforced their men recalls him to manly matters and he orders, unsentimentally, the killing of prisoners (4.6.33–37).

MISCEGENATION

It should not now need demonstrating that Princess Katharine is planted in the play as the reward for and final validation of Henry's manliness, the symbol of enforced French submission.[57] She is reported to be on offer to the English in the act 3 Chorus—directly before Henry's rape speech at Harfleur. Immediately after the entering of Harfleur, she is shown learning how to translate her body into language accessible to the English (3.4). In Henry's "wooing," he does not disguise that she is under compulsion. When she asks if she could possibly love the enemy of France, he finds opportunity for a joke: " I love France so well that I will not part with a village of it"; when she says it must be as it pleases her father, he replies "Nay, it will please him well, Kate; it shall please him, Kate." The deal has already been struck, and she is "our capital demand" (5.2.178–80, 261–63, 96). Nevertheless, critics have shied away from the thought that, after the princess's initial refusal to submit to the pretense that Henry is a courtly wooer, the king resorts to a sadistic exercise of power over her. The scene may certainly be played in that way. Henry is only too ready to repudiate once more the effeminate virtues of men who can dance and "rhyme themselves into ladies' favours" for those of the "plain soldier" (lines 134–73). The princess's inability to respond fluently leaves her vulnerable to long, cajoling speeches in which she is overwhelmed, like France before her, by the power of England. "It is as easy for me, Kate, to conquer the kingdom as to speak so much more French," Henry says (lines 191–92), but since he is the conqueror, he can use English when he wants to. For it doesn't really matter whether the princess understands him, though she must realize well enough that she is being browbeaten. Calling her so insistently "Kate" (twenty-eight times in the interview) is part of the humiliation: she cannot prevent the anglicization or the intimacy—Gary Taylor points out that the name was "associated with promiscuous women."[58] To be sure, an arranged marriage is only what one should expect; there is no precedent in the chronicles for any personal interaction. What complicates the betrothal ideologically is the attempt of the king to throw some kind of romantic veil over his conquest (as if they were Beatrice and Benedick just looking for an excuse to get together), and without even questioning male dominance (unlike Beatrice and Benedick). In *The Famous Victories of Henry the Fift,* from which the betrothal scene derives (printed in Walter's edition, pp. 165–67), the king is represented as falling genuinely in love with Katheren, to the point where he regards his defeat of the French as a disadvantage (likely to prejudice her against him), and she persuades him to abate his demands for territory; she has as many lines as he. In this scenario feminine values are made to win out, perhaps at a cost in plausibility. But in *Henry V* they tangle inconclusively: the text wants the king to display excellence in this skirmish as he has in all the others, but shrinks from allowing him to become contaminated with the effeminacy of wooing. (Of course, this is not Henry's individual failure, but another instance of the faultline, identified in chapter 2, whereby marriage was supposed to be both the means through which property and inheritance were arranged and also a fulfilling personal relationship.) Only when he has dominated Katharine by kissing her does Henry discover an element of yielding to her in himself; ominously enough, he attaches it to the most potent and demonized image for illegitimate female wiles: "You have witchcraft in your lips, Kate" (line 292). The peak of personal emotion in the play remains the love-death of Suffolk and York.

Commentators have said that Katharine is submissive,[59] but she need not be played quite like that. In fact, she may be seen as avoiding collusion with Henry's approaches through a minimalist strategy of one-line replies—the least that courtesy requires. "I cannot tell," she says three times. "I do not know," her father must decide. She declines to join in the pretense that her preferences matter—it is as much resistance as she can manage. In the customary masculine manner, Henry decides that her reluctance means yes: "Come, I know thou lovest me" (line 205). But there is no reason (only sexist assumptions) to believe that Katharine is coy or teasing. When she objects to the king kissing her hand—insisting on the power relations—that it is inappropriate for a conqueror ("mon très puissant seigneur") to abase his grandeur and kiss the hand of "votre seigneurie indigne serviteur"—he takes it as a pretext to kiss her lips. She objects that this is not the custom in France, but he overrides her ("nice customs curtsy to great kings"), stops her mouth (as such men like to say), and forces her: "therefore, patiently and yielding . . ." (lines 265–91).

I am not saying that this is the "right" way to play the scene. Rather, as was argued earlier, the text is implicated, necessarily, in the complexities of its culture, and manifests not only the strategies of power but also the anxieties that protrude through them, making it possible always to glimpse alternative understandings. The traditional reading—the triumph of personal and international peace and harmony through the betrothal of Henry and Katharine—is not a different scene from the one I propose, in which she is recognized as one figure in a far larger ideological structure of sexualities and genders. It is an alternative reading of the same scene, one the text cannot but license in some measure. As Lance Wilcox puts it in his essay on the play, with evident reference to the current state of the law in many countries, "When is a rapist not a rapist? When he's a husband."[60] Whether the betrothal of Katharine appears delightful or oppressive depends on the framework of assumptions readers and audiences bring to it. Even so, my story of Katharine's recalcitrance gains support from Henry's complaint when the others return: "I cannot so conjure up the spirit of love in her, that he will appear in his true likeness." She has not performed properly to his script, so he threatens to demand more French cities (lines 306–8, 334–37). Burgundy's solution is to engage Henry in a sequence of bawdy innuendoes that positions Katharine, apparently in her hearing, as the merest object of male use. Cities and maids, it is said once more, are the same: "for they are all girded with maiden walls that war hath never entered" (lines 339–41). The princess, Burgundy means, must be forced, and Henry will get the cities eventually through the marriage. They drop the pretense of seeking Katharine's consent; she does not speak again.

Despite the bullying of Henry and the other men—and this is the kind of point of ideological contradiction against which no text can entirely protect itself—the state cannot be secured against female influence. The betrothal, of course, is witness to that: it is to confirm his claim to France that Henry marries the French king's daughter. English unease at this is evident in the demand that the French king name Henry "Notre très cher filz Henry, Roy d'Angleterre, Héritier de France" (5.2.357–58). It sounds as if Henry is the lineal son of the French monarch, but actually such nomination depends on his wife. Henry is following the precedent of Edward III's father at the start of the story, inviting once more the embarrassment of the royal title passing through the female. In fact, fear of miscegenation—always a complication in imperialism—has been a major preoccupation all through the play; xenophobia and racism often accompany male homosocial insecurity. The archbishop's explanation of Salic law is that it was devised to prevent conquerors from marrying local women:

> Charles the Great having subdued the Saxons,
> There left behind and settled certain French;
> Who, holding in disdain the German women
> For some dishonest manners of their life,
> Establish'd then this law; to wit, no female
> Should be inheritrix in Salic land.
>
> (1.2.46–51)

The French draw upon this attitude to dismiss the English, regarding them as degenerate consequences of their men mating with native women after the Norman conquest of 1066 (it is another way of blaming women):

> O Dieu vivant! shall a few sprays of us,
> The emptying of our fathers' luxury,
> Our scions, put in wild and savage stock,
> Spirt up so suddenly into the clouds,
> And overlook their grafters?
>
> (3.5.5–9)

If this is a danger, Henry is courting it by grafting English virtues onto French stock. The French queen welcomes the prospect "That English may as French, French Englishmen, / Receive each other" (5.2.385–86). But such sexual mingling, in the terms the play has established, involves contamination of English masculinity with French effeminacy. Henry has hopes of a soldier son, he tells Katharine, typically writing a script for her:

> If ever thou beest mine, Kate, as I have a saving faith within me tells me thou shalt, I get thee with scambling, and thou must therefore needs prove a good soldier-breeder. Shall not thou and I, between Saint Denis and Saint George, compound a boy, half French, half English, that shall go to Constantinople and take the Turk by the beard? shall we not? what sayest thou, my fair flower de-luce?
>
> (5.2.211–18)

But the ideology of the play has made this unlikely, for it has maintained that the French (whom the princess is made to personify in the last phrase quoted) are *not* good soldier-breeders. The point is evidently in Henry's mind when he adds: "do but now promise, Kate, you will endeavour for your French part of such a boy, and for my English moiety take the word of a king and a bachelor" (lines 223–26). There is no problem (of course) about Henry's capacity, but Katharine must promise to make a special effort. "Take her, fair son," says the French king, "and from her blood raise up / Issue to me" (lines 366–67). The issue have to be French to strengthen the English claim to French territory, but by just so much, the rhetoric of the play has been saying, they will be effeminate, French-style men, and hence unable to defend that territory. Henry V cannot secure his imperial inheritance without putting it at risk from female influence. So the unfortunate reign of Henry VI, with its "weak" king and dangerous women, is biologically encoded through a kind of Social Darwinism. Immediately at the opening of *1 Henry VI* the son of Katharine and Henry V is called "an effeminate prince"; a campaign over the French cities ensues, concluding with their loss through an "effeminate peace."[61]

All this was important because contemporary monarchs, including Elizabeth and her presumed successor, James VI, relied on claims through the female line, albeit reluctantly. But the attribution of military failure to female influence through miscegenation found its most immediate current shape in respect of anxieties about the current imperial project in Ireland. The devastation of France described at length by Burgundy (once more in terms of a need for sexual control [5.2.29–67]) sounds much too extensive to be the outcome of Henry V's relatively limited operations along the coast of Normandy; far more like the consequences of English policy in Ireland as it was described in many contemporary accounts, with agriculture destroyed and the people grown "like savages" (line 59). In his *View of the Present State of Ireland*, Spenser laments that the English who have been settled there identify with Irish rather than English interests, to the point of preferring to speak Erse: "It seemeth strange to me that the English should take more delight to speak that language than their own, whereas they should (methinks) rather take scorn to acquaint their tongues thereto, for it hath been ever the use of the conquerer to despise the language of the conquered, and to force him by all means to learn his." This latter, of course, is the tendency manifested by Henry. The reason it did not work out in Ireland, Spenser says, is "fostering and marrying with the Irish." In Spenser's view, such intermingling is extremely undesirable; because of it "great houses . . . have degendered from their ancient dignities and now are grown as Irish as O'Hanlan's breech, (as the proverb there is)." Though some great men have successfully made "such matches with their vassals, and have of them nevertheless raised worthy issue . . . yet the example is so perilous as it is not to be adventured." For "how can such matching but bring forth an evil race, seeing that commonly the child taketh most of his nature of the mother, besides speech, manners, inclination, which are for the most part agreeable to the conditions of their mothers?" Henry VII and Elizabeth passed acts against intermarriage in Ireland, and other commentators confirmed the dangers—Richard Stanyhurst, Barnaby Rich, and William Herbert.[62] By this analysis, Henry's marriage is a considerable blunder. He tells Katharine: "England is thine, Ireland is thine, France is thine, and Henry Plantagenet is thine" (5.2.252–53). But each of those four imperial claims is fraught with the seeds of its own falsification. The dominant again proves inseparable from that which it seeks to control.

In some respects, my account has produced distinctions between ideas of genders and sexualities in early modern England and today. Nevertheless, there are also continuities: imperialist, xenophobic, and male homosocial ideologies still often reinforce each other, demonizing the female, the feminine, and the effeminate. The dominance of masculine attributes is represented as "order," and the answer when that order fails to carry conviction is said to be more order (rulers should be more manly). But because the order was of a kind that produces its own concomitant disorder, as the bellicosity of the English and French produces war, that answer must be futile. Nor, as critics have hoped, is a convenient resolution available in the "softening" or "balancing" of manly attributes such as appear in Henry V by placing him in negotiation with the French princess, or even with the love-death of Suffolk and York. For the terms of such negotiations still presuppose, not only the oppressive initial construction of genders and sexualities, but also the anxieties and power assumptions that remain inscribed within them. Critics who believe that Henry becomes more fully human through interaction with the feminine qualities of the princess do not dream of suggesting that the effeminate *as such* might in any way be redeemed: that remains the "wrong" kind of femininity, the "wrong" kind of compromise. The dominant, characteristically, takes from its others what it can incorporate, leaving the remainder more decisively repudiated.

7 Protestantism: Questions of Subjectivity and Control

ENGLIT AND CHRISTIAN HUMANISM

I arrived at a study of protestantism in early modern England through Philip Sidney. The image of him that prevailed in literary studies was that of the ideal courtier, poet, scholar, patron of letters, and soldier. He seemed to heal the rift between practical affairs and writing—he at least could not be called a sissy (see chapter 10 below). Further exploration showed an attractive modification of this image: Sidney was a political activist who annoyed the establishment of his time. He and his friends opposed Queen Elizabeth's foreign policy, wanting a principled rather than a prudent attitude to religion in Europe; supported puritan ministers; and held that subjects (admittedly only upper-class subjects) may resist monarchs when the latter are tyrannical.[1] The popular image had Sidney as the queen's favourite in an ideal administration without conflict, but actually she distrusted his politics, ignored his advice, and only reluctantly employed him.

The basis of Sidney's political commitment was religious: he belonged to the puritan party (I use *puritan* to mean those committed to the zealous maintenance and furtherance of the Elizabethan protestant settlement).[2] One might have expected this to involve a distinctive doctrinal perspective, but in fact the issue between most puritans and the government was not of that kind. The reformed English church, centrally and generally, was Calvinist; it looked not to Wittenberg, where Luther's successors had moderated his doctrine, but to Geneva. The "Thirty-nine Articles of Religion" were ordered to be read in church several times a year and repeated by the faithful as a condition of participation at the communion service. "Man . . . cannot turn and prepare himself, by his own natural strength and good works, to faith, and calling upon God," Article 10 states firmly: we cannot, of ourselves, move towards God. And, it continues, "we have no power to do good works pleasant and acceptable to God without the grace of God by Christ preventing us" (i.e., going before us).[3] God must *intervene before* we can become meritorious, such is our predisposition to evil. In principle, this is what many Christians have believed, but the emphasis is Calvinist. Such doctrine was propagated also in the Homilies, which were appointed to be read in churches whenever there was not a sermon. In "The Salvation of Mankind," congregations were told that "justification is the office of God only; and is not a thing which we render unto him, but which we receive of him." Protestants speak of "justification by faith," but this, says the homily, does not mean "that this our own act, to believe in Christ, or this our faith in Christ, which is within us, doth justify us and deserve our justification unto us; for that were to count ourselves to be justified by some act or virtue that is within ourselves. . . . We must trust only in God's mercy."[4] The corollary of this doctrine is election and reprobation, which were by no means specially puritan ideas. The seventeenth of the Thirty-nine Articles asserts: "Predestination to Life is the everlasting purpose of God, whereby (before the foundations of the world were laid) he hath constantly decreed by his counsel secret to us, to deliver from curse and damnation those whom he hath chosen." This article compromises only insofar as it leaves the loophole (which Milton was to exploit) that the end of some people might be undecided. Both Catholicism and neoplatonic humanism encouraged belief in a *continuity* between human and divine experience; that one might school one's soul and rise from one to the other. Protestantism insisted on the gap between the two, emphasizing the utter degradation of humankind and the total power of God to determine who shall be saved.

   No ideology can contain all the issues it releases, let alone those that might occur around or beyond its ostensible boundaries. Reformation orthodoxy was contested, eventually to the point where it was pushed to the margins of English thought. Nonetheless, around 1600 it was an overwhelmingly important part of the ideological field and had to be taken into account, not least by those who distrusted it. Literary studies have only recently recognized this, mainly because they were dominated by "Christian humanism." This latter was a genial, moderate (except when under threat), gentlemanly/ladylike attachment to something not too specific, but involving a loose respect for Jesus' Sermon on the Mount and an assumption that "redemption" will come to people of goodwill; it cultivated a calm superiority to worldly affairs. Rather more earnestly, it believed that these attitudes will be embodied in and transmitted by literature. Christian humanists were influential in selecting the canon, and when there was danger that a text might not fit in, it was forcefully "explicated" so as to produce an acceptable reading. A neat instance is witchcraft in *Macbeth*, for it implies a superstitious and violently polarized kind of Christianity. As I remarked in chapter 5, Kenneth Muir tries to deal with this by saying that the Witches "can yet symbolise the workings of evil in the hearts of men." Theodore Spencer, similarly, refers to the Witches in *Macbeth* as "abstractions that are developed from the human mind" and as "a final dramatic realisation of the Elizabethan dramatic convention which invariably tended to see individual human experience in relation to some power—God, the stars, or fortune— larger than itself."[5] But to most early modern audiences, the Witches were not symbol, abstraction, or convention; they were part of a pattern of superstitious, violent, repressive, and sexist attitudes. Muir and Spencer impose a genial gloss, evading consideration of the power relations inscribed in the religious ideology of the play.

Usually, Christian humanists allege that the Elizabethan religious settlement of 1558 was a typically wise English compromise, that the rigors of protestant experience are therefore scarcely relevant, and that the vast majority of early modern English people believed themselves to inhabit a stable, harmonious universe guaranteed by a manifestly benign deity, understudied by a manifestly benign monarch.[6] But this was not so, and it has implications not only for the context of many literary texts, but also for the kind of study Englit is taken to be. If religion and literature express not absolute values but culturally relative concerns that are very likely uncongenial to modern readers, and if they were contested, both in themselves and in their relations with each other, how may this affect modern ideas of what literary study is for?

Not just the Christianity but also the humanism in Christian humanism has been challenged, and I want to register that first. Hugh Kearney sets the development of a humanist pattern of study in sixteenth-century England alongside changes in the roles of the universities—the forbidding of the teaching of canon law, a stronger collegiate system, and the displacing of poor scholars by gentry and nobility. Together these changes facilitated an enhanced social and intellectual control by the Crown, and helped to establish the division between gentleman and non-gentleman, which during the sixteenth century became the crucial factor in the life-chances of a family.[7] There was in the period, in Kearney's view, a progressive, civic humanism, inspired by classical republicanism and adapted to a wide-ranging political engagement (exemplified by More's *Utopia*), but in England it was overwhelmed by a court humanism (exemplified by Elyot's *The Governor*) that depended on the patronage and support of the social hierarchy (pp. 34–35). Anthony Grafton and Lisa Jardine argue that scholasticism had been well adapted to practical training in diverse occupations, whereas the humanist learning that displaced it "fitted the needs of the new Europe that was taking shape, with its closed governing elites, hereditary offices and strenuous efforts to close off debate on vital political and social questions." By establishing an un-challengable superior culture, humanism "fostered in all its initiates a properly docile attitude towards authority."[8] Like the modern humanities, Grafton and Jardine add, early modern humanism thrived only by "overlooking the evident mismatch between ideals and prac-tice"—between exalted claims of human fulfillment and petty details of instruction (p. xv). Recently Jonathan Goldberg has developed a comparable analysis in relation to disputes among anthropologists and theorists about the ideological status of writing. Goldberg follows Claude Lévi-Strauss and Brian Street, rather than Jack Goody and (in this respect) Jacques Derrida, arguing that writing has to be seen as a tool not "of civilised knowledge but of ideological imposition." Goldberg quotes Lévi-Strauss:

> The systematic development of compulsory education in the Euro-pean countries goes hand in hand with the extension of military ser-vice and proletarianisation. The fight against illiteracy is therefore connected with an increase in governmental authority over the citi-zens. Everyone must be able to read, so that the government can say: Ignorance of the law is no excuse.[9]

Such an argument is familiar to British students of the extension of compulsory schooling in the nineteenth century, but its application to the high humanism that has seemed to ratify the modern human-ities is provocative. Goldberg is able to cite Keith Thomas's judgment that the uneven spread of literacy "gave a new cultural dimension to social differences previously founded on wealth and power. It rein-forced the existing social hierarchy by enabling the upper classes to despise their inferiors." However, Goldberg's account of "the instal-lation of the pedagogic apparatus as the arm of an increasingly centralised and bureaucratised power"[10] is in danger of making the case too total—as if the effect were unitary, coherent and purposeful, not embedded in conflict and contradiction and subject to negotiation. The same criticism may be attached to Grafton and Jardine (I discuss this further in chapter 8). Nevertheless, these are major assaults on the alleged humanist origins of Christian humanism.

The notion of Christianity that Christian humanism purports to find in the early modern period is traditionally organized around the poetry of Donne and Herbert. In the reading of Louis L. Martz, Donne's Holy Sonnets are meditations leading to the achievement of a state of "devotion."[11] In fact, although a few of these sonnets suggest such attainment, Donne's protestantism is strongly infused with the anxious contradictions of Calvinism. About half the Holy Sonnets end with with the condition of Donne's soul *in question*—unaffected by his devotional efforts, awaiting God's mysterious judgment: "Thy Grace may wing me to prevent his art, / And thou like adamant draw mine iron heart" (Holy Sonnet no. 1); "Oh I shall soon despair, when I do see / That thou lov'st mankind well, yet wilt not choose me" (no. 2); "burn me O Lord, with a fiery zeal / Of thee and thy house, which doth in eating heal" (no. 5); "Teach me how to repent; for that's as good / As if thou hadst sealed my pardon, with thy blood" (no. 7). All these conclusions are in conditional or imperative moods, and Holy Sonnets 4, 6, 8, 9, 14, 16, and 18 are in similar vein.[12] Grace, or any kind of reconciliation, has yet to be granted. Nor does the tone of these sonnets suggest what Martz says he hears—namely, "the perfect equipoise of a carefully regulated, arduously cultivated skill" (p. 56). The arduousness, rather, is in the Christianity and Donne's self-consciously nervous relation to it. For actually, Donne's theology is close to the center of English Calvinism, in the sense that any move towards God depends on God moving first, and this leaves the human person without influence over his or her salvation. In Holy Sonnet 4, Donne writes: "grace, if thou repent, thou canst not lack; / But who shall give thee that grace to begin?" And even when that grace is received, Donne says in a sermon of 1618, we cannot proceed without God's continuing intervention: "we are so far from being able to begin without Grace, as then where we have the first Grace, we cannot proceed to the use of that, without more."[13] "Impute me righteous," Donne cries (Holy Sonnet 6), echoing Saint Paul echoing King David on "the blessedness of the man, unto whom God imputeth righteousness without works" (Rom. 4:6).

Herbert has often been invoked as Donne's gentler counterpart, but he shared the orthodox commitment to election: it is God's decision, Herbert says in "The Water-course": he

$$\text{gives to man, as he sees fit} - \begin{cases} \text{Salvation.} \\ \text{Damnation.}^{[14]} \end{cases}$$

It is only through sheerly perverse reading that criticism avoids hearing the theology in these poems; rather than belabor the point here, I shall draw further upon Donne and Herbert in the discussion that follows.

As I show elsewhere, the dominant modern conception of literature in Britain and North America took much of its shape from its association with a partly dissident, leisured fraction of the middle and upper classes.[15] Members of this fraction might find Christian humanism congenial; they might even think of it as a progressive force, dispelling just such a violent theology as I have located in early modern England, and contributing to the establishment of more civilized values. This need not have been an entirely disinterested program, for by the late eighteenth century, Calvinistic Methodism was the creed, not of such as Philip Sidney, but of lower-class, nonconformist chapel communities—with the potential for political organization. In Wales and the border counties, Calvinist tenants who abstained from voting for Anglicans in parliamentary elections were driven off their farms; and, for instance, at Llanyblodwel in Shropshire, in 1840, the vicar and landowners combined to prevent the building of a nonconformist chapel.[16] Christian humanists might prefer to look back to the time when Sir Henry Sidney kept strict order as Lord President of the Welsh Marches; they would not notice too sharply that Philip Sidney and Fulke Greville studied Calvin's *Catechism* twice a day at Shrewsbury school, for that would confuse the picture. (Today there is no longer cause for alarm, since Shropshire, the Countryside Commission and county council inform tourists, is "the great natural theme park"—safely packaged by nature and history for convenient consumption; Sir Philip Sidney is "heritage," and the "twin town" of Shrewsbury is Zutphen.)[17] Christian humanists appease their anxieties by imagining, like Theodore Spencer, a mild-mannered Renaissance Man: "the ideal aristocrat, dutiful, learned, religious, temperate, constant, controlling passion with reason, and ruling sense with judgment" (*Shakespeare and the Nature of Man*, p. 81). They may even imagine the twentieth-century gentleman-don to be such a person.

Christian humanism is distinctively potent in England, where the state church derives itself from the Elizabethan settlement (clergymen still experience difficulty with the Thirty-nine Articles) and some universities retain the trappings of nineteenth-century religiosity. Michael D. Bristol presents it as the project of North American old historicism also, adducing Theodore Spencer, and also A. O. Lovejoy and Hardin Craig. Bristol remarks that Spencer "represses whatever knowledge he has of European history" when he describes "the Eucharist" as beyond contention.[18] The idea was to invoke not just Shakespeare but a whole society of which he was the ultimate manifestation, and to credit it with all the virtues of hierarchy, order, and stability that seemed to be lacking in modern times. For such critics, Bristol shows, the supposed "world view" of the Elizabethans was not merely a historical phenomenon: "By implication the 'great chain of being' has a privileged status as a genuine principle of social rationality, valid in differing socio-historical contexts" (p. 148). In this supposedly consensual outlook, conflict is eliminated and Shakespeare is discovered to be "the poet of tradition, of religious orthodoxy, and of a politically conservative view of the individual contained within the hierarchy of master and servant" (p. 145). This vision is offered, if not as attainable in the modern world, then as a reproach to the forces that impede it. Bristol relates it to "the interests of entrenched and privileged social groups and of the professional cadres affiliated with those groups" (p. 146)—meaning by the latter members of the Englit profession. As Louis Montrose has observed, a more or less unspoken respect for Christianity persists in literary studies today: "A gentle/manly—that is, benignly patriarchal—Anglo-Saxon, Protestant, Humanist ethos remains still today deeply ingrained," and much criticism celebrates "an apparently continuous tradition of religious, social and aesthetic values."[19] Richard Hooker's "moderate" *Of the Laws of Ecclesiastical Polity* still bulks large in the fifth edition of the *Norton Anthology of English Literature* (1986), with more pages than Hobbes and twice as many as Locke; the only other sixteenth-century theological prose included is one page of John Foxe.[20] This prominence is not justified by the status of the *Laws* in early modern England. In the process of defending episcopacy (which is what the bishops commissioned him to do), Hooker argued back towards the papist view of the individual's capacity to contribute towards salvation. This is the attraction for Christian humanists, but it is probably why publication of the *Laws* was held up. The 1593 edition was not sold out until 1606, whereas

William Perkins's *Golden Chain* was reprinted twelve times between 1591 and 1600; Perkins's work made up nearly a quarter of the 200 items published by the university press at Cambridge between 1590 and 1618. "For generations *The Laws of Ecclesiastical Polity* held few attractions for committed protestant laymen," Claire Cross says.[21]

Such considerations were in my mind when I wrote *Literature in Protestant England,* which aimed to confront Christian humanists with the remoteness of much early modern literature and religion from modern progressive values (on relations between that book and the present study, see p. x). In an associated essay, "Against Appropriation," I held that instead of effacing the ideological specificity of texts such as *Macbeth,* we should purposefully reconstruct them, so that their otherness might challenge and illuminate our own assumptions. The argument drew upon Brecht's project for enhancing political awareness through alienation rather than empathy.[22] I soon felt that this program was too optimistic, too dependent upon assumptions about how far the appeal of rationality and progressive values could be expected to shine through texts and histories. In "Four Ways with a Reactionary Text," I pointed out that Brecht did not in fact leave audiences to discover a progressive politics in themselves and their society, but organized his plays so that a desired political implication might emerge. Criticism, too, should take a stronger role, identifying the modes of ideological intervention implied in the text's representation of social reality, both at its initial production and in our culture today.[23] More significant than the argument of this essay was its association with the Literature Teaching Politics movement (it was published in the second issue of the movement's journal, edited by a group at Sussex after the example of Cardiff in the previous year). The collective ethos of LTP afforded a milieu in which it was not bad manners to address political issues in Englit teaching and writing.

Feminism and Black Studies apart (and even there professional codes remain important), political explicitness is still a difficulty in Englit in the United States, and in respect of religion particularly. Jonathan Culler has complained recently that Christianity seems to occupy there "a special, privileged place, as though it went without saying that any sort of challenge or critique were improper, in bad taste." Time is spent, Culler observes, "explicating literary works in religious terms and declining to challenge or contradict their teachings." Yet "religion provides a legitimation for many reactionary or repressive forces in the United States and is arguably a greater danger today than ideological positions critics do spend their time attacking."[24] This reticence continues despite the entry of non-gentry, non-Christian people into the profession, and largely despite the interest of new historicists in "power" (it may be that religion is too mainstream, too straight, whereas new historicism likes to uncover the weird). It may even be that literature, and especially the Shakespeare period, is partly attractive, still, because it invites a loose, nostalgic affiliation to a residual gentry ideology. But it means, Culler says, that "education has abandoned its historic tasks, of combating superstition, encouraging skeptical debate about competing religions and their claims or myths, and fighting religious dogmatism and its political consequences" (p. 78). It hardly entitles Western intellectuals to animadvert, as they do, upon Islam.

In a way, Reformation theology commands respect. Compared with the more user-friendly doctrines of Christian humanism, it does attempt to face up to the consequences of monotheism. If there is a creator (creatrix) in charge of the universe, he or she cannot evade ultimate responsibility for human suffering and frustration. Calvin does not try to shuffle off divine accountability; he positively insists upon it: "When afflicted with disease, we shall groan and be disquieted, and long for health; pressed with poverty, we shall feel the stings of anxiety and sadness, feel the pain of ignominy, contempt, and injury, and pay the tears due to nature at the death of our friends." But it is all God's will: "the rule of piety is, that the hand of God is the ruler and arbiter of the fortunes of all, and, instead of rushing on with thoughtless violence, dispenses good and evil with perfect regularity."[25] Calvin makes very little appeal to the consolation of life after death. Out of an unusually vivid awareness of the trials that beset us, he declares that everything is as God wills it. This theology confronts directly the principal difficulty for a religion that asserts a single deity of complete power and goodness: if God is omnipotent and good, why does he not make things better? One answer is that we have free will—he has left it to us to decide what to do, and we have spoiled things. But that answer diminishes God's power, with the danger that we might forget about him, attribute events to blind fortune, and drift towards secularism. Luther complained that in Erasmus's humanism, God has left it to men "to decide whether they want to be saved or damned; and in the meantime he has himself, perhaps, gone off to the banquet of the Ethiopians, as Homer says" (i.e., to the end of the world).[26] The reformers chose the other path: they emphasized God's control over the universe at the expense, or so it seems to most people now, of his goodness. It is easy for humanistic intellectuals today to condemn Reformation Christianity; it encourages a deceptive and complacent sense that we now think freely, and leaves the field open for Christian humanism. The more challenging task is to consider why many found Calvinism productive and comforting at that time.

WHY CALVINISM MADE SENSE

There was nothing intrinsically protestant about English people, and the Reformation doctrine of grace and predestination was not new—the reformers drew continually upon the church fathers, especially Augustine. Indeed, if God is the all-powerful creator, it is difficult to avoid the ultimate conclusion that he has determined everything—Aquinas granted as much.[27] It was the political and social conditions of the sixteenth century that precipitated an institutional split in Christendom; which countries "went protestant" depended on infighting among the ruling elite and the attitudes of powerful neighbors. However, once political conflict had become focused around religion, doctrine polarized and hardened. Issues that in other times had been accommodated by logical sleights of hand and evocative phraseology were teased out and stated in confrontational terms; each faction represented the other as seditious, devilish, atheistical, and immoral. Governments in all countries understood that religious allegiance was a key basis for social cohesion and disruption, and sought to control it.

Of course, we cannot tell what most people actually believed around the year 1600. People do not necessarily believe what they are told; indeed, the reiteration of a doctrine by authority probably indicates that it was widely ignored or mistrusted. Human thought and behavior are in practice crisscrossed by assumptions of which we are only half aware and which, if pressed, would prove radically divergent. Many uneducated people must have retained a perhaps confused attachment to Catholic practices, chance, and magic. In fact, there is considerable evidence that many had little comprehension of Christian thought of any kind. Church courts were exercised with bizarre cases of ignorance and irreverence, and protestant activists complained continually of the lack of preachers to inform the people. William Perkins listed some of the "errors" in a preface to *The Foundation of Christian Religion* (1590)—"That howsoever a man live, yet if he call upon God on his deathbed and say, Lord have mercy upon me, and so go away like a lamb, he is certainly saved"; "That a man may go to wizards, called wise men, for counsel, because God hath provided a salve for every sore."[28] However, educated people probably understood what they were expected to believe. Many of them were instructed at Oxford or Cambridge universities, which were mainly training centers for the ministry: all teachers there had to be approved by the church hierarchy and attendance at sermons was compulsory. At the same time, educated people had access to other discourses, including an atheist tradition going back to Epicurus and Lucretius, Renaissance neoplatonism, a whole pantheon of pagan writing of immense standing, and the nascent empiricism we associate with Machiavelli and Bacon. Thomas Nashe complained that some of the learned "fetch the articles of their belief out of Aristotle, and think of heaven and hell as the heathen philosophers, take occasion to deride our ecclesiastical state and all ceremonies of divine worship as bugbears and scarecrows."[29] (In chapter 8 I discuss the conflict of the "puritan humanist"; in chapter 9 I say more about the scope for writing disruptive of orthodoxy.) The official dominance of protestant theology did not render superfluous a continuous preoccupation with heresy, atheism, and irreligion; to the contrary, the threat of them was persistently invoked as the reason for censorship and other controls. Indeed, this was not just a scare tactic: choice in religion, Conrad Russell observes, "was a fact too established to be denied." As Montaigne remarked, once people notice "that some articles of their religion be made doubtful and questionable, they will soon and easily admit an equal uncertainty in all other parts of their belief."[30] The atheistical work of Pietro Pomponazzi was banned in England, but went through dozens of editions in France and Italy in the sixteenth century.

With all this said, what I have identified as Reformation orthodoxy was hardly disputed in the English church before 1600. The libraries of theological students at the turn of the century were stocked with works by Calvin, Peter Martyr, Theodore Beza, and Henry Bullinger; the sermons of the Calvinist preacher William Perkins were a chief feature of life at Cambridge between 1592 and 1602; the standard Bible was the Geneva version (1560).[31] In 1571–72, Archbishop Edmund Grindal insisted in a letter to the Strasbourg Calvinist Hierom Zanchius: "As for *doctrine*, hitherto we retain it unshaken and unadulterated in our churches. . . . all our controversy has flowed from *discipline*."[32] There was a discontented wing of puritan clergy and gentlemen, but they were concerned about organization and hierarchy, clerical training, and the wearing of vestments which could not be justified from scripture; there were noblemen and gentry at court and in Parliament, led by Leicester and Warwick (Sidney's uncles) who supported puritans and argued for an interventionist foreign policy. But doctrine was generally Calvinist. There were a few sectarians, who alarmed the government by developing the doctrine of election in an anti-authoritarian way, into the antinomian belief that the saved are not subject to earthly powers and may do as they wish; but puritans did not approve of that; they liked authority.[33]

When William Barrett and Peter Baro questioned predestination at Cambridge in the 1590s, this was thought a strange turn of events. Archbishop Whitgift (no puritan) sought to still the controversy by promulgating the Lambeth Articles (1595), which state unequivocally that "God from eternity predestined certain men to life and condemned others to death." Lancelot Andrewes expressed a reservation and the queen supported him, but Whitgift remarked to Archbishop Hutton of York that these matters "were never doubted by any professor of the gospel during all the time of your abode and mine in the university." He declared that the articles should be accepted as his authoritative judgment since, he believed, they were "true and correspondent to the doctrine professed in this church of England, and established by the laws of the land." He told the vice-chancellor at Cambridge "to take care that nothing be publicly taught to the contrary," and only this opinion was allowed into print.[34] The teaching at Oxford remained steadily Calvinist.[35] When James I came to the throne, he called the Hampton Court Conference (1604) to settle the structure of the church, but here the quarrel was again not doctrinal; James was a Calvinist, and so was George Abbott, whom he appointed as Archbishop of Canterbury in 1611 (Abbott held the post until 1633). Arminianism (espousing free will and a compromise with the Roman liturgy) arose in Holland but was uninfluential in England until Charles I came to the throne in 1625 and promoted John Laud, who eventually became Archbishop of Canterbury in 1633. If anything, it was these Arminians, rather than the puritans, who disrupted the English church in the 1630s and helped to cause the Civil War.[36]

Centrally, perhaps, protestants wished religion to be more *inward;* or, more precisely (since of course many Catholics experienced their religion inwardly), that it should be more inward for more people than hitherto. Protestants were not content with casual or external observance. Hence the attack on the mediatory functions by which the church had traditionally interposed itself—saints, the Latin Bible and ritual, the priest, indulgences. In the Homily "Of Good Works," Elizabethans were given a list—

of papistical superstitions and abuses, as of beads, of lady psalters and rosaries, of fifteen Os, of St Bernard's verses, of St Agatha's letters, of purgatory, of masses satisfactory, of stations and jubilees, of feigned reliques, of hallowed beads, bells, bread, water, palms, candles, fire, and such other, of superstitious fastings, of fraternities (or brotherhoods), of pardons, with such like merchandise.[37]

Protestants held that religion had become superstitious and routine, too often corrupted by the movement of cash. They sought to establish for all the faithful an intense and immediate relationship between the individual and God. This is the emphasis in the poetry of Herbert:

> But as I rav'd and grew more fierce and wild
>> At every word,
> Me thoughts I heard one calling, *Child*:
>> And I reply'd, *My Lord*.
>>> ("The Collar")

By taking from the church the responsibility for the quality of the relationship between people and God, Reformation Christianity placed a personal burden upon every believer. How could one gain God's favor? The only safe answer was that one could not: one could be pleasing to God only through his extraordinary generosity. Hence the emphasis on the need for grace to come first. Luther declared in *The Bondage of the Will* (1524): "No man can be thoroughly humbled until he knows that his salvation is utterly beyond his own powers, devices, endeavours, will, and works, and depends entirely on the choice, will, and work of another, namely, of God alone."[38] We cannot ascend, only be lifted up. Hence the abrupt ending of "The Collar." The liturgical imagery in the poem (a thorn, bloodletting, the wine and corn of the communion service) brings the poet no closer to God. He only becomes "more fierce and wild." The reversal is caused sheerly by divine intervention: "I heard one calling, *Child*: / And I reply'd." The poet's response is unexplored, even automatic; it is not his achievement but something God does to him.

If one experiences the basic protestant sense of human wretchedness (and who would not when God is aware of every repining at his arrangement of human affairs—of every wish, for instance, that it should stop raining?), then to be told that one may be saved nevertheless, entirely through divine mercy, is reassuring. The protestant who believed that he or she had received grace might rise above all the anxieties of this world and the next. Richard Sibbes explains that the faithful may eventually receive "a sweet spiritual security, whereby the soul is freed from slavish fears, and glorieth in God as ours in all conditions. And this is termed by the Apostle, not only *assurance,* but *the riches of assurance.*"[39] Herbert's poems present diverse experiences of distress, but they are held within an overriding confident tone, deriving evidently from assurance of election. This was apparently founded upon an early experience. In "The Glance," Herbert says God

> Vouchsaf'd ev'n in the midst of youth and night
> To look upon me, who before did lie
> > Weltring in sin.

Herbert felt "delight" "overrun my heart, / And take it in." He attributes his surviving "many a bitter storm" to that original call and God's continuing "work within" his soul:

> But still thy sweet original joy
> Sprung from thine eye, did work within my soul,
> And surging griefs, when they grew bold, control,
> > And got the day.

Assurance of election could confer a great sense of well-being, a trust in one's (that is, God's) powers, and an authority in dealing with people and nature. Of course, one was not to feel *too* secure—that would be pride—but to trust the promise one had received from God.

However, you could never be sure. The believer was supposed to attain a quiet assurance, but too much security was dangerous. Andrewes quotes Saint Bernard: "the only way to be secure in fear, is to fear security." Richard Rogers wrote in his diary: "when so ever I have weltred in any looseness or security, yes such wherein I have been unwilling to be awaked, yet I thought even in the same time that God would bring it against me some time or other, and the longer that I have deferred it, the greater is my torment, and then I have no sound peace until I return."[40] As George Herbert pointed out in *A Priest to the Temple,* it was dangerous to feel too safe:

> it is observable that God delights to have men feel, and acknowledge, and reverence his power, and therefore he often overturns things when they are thought past danger: that is his time of interposing.
> . . . So that if a farmer should depend upon God all the year, and being ready to put hand to sickle, shall then secure himself, and think all cock sure; then God sends such weather as lays the corn and destroys it.[41]

At any time God might throw a sulk because you had not been quite attentive enough to him. And there was no reason to suppose that he would let you off lightly. "There is nothing more lamentable, than to see a man laugh when he should fear," said Joseph Hall: "God shall laugh, when such a one's fear cometh."[42]

The dooming of the reprobate to hell is the ultimate difficulty with this religion for many people today. It had little to do with deterrence or reform, for one could not influence one's situation. It was simply that there are two categories, and the elect belong in heaven and the reprobate in hell. The best way I can explain this is to compare the distinction we make now between people and cattle: the latter have to stand out in the rain in fields and get eaten, and most of us accept that this is as it should be because cattle are born different. From the start, they are not like us. So with the reprobate: God had created them different, so it was not unreasonable that their lives (for they were supposed to live miserably) and eventual destination should be different. To the contrary, when they took their proper place in hell, the distressing confusion of life was sorted out and right made to prevail; the idea is still heard.

Finally, protestants thrived on irrationality; they did not expect divine judgments to be comprehensible to the human mind. In fact, the Reformation was in part a reaction against the incipient rationalism of humanists like Erasmus. Luther's early pronouncements provoked Erasmus's objections in *The Freedom of the Will* (1524): "Pious ears can admit the benevolence of one who imputes his own good to us; but it is difficult to explain how it can be a mark of his justice (for I will not speak of mercy) to hand over others to eternal torments in whom he has not deigned to work good works, when they themselves are incapable of doing good, since they have no free choice or, if they have, it can do nothing but sin."[43] If this seems unanswerable to the modern reader, it is because he or she shares Erasmus's tendency towards a rational, ethical, and ultimately secular worldview. But the whole aim of the reformers was to impose a rigor more intense than they found in the Catholic church. Hence Luther's reply: "This is the highest degree of faith, to believe him merciful when he saves so few and damns so many, and to believe him righteous when by his own will he makes us necessarily damnable."[44] Rational, humanistic objections are more than irrelevant to the protestant; they actually illustrate the inadequacy of human reason. God's inscrutable will *should* be incomprehensible to the "fallen" intellect.

CONSTRUCTING THE REFORMATION SUBJECT

The protestant determination to create a more immediate relationship between humanity and God placed a vast and uncertain gulf between them. The opposition is stark—we might say manic depressive: we are sunk in sin unless God reclaims us; then we are immediately among the saints. "There are two kingdoms in the world, which are bitterly opposed to each other," Luther declared. "In one of them Satan reigns. ... He holds captive to his will all who are not snatched away from him by the Spirit of Christ. ... In the other kingdom, Christ reigns, and his kingdom ceaselessly resists and makes war on the kingdom of Satan."[45] Hence the anxious and combative religion of Donne's besieged citadel, demanding to be taken by force:

> I, like an usurped town, to another due,
> Labour to admit you, but oh, to no end,
>
> . . . .
> Take me to you, imprison me, for I
> Except you enthral me, never shall be free,
> Nor ever chaste, except you ravish me.
>
> (Holy Sonnet 14)

Donne agonizes: "Oh I shall soon despair, when I do see / That thou lov'st mankind well, yet wilt not choose me" (Holy Sonnet 2). This is a formula for intensity rather than comfort: when you feel it, it is really there, when you don't you are lost. Medieval Catholics had proposed a harmonious cooperation between God and humanity. They too held that there can be no merit without grace, but also that there can be no blessedness without merit. The reformers rejected this compromise, and with it the sense of continuity and shared purpose between human and divine. They established instead a universe in deep and perpetual strife.

However, such spiritual insecurity was not a malfunction or unfortunate by-product, as commentators often imply, but the way many protestants wanted things to be. Hugh Latimer explained in a sermon of December 19, 1529:

> the more we know of our feeble nature, and set less by it, the more we shall conceive and know in our hearts what God hath done for us; and the more we know what God hath done for us, the less we shall set by ourselves, and the more we shall love and please God: so that in no condition we shall either know ourselves or God, except we do utterly confess ourselves to be mere vileness and corruption.[46]

We approach God by learning how distant, through our wickedness, we are from him. It is a formula for continual restlessness: the invitation to advance is conditional upon acknowledgment that we are unable, of ourselves, to do so. Again, here is Perkins:

> The principal worship of God hath two parts. One is to yield subjection to him, the other to draw near to him and to cleave unto him. By the first we put a difference between ourselves and God, by reason of the greatness of his majesty. By the other we make ourselves one with him as with the fountain of goodness.[47]

Perkins does not say that we first humble ourselves then become one with God, as might a medieval mystic. The two "parts," difference and oneness, are to be simultaneous and continuous, the tension is permanent. According to William Tyndale, a sense of inadequacy in the face of such contradictory demands is a good sign: "So long as thou findest any consent in thine heart unto the law of God, that it is righteous and good, *and also displeasure that thou canst not fulfil it,* despair not, neither doubt but that God's spirit is in thee."[48] It is a mistake to regard this brinkmanship as merely horrid. Indeed, though there are striking instances of people being thrown into despair by protestant doctrine, most found it rather satisfactory. As Michael Walzer remarks (with Weber in mind), we should ask why people "should adopt an anxiety-inducing ideology in the first place." Walzer suggests that they did not; rather, Calvinism was "an 'appropriate' option for anxiety-ridden individuals."[49]

In my view, the main impetus in the system derives from its attractiveness, at this date, as an instrument for the creation of self-consciousness, of interiority. "How could you resist looking at your mind to see if it was in the right state?" John Carey asks, and he regards this as "a recipe for anguish."[50] But anxious self-examination, surely, was the gratification. Rogers desired "to know mine own heart better, where I know that much is to be gotten in understanding of it, and to be acquainted with the diverse corners of it and what sin I am most in danger of and what diligence and means I use against any sin and how I go under any affliction."[51] The idea was not to relax, but to savor the nuances of one's spiritual condition. That is why Rogers was writing the diary—and why there is so much writing of all kinds, including poetry. For in a state simply of spiritual terror, one would not (Donne would not) write metrical and rhyming sonnets (even—or especially—sonnets where the meter evinces the roughness that is regarded, conventionally in Englit, as indicating mental stress). Such writing is not the innocent expression of spiritual anguish, but a self-conscious deployment and cultivation of self-awareness; it is part of a project for actualizing interiority. "Those are my best days, when I shake with fear," Donne says (Holy Sonnet 19), but the effect is modified by the consciousness of it that Donne produces in the poem. In such a process the soul is constituted. It is the place where uncertainty, speculation, anxiety, even anguish may occur, and they are the price of—proof of—the soul being in place. So the self-examination, self-consciousness, in protestant practice is not a by-product, or even a characteristic, but the goal; the orthodox god did not just demand self-awareness, he justified it. Samuel Ward in his diary thanks God that he is "not blind, stubborn minded, cast into a reprobate sense, as other people are," but he still finds plenty to worry about—"my desire of vain glory, when we were gathering herbs with Mr Downham . . . my overmuch quipping and desire of praise thereby. My negligence in my calling. My forgetfulness in noting my sins."[52] That last sentence gives it away: there must be some more sins for Ward to note.

Envisaging one's fate in the hands of the Reformation god of incomprehensible love and arbitrary damnation must have been a great provoker of self-consciousness. This is so even in Donne's Holy Sonnet 4, "Oh my black soul! now thou art summoned," which William H. Halewood says "moves surely from the soul's sin to Christ's redemptive power."[53] The soul facing death is

> like a pilgrim, which abroad hath done
> Treason, and durst not turn to whence he is fled.

Perhaps the pilgrimage is itself the treason, a recidivist attempt to gain divine favor. But the sense of entrapment is more general than that, it is part of the protestant pattern whereby any move that the believer might make of his or her own initiative would be futile and self-destructive:

> Or like a thief, which till death's doom be read,
> Wisheth himself delivered from prison;
> But damned and haled to execution,
> Wisheth that still he might be imprisoned.

There is no way Donne can make the right move. God must move first:

> Yet grace, if thou repent, thou canst not lack;
> But who shall give thee that grace to begin?

The answer goes without saying, and it makes Donne's efforts irrelevant; yet the poem concludes with self-exhortation:

> Oh make thyself with holy mourning black,
> And red with blushing, as thou art with sin;
> Or wash thee in Christ's blood, which hath this might
> That being red, it dyes red souls to white.

Christ's blood may have "this might," but the question is still whether it is to be deployed for Donne. The mourning and blushing are not achieved states; they are imperatives addressed by Donne to himself: "Oh make thyself. . . ." But, as he has just said, he cannot *make himself*: grace is necessary first. Donne is telling himself to do something that he cannot, again the ending is provisional. Also, does it help to envisage mourning and blushing at the same time? And is not the paradox of red and white, for Donne, rather conventional? It is used by Perkins: one's sins are great, "I grant. But Christ's passion is far greater and although my sins were as red as scarlet and as purple, yet they shall be as white as snow and as soft as wool."[54] If Donne's imagery here is at once empty and strained, reverting to standard tropes, it is because it can only be gestural and ritual repetition cannot make any difference. For although it is said that these paradoxes are reconciled in God, it is not known how he will apply his "might" to Donne. As in many of these poems, the conclusion substitutes spiritual exhaustion for closure.

The elaborate rationalizations of Reformation theology, which we might regard as evidence of intellectual embarrassment, are of a piece with the program of self-examination: they foreground mental activity. It is incoherence that makes the self aware of itself, that sets it to work in the endlessly deferred task of discovering coherence. In Holy Sonnet 9, Donne says it is consciousness and rationality that give him a place in the protestant scheme, thereby rendering him liable to damnation:

> Why should intent or reason, born in me,
> Make sins, else equal, in me more heinous?

He straightaway exemplifies the problem by broaching one of the trickier questions:

> And mercy being easy, and glorious
> To God, in his stern wrath, why threatens he?

Why should not a loving god save everyone? There is no good answer, and Donne does not pretend otherwise:

> But who am I, that dare dispute with thee
> O God? Oh! of thine only worthy blood,

> And my tears, make a heavenly lethean flood,
> And drown in it my sin's black memory.

"Thine only worthy blood" suggests Christ's generous sacrifice, but "dare dispute" suggests power rather than goodness: threat and beneficence are inseparable, the argument is not resolved. Donne's best chance might be to evade entirely the dialogue with God and the rational activity it provokes: "I think it mercy, if thou wilt forget." Yet still this very wish promotes not oblivion but self-consciousness.

Herbert's tone is quite different, but he too relishes the intricate contradictions of protestantism. In "The Holdfast," he thinks to observe God's law but is told that he cannot, he may only trust in God. However, even this is not in Herbert's power, for it is up to God who may conceive a full faith:

> Then will I trust, said I, in him alone.
>   Nay, ev'n to trust in him, was also his:
>   We must confess, that nothing is our own.
> Then I confess that he my succour is.

But there is still a problem: "But to have nought is ours, not to confess / That we have nought." There is no move that Herbert can legitimately make; he can only recognize "That all things were more ours by being his." In theory this might produce an extreme of self-denial, but the baffled consciousness of the poet is foregrounded once more as the case is worked through.[55] The frustration in "The Cross" is more anguished. Herbert writes: "These contrarieties crush me: these cross actions / Do wind a rope about, and cut my heart." This poem too ends with acknowledgment of divine control, but not with achieved closure. Rather there is a gesture, one that does not try to conceal its abruptness, towards where closure ought to be:

> And yet since these thy contradictions
> Are properly a cross felt by thy son,
> With but four words, my words, *Thy will be done.*

The poet's words are recognized as Jesus' words, rendering the syntax ambiguous: if the reader brackets "With but four words, my words," then the sentence completes itself, but if those words are understood as elaborating on "a cross felt by thy son," the sentence is left hanging. The issue, once more, is whose speech can be effective, and the answer must be God's alone. But although this seems like an abnegation of self, releasing Herbert from the burden of consciousness, its arbitrariness leaves the self exposed as the site upon which difficulty has been painfully registered.

Foucault presents the technique of confession, as it developed through the Middle Ages, as a comparable process of self-construction:

> The confession is a ritual of discourse in which the speaking subject is also the subject of the statement; it is also a ritual that unfolds within a power relationship, for one does not confess without the presence (or virtual presence) of a partner who is not simply the interlocutor but the authority who requires the confession, prescribes and appreciates it, and intervenes in order to judge, punish, forgive, console, and reconcile; a ritual in which the truth is corroborated by the obstacles and resistances it has had to surmount in order to be formulated; and finally a ritual in which the expression alone, independently of its external consequences, produces intrinsic modifications in the person who articulates it: it exonerates, redeems, and purifies him; it unburdens him of his wrongs, liberates him, and promises him salvation.[56]

That such a process must be powerfully constitutive of subjectivity is beyond question (more insidious, surely, than the bodily rigors Foucault identifies as soul-forming in *Discipline and Punish;* protestants cultivated physical torture as well, though it was Oliver Cromwell who abolished its judicial use in England). Protestant self-examination is in a way confessional, but it shifts the whole business inside the consciousness. The interlocutor is now, in one sense, simply God; and as such, an other vastly more powerful and unpredictable than the human confessor. In another sense, of course, the other is internal, the conscience. But in a further sense, God and the conscience are the same thing—Perkins, with a nervous, parenthetical hesitation, says conscience is "(as it were) a little God sitting in the middle of men['s] hearts."[57] This made the whole process more manipulable, but it also made it more indefinite, for since there was no external resistance there could also be no external reassurance. It was a powerfully unsettling pattern. Foucault's confession culminates in absolution, and seems designed to produce a docile soul. The protestant could fight the battle over and over again, and might remain perpetually on edge.

Insecurity was the sign of an authentic encounter with divine rigor, and at least suggested that God was concerned about one. "How should I know that I loved God if I never suffered for his sake? How should I know that God loved me if there were no infirmity, temptation, peril, and jeopardy whence God should deliver me?" Tyndale asks.[58] So God creates difficulties in order to make people feel wanted.

That is why Donne almost dares God to batter his heart, not content with gentler handling. If it seems that Donne is picking a fight with God, it is because the self is constituted by being pitted against this powerful other. As Althusser observes, "the interpellation of individuals as subjects presupposes the 'existence' of a Unique and central Other Subject, in whose Name the religious ideology interpellates all individuals as subjects." In Exodus (3:14), God says "I am that I am," and from this position as "the Subject *par excellence*" he calls and nominates Moses, who, "having recognised that it 'really' was he who was called by God, recognises that he is a subject."⁵⁹ For this effect, a strong deity is an advantage, but many protestants went further. They made God so powerful and intrusive that the subject is constituted not passively, as Althusser rather supposes ("The proof: [Moses] obeys [God]"), but in manifest violence; it is an explicitly aggressive technology of the soul. Two conditions that Greenblatt proposes for self-fashioning are "submission to an absolute power or authority situated at least partially outside the self," and "relation to something perceived as alien, strange, or hostile."⁶⁰ The protestant god was both at once—both the absolute external power and the unappeasable, alien other.

Endlessly manipulating the contradictions in this astounding deity might produce one further outcome, though probably few could afford to contemplate it. The most profound and destructive thought— destructive of the whole system—would be that it is all in the believer's imagination. If one is elect, or reprobate, one is at least distinct from God. But if God is a projection of the believer's need then there is no opposition, no outside against which to define the self. Yet if there was, for some, such an undercurrent of skepticism about the whole exercise, it would not destroy the enhancement of inwardness. On the contrary, the most vivid self-consciousness occurs at that point where God and Man slide away: it is constituted in the attempt to retrieve them, and in realizing, more or less dimly, that it cannot be done.

PROTESTANTISM AND SOCIAL CONTROL

Luther "shattered the faith in authority by restoring the authority of faith. He transformed the priests into laymen by turning laymen into priests. He liberated man from external religiosity by making religiosity the innermost essence of man. He liberated the body from its chains because he fettered the heart with chains": so Marx.⁶¹ The production of self-consciousness in protestantism was a high-stakes, high-risk strategy. In some instances it might set distinctively subtle hooks in the psyche, interpellating docile subjects in a specially intricate way; in other instances its blatant contradictions might allow its constitutive project to become apparent, and hence afford access to an identity sufficiently unbeholden to any one ideological pattern to form a feasible ground for critique and dissidence. Many of the expounders of protestantism aspired to produce acquiescent subjects, and did so. But they also stimulated a restless self-awareness, one that might allow, in some, a questioning of the system. It is not straightforward to say whether the Reformation tended to free or repress people.

Logically, Luther's demand that he be "convicted by the testimony of scripture or plain reason" since "it is neither safe nor honest to act against one's conscience"[62] enabled anyone to justify any belief. The ultimate warrant for the truth of the Bible could only be that the individual believer was convinced in his or her soul. However, few reformers were prepared to leave it there. Tyndale says that every member of the congregation should be able to criticize the preacher if need be, and that we must "desire God, day and night, instantly, to open our eyes and make us understand and feel wherefore the scripture was given." However, Tyndale also warns that "the scripture speaks many things as the world speaks, but they may not be worldly understood," and therefore prefaces his translations of the Bible with interpretive guidance and sprinkles them liberally with marginal glosses. He does not trust individual intuition. For these were bitterly contested matters, and to establish your gloss was to win a point. In his "Prologue upon the Gospel of St Matthew," Tyndale writes: "I thought it my duty, most dear reader, to warn thee before, and to show thee the right way in, and to give thee the true key to open it, and to arm thee against false prophets and malicious hypocrites; whose perpetual study is to blind the scripture with glosses, and there to lock it up."[63]

The Althusserian assumption that religion helps to produce law-abiding subjects is substantially right in respect of early modern protestantism. Robert Burton asks: "What power of prince, or penal law, be it never so strict, could enforce men to do that which for conscience' sake they will voluntarily undergo?" This, Althusser argues, is the effect ideology strives for: subjects work, like a marvelous toy, "all by themselves."[64] This constitutive effect is notably apparent in respect of writing proposed for reading experientially, as a self-conscious aid to self-examination and spiritual development. This is how protestants said the Psalms should be used, since the poems of despair and rebellion there could hardly be taken as the straightforward presentation of God's word (it is one way to read Donne's Holy Sonnets and Herbert's *Temple*). In his preface to the Psalms, Calvin called them "the anatomy of all the parts of the soul, in as much as a man shall not find any affection in himself, whereof the image appeareth not in this glass"; thus the Psalms enable the believer to practice or rehearse, as it were, his or her relationship with God.[65] However, this would have little point if the reader saw in the glass only what he or she already knew. Actually, the soul is being produced by the writing targeted on it. The Psalms, Calvin says, "call or draw every one of us to the peculiar examination of himself, so as no whit of all the infirmities to which we are subject, and of so many vices wherewith we are fraughted, may abide hidden."[66] This mirror does not merely give back what we know already to be there, it focuses aspects that have been "hidden." It does not merely reflect subjectivity, it organizes it. Luther also describes the Psalms as a mirror that does more than reflect: "You will see your own self in it, for here is the true [Know thyself], by which you can know yourself as well as the God himself who created all these things."[67]

However, many subjects did not "work by themselves." Indeed, the government took the possibility of religious contention as a reason for urgent law enforcement. "Those which now impugn the ecclesiastical jurisdiction [will] endeavour also to impair the temporal and to bring even kings and princes under their censure," Whitgift warned Queen Elizabeth. James I summed up the anxiety: "No Bishop, no King." He feared that if people were allowed their preferred modes of religious organization, "Jack and Tom, and Will and Dick, shall meet, and at their pleasure censure me and my Council and all our proceedings."[68] Francis Bacon wanted "unity in religion" but opposed any encouragment of "conspiracies and rebellions" in Catholic countries, and above all anything that might "put the sword into the people's hands; and the like; tending to the subversion of all government, which is the ordinance of God."[69] The maintenance of existing authorities took first priority. Precisely because the Reformation had overturned the ideology of the unity of Christendom, it seemed essential that the new establishment insist on the absolute authority of its doctrine. Luther did not grant to Anabaptists the scope of scriptural interpretation that he claimed for himself; Henry VIII passed an act "for abolishing diversity of opinions."[70] Mainly in the name of religion, communications were tightly policed. School and university teachers had to be approved by the bishops. Preachers had to be licensed and were forbidden to talk about controversial topics or to hold private meetings; a deprived minister lost his audience and his livelihood at a stroke. Church attendance was compulsory and was enforced with large fines. Plays were subject to the approval of bishops and other state officials, and playwrights were forbidden to deal with religion. Printing presses had to be registered and new books inspected by the Archbishop of Canterbury or Bishop of London. When opponents of episcopacy set up a secret press in 1588–89, they were hunted down and subjected to indefinite imprisonment, torture, and heavy fines; John Penry was killed. Simply being a Catholic priest was deemed treasonable. Between 1570 and 1603, nearly two hundred Catholics were killed by the government, often with great cruelty.[71] And unfortunate fanatics who claimed divine inspiration independent of any church were imprisoned, whipped, tortured, and killed.

Puritan ministers and gentry were not against the authority of church or state; until the 1630s, they believed generally that they could make the national church take their direction. Patrick Collinson's research shows that "urban magistrates, gentlemen, and noblemen too, perceived no conflict between evangelical protestantism and the social status and public responsibilities of magnates and nobles."[72] John Morgan quotes the Earl of Huntingdon's recommendation of protestant commitment on the ground that "where there is a preaching pastor, the people, for the most part, are very well given."[73] The security of the protestant settlement seemed to depend upon strong social discipline, so most of the godly sought to help the government clamp the lid back on the forces of dissidence that they might seem to have licensed. As Christopher Hill observes, the "fall" legitimates a coercive state by making it "necessary to prevent sinful men from destroying one another. Private property is likewise a consequence of sin; but since it inevitably exists, it must be defended against the greedy lusts of the unpropertied, who must be held in subordination."[74]

The providential care attributed to the violent and unchallengable deity of the Reformation is, of course, very like that which people often experienced in the human power system. Both cultivated a hierarchical, punitive, and tyrannical concept of ruler and ruled, while claiming that it was all for the best. Relations between the strong and the weak—in the household, at school, at work, in the local community and the state—were characterized by personal cruelty and the exercise of autocratic power. Whipping was the customary response to infringements in all parts of society, and religious writers refer continually to God's "chastening rod." Lawrence Stone believes that such attitudes were more pronounced in the period 1500–1660 than before or after.[75] It was usual to explain earthly afflictions as divine punishment. Shakespeare's Henry IV is altogether in the spirit of protestantism when he envisages a god who avenges himself at the expense of succeeding generations:

> I know not whether God will have it so
> For some displeasing service I have done,
> That in his secret doom out of my blood
> He'll breed revengement and a scourge for me;
> But thou dost in thy passages of life
> Make me believe that thou art only mark'd
> For the hot vengeance and the rod of heaven,
> To punish my mistreadings.[76]

To be sure, this divine violence extends beyond those to whom it is due, but only in the way anticipated in the second commandment, where God promises to visit "the iniquity of the fathers upon the children unto the third and fourth generation" (Deut. 5:9). Protestants did not believe that the Old Testament god of wrath had been superseded; they relied equally upon all parts of the Bible for illustrations of God's way with his people, and did not play down the violent and punitive elements in the New Testament. A stern but decisive deity seemed preferable to a universe without manifest moral order, and was not thought incompatible with the principle of divine love. Joseph Hall found that his patron was being influenced against him by "a witty and bold atheist": "I bent my prayers against him; beseeching God daily, that he would be pleased to remove, by some means or other, that apparent hindrance of my faithful labours: who gave me an answer accordingly; for this malicious man, going hastily up to London to exasperate my patron against me, was then and there swept away by the pestilence, and never returned to do any farther mischief."[77] Such glee at the intricate misfortunes of enemies (perceived of course as just judgments) was customary. The protestant god has been spoken of as a *deus absconditus,* but that is quite misleading in respect of early modern England. True, he was no longer supposed to be vaguely infusing all things, but he did not hesitate to make his presence felt. John Carey sees Donne as "particularly relishing dwelling on" God's destructive power, but Donne's preoccupation is not extraordinary. In fact, it may indicate an unusual sensitivity rather than special rigor in his personality.[78]

Probably the queen and some of her advisers did not care much what people believed so long as they kept quiet. Within certain limits, it may not matter what the orthodoxy *is:* the bid for total authority feeds on any polarizing of alternatives—especially if they can be correlated with a threat of foreign invasion. Communism, the Cold War, and the "evil empire" have worked in this way in our own time. But protestant orthodoxy came packaged with a theory of deference. Since God has arranged everything, we must assume that he wants us to be where we are. Therefore, says the homily "Against Wilful Disobedience," he has "not only ordained that in families and households the wife should be obedient unto her husband, the children unto their parents, the servants unto their masters, but also, when mankind increased and spread itself more largely over the world, he by his holy word did constitute and ordain in cities and countries several and special governors and rulers, unto whom the residue of his people should be obedient" (p. 589). Everyone has someone to tell them what to do. William Pemble records a conversation with a man on his deathbed: "Being demanded what he thought of God, he answers that he was a good old man; and what of Christ, that he was a towardly young youth; and of his soul, that it was a great bone in his body; and what should become of his soul after he was dead, that if he had done well he should be put into a pleasant green meadow."[79] Was this foolish? This man had heard two or three thousand sermons commanding him to obey God and his political superiors, and he sought to integrate these injunctions with his social experience. Was it not reasonable to deduce that God was like the lord of the manor and his son like the heir? After all, Herbert has a poem in this vein, "Redemption"—with the difference that Herbert, doubtless because he is a gentleman, is able to envisage the lord finally granting his suit for a "small-rented lease." Pemble's old man did not consider himself so favored; he saw that the position allocated to him in the socioreligious order was like that of a faithful workhorse.

A personalized imperative to stay in one's place was added by the doctrine of callings. "Let every man therefore wait on this office wherein Christ has put him, and therein serve his brethren. If he be of low degree, let him patiently abide therein, till God promote him," Tyndale enjoined.[80] There seems little scope for independent initiatives. Yet not all class fractions and categories were subdued by Reformation orthodoxy. Some people would derive from the doctrine of callings a sense of righteous dignity, a conviction of their distinctive value to society and to God. Tyndale declares: if you are but a kitchen page, "thou knowest that God hath put thee in that office; thou submittest thyself to his will, and servest thy master not as a man, but as Christ himself," and this certainly tends to discourage the page from aspiring to become a chef.[81] But if he feels himself to be among the elect, he may begin to develop a sense of his own worth not tied to his role in the kitchen, not dependent on the social hierarchy. The doctrine of callings tends to reduce all to the common position of subjects, ignoring and superseding the elaborate apparatus of late feudal relations. At the same time, since puritanism was always a minority commitment (though not at odds with official doctrine), and very many people remained manifestly unmoved by its claims, those who believed themselves to be among the elect might feel very special indeed. As Christopher Hill puts it, "the elect form a spiritual aristocracy, which bears no relation to the worldly aristocracy of birth." The effect was not egalitarian, therefore, so much as the validation of a new kind of elite, founded in righteousness rather than conventional social standing. "Puritans understood their immediate world to be polarised between themselves and their religious enemies, two undifferentiated masses of good and evil," Patrick Collinson argues.[82]

So the doctrine of callings had a contradictory effect: though it said that people should stay in their places, it seemed to legitimate the efforts of the more determined. For some this would be an economic impetus—particularly for "those smaller employers and self-employed men, whether in town or country, for whom frugality and hard work might make all the difference between prosperity and failure to survive in the world of growing competition."[83] For some of the gentry, who were embarking at this point on the long trek towards parliamentary rule, it enhanced their self-importance by offering new responsibilities to replace feudal status and military prowess, which were declining in importance. The protestant gentleman gained social and civil functions as the maintainer of true religion; the old knight and even the Renaissance courtier seemed irrelevant in comparison with the Christian gentleman and pious magistrate. A prime instance is Philip Sidney, whose orientation may be observed when he urges his brother Robert to use travel and reading to develop his powers: "Your purpose is, being a gentleman born, to furnish yourself with the knowledge of such things as may be serviceable to your country and fit for your calling."[84]

A particular responsibility of the godly magistrate was to support learned and committed ministers (Sidney did this).[85] The latter were the ideological workers in the enterprise (though the gentleman or lady might also be learned and a writer, as in the instances of Sidney, the Countess of Pembroke, the Earl of Huntingdon, Lady Margaret Hoby, Charles Blount, and the Earl of Bedford; and the minister might be from a gentry family). The role assigned to the clergy in protestantism tended to produce among them a new confidence, vigor, and sense of relevance, as well as a sense of special calling. Latimer, in his famous "Sermon on the Plough," complained that churchmen were running after secular honors and rewards—"placed in palaces, couched in courts, ruffling in their rents, dancing in their dominions, burdened with ambassages, pampering of their paunches . . . loitering in their lordships." This, he says, is not their calling. They should be laboring for spiritual needs as a ploughman does for physical, bringing their flock to a right faith—

> now casting them down with the law, and with threatenings of God for sin; now ridging them up again with the gospel, and with the promises of God's favour: now weeding them, by telling them their faults and making them forsake sin; now clotting them, by breaking their stony hearts, and by making them supple-hearted . . . now teaching to know God rightly, and to know their duty to God and their neighbours: now exhorting them, when they know their duty, that they do it, and be diligent in it; so that they have a continual work to do.[86]

If all the population are going to become thoroughgoing protestant subjects, it is going to take a lot of effort. Latimer was proposing a new, enhanced role for the clergy, and with it a new expertise and authority. Where the Catholic priest had confessed and absolved people in his parish through the magical properties of the sacrament, the protestant minister was to interpret the scriptures to them, intervening specifically in their states of mind. This new priest might, therefore, be quite a different kind of person. He had to be educated—whereas the bishop of Gloucester had found in 1551 that of 311 clergy examined, 171 could not repeat the Ten Commandments, 33 could not say where they occur in the Bible, 10 did not know the Lord's Prayer, and 27 did not know its author.[87] So a different kind of mediator was interposed between God and most believers. Though in theory every individual was responsible for his or her own soul, no minister felt that his flock could be left without expert guidance from himself. John Brinsley the Younger wrote that ministers were "agents betwixt God and his people," and should preach "as heralds, in the name, in the authority of him that sendeth them."[88]

Rosemary O'Day has argued that under these conditions the clergy became a profession—a distinct group with its own internal hierarchy, regulations, training program, machinery for association, and career structure, consolidated by kinship and social connections, and distinguished from other people in the locality by its obligation to intellectual work.[89] I think the topic may be widened still further, for we may link this increase in preaching and writing to the general burgeoning of reading, writing, and oral production in the period, including theater, printed books, poems, diaries, letters, and pamphlets. We may date from this point the appearance of "the writer," under patronage and in the market, as a recognizable social and economic role. Indeed, we may without exaggeration speak of the formation and consolidation of a stratum of *intellectuals*. I use this term to cover the range of cultural producers—people whose role in society is to help confirm or change the stories through which we tell ourselves who we are, to set the boundaries of the thinkable, to maintain or undermine belief in the legitimacy of the prevailing power arrangements.[90] The appearance of the category of intellectuals at this date signals a vastly enhanced scale of cultural production, facilitated by improvements in communications, through which early modern English people conversed among themselves about spiritual and secular authority. Protestant conviction conferred the personal and institutional confidence for a part of this work. It all marks a decisive change in the conditions of cultural production; one occurring, necessarily, at a point where fundamental matters of economic, social, cultural, and political organization were in question.

I suggested in chapter 4 that if Philip Sidney conceived a relatively independent view of the Elizabethan state, it might derive from his experience of an uneven and mobile overlap of classes, roles, and aspirations, and in particular from his ambivalent structural position as a functionary in the developing Tudor bureaucracy. And I argued that intellectuals similarly, as a category, might well find themselves situated at a point of conflicting affiliation and hence relative autonomy; in particular, they would have concerns *as intellectuals* that might not altogether suit the interests they ostensibly served. Ministers, like other cultural workers, might have access to a distinctive perception of power relations. The churchman's career very likely detached him from one class allegiance and invited him to adopt others; and the role of minister as such would produce its own specific interests. Of course, these intellectuals, like others at other times, were in many ways dependent on the social hierarchy, and relatively few ministers were dissident; but some were (and some were at one conjuncture though not at another).

As well as holding this structural position on the margin of other groups, the activist theology of puritan ministers made friction likely.

The sense of most other people as unregenerate justified an aggressive attitude towards insufficiently enthusiastic members of congregations (Hill reports numerous quarrels as godly magistrates and municipalities sought to appoint appropriate ministers or lecturers—these were battles "for key positions of political influence").[91] The doctrine of callings and industriousness could lead to the thought that the upper classes, even, were reprehensibly idle. Disputes between ministers and bishops might occur at any time as the latter tried to implement shifting government policies. And even respect for the Crown might be tested when royal commands seemed at odds with those of God.[92] The whole theology was steeped in contentiousness, so the godly must have expected conflict in social relations. The struggle with God was continuous with the struggle in society—God was to batter Donne's heart, and Donne in turn was an aggressive preacher. Ministers may have been personally conservative, then, but the structural tendency was to make possible the development of a dissident minority. Collinson says puritans were conservative, but also that the vigorous alliance of gentry and ministers was an index of instability and "vulnerability in the social fabric rather than of security."[93] William Haller's argument seems right: the object of preachers was "to instill in the minds of country gentlemen, merchants, lawyers and their followers the idea that, over against the carnal aristocracy which ruled the world, there was an aristocracy of the spirit, chosen by God and destined to inherit heaven and earth. . . . Thus the preachers were in effect organising a discontented minority into an opposition."[94]

With all this in mind, we may be able to revise a little Stephen Greenblatt's important account of protestant politics and theology in *Renaissance Self-Fashioning*. Greenblatt discerns two self-constituting processes: "submission to domination" and "negation" (saying No; pp. 123–28). This is not unlike the technology of subjectivity that I proposed earlier, but it presents power and ideology as too unified in their impetus and effects. As Dollimore says, "ideology typically legitimates the social order by representing it as a spurious unity, metaphysically ordained, and thereby forestalls knowledge of the contradictions which in fact constitute that order."[95] The unity is always spurious; conflict and contradiction cannot be filtered out. Refining protestant subjectivity to dominance and negation makes it appear too coherent: Greenblatt at this point allows it to sound as if the circuit of power runs through one primary source, with which the relation is either domination or negation (perhaps a metaphor of electrical wiring is running through this: power reaches the consumer through a master switch belonging to the great power corporation in the sky, and people are energized by being connected to its positive and negative terminals). Rather, we have to envisage power and ideology in modern societies as proceeding through a network of diverse, interconnecting, but partly competing, substructures. The influences of church, state, family, faction, humane learning, discourses of gender and sexuality, and so on, to which a person such as Wyatt or Donne is subject, exert *divergent* pressures. However much the state or the church may aspire to unify them, these institutions and discourses tend to construct alternative, potentially rival, subjectivities. And hence they produce inwardness: for, as I argued in chapter 3, this is not an effect of unitary power, but of incoherent power. The protestant subject arises, not in the accomplishment of domination or negation, but in the *thwarting* of harmony, cogency, common sense. To be sure, in Greenblatt's account subjects are by no means simple, but their complexity is not traced to the social order. Rather, it appears as a complication on the surface of the already-constructed subject—constructed in those broad processes of domination and negation and now coping with the consequences. The self is described in *Renaissance Self-Fashioning* as experiencing apparently incompatible impulses, complex interweavings, nuances of feigning, alienated feelings revolving uneasily around a center of power, forces intertwined in complex relation, a fathomless and eerily playful self-estrangement, the will to play.[96] We may detect here a residue of Greenblatt's initial interest in how sixteenth-century writers "created their own performances" (p. 256): just a little of this scope for play seems to be retrieved after the deep structure has been laid down through domination and negation. Furthermore, it is because the dominance/negation paradigm is conceived so abstractly, and as working at such a fundamental level, that it seems reasonable to envisage it as reversible. So Greenblatt writes that "acts of negation not only conjure up the order they would destroy but seem at times to be themselves conjured up by that very order" (p. 210). It is the entrapment model again (see chapters 2 and 10): power seems to head off dissident activity even before it is conceived.

Protestantism proved itself accessible to both dissidence and control. Walzer sees puritan activism as the first instance in Western societies of "a politics of party organisation and methodical activity, opposition and reform, radical ideology and revolution."[97] Previously, Walzer elaborates, "feudal wars were largely the chaotic struggles of aggressive noble families, 'over-mighty subjects' of weak kings. Rebellions were most often the desperate, furious risings of nonpolitical peasants or proletarians, unorganised, helpless, with only the crudest of programs" (p. 8). The puritans' sense of party derived perhaps from the exile some had experienced, but it depended also upon the novel idea that there might be a basis for alliance and commitment outside the traditional ties of family, guild, locality, and hierarchy. It was the beginning of modern politics. Dissent previously had hardly been organized or theorized; it had been difficult for people to think so purposefully *to one side* of social norms. Puritans cultivated a distinctive "discipline"—a pattern of ethical, organizational, and social coercion that they deemed necessary to sustain "fallen" people in a dangerous world; they formed associations that were impersonal, ideological, goal-oriented—produced rather than inherited. Membership of the old village communities had been compulsory (this, it should be remembered, is a powerful kind of totalitarianism). The transition from parish to the wider and looser network of the godly was a shift from local community to voluntary organization.[98] (Much of this is still apparent in the situation of modern intellectuals, and correlates with the argument I make in chapters 2 and 10 about subcultures and milieux as constitutive of dissidence.) Puritans were inspired, then, by individual zeal of election, but their intricate protestant subjectivities depended upon mutual reinforcement in groupings of the faithful. So they were socialized into a potentially oppositional subculture.

WINSTANLEY AND THE SELFISH IMAGINARY POWER

I have argued that the rigors and intricacies of protestant orthodoxy did not render it ineffective. To the contrary, precisely these difficulties required that doctrinal nuances be endlessly pondered and debated in attempts to get the pattern adequately to constitute itself, and in the process appropriate subjectivities were constituted. It is the kind of interaction that bonds together an ideology and a social system. Nevertheless, the changes of the seventeenth century were ultimately at the expense of Calvinism. It proved inadequate to the historical situation—to the extent, in fact, that it actually became a stimulant to heterodoxy and dissidence. Briefly, its social theory, based on notions of stability, order, and unanimity in religious and political purposes, could hardly accommodate the social mobility that it helped to cause.[99] And its theology, though it attempted a bold and provocative resolution of certain characteristic problems of monotheism, and seems to have persuaded many, could not sustain indefinitely the special acuity of its contradictions (I show some of this process in chapter 9). Hobbes observed: "That which taketh away the reputation of wisdom in him that formeth a religion . . . is the enjoining of a belief of contradictories."[100] The conjuncture, always, determines whether or not dissident potential is mobilized. But since protestantism contained elements of disintegration as well as social cohesion, it could not be held inert by the powerful forces that informed it. The insistence of the English church—or at least of most of its prominent members—upon a theory of divine justice that it could not render satisfactory created profound disjunctions, both in religious experience and in contemporary writing. Theologians shuffled their texts and arguments to make it appear gracious and logically consistent; writers wrestled, with more and less conviction, to accommodate it to more generous ideas of relationships. Eventually many people edged towards a vaguer, more secularist outlook.

The ultimate perspective here is a shift in awareness of human potential. Even election and reprobation, a rebarbative feature of Calvinism to most modern thought, may have signified not the closing of minds but a fraught awareness of the extent to which they might become opened. Kierkegaard suggests that attention to predestination supposes a developing perception of freedom: "So long as there is no question of freedom asserting its rights in the world, it is impossible for the question of predestination to arise. It was only when the conception of human freedom developed and was then brought into relation with the conception of divine providence that the doctrine of predestination arose, and had to arise, as an attempt to solve the problem."[101] The enhanced sense of entrapment in protestant thought signified not a collapse of belief in human initiative, but a new awareness of just how far it might reach and of the recalcitrance of Christian theodicy. That this is so is evidenced by the apparently sudden emergence of libertarian ideas among sectarians in the 1640s, for, as Keith Wrightson observes, they drew intimately upon resources that orthodox protestantism itself had put into circulation:

> In the proliferation of the sects and in the vitality of debate over religious belief we have incontrovertible evidence of the extent to which one part of the common people—notably the literate "middling sort"—had become closely involved with the central issues of the day. Steeped as some of them now were in scriptural knowledge, they were prepared to take up positions of their own on matters of faith, to the very evident discomfiture of clergymen who regarded themselves as the guardians of Protestant orthodoxy.[102]

Like other ideological formations, protestantism was appropriable. The breakdown of censorship in the 1640s produced a flood of pamphlets questioning original sin and proposing universal salvation. In my view, it is the same with the preoccupation with entrapment in new historicism and cultural materialism: they indicate, at least potentially, a renewed sense of freedom from some traditional political thinking among sectors of the professional intelligentsia.

Hobbes took Reformation orthodoxy to one kind of logical conclusion. He abandoned the claim that God is good, just, and concerned about mankind, and identified as the source of divine sovereignty nothing other than power: "The right of nature, whereby God reigneth over men and punisheth those that break his laws, is to be derived, not from his creating them, as if he required obedience as of gratitude for his benefits; but from his *irresistible power*" (*Leviathan,* p. 397). Calvinists declared that God has total power over his creation, but held at the same time that human afflictions are providential, contained within a divine beneficence. How to square this, I have suggested, is the eternal problem for theodicy. Hobbes, more logically, simplified the issue by retaining only half the doctrine. He pointed out that Job was innocent and that God's resort was to "arguments drawn from his power, such as this, *Where wast thou when I laid the foundations of the earth?*" (p. 398, quoting Job 38:4). Hobbes cut the knot of God's contradictory power and goodness by dropping the goodness.

Gerrard Winstanley, like other sectarians, demystified orthodoxy from the opposite direction. He took the idea of the individual's inner light of conscience as license to reject unjust political structures; for, as Hobbes pointed out, if every person can claim to derive an individual faith from his or her own insight, there is no reason why "any man should take the law of his country, rather than his own inspiration, for the rule of his action" (*Leviathan,* p. 366). Winstanley's "inspiration" was unusually alert to mystifications of power and ideology. In *Fire in the Bush* (1650), he opposes the Hobbesian view that the "power in man, that causes divisions and war" is properly called "the state of nature"; on the contrary, "the living soul is in bondage to [such power], and groans under it, waiting to be delivered from it, and is glad to hear of a saviour."[103] In *The Law of Freedom* (1652), Winstanley recognizes two principles necessary for human societies: common preservation and self-preservation (p. 537). A society that emphasized the former would, through an ethic of mutual aid and community supported by an appropriate political and legal structure, protect the weak and share its resources for the benefit of all; one emphasizing the latter would center on individualism and competitive striving and hence would favor the strong and the wealthy. The distinction is familiar enough in modern arguments about socialism and capitalism. Enthusiasts for the latter maintain a Hobbesian claim that it is natural to "Man." In Britain the neofascist National Front asserts: "Sociobiology has shown us that evolutionary processes have genetically and therefore immutably programmed human nature with instincts of competitiveness, territorial defence, racial prejudice, identification with one's group (nation), instincts which the Marxist fantasy said were socially determined and which could and should be eradicated."[104] Actually, of course, if the exercise of individual power were the primary human impulse, we would be living in continual danger and would surely have destroyed ourselves aeons ago. Amity and cooperation must be as important in the survival of human societies as aggression and competitiveness. This is recognized among modern anthropologists; Richard Leakey believes on the evidence of paleontology that "reciprocal altruism" is the source of the ascendancy of the human species: "We are human because our ancestors learned to share their food and their skills in an honoured network of obligation."[105] Capitalism itself in part exploits such amiability.

Winstanley bases his insights on a total re-vision of Christianity. The "fall," he says, is not Adam's and once and for all: it is for each person, into a bad way of thinking. Winstanley takes protestant insistence upon inwardness that one, crucial step further: he undercuts the whole system of anxiety and self-absorption by declaring that "out of mankind arises all that darkness and tyranny that oppresses itself" (p. 464). Satan, he says, is not a force wielded by God, but a destructive state of human minds; it is imagination that "fills you with fears, doubts, troubles, evil surmisings and grudges, he it is that stirs up wars and divisions. . . . So that the selfish imaginary power within you, is the power of darkness; the father of lies, the deceiver, the destroyer, and the Serpent that twists about everything within your self, and so leads you astray from the right way of life and peace" (pp. 452–53). The besieger and the citadel were in Donne's head. But this is not a new solipsism for, Winstanley adds, breathtakingly, such bad states of mind derive from and sustain a bad social system. Both must be overthrown, and that would be a real reformation: "Then that great reformation, and restoration spoken of, shall be made manifest in the nations of the world; then those pluckings up, shakings down, tearing to pieces of all rule, power and authority shall be known" (p. 455). A true reformation would transform not only the church, but also economic, political, and social relations throughout the commonwealth. Like protestants generally, Winstanley proclaimed that God was working out a vast plan for England, but he argued that its true agents were the common people, from whom the land had been taken (pp. 521–22). As much as George Herbert, he held that God's spirit moves in every individual and experienced a sustaining belief in his own personal calling; but Winstanley felt called to critique the institutions that Herbert had taken for granted.

Of course, Winstanley did not get these ideas just out of his head. He drew upon the Baptist undercurrent that the English government had never managed entirely to suppress; and he reoriented elements from the orthodox preaching of the time. Spectacularly, he derived his revolutionary theory from just those texts and images that in conventional protestant writing legitimated an oppressive church and state.[106] Luther wrote of "two kingdoms in the world," Satan's and Christ's; Winstanley restates this binary as property on the one hand, "called the Devil, or covetousness," and "community on the other hand, called Christ, or universal love" (p. 493). This exemplifies very well how an ideology may be infiltrated and appropriated, brought through its own resources to reorient itself. Indeed, Winstanley understood this. Granting that there should be magistracy in his commonwealth, he observes that it is not the concept that is the trouble, but the way it has been used, for the power of darkness "puts bad names upon things that are excellent" so that "under a good name he may go undiscovered" (p. 472).

This awareness of ideology leads Winstanley to attack above all abuses of intellectual power by lawyers and, especially, preachers. "Kingly power depends upon the Law, and upon buying and selling; and these three depend upon the Clergy, to bewitch the people to conform; and all of them depend upon Kingly power by his force, to compel subjection from those that will not be bewitched" (p. 470). This is a fair statement of the relation between ideological and repressive state apparatuses. Winstanley saw that protestantism afforded specially subtle hooks into the psyche: "This divining doctrine, which you call spiritual and heavenly things, is the thief and the robber; he comes to spoil the vineyard of a man's peace, and does not enter in at the door, but he climbs up another way" (p. 567). He saw that protestantism tended to sustain power relations because the weak in spirit may be terrified and submit "himself to be a slave to his brother, for fear of damnation in Hell" (p. 569). And he saw that one effect was an increase in the social authority of the clergy, for while the old priesthood had indeed interposed its ritual between people and the truth, the new intellectuals claimed, more insidiously, learning that would enable the believer to comprehend his or her salvation: "The former hell of prisons, whips and gallows they preached to keep the people in subjection to the King: but this divined Hell after death, they preach to keep both King and people in awe to them, to uphold their trade of tithes and new-raised maintenance."[107] Yet the political effect is still not unitary, for Winstanley himself was a persuasive intellectual leader. Though outside establishment institutions, he derived some of his political authority and even some of his insight, though in upside-down fashion, from the same resources as the puritans.

Protestant activism has implications for our understanding of political possibilities today. For John Carey, the moral is largely quietist: "Calvinism has been compared to Marxism, and resembled it in the revolutionary enthusiasm it bred, as well as in its fatalism and the scope it offered to self-righteousness and hate"; and for Stephen Greenblatt there is something fearful about the determination that can sustain a political commitment.[108] Socialists have reason to be conscious of such dangers. Christopher Hill sees puritan emphasis on predestination and discipline as an attempt "to carry hierarchical social subordination and national thought-control over into the modern world," and Michael Walzer suggests that in Calvinism we may locate the rationale for the state as an order of repression.[109] However, Walzer also presents protestant activism more positively: while "other men remained subjects, condemned to political passivity," puritans developed the conviction and commitment that enabled them to conceive a program and organization in some degree independent of the social hierarchy.[110] They took political structures, not as natural or as the prerogative of the powerful, but as affording opportunity for debate and change. Winstanley shows how productive this might be. As well as leading a movement that briefly challenged the might of the state, he demystified the orthodox regime of superstition and fear, held that almost all people may share a response to ideas of community, and argued that a different kind of society might be organized on the basis of rationality and only minimum force. All this belongs to the historic program of socialism. Winstanley and his ilk contributed to what Hill has called the "revolution which never happened, though from time to time it threatened."[111] For the present conjuncture, it is encouraging to take him as one figure in an urgent debate, which we may continue, about the kind of place England might become.

8 Sidney's *Defence* and the Collective-Farm Chairman

*Puritan Humanism
and the Cultural Apparatus*

> The works of authors devoted to the military theme foster love of country and staunchness in hardship. . . . The heroes of these works are people from different walks of life: a building team leader, a collective-farm chairman, a railway worker, an army officer, a pilot, or an eminent scientist. But in each of them the reader or the viewer sees his own thoughts and feelings, and the embodiment of the finest qualities of the Soviet character.

So Leonid Brezhnev in his *Report of the Central Committee of the CPSU to the XXVI Congress of the Communist Party of the Soviet Union* (1981).[1] He discovers in Soviet writing at once a truthful representation of reality and an incitement to readers who do not match up to an ideal. The proclaiming of ideal images in literature, with the hope that they will move the rest of us to virtue, has characterized not only Soviet realism. Nature has not produced "so true a lover as Theagenes, so constant a friend as Pylades, so valiant a man as Orlando, so right a prince as Xenophon's Cyrus, so excellent a man every way as Virgil's Aeneas": so Philip Sidney, in his *Defence of Poetry*. And again: "If the poet do his part aright, he will show you in Tantalus, Atreus, and such like, nothing that is not to be shunned; in Cyrus, Aeneas, Ulysses, each thing to be followed."[2] Both theorists suppose that truth, right, and goodness are organized in an ideal, universal hierarchy, that this is displayed especially in the works currently recognized as good culture, and that the role of that culture is to incite people to aspire to the ideal.

I call this "aesthetic absolutism" because, like an absolutist political ideology, it posits an ultimately static model for societies and their

181

values. Also, both absolutisms acknowledge a directly propagandist function for culture—for if societies and their values are fixed, people had better adjust themselves to their proper slots. An absolutist aesthetic is attractive, though by no means limited, to regimes that aspire to absolutism. In early modern England (although it was not actually an absolutist state) an ideology of ineluctable, unified hierarchy and value, with a precise, ideal position for each subject, was propagated through what we now call art and literature. Stalin and Zhdanov (his minister of culture) held that a socialist society had already been achieved, or as much of it as could be expected for the foreseeable future, so the ideal images proposed in Soviet realism could be regarded as actualities for the most heroic citizens and feasible goals for the rest. So Stephen Greenblatt's remark that the survival rate of those close to Henry VIII resembles that of the first politburo is pertinent; John N. King shows how Henry's court produced a mid-Tudor genre, the prison biblical paraphrase or meditation, anticipating, almost, writing from Stalin's prisons.[3]

Queen Elizabeth I spent relatively little money on what C. Wright Mills called the cultural apparatus, but was adroit at provoking others to do it for her.[4] Courtiers sponsored progresses, pageants, tournaments, interludes, masques, and plays; portraits and tombs; palaces and houses; music from masses to madrigals; and the whole range of literary forms. Patronage and censorship persuaded artists to incorporate secular and religious symbolism that ratified the prevailing power arrangements and projected them onto a supernatural dimension. The system filtered down through the gentry, the universities, and local patronage, and was disseminated across the country through churches and schools. Modern lovers of literature who value good culture as the product of free individual creativity, and who regard the early modern period as the finest flowering of the English imagination, sometimes find it disconcerting that this culture was subject to political organization such as we associate now with authoritarian regimes. But then it has generally been something of an embarrassment for essentialist humanism that art and literature are so highly prized in authoritarian states; the commonest attempt at explanation, making a virtue of oppression, implies the enlightened wisdom and sensibility of the ruling elite when untrammeled by the distractions of democracy.

Analysis of all absolutisms is complicated by the fact that they must actually be fantasies. Neither the Communist Party nor the Tudor power elite could hold history trapped. Concomitantly, the unity proposed in absolutist aesthetics is a chimera. Prescriptions for human behavior and for what is currently recognized as good culture are necessarily embedded in the contradictions and conflicts of the historical moments of their initial production and of subsequent reading. That is why, despite the clean-cut line it cultivates, aesthetic absolutism is always disintegrating as a theory. Brezhnev manages to build a contradiction even into his brief acccount: he says the reader finds in the text, at the same time, both the finest conceivable qualities *and* the reader's own thoughts and feelings. In Sidney's version this is not the problem—he believes people live in a "fallen" world and that the ideal instantiated in poetic images is unlikely to be achieved or even wholly imagined by most people. Even so, its properties may be known through such authoritative discourses as the Bible, theology, philosophy, and poetry, and people are said to discover their "true" natures when they move towards it, so it still constitutes a standing reproach to dissident behaviors and writing. (Of course, locating the ideal beyond the observable world may be more persuasive, since it evades empirical testing such as undermined Brezhnev's state.) Sidney's program runs into difficulty because he wants to reinforce the authority of his ideal images by locating them in classical texts. To be sure, these were written in very different cultures (that this matters is what an absolutist aesthetic needs to deny). Hence some strenuous reading. "If evil men come to the stage," Sidney says, "they ever go out (as the tragedy writer answered to one that misliked the show of such persons) so manacled as they little animate folks to follow them."[5] But this is not quite right in respect of the tragedies most remarked by Sidney and his contemporaries: those of Seneca. Atreus at the end holds the stage triumphantly, and so does Medea. Seneca's plays derive from a political situation in which it was important to say that evil might well triumph (Seneca was forced by Nero to commit suicide). Sidney's suppression of this situation is not incidental. It had more in common with early modern England than he quite wanted to admit—perhaps that is why he wanted to rewrite, and did not finish, the *Arcadia*.

Such snags in the *Defence* point towards complications in Sidney's relation to the contemporary cultural apparatus. There were factors that tended to strengthen centralized power—the financial and military independence of great magnates was reduced and there was a growth in loyalty to and dependence on the Crown; rebellion became disreputable.[6] But these very changes facilitated the development of discourses and institutions—centered upon the Court but also involving Parliament, the church, the universities, the legal system, printing, and the theater—in which an elaborate culture of *political* maneuvering might flourish. At the same time, the simultaneous arrival in England of Renaissance and Reformation influences conferred upon writing and visual display an extraordinary status. For both movements, the word seemed to speak an exhilarating ultimate truth, and printing and the market projected and dispersed exciting ideas into situations where the conditions of reception could not be controlled, or even envisaged. John N. King has shown the extent to which the Edwardian Reformation was a "cultural revolution," accomplished in part by "a tightly knit faction of Protestant lords and prelates."[7]

Philip Sidney belonged to such a faction, committed to defending and enhancing the reformed religion in England, and to doing this in part through cultural intervention.[8] The Earls of Leicester, Huntingdon, and Bedford, and Sidney's sister Mary, Countess of Pembroke, supported determined protestant writers like Arthur Golding; Sir Walter Mildmay and Frances, Countess of Sussex (Sidney's aunt), founded Cambridge colleges;[9] the protestant orientation of Sidney's literary patronage has often been detailed. Cultural intervention also included protecting puritan ministers. For Lawrence Humphrey, this task was "peculiar to noblemen, to relieve the cause of the gospel fainting and falling, to strengthen with their aid impoverished religion, to shield it forsaken with their patronage."[10] In several instances, Sidney favored puritans who had caused difficulties for the authorities. In 1570 he solicited a living on behalf of Christopher Goodman; in 1575 he agreed that John Buste should be involved in tutoring his brother; and in 1582 he appointed as his chaplain the controversial lecturer James Stiles.[11] Sidney and his circle sponsored and produced writing, preaching, teaching, and printing; they constituted a determined pressure group within the cultural apparatus. The importance Leicester and Sidney attached to such efforts may be gathered from their activity when they arrived in the Netherlands: they immediately set about the same project.[12]

That some such task devolved upon Sidney as a part of his "calling" was often urged. The French reformer Hubert Languet pressed him to place his powers "in the service of your country, and of all good men; since you are only the steward of this gift, you will wrong him who conferred such a great benefit on you if you prove to have abused it." In the dedication of his *History of Wales* to Sidney in 1584, the Bishop of St. Asaph reminded him that he must eventually render an

account of the use of his talents and therefore should devote himself
to God and his country.[13] Sidney's Huguenot friends theorized the
matter—François Hotman in his *Franco-Gallia* (1573) and Mornay
in his *Vindiciae contra tyrannos* (1576). The first assumption was that
a man of Sidney's class should deploy his skills as a statesman; literary
work was his response to the queen's refusal to use him seriously
between 1577 and 1585. "To what purpose should our thoughts be
directed to various kinds of knowledge unless room be afforded for
putting it into practice so that public advantage may be the result?—
which in a corrupt age we cannot hope for," he wrote to Languet in
1578.[14] Sidney found in writing the best answer he could. In 1578
he wrote *The Lady of May* to entertain the queen at Leicester's house
at Wanstead, but it was also an attempt to urge an activist protestant
policy upon Elizabeth. However, although the contemplative and active qualities embodied by the shepherd and forester appear as absolutes, in the manner proposed in the *Defence,* the queen resisted
Sidney's implication and chose, against the grain of the text, the cautious shepherd rather than the lively forester. Thus she repudiated
protestant activism.[15] This failure of an absolutist aesthetic to secure
its reading illustrates, in the one instance, the implication of cultural
production in a contested political milieu, the scope for negotiation
that was available to a man like Sidney, and the kind of intervention
to which he was committed. For although Sidney's aesthetic correlated
broadly with the absolutist aspirations of the Elizabethan state and
with the principal modes of its cultural apparatus, he was trying to
turn that apparatus in a particular direction in order to reinforce a
sectional stance within that state. An absolutist aesthetic never represents the totality that it claims, but a strategic position within a
contested arena.

We should therefore be more cautious than Anthony Grafton and
Lisa Jardine when they write of the new, Italianate humanism as suit-
ing the ruling elites of fifteenth- and sixteenth-century Europe, or
than Jonathan Goldberg when he says the new pedagogy "represents
and reproduces the state in its differentiated and bureaucratized
forms, and attempts to secure for itself a sphere of power as the place
from which and within which the state is reproduced."[16] Such accounts make the effects of cultural production more coherent than
they ever can be. At the least, we should notice the potential for
disturbance between two features in Goldberg's formulation: the attempts of pedagogy to secure its own position may well, at certain
points, diverge from the interests of the state. This is the point I was

making in chapters 4 and 7, following Pierre Bourdieu's argument that ideologies owe their characteristics not only to the interests they serve "but also to the specific interests of those who produce them" (see p. 92 above). In fact, Goldberg's whole argument shows that writing can never make safe its absolutist aspirations; it is always sliding towards a confession of its own construction in ideology, and on occasion Goldberg remarks how distinctively situated groups manifested distinctive relations with the dominant formation. For instance, he observes that the hand of the writing master cannot aspire to the scope of the noble hands that he guides, and that "the female hand makes the rifts in the ideology more apparent" (pp. 116, 145). Rupture in dominant discourses is indicated by Grafton and Jardine also when they remark: "The fact that Erasmus returns again and again in his letters to the connection between his publishing activities in the secular sphere and his scriptural and doctrinal studies suggests that the welding of profane learning to lay piety requires a certain amount of intellectual sleight-of-hand."[17] The present chapter addresses a disturbance in precisely this region, in the relation between the twin Elizabethan orthodoxies of humanism and protestantism.

PURITAN HUMANISM

The Reformation, by problematizing many preexisting stories, hugely stimulated cultural production of all kinds. Literary endeavor burgeoned in the reign of Edward VI, remaining generally close to native English traditions, adapting them to protestant purposes. Often this writing achieved popular appeal through a combination of ecclesiastical and social reform in the tradition of Lollardry and *Piers Plowman*.[18] At this time humanistic learning was still establishing itself in England, but often it seemed allied with protestantism, in opposition to scholasticism and the Catholic church. Robert Barnes, an Augustinian friar, studied under Erasmus and returned to Cambridge to teach Terence and Cicero alongside the Pauline epistles; he was martyred in 1540.[19] Even so, there was a fundamental divergence of interests between pagan and Christian writing, as Luther at once perceived. "It grieves me to the heart that this damned, conceited, rascally heathen"—Aristotle—"has with his false words deluded and made fools of so many of our best Christians. God has sent him as a plague upon us for our sins," Luther wrote, and Erasmus complained: "Wherever Lutheranism is dominant the study of letters is extinguished."[20] Pagan writing had bothered earlier Christians—Petrarch, for instance—but the co-occurrence of the Reformation with humanistic enthusiasm for classical letters posed the problem with enhanced intensity. In 1552 Roger Ascham, though recommending diverse Greek and Latin authors to the schoolmaster, complained of the secular slant of "our Englishmen Italianated": "they have in more reverence the *Triumphs* of Petrarch than the Genesis of Moses; they make more account of Tully's *Offices* than St Paul's Epistles, of a tale in Boccaccio than a story of the Bible."[21]

This disturbance is found, in varying degrees of strength, all through protestantism. Hence my term *puritan humanist*—which might be written more disjunctively as *puritan/humanist*, were it not that such persons are often discovered trying to manipulate and efface the conflict, rather than admit it. Sidney displays his Italianate frame of reference on the first page of the *Defence* by invoking "the fertileness of Italian wit" (p. 73); that this is by way of an elegant and rather oblique joke only confirms the orientation. His main pitch in the *Defence* is towards courtiers, aristocrats, and gentry—as we see from the restricted manuscript distribution, the derogation of the native English tradition as the work of "base men with servile wits" and lacking unity and decorum (pp. 111, 113–15), and the appeals to the experience of rulers, captains, and courtiers.[22] Thus Sidney signaled a new phase of anxiety and contest over the role of humane—pagan—learning in protestant culture. In 1582 the Privy Council ordered that Christopher Ocland's new Latin textbook be used in schools, "where diverse heathen poets are ordinarily read and taught, from which the youth of the realm doth rather receive infection in manners than advancement in virtue."[23] I use the term *puritan humanist* to identify those who experienced with special intensity the disjunction between humane letters and protestantism.

The ultimate question is whether pagans may be saved. The humanist position is offered in Thomas Starkey's *Dialogue between Reginald Pole and Thomas Lupset* (c. 1535). "None there is so rude and beastly, but, with cure and diligence, by that same sparkle of reason given of God, they may subdue their affections and follow the life to which they be institute and ordained of God," Starkey asserts. Even pagans, then, may be saved "so long as they live after the law of nature, observing also their civil ordinance."[24] Of course, this means that Adam and Eve cannot have "fallen" too far, and that the incarnation of Jesus, though a help, was inessential. Lord Herbert of Cherbury reached just these conclusions. He explicitly repudiated the "fall," declaring that "the Christians and the heathens are in a manner agreed concerning the definitions of virtues ... they being doctrines imprinted in the soul in its first original and containing the principal and first notices by which man may attain his happiness here or hereafter."[25] Protestants generally said the opposite, denying that there can be salvation without the Christian revelation, which pagans could not have anticipated. Tyndale declared: "The spirit of the world understandeth not the speaking of God; neither the spirit of the wise of this world, neither the spirit of philosophers, neither the spirit of Socrates, of Plato, or of Aristotle's ethics."[26] John Donne warned: "The scriptures will be out of thy reach, and out of thy use, if thou cast and scatter them upon reason, upon philosophy, upon morality, to try how the scriptures will fit all them."[27]

In an influential essay, D. P. Walker has alleged that Sidney in particular was engaged by "a purely rational 'natural' theology," using the *prisca theologia*—pre-Christian hermetic writings—"to integrate Platonism and Christianity."[28] But the argument rests on *De la vérité de la religion chrestienne* by Sidney's friend Philippe de Mornay, which Sidney began to translate, and which actually maintains the opposite. Mornay's aim is to refute atheists, and to this end he demonstrates that pagans are obliged to recognize certain Christian propositions. But this is only half the argument: the second half of the book states that the sole hope of retrieving the "fall" is through the Christian revelation, which even Jews do not have. Mornay insists that Pythagoras, Thales, and Xenophanes "have spoken nothing of [God] but dreamingly, nor deemed of him, but overthwartly, nor knowen ought of him but that little which they learned of the Aegyptians. . . . And what learned they there but superstition, as I have showed before?"[29] The whole structure of his book follows the principle Mornay lays down in his preface: human reason "is so far off from being the measurer of faith, which very far exceedeth nature, that it is not so much as the measurer of nature, and of the least creatures which lie far underneath man, because of the ignorance and untowardness which is in us and reigneth in us." The question of whether Sidney's pagan characters in the *New Arcadia* will be saved sounds like the ultimate numbering of Lady Macbeth's children, but it indicates Sidney's stance. In fact, as Walker is obliged to admit, Sidney does not make his characters draw upon the *prisca theologia* or allow them any distinctive Christian insight. Pamela's arguments against the atheism of Cecropia bear directly upon the point. They read as if Sidney had open before him a book Mornay often quotes, Cicero's *De natura deorum*.[30] Like Cicero's Stoic spokesman Balbus, Pamela asserts that an ordered universe could not have occurred fortuitously and that design in the stars and the world indicates the presence of a providential nature. Like Balbus, she infers reason in nature from the fact of human intelligence, since the whole must contain that which is in the part and be superior to the part, and she anticipates the peculiar objection made by Cotta, Cicero's Academic, that if the world is rational then it must be able to read a book (*De natura deorum* 3.9). Yet Pamela does not follow Balbus all the way: she does not claim that the world and mankind are perfect and perfectly adapted to each other, or that human reason is perfect. Those ideas were too humanist. Sidney brings Pamela precisely as close to protestant ideas as he feels he can, while pointedly denying her any specifically Christian revelation.

Though they would condemn pagans to hell, early modern protestants could not easily set aside classical letters—they were ingrained far too deeply in the culture. In the dedication to his *Commentaries on Genesis* (1563), Calvin asserts that Aristotle "applied whatever skill he possessed to defraud God of his glory," and that Plato "corrupted and mingled with so many figments the slender principles of truth which he received, that this fictitious kind of teaching would be rather injurious than profitable"; we should attend to Genesis instead.[31] But a mere two pages before, Calvin has enthused about the humanistic attainment of the ten-year-old Henry of Navarre, to whom these *Commentaries* are dedicated: "liberal instruction has been superadded to chaste discipline. Already imbued with the rudiments of literature, you have not cast away (as nearly all are wont to do) these studies in disgust, but still advance with alacrity in the cultivation of your genius" (1:47). There is no need to decide whether deference towards the classics or towards the court of Navarre motivated Calvin here: the cultural apparatus works to render such considerations inextricable. The heathens could not be repudiated; they were too firmly established—not merely such that they could not be dislodged, but that cultural work could not otherwise envisaged. Only radical sectarians rejected secular learning altogether;[32] the overwhelming proportion of protestants worked to capture it for their own purposes. An educated ministry was the most persistent demand of protestants, for the preacher had to interpret and explain the scripture; also, the education system was the place to influence young people. "It was this infiltration of the universities which turned Puritanism from the sectional eccentricity of a few great households in the countryside and groups of artisans and small traders in the towns into a nation-wide movement affecting all classes of society," Lawrence Stone observes.[33]

But such infiltration inevitably involved negotiation, perhaps contamination. "It may be lawful for Christians to use philosophers and books of secular learning, but with this condition, that whatsoever they find in them that is profitable and useful, they convert it to Christian doctrine and do, as it were, shave off, and pare away all superfluous stuff," John Rainolds cautioned.[34]

The scope of the problem was nothing less than God and Man. The protestant idea of god was affronted by pagan deities, who were not only too numerous, but given to immoral behavior. Thomas Becon specified carefully in his *Catechism* (1560) that after "the word of God," the schoolmaster will teach

> good letters, I mean poets, orators, historiographers, philosophers, &c. . . . But, in reading these kinds of authors in his discipline, the school-master must diligently take heed that he read only those to his scholars that be most profitable and contain in them no matter that may either hinder the religion of God or the innocency of manners. Such writers in many places of their works are wanton and unhonest, as Martialis, Catullus, Tibullus, Propertius, Cornelius Gallus, and such-like; some wicked and ungodly, as Lucianus, &c.[35]

It was unclear where the line should be drawn. Lawrence Humphrey in *The Nobles* (1563) recommends many secular authors for the education of the puritan gentleman, but complains that too many read "human things, not divine, love toys, not fruitful lessons, Venus' games, not weighty studies tending to increase of godliness, dignity, or true and sound commodity; as Ovid, *Of the Art of Love.*" Humphrey excludes Homer, Horace, Lucian, Ovid, and Virgil's *Aeneid* (but not the workaday *Georgics*) because they present un-Christian values too eloquently (sig. x, y). Hugh Kearney compares Humphrey's approach to Sir Thomas Elyot's in *The Governor*, where the preference is for classical rather than biblical texts and models of conduct.[36]

So one answer was to select; another was allegorical interpretation. For protestants, this had to be moral allegory—the medieval and Catholic practice of finding theological allegory in pagan texts attributed too much spiritual wisdom to them.[37] "Undoubtedly there is no one tale among all the poets, but under the same is comprehended some thing that pertaineth either to the amendment of manners, to the knowledge of truth, to the setting forth of Nature's work, or else to the understanding of some notable thing done," Thomas Wilson asserts in *The Arte of Rhetorique* (1553) (fol. 104r). By this strenuous claim ("undoubtedly . . . no one tale but"), Wilson hoped to justify the sexual escapades of the gods—Jupiter's assault on Danaë shows that women will be won with money; his changing into a bull to abduct Isis, that beauty may overcome the beast (fol. 104v). Wilson asserts these strained interpretations because he is struggling to square religion and literary interests. Arthur Golding was similarly situated— he translated Theodore Beza's tragedy *Abraham sacrifiant* (in 1577) and at Sidney's request completed the translation of Mornay's *De la vérité de la religion chrestienne*.[38] In the preface and epistle to his translation of Ovid's *Metamorphoses* (1567), Golding takes the same line as Wilson, trying to retrieve those stories through ethical allegory:

> The snares of Mars and Venus show that time will bring to light
> The secret sins that folk commit in corners or by night.
> Hermaphrodite and Salmacis declare that idleness
> Is chiefest nurse and cherisher of all voluptuousness,
> And that voluptuous life breeds sin: which linking all together
> Make men to be effeminate, unwieldy, weak and lither.[39]

On his title page Golding warns: "With skill, heed and judgment, this work must be read, / For else to the reader it stands in small stead." He means it must be read with a protestant slant if the reader is not to be tempted by pagan values.

While the classical idea of deity seemed all too human for protestants, the idea of human potential was often too godlike. Epic was the most highly valued poetic form partly because an exalted conception of what today might be called "Renaissance Man" could be derived from it. Tasso asserts in his *Discourses on the Heroic Poem* that "epic illustriousness is based on lofty military valour and the magnanimous resolve to die, on piety, religion, and deeds alight with these virtues." Ficino alludes to an epic idea of human potential when he declares, "In certain ages there are great and powerful men, gods in the guise of humans, or humans who are gods, but they are rarer than the Phoenix."[40] The contrast with Christianity was appreciated by Machiavelli: "Our religion has glorified humble and contemplative men, rather than men of action. It has assigned as man's highest good humility, abnegation, and contempt for mundane things, whereas that other hath identified it with magnanimity, bodily strength, and everything else that conduces to make men bold."[41] William Perkins agreed, though unlike Machiavelli he did not regret the Christian attitude:

> the Philosopher [Aristotle, *Nichomachean Ethics* 4.3] calls *Magnanimity* (whereby a man thinks himself worthy of great honours, and thereupon enterpriseth great things) a virtue; which notwithstanding is to beholden a flat vice. For by the law of God, every man is to range himself within the limits of his calling, and not to dare once to

go out of it. Whereas, on the contrary, the scope and end of this virtue (as they term it) is to make men attempt high and great matters above their reach, and so to go beyond their callings. Besides, it is directly opposite to the virtue of humility, which teacheth that a man ought always to be base, vile and lowly in his own eyes.[42]

Puritan humanists felt they should adapt epic to meet these reservations. In the *New Arcadia,* Musidorus and Pyrocles seem to be the perfect heroic princes; indeed, they have been reared in the manner proposed in Sidney's *Defence,* on "all the stories of worthy princes, both to move them to do nobly and teach them how to do nobly." They set out on their adventures to excel the classical models, "thinking it not so worthy to be brought to heroical effects by fortune or necessity, like Ulysses and Aeneas, as by one's own choice and working."[43] But their love slides towards lust, and they are unable to defeat Amphialus; they are subjected to suffering, impotence, and failure, and they begin to develop a more inward and spiritual strength, based on a recognition of their limitations; they learn patience from the princesses. It seems that eventually they must be rescued by providence when their own efforts fail. Milton in *Paradise Lost* faces a similar task. He says his argument is "Not less but more heroic" than the classical epics, and that knights in battle are "tedious"; he prefers "the better fortitude / Of patience and heroic martyrdom."[44] The word *stand* rings through *Paradise Lost.* It connotes a heroism that does not overrate the potential for human achievement. "They also serve who only stand and wait" ("On his Blindness").

The most radical solution was to admit only literature on divine subjects—which meant, in the main, translating, rewriting, and reworking biblical material in secular forms (lyric verse, tragedy, epic). A great deal of early protestant writing was of this character; for Sidney's generation, the Huguenot poet Du Bartas (who, like Mornay, was at the court of Navarre) became the spokesman for "divine poetry." In *Urania* (1574), translated by James VI of Scotland in 1584, Bartas nominates Urania the muse of the divine poem; she exhorts him:

> If ye be heavenly, how dare ye presume
> A verse profane, and mocking for to sing
> 'Gainst him that leads of starry heavens the ring?
> Will ye then so ingrately make your pen
> A slave to sin, and serve but fleshly men?[45]

The white dove of the Holy Spirit should replace Pegasus, the winged horse, as the emblem of poetic inspiration (p. 35). The Scottish connection was strengthened by the writings of George Buchanan, whose tragedies *Baptistes* and *Jepthes* were published in London in 1577–78 and 1580. Such insistence on divine poetry constituted a coherent puritan humanist position, and its influence was powerful in English writing. George Herbert asked God: "Why are not sonnets made of thee? and lays / Upon thine altar burnt?" (they already were being, of course), and resolved that his poetic abilities should be "ever consecrated to God's glory";[46] he held to that line. Spenser wrote divine poetry; several titles showing this are listed in the printer's note to the *Complaints*. His *Fowre Hymnes* (1596) are prefaced with a dedication to the puritan countesses of Cumberland and Warwick, in which Spenser attributes the first two hymns, on earthly love and beauty, to his green youth and offers the second two, on heavenly love and beauty, as a corrective. These latter begin with a repudiation:

> Many lewd lays (ah woe is me the more)
> In praise of that mad fit, which fools call love,
> I have in th'heat of youth made heretofore,
> That in light wits did loose affection move.
> But all those follies now I do reprove,
> And turned have the tenor of my string,
> The heavenly praises of true love to sing.[47]

However, Spenser did not settle to divine poetry; indeed, despite this repudiation, he prints all four hymns—the lewd lays as well as the heavenly praises. The humanist is reluctant, here, to submit to the puritan. Such wavering is not uncharacteristic, for the puritan humanist stance was by definition anxious and indeterminate, inviting diverse resolutions, none of which was quite satisfactory. Some writers moved towards divine or severely instructional writing as they grew older; this was the pattern taken by Fulke Greville and Joseph Hall, and perhaps by Sidney as well, for near the end of his life he translated Bartas's long poem *La création du monde ou première sepmaine*[48] and began translating the Psalms and Mornay's *De la vérité*. Milton moves steadily across the spectrum from humanist to puritan. *Comus* and "Lycidas" use pagan imagery in ways that may be justified by their ethical purport; *Paradise Lost* is a divine poem, but it is the unstable mixture of Christian theme and pagan imagery that makes it so astounding; *Samson Agonistes* and *Paradise Regained* cultivate an austere, though not quite complete, repudiation of secular reference.

However, appropriation is never one-way: the pagan genres adapted by puritan humanists inevitably leave in the Christianizing texts traces of their prior implication. Hence, perhaps, readers' unease with Acrasia's Bower of Bliss (*Faerie Queene* 2.12). Milton in *Paradise Lost* juxtaposes pagan gardens with Eden while denying that there is any comparison (4.268–87; 9.439–43). But the connotations run riot when Spenser evokes the garden round the dwelling of Acrasia, the wicked seductress:

> More sweet and wholesome than the pleasant hill
>   Of *Rhodope*, on which the nymph that bore
>   A giant babe herself for grief did kill;
>   Or the Thessalian *Tempe*, where of yore
>   Fair *Daphne Phoebus'* heart with love did gore;
>   Or *Ida*, where the gods loved to repair,
>   Whenever they their heavenly bowers forlore;
>   Or sweet *Parnass*, the haunt of Muses fair;
>   Or *Eden* self, if ought with *Eden* mote compare.
>   (*Faerie Queene* 2.12.52)

Douglas Brooks-Davies invites readers to "note the interpretative problem posed here."[49] Rhodope and Thessaly were the scenes of disasters, and so might point towards the dangerous character of Acrasia's garden; Ida and Parnassus, on the other hand, had mystical, neoplatonic, and poetic associations, and thus might set an ironic frame for Acrasia's activities. But the two strategies undermine each other: contradictory analogues stand together, without formal distinction, in the one list. Critical ingenuity might propose that Acrasia inhabits a place of moral confusion; but then what of the final comparison with Eden? The question is recognized ("if ought with *Eden* mote compare"), but not resolved. Pagan, neoplatonic, and Christian images jostle together without an apparent hierarchy. Despite his professions at other points—for instance when the Bible is presented to Redcross as "heavenly documents . . . That weaker wit of man could never reach, / Of God, of grace, of justice, of free will" (1.10.19)— Spenser allows pagan poetry to disturb the priority of Christian imagery. Generally, with Greenblatt, I see Spenser now as a far more *opportunistic* poet than the modern critical tradition, with its commitment to the discovery of structure, has wanted to envisage.[50]

Anti-puritan traces in Acrasia's setting may derive also from the sixteenth-century Italian reworkings of epic upon which Spenser was drawing. The equivalent to Acrasia in Ariosto's *Orlando Furioso* (1532) is Alcina: she is presented similarly, with a full catalogue of her attractions, but without serious disapproval of her or her island being suggested (7.11–15; 6.20–22). Ariosto encourages the reader to forgive Ruggiero for being ensnared (7.18); he is tolerant of his heroes' frequent sexual lapses and does not begrudge Alcina her beauty. The humanist *Spenser* wants to adopt Ariosto's image, but the puritan must build in evaluative phrases:

> Upon a bed of roses was she laid,
>   As faint through heat, or dight [dressed] to pleasant sin,
>   And was arrayed, or rather disarrayed,
>   All in a veil of silk and silver thin,
>   That hid no whit her alablaster skin,
>   But rather showed more white, if more might be.
> (2.12.77)

The moral tone here is quite finely balanced: replace *sin* with a merely ambiguous word such as *dalliance* and many readers might not worry about the disarray or the hint of excess and falsification in the last two lines. Spenser is following and partly revising Ariosto's practice, but traces of Ariosto's ethic remain embedded in the language. Spenser's other main source here, Tasso's *Gerusalemme liberata* (1575), is closer to puritan purpose—Tasso disapproved of Ariosto's casual treatment of Alcina's charms, and his parallel account of Armida and her island is qualified by a moral commentary like Spenser's.[51] But Tasso's Rinaldo is readily persuaded to leave Armida by a mirroring of his debased condition and an appeal to his honor; Tasso and his hero seem quite at ease in the world of epic achievement (16.29–34). Guyon's good behavior, in contrast, seems always precarious—in Acrasia's garden, he

>   suffered no delight
> To sink into his sense, nor mind affect,
> But passed forth, and looked still forward right,
> Bridling his will, and maistering his might.
> (2.12.53)

Guyon resisted the temptations of the Cave of Mammon without difficulty, but here his bridling and maistering is not secure; his defeat of sensuality is both harder-won and more decisive than Ruggiero's. Indeed, it is positively destructive:

> But all those pleasant bowers and palace brave,
>   *Guyon* broke down, with rigour pitiless;
>   Ne ought their goodly workmanship might save
>   Them from the tempest of his wrathfulness,
>   But that their bliss he turn'd to balefulness:
>   Their groves he felled, their gardens did deface,
>   Their arbours spoil, their cabinets suppress,

> Their banquet houses burn, their buildings raze,
> And of the fairest late, now made the foulest place.
> (2.12.83)

The reversed evaluation of "fairest" and "foulest" in the last line (readers are asked to approve the displacement of fair by foul) is the demand of an extremist. This may just be protestantism: in Reformation thought any virtue in "fallen" humanity must be strenuous and controversial. What is nonetheless perverse, however, is that the zealous Guyon is supposed to be the knight of temperance! But then, while Spenser has portrayed Acrasia's environment as in some ways excessive, he has also allowed it to appear *temperate:* the heavens "suffered storm nor frost on them to fall,"

> Nor scorching heat, nor cold intemperate
> T'afflict the creatures, which therein did dwell,
> But the mild air with season moderate
> Gently attempered, and disposed so well,
> That still it breathed forth sweet spirit and wholesome smell.
> (2.12.51)

In the first line of the next stanza, *wholesome* is repeated (introducing the comparison with Rhodope, already quoted). The birdsong around the bower also seems to be a good thing, harmonious and temperate:

> The joyous birds shrouded in cheerful shade—

(but look at the disjunctions—shrouds are deathly, and shade is often gloomy—is this comforting or threatening?)—

> The joyous birds shrouded in cheerful shade,
> Their notes unto the voice attempered sweet;
> Th'angelical soft trembling voices made
> To th'instruments divine respondence meet.
> (2.12.71)

This is what Guyon has to overthrow. It is not surprising that he does not do it temperately, for it is itself partly temperate.

Puritan and humanist values cannot be merged, but they refuse, in Spenser's handling, to separate out. After all, temperance is a pagan virtue, most famously defined in Aristotle's *Ethics* (2.6) as the rational achievement of a mean between extremes of excess and defect in passions and actions, and it is by no means obvious how it should sort with protestant zeal. The violence with which Guyon breaks up the bower may be not only religious fervor, therefore, but an anxiety that the place of pagan letters, together with the palaces, arbors, banqueting halls, and fine workmanship of courtly culture, is not altogether set-tled. One of the temptations Guyon has to survive on his way to Acrasia's bower is the Mermaids, and they are related to the Muses: "They were fair ladies, till they fondly striv'd / With th'*Heliconian* maids for maistery." This presumption caused them to be transformed half to fish,

> But th'upper half their hue retained still,
> And their sweet skill in wonted melody;
> Which ever after they abused to ill,
> T'allure weak travellers, whom gotten they did kill.
>
> (2.12.31)

It must be hard to tell, then, when melody is legitimate and when not. The temptation that is repelled when Acrasia's bower is broken up is integral with one half of the puritan humanist poetic. Guyon is both temperate and intemperate; he is destroying a part of himself. The canto and book close with the complaint of the beastly Grill at being transformed into the kind of creature that Guyon approves: Grill "Repined greatly, and did him miscall, / That had from hoggish form him brought to natural" (2.12.86). This recalcitrance affords Guyon, even in his moment of success, pretext for further immod-erateness, further strain and agitation. He and the Palmer do not forego the opportunity for intemperate taunts—

> The dunghill kind
> Delights in filth and foul incontinence;
> Let *Grill* be *Grill*, and have his hoggish mind.

Such compulsion to discover yet further resistance to vilify, in the last moment of the book, suggests once more an excess, an instability, in the puritan humanist project.

SIDNEY'S *DEFENCE* FOR PURITANS

Poetry, Sidney wants to show in his *Defence of Poetry*, "being rightly applied, deserveth not to be scourged out of the Church of God."[52] His initial move is to propose three kinds of poetry—divine, philo-sophical, and (the type he mainly discusses) "that feigning notable images of virtues, vices, or what else, with that delightful teaching" (p. 81). This enables him to revere, yet at the same time to bracket off, divine poetry: it is "the chief, both in antiquity and excellency" (p. 80), yet need not interfere with the main argument. This is not casual lip service though, for Sidney maintains with considerable care a major protestant distinction by accepting only Christian poetry as divine. He adds and prefers biblical instances (David, Solomon, Moses, Deborah, Job) to the pagans listed by Scaliger—the latter were "in a full wrong divinity" (pp. 80, 190); he does not, like Plato, Scaliger, and the Pléiade, claim heavenly inspiration for the poet; nor, like George Puttenham in the opening paragraph of his *Arte of English Poesie* (1589), does he draw an unqualified analogy between the poet and God. Like Sir Thomas Elyot, he employs to the general credit of poetry the fact that the Romans called any poet a *vates,* but he insists that the use of Virgil for fortune-telling was "a very vain and godless superstition"; and verse in oracles, he says, only *seemed* to have some divine force (pp. 76–77). Sidney apparently read Bartas after writing the *Defence,* but he places Buchanan in a list of distinguished people who have not disdained poetry and writes, punningly: "the tragedies of Buchanan do justly bring forth a divine admiration" (pp. 110, 116).

Sidney's main case, though, is not for divine poetry, but for the ethical validity of secular poets: "For these indeed do merely make to imitate, and imitate both to delight and teach; and delight, to move men to take that goodness in hand, which without delight they would fly as from a stranger; and teach, to make them know that goodness whereunto they are moved" (p. 81). He grants the priority of divine poetry, but does not want poetry restricted to biblical subjects; it is a distinctively puritan humanist project. His key move is to claim for secular poetry ethical insight, for this, according to protestants, was entirely within the competence of pagan reason. "Nothing, indeed, is more common," Calvin allowed, "than for man to be sufficiently instructed in a right course of conduct by natural law."[53] Pagans could not reach spiritual insight—that would be the province of revelation and divine poetry; but "the admirable light of truth displayed" in pagan writings, Calvin writes with unusual enthusiasm, "should remind us that the human mind, however much fallen and perverted from its integrity, is still adorned and invested with admirable gifts from its Creator" (*Institutes* 2.2.15). This gives Sidney much of what he needs to defend pagan poetry. He maintains the demarcation between revealed religion and the ethical philosophy naturally available to "fallen" humankind when he remarks that "in nature we know it is well to do well, and what is well, and what is evil, . . . for out of natural conceit the philosophers drew it," and adds, "*I speak still of human, and according to the human conceit*" (p. 91; emphasis added). The same idea is at work when Sidney indicates the respective roles of biblical and secular reading in his letter of May 22, 1580, to Edward Denny: the scriptures "are certainly the incomparable lantern in this fleshly darkness of ours. . . . To them if you will add as to the help of the second table (I mean that which contains the love of thy neighbour, and dealing betwixt man and man) some parts of moral philosophy, I think you shall do very wisely."[54] From such a basis, Sidney may claim "wisdom and temperance in Ulysses and Diomedes, valour in Achilles, friendship in Nisus and Euryalus" (*Defence,* p. 86).

Yet the *Defence* remains vulnerable to the argument, which Sidney knew others were making, that divine subjects would better suit the dignity of poetry and avoid the danger of heathen temptations. Psalm-singing, he says, is recommended by Saint James for times of merriment, and "I know is used with the fruit of comfort by some, when, in sorrowful pangs of their death-bringing sins, they find the consolation of the never-leaving goodness" (p. 80). This seems to echo the well-known preface to the metrical version of the Psalms by Thomas Sternhold and John Hopkins (1562), but notice the corollary that they draw: psalms are "to be used of all sorts of people privately for their solace and comfort: laying apart all ungodly songs and ballads which tend only to the nourishing of vice and corrupting of youth." Patrick Collinson notes this yearning towards an exclusively religious culture—he quotes Miles Coverdale's wish "that our minstrels had none other thing to play upon, neither our carters and ploughmen other thing to whistle upon, save psalms, hymns, and such godly songs as David is occupied withal!"[55] Sidney, however, does not want to lay apart ungodly songs. Even so, he declares later on that songs and sonnets of love might better be employed "in singing the praises of the immortal beauty; the immortal goodness of that God who giveth us hands to write and wits to conceive" (p. 116). The question has not gone away. If Sidney's argument for ethical poetry is sometimes forced, as I think it is, then it is partly because although few people seriously imagined dispensing with pagan learning, the case for the exclusive validity of divine poetry was lurking just out of sight.

In the medium term, indeed, the separation of spiritual and terrestrial concerns, which was designed to protect the former, helped make space for empirical and other scientific study that eventually produced a more persuasive secular view of the universe. The separation was Francis Bacon's justification in *De augmentis scientiarum,* but he hardly admits that the quest for natural laws seems to narrow the scope for divine intervention in the world. However, he does say that "we are not to give up the investigation, until the properties and qualities found in such things as may be taken for miracles of nature be reduced and comprehended under some Form or Fixed Law,"[56] and this must leave little space for specific operations of God's "special providence" such as protestants envisaged. Even Calvin and Perkins invite admiration for the marvelous *design* of the universe, not seeing that regularity must undermine the scope for an intrusive deity. Perkins compares the universe to a watch with many wheels, as deists were to do, not noticing that a good watch does not require the continual tinkering of the watchmaker.[57] The separation of divine and secular learning enabled Calvin to say that God wants us to study his creation and assists us even "by the work and ministry of the ungodly in physics, dialectics, mathematics and other sciences" (*Institutes* 2.2.16). But he was helping the ungodly to get the better of the argument: gradually the secular slipped free from religious domination and, by promising advances in understanding and control of the natural world, made religious superstition seem less relevant as an explanation. Similarly, Calvin's freeing of ethics from total subjection to religion permitted people to construct, with some help from pagan thought, an autonomous secular morality that repudiates supernatural sanctions as destructive of true moral choice. The Reformation unwittingly made possible the modern situation, which is generally more advanced in the countries that were protestant, wherein many people conduct a moral life with little or no reference to a spiritual dimension.

That the *Defence* is subject to a structural difficulty, arising from tension in the puritan humanist situation rather than incidental awkwardnesses, is apparent from other strains in Sidney's argument. With respect to misguided ideas about god(s), he is, of course, not obliged to attribute religious wisdom to pagan poets: "The poets did not induce such opinions, but did imitate those opinions already induced. For all the Greek stories can well testify that the very religion of that time stood upon many and many-fashioned gods, not taught so by the poets, but followed according to their nature of imitation" (p. 108). At this point Sidney becomes a historical relativist, and potentially a materialist; it is a position altogether incompatible with the absolute aesthetic he propounds elsewhere. Moreover, it does not address the question of whether reading such opinions—with all the moving power Sidney attributes to poetry—might be harmful. Much of the anxiety about the gods concerned their sexual behavior, as I have remarked, and on love poetry Sidney is distinctly ambivalent. He suppresses it from his definitions of elegy and lyric—the former is taken solely as lament, ignoring Ovid and the Latin elegists; the latter is said to praise, not sexual love, but virtue and sometimes God (pp. 95, 97). However, Sidney knows that this is partial, and not only in respect of those genres. As he admits later on: "They say, the comedies rather teach than reprehend amorous conceits. They say the lyric is larded with passionate sonnets; the elegiac weeps the want of his mistress; and that even to the heroical, Cupid hath ambitiously climbed" (p. 103). His answer to this is notably indirect. He grants two objections while hinting at parenthetical reservations, but his appeals to "love and beauty" and "philosophers" support Platonic, not sexual love. Finally he grants that lust, vanity, and scurrility possess much love poetry—but yet that we may "not say that poetry abuseth man's wit, but that man's wit abuseth poetry" (p. 104). So poetry in principle is vindicated at the expense of most actual love poetry.

That Sidney's caution here is more puritan than the standard currency of Elizabethan critical thought may be observed through comparison with some less zealous writers. Sir Thomas Elyot recommends that the noble youth study the parts of Lucian "which be without ribaldry or too much scorning" and the episodes with Dido in the *Aeneid,* and Ovid's *Metamorphoses;* he says they will appeal to "that affect or desire whereto any child's fantasy is disposed." Elyot denies that in Terence, Ovid, Catullus, and Martial "is nothing contained but incitation to lechery," and holds that no ancient poet should "be excluded from the lesson of such one as desireth to come to the perfection of wisdom." Puttenham is openly liberal. He says poetry provides instruction, but sees it also as "the common solace of mankind in all his travails and cares of this transitory life." As such, it may "allowably bear matter not always of the gravest, or of any great commodity or profit, but rather in some sort vain, dissolute, or wanton, so be it not very scandalous and of evil example."[58]

The epic idea of the hero was also, as I have said, problematic. Here Sidney confronts the puritans more directly, perhaps because magnanimity is a more appropriate virtue for his class than for the social groups envisaged by Perkins as his likely readers. Even so, in his account of "the Heroical," Sidney says it "maketh magnanimity and justice shine," supplying a distinctive second quality—justice—to make the epic hero seem less grandly amoral than he often is. Sidney then offers the noticeably vaguer claims that epic instills "virtue" and "inflameth the mind with desire to be worthy," instancing Aeneas's behavior—"how he governeth himself in the ruin of his country; in the preserving his old father, and carrying away his religious ceremonies; in obeying God's commandment to leave Dido" (*Defence,* p. 98). This is surely the best protestant case that could be made for epic. When Sidney ventures a wider range of heroes, his claim for their virtue is less convincing: he declares that, hearing "the tales of Hercules, Achilles, Cyrus, Aeneas," one "must needs hear the right description of wisdom, valour, and justice" (p. 92). Such an appropriation obliges us to concede a point to Stephen Gosson, who in his *Schoole of Abuse* (1579) complains that defenders of Homer wrest "the rashness of Ajax to valour, the cowardice of Ulysses to policy, the dotage of Nestor to grave counsel."[59] Sidney's material reveals its intractability.

The boldest gambit in the *Defence* is the account of the provenance of the poet's vision. The main competitors to poetry are restricted severely by the "fallen" condition of humanity. History, "being captived to the truth of a foolish world, is many times a terror from well-doing, and an encouragement to unbridled wickedness." Philosophy is subject to a comparable drawback: it does not move us, and "to be moved to do that which we know, or to be moved with desire to know, *hoc opus, hic labor est.*"[60] Poetry's competitors, then, are vitiated by the "fall"; so Sidney sets aside the optimistic view of human potential that we associate with "Renaissance humanism." And poetry too, he says at one point, can only "draw us to as high a perfection as our degenerate souls, made worse by their clayey lodgings, can be capable of" (p. 82). But the powers of the poet, a few pages earlier, seem to be miraculously unhampered: he alone is found "freely ranging only within the zodiac of his own wit" (p. 78). This sounds a far larger claim than the ethical and practical insight with which protestants were happy to credit ancient writers. Sidney asserts special scope for the poet, Christian or pagan—that he is "lifted up with the vigour of his own invention" and transcends "fallen" nature, growing "in effect another nature, in making things either better than nature bringeth forth, or, quite anew, forms such as never were in nature" (p. 78). This is evidently designed to deal with objections by some protestants to the fictive character of much poetry: it does not only copy the world, but imagines ideal conditions—such as might have pertained before the "fall." Hence, in part, Sidney's commitment to the idea that absolute virtues and vices are displayed in poetry: it creates a golden world (of heroes, demigods, furies, and the like) where qualities are unalloyed. But how does such visionary perception fit the protestant categories that Sidney seems elsewhere to be using?—it sounds almost like Ficino's belief that in his inherent drive towards immortality Man "imitates all the works of the divine nature, and perfects, corrects and improves the works of the lower nature. Therefore the power of man is almost similar to that of the divine nature, for man acts in this way through himself. Through his own wit and art he governs himself, without being bound by any limits of corporeal nature."[61] Sidney is evidently aware of the danger of appearing to claim improper scope for lapsed humanity, for he moves quickly to "give right honour to the heavenly Maker of that maker." In fact, he says, so far from contradicting the "fall," the poet's vision affords "no small arguments to the credulous of that first accursed fall of Adam" (p. 79). This seems to mean that the poet's intuition reminds us of what our condition might have been had the "fall" not occurred; it is Calvin's thought when he remarks that "it is impossible to think of our primeval dignity without being immediately reminded of the sad spectacle of our ignominy and corruption, ever since we fell from our original in the person of our first parent" (*Institutes* 2.1.1). Here I agree with Andrew Weiner: Sidney is "declaring poetry's lack of complicity in that corruption of nature, following man's first disobedience, into her present 'brazen' state."[62] However, the question is how the *pagan* poet—and it is he who is the problem—could achieve such a vision. Weiner cites Calvin's principle that the "fall" may be reversed through "the grace of regeneration" (*Institutes* 2.2.12) and quotes Sidney's statement that the poet sees with "the eyes of the mind, only cleared by faith" (*Defence,* p. 77). But Sidney says this of David in the Psalms—*of the divine poet.* The pagan poet cannot be following "the promptings of the Holy Spirit."[63] Protestant admiration for pagan capacity in ethical affairs, on which Sidney's case is generally based, cannot be stretched so far. Perkins insists:

> though those virtues of the heathen be graces of God, yet they are
> but general and common to all: whereas the virtues of Christians are
> special graces of the spirit, sanctifying and renewing the mind, will
> and affections. For example, chastity in Joseph was a grace of God's
> spirit, renewing his heart; but chastity in Xenocrates was a common
> grace, serving only to curb and restrain the corruption of his heart.
> And the like may be said of Abraham, a Christian, and of Aristides, a
> heathen.[64]

Pagan virtue is *by definition* different, and elsewhere Sidney allows, indeed depends upon, the distinction. But here, in the passage about the "fall of Adam," he does encourage confusion, for he says that the poet—not just the biblical writer—has "the force of a divine breath" (p. 79). This sounds like the Holy Spirit: although Sidney claims, in the main, only ethical provenance for pagan poetry, he does at this point allow the distinctive inspiration of the divine poet to slide across.

That this is not a position he could defend explicitly is apparent later, when he bluntly repudiates Plato's claim that poetry is "a very inspiring of a divine force, far above man's wit" (p. 109).

So Sidney arrives at his celebrated formula: "our erected wit maketh us know what perfection is, and yet our infected will keepeth us from reaching unto it" (p. 79). This has proved of great appeal to Christian humanists as securing somehow both godlike aspirations and postlapsarian degradation. It has the ring of profound paradox, vague nobility, and inevitably thwarted idealism that appeals to traditional critics, promising imaginative potency at the expense of actual attention to human affairs. Had Sidney indeed reconciled the most exalted humanist conception of poetry and the protestant conviction that people are thoroughly "fallen," it would be an achievement on the order of reconciling science and religion, or Marx and Freud (or even literature and politics). But the same conditions pertain as before: either "erected wit" is a property of pagans, in which case it is still a limited faculty in comparison with the divine revelation available to regenerate Christians; or it is a property of the elect, in which case it cannot afford a defense of pagan poetry.

There was, in fact, a celebrated pagan use of the word *erect*. In Ovid's *Metamorphoses,* when Man is first created, his divine origin is celebrated and it is said that the god gave him an uplifted face and bade him see the sky and lift his countenance erect to the stars ("Os homini sublime dedit: coelumque videre / Iussit, & erectos ad sidera tollere vultus": 1.85–86). Calvin quotes this in the *Institutes,* applying it to "the integrity with which Adam was endued when his intellect was clear, his affections subordinated to reason, all his senses duly regulated, and when he truly ascribed all his excellence to the admirable gifts of his Maker" (1.15.3). That is when Man was erect. (Milton uses Ovid's verse in the same way when he adapts it in writing of the creation of Adam.)[65] Created man, Calvin continues, exhibited "the entire excellence of human nature," but at the "fall," this was "vitiated and almost destroyed, nothing remaining but a ruin, confused, mutilated, and tainted with impurity"—and hence the limits upon natural intellect. The one qualification is that Man's original condition "is now partly seen in the elect, in so far as they are regenerated by the Spirit" (*Institutes* 1.15.4). They may have erected wits; but not pagan poets. Even Ovid was speaking of the golden age, not of current human faculties.

There are two ways of reading Sidney's formula, then: it either addresses the condition of pagans (in which case despite the exalted tone, their work is still inferior to divine poetry); or it addresses the condition of the regenerate (in which case it cannot defend the pagan writing that figured so largely in the Elizabethan cultural apparatus). By allowing a confusion of the two, the formula sounds like a triumphant justification, the best of all worlds; but it does not stand up to analysis.

At this point the skeptical reader might say: Ah yes, but have you not been paying too much attention to Calvin anyway—was not Richard Hooker, after all, the central religious thinker of the period?

Supposing that were so, it still would not make Sidney's formula coherent. For while the erected wit is compatible with Hooker's conception of human capacity, the infected will is not. To Hooker, will is defined as following reason: "the object of Will is that good which Reason doth lead us to seek ... neither is any other desire termed properly Will, but that where Reason and Understanding, or the show of Reason, prescribeth the thing desired."[66] It is Calvin who insists, contrary to Aristotle and Aquinas as well as to Hooker, that the will is depraved to the extent that it is likely to resist the reason.[67] Alternatively we might say that "erected wit" sounds like Erasmus, who holds in his *Handbook of the Militant Christian* that "the soul, mindful of its celestial nature, struggles strenuously against the weight of the earthly body to press upward." But such a view correlates, again, with a general sense that the will also is not too damaged by the "fall": none of our passions, Erasmus believes, "is so violent that it cannot be restrained by reason or redirected towards virtue."[68] So Sidney's sentence deposits him between the two stools of contemporary thought. His idea of the scope of the reason approximates that of Hooker or Erasmus; but the recalcitrance of the will is the position of Calvin and Perkins. His poet meets the criteria of neither of the main contemporary ideas of Man; he is more "fallen" than is allowed in the one, less than in the other. "Our erected wit maketh us know what perfection is, and yet our infected will keepeth us from reaching unto it" effects not a resolution, but a clash of rival absolutes. It is a precise epitome of the struggle over God and Man at the center of puritan humanism.

POSITIVE IMAGES

It may now be apparent that, at least in the forms in which they offered themselves to Sidney, puritanism and humanism, for all their rivalry, finally *share* the same authoritarian deep structure. For each asserts an absolute notion of humanity—either sunk in spiritual degradation or blessed with godlike vision. And this entire way of thinking is of a piece with Sidney's determination to efface the historical and ideological specificities of pagan writing and discover ideal, ahistorical, exemplifications in poetry: Man is *essentially, ultimately, really,* thus (or thus)—it is guaranteed by God. Absolutes are ideological: Anthony Giddens proposes that the three principal ideological forms are "the representation of sectional interests as universal ones," "the denial or transmutation of contradictions," and "the naturalisation of the present."[69] Sidney in the *Defence* manifests all three. Despite his awareness that pagan gods are what we should expect in pagan society, he naturalizes the present to the extent that no difference in ethical values between protestants and pagans is acknowledged. To do this, he denies or transmutes the contradictions within pagan literature, between that literature and his society, and within his society. And his aim is to construct a relationship between the cultural apparatus and a particular point of view in Elizabethan culture and politics, but this is not admitted: sectional interests are represented as universal ones. Theories of Man are strategies of political power.

Sidney's strategic choices in his attempt to negotiate a relationship between the cultural apparatus and his political project are not without relevance for those who would do the same today. If I have been able to show partiality in his treatment of some classical texts, it is because their role is like that which Terry Eagleton attributes to Richardson's novels: they are "pitched standards around which battle is joined, instruments which help to constitute social interests."[70] But Sidney cannot altogether efface contradiction. The condition for the propounding of an absolutist aesthetic is a contest that must belie its claims. The *Defence,* like Spenser's Bower of Bliss, is problematic because it is not, in fact, a unified construction of absolute qualities, but a piecing together of divergent discourses within an unsettled cultural apparatus. This is characteristic of the way cultures develop: "The process of ideological elaboration is thus closer . . . to Lévi-Strauss' process of *bricolage* than it is to the consistent elaboration of theoretical or philosophical 'world views,' " Stuart Hall has observed. Ideologies "will frequently be extended and amplified to deal with new situations by 'putting together', often in an illogical or incoherent way, what were, previously, the fragments of more ordered or stable meaning-systems."[71] For, despite his language of high principle, Sidney is ratifying a program of compromise within the prevailing cultural apparatus. In the face of its absolutist statements, the *Defence* actually both proposes and instantiates mixed modes: its project demands, and itself exhibits, negotiation and appropriation of existing forms, not a sudden, unfettered intuition of ultimate truth. (And that is why Sidney's other writing does not achieve the ideological purity that the *Defence* seems to demand.) Doubtless all this was, for Sidney, a necessary personal accommodation. Also, I am arguing, we may discern a purposeful intervention. Sidney aimed to make space in the Elizabethan cultural apparatus for writing that might address the spectrum of concerns articulated at the interface between protestantism and pagan writing; to establish a courtly culture that, although less restricted than Bartas would have had it, was nonetheless a vehicle for earnest protestantism.

Upon his death in 1586, Sidney's admirers hastened to exploit his image, representing him as just such an absolute figure as he had sought to celebrate in pagan literature—an ideal hero in the epic struggle for protestantism and an example for his time. Dispute over the precise defensible balance for poetry and religion continued, for it was imperative for that culture to continue talking to itself about such a central and unresolved issue. Diverse emphases were derived from Sidney's work. Spenser is close on his heels in the Letter to Raleigh about the *Faerie Queene,* where Spenser claims to be following classical tradition wherein Homer "in the persons of Agamemnon and Ulysses hath ensampled a good governor and a virtuous man." Here puritans are Spenser's reference point, and are answered in their own terms when he says that those who may prefer "good discipline delivered plainly in way of precepts or sermoned at large" should consider that the poetic method is suitable for "these days, seeing all things accounted by their shows, and nothing esteemed that is not delightful and pleasing to common sense."[72] This is very like Sidney's case for delightful teaching.

Sir John Harington in the preface to his translation of *Orlando Furioso* (1591) uses the argument less straightforwardly. He borrows, with some acknowledgment, various of Sidney's points, but makes the tone teasing and debunking, for instance in respect of the belief of some opponents that all but divine poetry is "vain and superfluous," and in an absurdly elaborate array of allegorical readings of Perseus slaying Gorgon.[73] On love poetry, which as translator of *Orlando Furioso* he must address, Harington rehearses Sidney's embarrassment, but jovially sets it aside: "As for the pastoral with the sonnet or epigram, though many times they savour of wantonness and love and toying, and, now and then breaking the rules of poetry, go into plain scurrility, yet even the worst of them may be not ill applied, and are,

I must confess, too delightful." He reckons that even the blushing matron will read them when no observer is by (p. 209). While Sidney justifies the *Aeneid* by pointing out that Aeneas virtuously deserts Dido, Harington appeals to Aeneas's lapse with Dido to justify sexual license in *Orlando Furioso* (p. 214). As T. G. A. Nelson says, it amounts to a parody of Sidney's *Defence,* a repudiation of "the rather serious-minded aspirations" of Sidney and Spenser.[74] Fulke Greville, at the other extreme, also framed his argument about secular poetry in Sidneyan terms. He declares that in the *Arcadia,* Sidney's end "was not vanishing pleasure alone, but moral images and examples, as directing threads, to guide every man through the confused labyrinth of his own desires and life." Yet Greville does not present this as a program for more such writing; rather, he wishes that *Arcadia* "may be the last in this kind, presuming no man that follows can ever reach, much less go beyond, that excellent intended pattern of his."[75] In this version, Sidney's own image and example produce not a model to follow but a reason why there should be no more such; his instance was so ideal that none can emulate it. These diverse appropriations of the *Defence* show how a firm and accomplished statement, rather than closing an issue, very often instigates a further phase of cultural negotiation.

The moment of the Sidney circle was relatively brief, for courtly protestantism was overtaken by events. The defeat of the Armada diminished the need for heroic knights to oppose an evil empire; the Earl of Essex, having the queen's favor, fashioned a more exuberant, less thoughtful image of aristocratic virtue; most puritan ministers learnt to live with periodic intrusions from the bishops; a protestant succession was secured. Jacobean court culture became far more elaborate and expensive, and the commercial stage vastly more influential, than Sidney could have envisaged, producing a culture more ambitious and demotic, and more sexy and violent, than the *Defence* contemplates. Mixed genres became the norm; plays and masques merged pagan and Christian imagery and contexts, often with casual disregard for historical and philosophical consistency. If my thesis is right, Sidney would have been disconcerted to find the *Defence* inspiring Theseus's evocation of how "The poet's eye, in a fine frenzy rolling, / Doth glance from heaven to earth, from earth to heaven" at the start of act 5 of *A Midsummer Night's Dream.* And however much he might have admired the scope and poetry of *King Lear* and *The Duchess of Malfi,* which draw specifically upon the *Arcadia,* he would have been uneasy about the attitudes to Christianity that may be inferred from those plays.

It seems obvious now that Sidney's largest influence occurred because his texts were printed, initially in pirated editions. But the rapid growth in the demand for printed books marked a limit to the significance of the court in the cultural apparatus. Joseph Hall in his *Virgidemiarum* (1597–98) satirizes every kind of poetry in the name of unmasking the ugly face of vice, but says in a postscript that "poetry itself" scarcely needs defending "after the so effectual and absolute endeavours of her honoured patrons," Sidney and Spenser.[76] So the erected wit was recycled for the infighting of city wits (Hall later became a bishop and more solemn). The nodes of cultural power were becoming more dispersed—not necessarily very far down the political hierarchy, but into diverse networks and milieux that gained the intellectual and educational confidence to put together their own particular *bricolage*. As the Caroline court embraced Laudian Anglo-Catholicism, the kind of principled stance adopted by Sidney in the *Defence* became important again, but now in a gentry culture that cultivated godly earnestness against court excess. Perhaps in a purposeful appropriation, it is *Astrophil and Stella* that may be heard through George Herbert's religious verse:

> There is in love a sweetness ready penned:
> Copy out only that, and save expense.
>   ("Jordan [II]")

Compare *Astrophil and Stella*, sonnet 3:

> in *Stella's* face I read
> What Love and Beauty be, then all my deed
> But copying is, what in her Nature writes.[77]

Milton is close to the *Defence* in his *Reason of Church Government* (1641), where he asserts that poetry teaches "over the whole book of sanctity and virtue through all the instances of example, with such delight to those especially of soft and delicious temper who will not so much as look upon truth herself unless they see her elegantly dressed." For himself though, picking up what I have said is an indeterminacy in the *Defence*, Milton finds the logic of divine poetry more compelling: he contemplates a work not "to be obtained by the invocation of Dame Memory and her siren daughters, but by devout prayer to that eternal Spirit."[78] In *Paradise Regained* (1671), Milton adds a fourth temptation to the biblical account of Jesus in the wilderness: the temptation to study pagan letters. Satan says tragedians instruct and delight in the manner proposed by Sidney (4.261–66), but Jesus will have none of it:

> He who receives
> Light from above, from the Fountain of Light,
> No other doctrine needs, though granted true;
> But these are false, or little else but dreams,
> Conjectures, fancies, built on nothing firm.
> (4.288–92)

Jesus allows just one reservation, two lines out of 78: there may be pagan writing "where moral virtue is expressed / By light of nature not in all quite lost" (4.351–52). In these extensive references to Sidney's ideas we see not the triumph of absolutism but appropriations that precisely undermine its pretensions.

Sidney himself became a powerful cultural token, a figure through whom subsequent generations might propagate and contest significant values. The *Defence* brings into focus two strategies: the appropriation of prestigious cultural tokens (in Sidney's text, pagan letters), and the representing of supposedly absolute human qualities (the move also of Soviet realism). The history of the idea of Sir Philip in English culture shows, very often, these two strategies working together: he is appropriated as a statusful instantiation of supposedly absolute qualities. (I adopt Sidney's knightly title at this point, for although it was not his at the time of much of his writing, and its conferral was rather a formality,[79] those who deploy his image have evidently believed that adding social status to literary status helps their case.) Protestant activists initiated such appropriation. Arthur Golding, dedicating the *Trewness of the Christian Religion* to Leicester, declares that Sidney died "the honourablest death that could be desired, and best beseeming a Christian knight, whereby he hath worthily won to himself immortal fame among the godly, and left example worthy of imitation to others of his calling." That such deployments of the idea of Sidney are very like the theory of poetry that he himself proposed was noticed by Fulke Greville, who writes that Sidney's life "did (by way of example) far exceed the pictures of it in any moral precepts."[80] But, of course, although the theory suggests that Sidney's life will do this spontaneously, of itself, actually it must be scripted to produce the desired effect—as Greville was scripting it. Description creates the effect it pretends to reveal. In Ben Jonson's "To Penshurst,"

Sidney appears rather obliquely as a guarantor of the quality of the woodlands—

> That taller tree, which of a nut was set,
> At his great birth, where all the Muses met.[81]

It is perhaps surprising that he has no larger role; perhaps he has to remain significantly on the margin (in the woods outside the house) because as a writer who was also a nobleman he threatens to disrupt the poem's ethos of mutual deference between professional authorship and social power.

And so through the centuries, for other perspectives. Shelley coopted Sidney as one of the "inheritors of unfulfilled renown" who welcome Adonais to his "winged throne":

> Sidney, as he fought
> And as he fell and as he lived and loved
> Sublimely mild, a Spirit without spot.

Some Shelleyan self-justification—the mild, spotless lover—seems to have crept into this romantically ardent, yet ethereal, Sidney. For the twentieth century, the combination of poet and action-man has seemed to typify the complete English gentleman; Yeats thought of Major Robert Gregory as "Our Sidney and our perfect man."[82] With such a pedigree one might justifiably inherit large estates and fly around in airplanes trying to kill people. Sir Arthur Quiller-Couch (knighted for his services to literature, the Cornwall education committee, and the Liberal Party) offered Sir Philip to his students at Cambridge as an image of the gentleman his university aspired to produce. He describes him as a "perfect young knight," accomplished in both literary sensibility and "bodily games"—"perhaps no Englishman ever lived more graciously or, having used life, made a better end." Sir Arthur chose to print the version of his lecture delivered in February 1913, which related Sir Philip to Captain Robert Scott's Antarctic expedition: "But you have seen this morning's newspaper: you have read of Captain Scott and his comrades, and in particular of the death of Captain Oates; and you know that the breed of Sidney is not extinct. Gentlemen, let us keep our language noble: for we still have heroes to commemorate!"[83] (The appeal to "gentlemen" was Quiller-Couch's customary way of refusing to recognize that most of his students were women.)

John Buxton, too good a scholar to ignore Sidney's earnest protestant commitment, finds it not quite what one expects of a modern
English gentleman and sets it discreetly to one side:

> For himself, the hard clarity of Calvin's logic suited him, as did a
> similar quality in the mind of Ramus; but in poetry he never made
> the mistake that so many Puritans make, of emphasising the *utile,* the
> propaganda, at the expense of the *dulce,* the delight. . . . Sidney was
> much too civilised a man to fall into the ancient heresy of demand-
> ing that poetry should be "socially engaged," of insisting that the
> poet should accept his readers' dogmas and prejudices.[84]

Buxton's own "dogmas and prejudices" lead him to recruit Sidney
to his own viewpoint—which is then naturalized (these engaged fellows push their prejudices, whereas civilized chaps just see the world
as it is). Even Sidney's religion is aestheticized: "Calvin's logic suited
him." More recent criticism disguises its politics more thoroughly as
aesthetics, typically constructing "a totality without struggle and historical movement."[85] In such a perspective, Sidney's texts become
ideal, harmonious icons that both represent and move the reader
towards a reflective, disengaged stasis that aspires to leave the world
as it finds it. D. H. Craig sees that Sidney in the *Defence* "has drawn
on traditions that are at odds with each other," but finds them nevertheless resolved in "the humanist spirit of flexibility and clear-sighted
purposefulness"; Martin N. Raitiere finds the *Defence* "transcending
these antinomies and gathering the entire oration into the brilliantly
focussed work of art we always knew it was."[86] We still have heroes
to commemorate.

My account of the ideological maneuvering of Sidney and his admirers is not meant as a complacent attack on our benighted, be-
knighted, forebears; but it aims to see the *Defence* as, not an accomplished selection from current commonplaces (for who would bother
to write that?), but a purposeful intervention at a particular cultural
and political conjuncture—like Wordsworth's Preface to *Lyrical Ballads* or Eliot's "Tradition and the Individual Talent." The *Defence* is
still an intriguing text, and if it discloses with particular sharpness
the irreconcilability of certain serious questions, that is because Sidney
has assayed a uniquely ambitious, high-risk thesis. And it still has
resonances today. "Whatsoever the philosopher saith should be done,"
Sidney says, the poet "giveth a perfect picture of it in someone by
whom he presupposeth it was done" (*Defence,* p. 85). "A building
team leader, a collective-farm chairman, a railway worker, an army
officer, a pilot, or an eminent scientist . . . in each of them the reader

or the viewer sees his own thoughts and feelings, and the embodiment of the finest qualities of the Soviet character." Although it is rarely admitted, mainstream Anglo–U.S. literary criticism has followed a variant of this strategy. Authors and texts have been *interpreted* so as to construct pictures that bespeak approved-of values (though of course not so straightforwardly as is envisaged by Sidney and Brezhnev). And the authority of art and literature (partly freed from religion) has allowed critics to imply that they are producing, not a historically located preference, but a universal perception of the human.

It is not a good way to get a critical culture. Spenser's Grill, dubbed bestial for not welcoming the intense authoritarian regime of commissar Guyon, was right to resist being magicked into the approved ideal image—"from hoggish form . . . to natural." For what is more coercive, more ideological, than the demand to conform to an absolute idea of the natural? We would do better with the procedure Sidney himself adopts briefly with the pagan gods—acknowledging and exploring historical and political difference and remaining alert to the danger of cooption. Let Grill be Grill.

9 Tragedy, God, and Writing

Hamlet, Faustus, Tamburlaine

TENNIS BALLS

"It is impossible to understand the concrete utterance without accustoming oneself to its values, without understanding the orientation of its evaluations in the ideological environment": so Mikhail Bakhtin.[1] My case on protestantism is not that writers were all Calvinists. Rather, this orthodoxy hugely influenced the ideological field within which they produced diverse relations—of incorporation, conformity, negotiation, disjunction, subversion, and opposition—between religious orthodoxy and other, divergent ideological formations. Theater may well have been at times a radical medium (and at other times not; there is no reason to expect stage writing, or any genre of it, to be harmonious in outlook).[2] The church perhaps encouraged dissident tendencies in drama by forbidding it to deal with religious matters: theater was driven into the arms of secularism, which was just about ready to receive it. And although the censor could delete "See, see where Christ's blood streams in the firmament" from Marlowe's *Faustus,* he could not so easily assess the general tendency of the action.

I argued in the previous chapter that parts of the classical corpus were authoritative yet potentially subversive. Seneca was the principal model for tragedy; he was taught in schools and universities, and his presence was consolidated by the collection of translations of his plays published as *Seneca His Tenne Tragedies* by Thomas Newton in 1581. Seneca's plays seem designed for recitation and quite unlike the busy plots of the popular theater; their biggest influence was on closet dramas written in and for the Inns of Court and universities. However, the academic and popular traditions were not, initially, altogether separate. *Gorboduc* (1561), *Tancred and Gismund* (1568), and *The Misfortunes of Arthur* (1587–88) were played in the Inns and before the queen, but influenced popular theater; the French Senecan Robert Garnier was translated by both Thomas Kyd and the Countess of Pembroke (the former's *Cornelia* was printed in 1594, the latter's *Antonius* in 1592). G. K. Hunter disputes Seneca's importance on thematic grounds—because he believes that early modern drama is distinguished by a strong assertion of "the redeeming feature of a tragic existence: the gratuitous loyalties, the constancy under pressure, the renewed faith."[3] And this he does not find in Seneca. But this is to prejudge the issue; not all commentators on early modern plays have discerned such faith. Also, Hunter scarcely considers the Stoic motif in Senecan writings—I think because it might offer a more reasonable challenge to Christianity. However, as T. S. Eliot pointed out, Seneca's significance is indicated by the frequency with which early modern tragedies quote him for moral reflection.[4]

To some extent, Seneca's moral and philosophical writings could be reworked for Christianity. "If you read him thinking of him as a pagan, then he appears to have written like a Christian; but if you read him as a Christian then he appears to have written like a pagan," Erasmus remarked.[5] But the attitudes in Seneca's plays were an embarrassment. They represent the supernatural as fairy-tale spookiness, allow terrible violence by such as Atreus and Medea to go unpunished, offer to validate Stoic ethics entirely on rationalist grounds, and show humankind and the universe to be devoid of transcendent purpose. Thomas Newton felt it necessary to deny that they tend "sometime to the praise of ambition, sometime to the maintenance of cruelty, now and then to the approbation of incontinency, and here and there to the ratification of tyranny." John Studley even introduced his translation of *Medea* with the claim that it is "a small pearl of the peerless poet and most Christian ethnic Seneca, wherein no glutting but sweet delectation is offered unto the mind that doth hunger after virtue."[6] Philip Sidney worked harder at rendering Senecan tragedy acceptable. He said it is the form "that openeth the greatest wounds, and showeth forth the ulcers that are covered with tissue; that maketh kings fear to be tyrants, and tyrants manifest their tyrannical humours; that, with stirring the affects of admiration and commiseration, teacheth the uncertainty of this world, and upon how weak foundations gilden roofs are builded."[7] Thus slanted, a Senecan action might allow a broadly Christian moral.

Fulke Greville, writing later, with considerably more modern tragedies in view, demystified the issue by abandoning the idealist attempt
to see tragedy as a unitary category beyond history: he distinguishes
ancient and modern tragedy. The former would certainly include
Seneca's plays—it exemplifies "the disastrous miseries of man's life,
where order, laws, doctrine and authority are unable to protect in-
nocency from the exorbitant wickedness of power, and so, out of that
melancholy vision, stir horror, or murmur against divine providence."
Modern tragedy, conversely, is Christian, Greville says: it seeks "to
point out God's revenging aspect upon every particular sin, to the
despair or confusion of mortality."[8] In this view, modern tragedy
retains the Senecan illustration of presumption and destructiveness
in worldly affairs while asserting also the overarching control of
providence.

There was, then, a sufficient protestant theory of tragedy; so, as
recent commentators have remarked, reformers did not have to reject
drama as in principle irreligious. John Bale was altogether ready to
use it for protestant polemic in *The Comedy of John the Baptist, The
Tragedy of God's Promises to Men,* and *King Johan* (all written in 1538—
the last alludes to Henry VIII as a reforming monarch). Puritan attacks
on the stage began with the public, commercial theater; the question,
in the main, was not whether drama was irreligious as such, but
whether such a *disorderly and disreputable institution* could be tolerated
in the light of the high demands made by the protestant god. Phillip
Stubbes exclaimed in *The Anatomie of Abuses* (1583): "Oh blasphemy
intolerable! Are filthy plays and bawdy enterludes comparable to the
word of God, the food of life, and life itself?"[9] Nor need we assume
that the dire events and despairing attitudes in tragedies were inevitably in conflict with protestantism. Calvin did not hesitate to confront and appropriate what we might think of as a tragic universe:

> Various diseases ever and anon attack us: at one time pestilence
> rages; at another we are involved in all the calamities of war. Frost
> and hail, destroying the promise of the year, cause sterility, which re-
> duces us to penury; wife, parents, children, relatives, are carried off
> by death; our house is destroyed by fire. These are the events which
> make men curse their life, detest the day of their birth, execrate the
> light of heaven, even censure God, and (as they are eloquent in blas-
> phemy) charge him with cruelty and injustice.
>
> (*Institutes* 3.7.10)

Calvin is well aware that such a vision had inspired pagan tragedians:
"I confess, indeed, that a most accurate opinion was formed by those

who thought, that the best thing was not to be born, the next best to die early" (3.9.4). But in his view they could not pass beyond this perception because they lacked the Christian revelation, which shows that "the hand of God is the ruler and arbiter of the fortunes of all, and, instead of rushing on with thoughtless violence, dispenses good and evil with perfect regularity" (3.7.10). The whole achievement of faith is to assert providence in the face of an apparently violent and arbitrary universe.

Yet the topic could not so easily be tidied away. The value of Senecan tragedy, despite assertions to the contrary, was that it facilitated engagements with religious unorthodoxy.[10] Plays such as *King Lear* and *The White Devil* seem to advance, yet at the same time to problematize, the protestant god. The violent, irrational, and yet fateful world they depict seems like the providential dispensation Calvin envisages, but with a scandalous excess. When Marlowe's Ferneze concludes *The Jew of Malta* by proclaiming "Now march away; and let due praise be given, / Neither to Fate nor Fortune, but to Heaven," he is invoking precisely the alternatives that protestantism was striving to suppress.[11] In Kyd's *Spanish Tragedy* (c. 1586), Revenge, in the manner of Tantalus and Megaera in Seneca's *Thyestes,* sponsors the action. Nonetheless, much of the play is phrased in specifically Christian terms. The two languages clash when Hieronimo assumes heavenly collaboration in revenging his son:

Why, then I see that heaven applies our drift,
And all the saints do sit soliciting
For vengeance on those cursed murderers.[12]

The play ends with a distribution of the characters in partly pagan and partly Christian terms: Hieronimo's friends will consort together happily in Proserpina's underworld, while his enemies, Revenge promises, will be punished in "deepest hell, / Where none but Furies, bugs, and tortures dwell" (4.5.27–28). This instance may be parody or happy confusion; in either event there is a break beyond—which is yet dependent upon—the terms of contemporary orthodoxy.

An interaction between protestant and Senecan views may be briefly illustrated by divergent deployments of the tennis balls trope. In the *Institutes,* Calvin acknowledges: "Occasionally as the causes of events are concealed, the thought is apt to rise, that human affairs are whirled about by the blind impulse of Fortune, or our carnal nature inclines us to speak as if God were amusing himself by tossing men up and down like balls" (1.17.1). The French is *pelottes,* and Thomas Norton's translation of 1561 has "toss them like tennis balls." The protestant move was to disallow such a sentiment, as Sidney does by the way he frames it in the *Arcadia:* "The chief man they considered was Euarchus, whom the strange and secret working of justice had brought to be the judge over them. In such a shadow or rather pit of darkness the wormish mankind lives, that neither they know how to forsee nor what to fear, and are but like tennis balls, tossed by the racket of the higher powers."[13] In the manner of Calvin and his own Christianizing idea of tragedy, Sidney contains the tennis balls idea by relating it to "the strange and secret working of justice." However, in *The Duchess of Malfi,* providential care is far more difficult to discern. It seems that something like divine purpose may after all be working itself out when Bosola is inspired by the duchess's death to work for Antonio's safety and revenge, but then Bosola kills Antonio by mistake:

> Antonio!
> The man I would have sav'd 'bove mine own life!
> We are merely the stars' tennis-balls, struck and banded
> Which way please them.

At the end of the play Bosola finds no consolation, and says so with a reminiscence of *Arcadia*'s "shadow or rather pit of darkness":

> O this gloomy world!
> In what a shadow, or deep pit of darkness,
> Doth womanish and fearful mankind live?[14]

Bosola, and Webster insofar as he allows the action of the play to endorse Bosola, is voicing just that view of life that Calvin and Sidney tried to repudiate; he takes up the protestant claim that even disastrous events are ordered by God, and shows the disasters but not the order.

A play such as *The Duchess of Malfi* suggests that the protestant god was not persuasive to all the people all the time. "Who will be able to bring himself to love God with all his heart when he created hell seething with eternal torments in order to punish his own misdeeds in his victims as though he took delight in human torments?" Erasmus asked.[15] The answer I suggested in chapter 7 is that the reprobate are created different, like cattle, and hence it is reasonable that their life chances should be different. However, not everyone today believes it right that cattle should be treated as they are, and not everyone in early modern England thought it fair that the doctrine of election allowed the reprobate no opportunity to avoid condemnation.

In 1587 Christopher Fetherstone's translation of William Lawne's *Abridgement* of Calvin's *Institutes of the Christian Religion* (1583) was published. This is, in fact, not a précis but a dialogue in which objections to the *Institutes* are raised and answered in Calvinist terms. Predestination is evidently an issue. The objector says it is "a fearful decree to inwrap so many nations together with their children being but infants, in eternal death, by the fall of Adam, without redemption, and that because it pleased God." The answer privileges the rigor of logic over the luxury of fellow-feeling (and is not, I think, easy to evade): "I grant: and yet no man can deny but that God knew before what end man should have before he created him." It is explained:

> All are guilty: but the mercy of God relieveth and succoureth certain.
> *Objection.* Let it succour all.
> *Answer.* It is meet that by punishing he likewise show himself to be a just judge.[16]

It is important to keep in mind that Calvin, Lawne, and many others thought this an adequate reply. In the punitive outlook of many people in the sixteenth century, God was inseparable from justice, and justice from punishment. Yet the question was raised; concepts of good and justice were under contest. For some people Lawne's dialogue satisfactorily established a deity that others wanted to repudiate. The conflict manifests a society agitated by an ideological faultline.

The disturbance that protestant orthodoxy might produce is evident when Robert Burton, in *The Anatomy of Melancholy,* discusses doubt about election as a cause of despair: "The more they search and read scriptures, or divine treatises, the more they puzzle themselves, as a bird in a net, the more they are entangled and precipitated into this preposterous gulf." The trouble, Burton says, is texts such as "Many are called, but few are chosen": "This grinds their souls; how shall they discern they are not reprobates?"[17] Against this, with the avowed intention of comforting the anxious, Burton places other texts: "God will that all men be saved, and come to the knowedge of the truth," Saint Paul writes.[18] But scriptural authority then appears in conflict with itself, as Burton notes with some unease: "Now there cannot be contradictory wills in God; he will have all saved, and not all; how can this stand together?" Our best chance, he suggests, is to bet on the favorable texts: we should "be secure then, believe, trust in him, hope well, and be saved" (pp. 420–21). *Yet* . . , —and at this point the characteristic indeterminacy of Burton's writing seems to match the characteristic instability of protestant doctrine—the problem does not go away. "This furious curiosity, needless speculation, fruitless meditation about election, reprobation, free will, grace, such places of scripture preposterously conceived, torment still," Burton says, "and crucify the souls of too many, and set all the world together by the ears." So much so that an alternative theology has appeared:

> To mitigate those divine aphorisms (though in another extreme some), our late [i.e., recent] Arminians have revived that plausible doctrine of universal grace, which many fathers, our late Lutherans and modern papists do still maintain, that we have free will of ourselves, and that grace is common to all that will believe. Some again, though less orthodoxical, will have a far greater part saved than shall be damned (as Caelius Secundus stiffly maintains in his book *De amplitudine regni coelestis,* or some impostor under his name).
>
> (p. 421)

It is not at first clear what the status is of Arminian ideas in this passage. Only "some" are "extreme"; universal grace is "plausible" (meaning either "specious" or "agreeable")—it seems to have a lot of support. Burton goes on to expound Caelius at some length, pointing out that he too has juxtaposed Pelagian and predestinarian biblical texts, and that others also have said that pagans might be saved. So Burton arrives eventually at Caelius's vivid question: "How can he be merciful that shall condemn any creature to eternal unspeakable punishment, for one small temporary fault, all posterity, so many myriads for one and another man's [i.e., Adam's] offence?" (p. 423). It all seems at least open to discussion; but then, abruptly, Burton beats a total retreat: "These absurd paradoxes are exploded by our Church, we teach otherwise." And he restates as definitely as he can the orthodox belief in God's immutable, eternal, just decree whereby "all are invited, but only the elect apprehended" (p. 424). Surely we have Burton in a mood of vacillation. He is stirred by the problems but unwilling to repudiate the prevailing doctrine. The ensuing passage is altogether equivocal: Burton says he might have written more had not the Laudian articles of 1633 forbidden discussion in order to "avoid factions and altercations"; and quotes Erasmus (who of course had argued for free will) to the effect that the prevailing laws should be observed rather than "spread suspicions of the public authority."

That secular authority might come into question was the wider anxiety. The thought, often associated with Marlowe, that "the first beginning of religion was only to keep men in awe" was commonplace enough. Calvin, with typical ingenuity, acknowledges "that designing men have introduced a vast number of fictions into religion, with the view of inspiring the population with reverence or striking them with terror, and thereby rendering them more obsequious." But this, of course, is the other theologians—Calvin has the genuine article (he holds that rulers, even bad ones, exercise "an authority which God has sanctioned by the surest edicts").[19] However, the sheer dependence of Calvinism upon subservience to established authority was a weakness. Lawne makes a characteristic move when, pressed on election and reprobation, he falls back on this: "It is a point of bold wickedness even so much as to inquire the causes of God's will" (p. 222). The thought is from Saint Paul (Rom. 9:20), echoing Elihu's rebuke to Job (33:13), and was the cut-off point for Donne also: "But who am I, that dare dispute with thee / Oh God?" (Holy Sonnet 9).

Hobbes was to expose just these weaknesses. He remarks that the question of how God distributes prosperity and adversity was disputed by the ancients, and "hath shaken the faith, not only of the vulgar, but of philosophers, and what is more, of the saints, concerning divine providence." Hobbes observes that Job suffered notwithstanding his righteousness, and that God justified such affliction with "arguments drawn from his power"—such as "Where wast thou when I laid the foundations of the earth?"[20] On such evidence, God's claim rests not on his love but on his power—and that, Hobbes concludes, is the only logical kind of deity. And so with civil authority, which religion was invoked to legitimate: if God is not good, only powerful, how could the king be better? Calvinism pointed the way to this conclusion, which deprived both the deity and monarchs of the justification of providential concern for their subjects.

I wish to discuss particularly three plays that focus the kinds of ideological complexity I have been noting—the juxtaposing of overlapping but competing discourses, the foregrounding of contradictions within Christianity, and the relation of such disruptions to the legitimizing of secular authority. Lastly, I address the scope of writing and politics in the early modern state. There are some dangers here; to be sure, plays are not prose tracts. Nevertheless, they are sited, necessarily though not passively, on the ideological terrain that constitutes the contemporary cultural possibilities. Prose tracts, as we have seen, are not straightforward either, but play texts do involve the further indeterminacy of performance. However, I have tried not so much to offer interpretations (though it is hard to avoid writing as if that were the goal) as to map the field within which certain plays might have made certain kinds of sense. All texts, I have already said, cannot but produce meaning in excess of any ideological project; this may be specially true of plays, and specially in respect of religious ideas and attitudes in early modern England.

HAMLET'S SPECIAL PROVIDENCE

> We defy augury. There is a special providence in the fall of a sparrow. If it be now, 'tis not to come; if it be not to come, it will be now; if it be not now, yet it will come. The readiness is all. Since no man, of aught he leaves, knows aught, what is't to leave betimes? Let be.
>
> (*Hamlet* 5.2.215–20)[21]

> [God is] a Governor and Preserver, and that, not by producing a kind of general motion in the machine of the globe as well as in each of its parts, but by a special Providence sustaining, cherishing, superintending, all the things which he has made, to the very minutest, even to a sparrow.
>
> (Calvin, *Institutes* 1.16.1)

> Fate guides us, and it was settled at the first hour of birth what length of time remains for each. Cause is linked with cause, and all public and private issues are directed by a long sequence of events. Therefore everything should be endured with fortitude, since things do not, as we suppose, simply happen—they all come.
>
> (Seneca, *De providentia* 5.7)[22]

Seneca and Calvin both seem relevant when Hamlet says, "There is a special providence in the fall of a sparrow." Indeed, rival views of the play have amounted to glosses on their divergent implications for its interpretation. A. C. Bradley recognizes Hamlet's phrasing as Christian but regards its tone and the play generally as pagan in tendency: Hamlet expresses "that kind of religious resignation which, however beautiful in one aspect, really deserves the name of fatalism rather than that of faith in Providence, because it is not united to any determination to do what is believed to be the will of Providence."[23] Roland Mushat Frye holds that these lines show Hamlet "relying upon an unmistakably Christian providence" and hence achieving true faith.[24] Roy W. Battenhouse agrees with Frye that the play has a Christian tendency, but also with Bradley that Hamlet's own attitude is un-Christian: "A biblical echo, the sparrow reference, when found in this upside-down context, alerts us to the tragic parody in Hamlet's version of readiness."[25] So Hamlet is either a pagan in a pagan play, a good Christian in a Christian play, or a reprobate in a Christian play.

A Senecan frame of reference seems appropriate in the first four acts of *Hamlet*, for the dialogue puts Stoic tranquility of mind firmly on the agenda. This is more the Seneca of the *Moral Essays*—the proponent of a calm, rationalist worldview that the plays invoke but scarcely validate. For Hamlet, Stoicism is an ideal he hopes to see achieved. He values Horatio because he perceives in him "a man that Fortune's buffets and rewards / Hast ta'en with equal thanks; . . . not a pipe for Fortune's finger / To sound what stop she please . . . not passion's slave" (3.2.67–72). By subduing his emotions, Horatio is said to free himself from the effects of fortune and become the Stoics' wise and happy man. If Hamlet could do that then revenge might not be a problem. The principle of revenge was one issue between Stoicism and protestantism—it is raised in the *Spanish Tragedy,* where the Christian text "Vindicta mihi!" is juxtaposed with the Senecan injunction "Per scelus semper tutum est sceleribus iter: / Strike, and strike home, where wrong is offer'd thee."[26] Typically, in the provocative manner I have already observed in Kyd's play, Hieronimo chooses Seneca rather than the Bible. However, Hamlet's problem seems prior to such considerations: it is the achievement of a state of mind where he can act purposively at all, and especially upon the Ghost's allegations. Seneca declares: "The good man will perform his duties undisturbed and unafraid; and he will in such a way do all that is worthy of a good man as to do nothing that is unworthy of a man. My father is being murdered—I will defend him; he is slain—I will avenge him, not because I grieve, but because it is my duty."[27] This is the kind of mood Claudius recommends to Hamlet in respect of his grief for his father, but not what he achieves. His baiting of Claudius is all improvisation and he cannot follow it through; when he believes he has the evidence he has sought, he allows himself to be shipped to England.

It is quite appropriate, therefore, that Hamlet presents himself as a failed Stoic in his first exchange with Rosencrantz and Guildenstern. The dialogue here is in a mode of light-hearted philosophical banter (such as might have occurred when they were students), but the sub-text is maneuvering to discover each other's purposes. Rosencrantz denies that Denmark is a prison; Hamlet replies, "Why, then 'tis none to you; for there is nothing either good or bad but thinking makes it so" (2.2.249–50). This characteristically Stoic notion usually has a contrary import—that one can be happy and free if the mind chooses. So Rosencrantz should be amused, but he is determined to turn the discussion to ambition. Hamlet's response is more earnest: "O God, I could be bounded in a nutshell and count myself a king of infinite space—were it not that I have bad dreams" (2.2.254–56). This also sustains a Senecan framework—the Chorus in *Thyestes* says: "It is the mind that only makes a king. . . . A king he is that feareth nought at all. / Each man himself this kingdom gives at hand."[28] It is Stoic reluctance to live with the mind in chains that puts suicide on the agenda. Horatio, wanting to die with Hamlet, terms himself "more an antique Roman than a Dane" (5.2.346). To Seneca, it is indeed a "question" whether it is nobler in the mind to suffer or to make a dignified exit; death is always a way of escaping intolerable pressure, yet it is base to flinch: "The brave and wise man should not beat a hasty retreat from life."[29] Seneca's point is that it is superstitious and irrational to fear death or what might follow it, but just such anxieties preoccupy Hamlet, who again falls short of Stoic detachment.

For Seneca, the man who achieves Stoic mastery is godlike: "The wise man is next-door neighbour to the gods and like a god in all save his mortality. As he struggles and presses on towards those things that are lofty, well-ordered, undaunted, that flow on with even and harmonious current, that are untroubled, kindly, adapted to the public good, beneficial both to himself and to others, the wise man will covet nothing low, will never repine."[30] Such presumption, of course, ran precisely counter to the protestant doctrine of human wretchedness. Henry Smith complained that the proud man "maketh himself equal with God, because he doth all without God, and craves no help of him."[31] But Hamlet is perplexed and disillusioned at the failure of the Stoic ideal in others and himself. Man is said to be "in apprehension how like a god: the beauty of the world, the paragon of animals—and yet, to me, what is this quintessence of dust?" (2.2.306–8). Hamlet would like to believe that human reason is a godlike instrument by which people may act in the world:

> Sure he that made us with such large discourse,
> Looking before and after, gave us not
> That capability and godlike reason
> To fust in us unus'd.
>
> (4.4.36–39)

At issue here is optimistic humanism—the strand in Renaissance thought that exalted human capacity to achieve, through the exercise of rational powers, a moral stature that the incautious termed godlike. Neoplatonists had not even Seneca's ambivalence. "The soul desires, endeavors, and begins to become God, and makes progress every day. . . . Hence our soul will some time be able to become in a sense all things; and even to become a god," Ficino enthused.[32] Such an aspiration is at stake when Ophelia laments "that noble and most sovereign reason / Like sweet bells jangled out of tune and harsh"

(3.1.159–60.) In the play this is not Hamlet's failure alone. In some ways he contrasts with the other young men, but Laertes is no more successful in establishing and pursuing rational purposes (he kills Hamlet but wishes he had not), and Fortinbras is elected king of Denmark (presumably) not because of the schemes of his father and himself but by default and by arriving at the right time. Even Horatio has to be dissuaded from suicide. At this point, *Hamlet* seems Calvinist rather than Senecan. Calvin termed "absurd" the Stoic hero "who, divested of humanity, was affected in the same way by adversity and prosperity, grief and joy; or rather, like a stone, was not affected by anything" (*Institutes* 3.8.9). Joseph Hall seems almost to take up Hamlet's speech:

> There is nothing more wretched than a mere man. We may brag what we will; how noble a creature man is above all the rest; how he is the lord of the world, a world within himself, the mirror of majesty, the visible model of his Maker; but let me tell you, if we be but men, it had been a thousand times better for us to have been the worst of beasts.[33]

According to such an analysis, the failure of the Stoic ideal in *Hamlet* should cause no surprise.

The plausibility of the godlike Stoic hero is questioned also in John Marston's Antonio plays, which satirize positions like those taken up by characters in *Hamlet*. In *Antonio and Mellida,* Andrugio affects indifference to the loss of his kingdom but falls at once into a rage when it is mentioned: "Name not the Genoese; that very word / Unkings me quite, makes me vile passion's slave."[34] In *Antonio's Revenge,* Pandulpho for many scenes remains tranquil about the murder of his son, but suddenly declares, "Man will break out, despite philosophy. . . . I spake more than a god, / Yet am less than a man."[35] And in *The Scourge of Villainy* 4, Marston exclaims:

> Peace *Seneca,* thou belchest blasphemy.
> *To live from God, but to live happily*
> (I hear thee boast) *from thy Philosophy,*
> *And from thy self,* O raving lunacy![36]

Senecan attitudes were deeply incoherent. Miriam T. Griffin writes of "the schizophrenia endemic in Stoic philosophy, with its vision of the *sapiens* and its code of behaviour for the *imperfectus.*"[37] There was therefore a double dispute with protestantism. While the optimistic estimate of Man contradicts the doctrine of the "fall," Senecan pessimism about how the world goes contradicts the doctrine of providence. It is against Stoic fate or fortune that Calvin is arguing when he speaks of special providence and the fall of a sparrow—both in the quotation with which I began this section and during the supporting argument:

> The Christian . . . will have no doubt that a special providence is awake for his preservation, and will not suffer anything to happen that will not turn to his good and safety. . . . Hence, our Saviour, after declaring that even a sparrow falls not to the ground without the will of his Father, immediately makes the application, that being more valuable than many sparrows, we ought to consider that God provides more carefully for us.
>
> (*Institutes* 1.17.6)

In Calvin's Latin the words are usually *singularis providentia*; his French has alternately *la providence singulière* and *la providence spéciale*; the translation by Thomas Norton (1561) has both "singular providence" and "special providence." Jesus' remark about the sparrow was a favorite for arguing God's beneficent control of his creation. For instance, Arthur Golding repudiated both chance and natural causes when considering the earthquake of 1580: "Know we not (after so long hearing and pretelling of the Gospel) that a sparrow lighteth not on the ground without God's providence?"[38] Conversely, Erasmus, trying to establish free will against Luther, was obliged to take Jesus' saying as "hyperbole" (this latter tactic would wreak havoc if applied generally to the Bible).[39]

Upon his return from England, Hamlet seems to have abandoned his Stoic aspirations and become a believer in providence. Now sermon tags roll off his tongue—"There's a divinity that shapes our ends, / Rough-hew them how we will"; "even in that was heaven ordinant" (i.e., "directing, controlling": 5.2.10–11, 48); "There is a special providence in the fall of a sparrow." This is very strong phrasing. In fact, in the first quarto Hamlet says, "theres a predestiuate prouidence in the fall of a sparrow." Even if that is no more than a faulty memorial reconstruction, it shows how one well-placed contemporary read the prince's thought: it is Calvinist.

Hamlet seems to have changed. To say this is to *expect* (but not necessarily to find) some continuity in his character. I argued in chapter 3 that many dramatis personae in Shakespearean plays are written, at least for some of the time, in ways that suggest that they have continuous subjectivities. This is not to suppose, in a Bradleyan or essentialist-humanist manner, that these dramatic personae are unified subjects, or independent of the multiple discursive practices of the culture. Indeed, I have been trying to locate Hamlet at the intersection point of Senecan and Calvinist discourses, and it is in their terms that I perceive a break upon his return from England. (I do not say that these are the only relevant discourses; but they were powerful enabling systems through which, in some measure, subjectivities were constructed.) It is recognizing cues that some continuity in the character of Hamlet is to be expected that makes it possible to allege a break (as, for instance, Francis Barker does).[40]

At such a breaking point, readers and audiences may either declare the play incoherent or attempt to intuit an appropriate linking factor. If we do the former, we may either complain about artistic quality (as did T. S. Eliot) or triumphantly discover once more (with some poststructuralists) the twin instabilities of subjectivity and textuality. Wishing to push further than either of these, I try instead to envisage a linking factor through which an audience might (having in mind Hamlet's changed mode of utterance and the play so far) plausibly renew the sense of Hamlet as a continuous subjectivity. This, again, sounds Bradleyan but is in fact only a specially determined application of the process through which any story is understood. The mistake would be to efface the work required, and to imagine that one is uncovering the inner truth of Hamlet's character. I am observing that, as well as producing a breaking point, the text does suggest at least one plausible link.

This is Hamlet's awareness, which is in the dialogue, of the extraordinary turns events have taken—the appearance of the Ghost when Claudius seemed secure, the arrival of the Players prompting the test of the king, Hamlet's inspired discovery on the boat of the plot against his life, and then his amazing delivery from the pirates. The latter is so improbable, and unnecessary to the plot, as to suggest the specially intricate quality of divine intervention wherein even a sparrow's death is purposive. It is when explaining how he found Claudius's letter and changed it that Hamlet attributes events to "a divinity that shapes our ends"; and when describing how he was able to seal the altered instructions that he says heaven was "ordinant." The sequence seems to require the providential explanation; so the prince recognizes the folly and pretension of humanistic aspiration and the controlling power of God.

For so much strenuous narration to be necessary, and with such sudden consequences for character and theme, the play must be laboring at a particularly awkward ideological moment. The strain, it appears, is getting Hamlet to the point where he can express belief in a special providence. This could produce a Christian moral such as Sidney might have approved. The "carnal, bloody, and unnatural acts" and "purposes mistook / Fall'n on th'inventors' heads" (5.2.386, 389–90) are quite compatible with a violent and punitive deity. In Calvin's view, both believers and the wicked must expect such afflictions (for the former, "it is not properly punishment or vengeance, but correction and admonition"; for the latter, God is "confounding, scattering, and annihilating" his enemies [*Institutes* 3.4.31]). So we may envisage an Elizabethan audience not finding *Hamlet* sad and bleak (or even strangely uplifting in its sense of wasted human potential), but being satisfied by the working out of events in the providential manner described in the sermons they had heard. The same might be true of other tragedies. Yet all texts, I have said, produce meaning in excess of any ostensible ideological project. In *Hamlet* the difficulties emanate from the concept of special providence.

The problem, as in respect of Stoic theory earlier, is focused by Hamlet's state of mind. For as Bradley said, the tone and implication of the sparrow speech, however Christian its phrasing, are fatalistic. Of course, predestination means that individual actions can make no difference, but protestant sermonizers, always afraid of antinomianism, urged all the more that the believer should show his or her delight in God's will by cooperating as far and as eagerly as possible. As Henry Bullinger put it, though "men's affairs and state are wholly governed by God's providence, so yet that they must not therefore sit (as we say) with their hands in their bosoms idly, and neglect good means."[41] Hamlet believes that providence wants Claudius removed, and that he should do it. He rehearses the king's manifold crimes and asks:

> is't not perfect conscience
> To quit him with this arm? And is't not to be damn'd
> To let this canker of our nature come
> In further evil?
>
> (5.2.67–70)

However, when he says, "The readiness is all," he means not for action but for death. He is not making a reverent general statement about the rightness of God's control of the world, but dismissing Horatio's very reasonable suspicion about the duel. He plays with Osric (this scene seems purposefully desultory), competes recklessly with Laertes, makes no plan against the king. The final killing occurs in a burst of passionate inspiration, and when Hamlet himself is, in effect, slain. He seems to have fallen into the fatalistic heresy of Lawne's objector, who is made to ask: "If God have assigned the point and very time of our death, we cannot escape it: and therefore it is vain to use any circumspection." The Calvinist answer is that "the Lord has furnished men with the arts of deliberation and caution, that they may employ them in subservience to his providence, in the preservation of their life."[42] Hamlet manifests the tendency of the objector: he sees no point, now, in bothering. He acknowledges divine determination, but without enthusiasm. At this point the play turns back upon itself, retrieving the Stoicism that it has seemed to dismiss, for the tone and context of the speech and Hamlet's subsequent inactivity are more in keeping with the quotation from Seneca's *De providentia* that I presented initially: "It was settled at the first hour of birth what length of time remains for each. . . . Therefore everything should be endured with fortitude, since things do not, as we suppose, simply happen— they all come." So Hamlet: "If it be now, 'tis not to come; if it be not to come, it will be now; if it be not now, yet it will come. The readiness is all. . . . Let be." Hamlet falls back upon the fatalism that often underlies the Stoic ideal of rational self-sufficiency.

There is no speech saying that Hamlet feels thus because he feels alienated from the protestant deity; probably that could have been said on a stage only by a manifest villain. But as members of an audience try to make sense of events in the play and Hamlet's responses to them, it may appear that the divine system revealed in the action is not as comfortable and delightful as protestants proclaimed. It makes Hamlet wonder and admire; temporarily, when he is sending Rosencrantz and Guildenstern to their deaths, it exhilarates him; but ultimately it does not command his respect. The issue in Stoicism, for Hamlet, is how the mind might free itself, for to him Denmark and the world are a prison. But protestantism offers no release from mental bondage, as William Perkins allows us to see in a revealing analogy:

> God hath watch over all men by a special providence. The master of a prison is known by this to have care over his prisoners; if he send keepers with them to watch them and to bring them home again in time convenient: and so God's care to man is manifest in this, that when he created man and placed him in the world, he gave him conscience to be his keeper, to follow him always at his heels, and to dog him (as we say) and to pry into his actions, and to bear witness of them all.[43]

The governor of the prison may be divine and may appoint his keepers with special providential care, but it is still a prison, and Hamlet cannot be made to co-operate.

As I will argue of Marlowe's *Faustus, Hamlet* exploits the shared ground, the embarrassing overlap, between protestantism and the doctrines it seeks to repudiate. Hamlet's slide into Senecan fatalism is accomplished in the very teeth of orthodoxy, for, as I have shown, it is actually while repudiating Stoic thought that Calvin refers to special providence and the sparrow. His particular anxiety was that a predestinating god might sound merely like fate—an impersonal force operating only a crude mode of justice, indifferent to mankind; "Those who cast obloquy on this doctrine [of special providence], calumniate it as the dogma of the Stoics concerning fate" (*Institutes* 1.16.8). And that might lead to detachment, alienation, irresponsibility, antinomianism, disregard for authority, free-thinking, disorder, social disintegration. It is with such thoughts that Faustus finds his way to conjuring, and that Despayre drives Redcrosse to the brink of suicide in the *Faerie Queene* (1.9.37–54). It is the story Calvin has to suppress, and hence his insistence on the sparrow and God's intimate and personal concern at every point. But members of an audience watching *Hamlet* may come to feel that this Christianity cannot separate itself satisfactorily from a Stoic paganism that claims no divine revelation and no divine beneficence; that insofar as the protestant deity is distinguished by an intricate determination of human affairs, it is intrusive and coercive; and that such a tyrannical deity need inspire no more than passive acquiescence.

READING FAUSTUS'S GOD

The Tragical History of Doctor Faustus has afforded a marvelous interpretive challenge to Christian humanists who feel they should discover Marlowe to be endorsing a nice, decent kind of god.[44] However, my argument thus far should suggest another plausible Christian reading. Elizabethan orthodoxy would make Faustus's damnation more challenging than most modern readers might expect, by denying that Faustus had a choice anyway: it would regard Faustus, not as damned because he makes a pact with the devil, but as making a pact with the devil because he is already damned. "Before the foundations of the world were laid," it says in the seventeenth of the Thirty-nine Articles, "he hath constantly decreed by his counsel secret to us, to deliver from curse and damnation those whom he hath chosen." And Faustus, an Elizabethan might infer from his blasphemous, dissolute, and finally desperate behavior, exemplifies the fate of the reprobate. The article continues: "So, for curious and carnal persons, lacking the Spirit of Christ, to have continually before their eyes the sentence of

God's predestination is a most dangerous downfall, whereby the devil doth thrust them either into desperation, or into wretchlessness of most unclean living, no less perilous than desperation." In Kyd's *The First Part of Hieronimo* (c. 1585), the villainous Lazarotto declares himself just such a person:

> Dare I? Ha! ha!
> I have no hope of everlasting height;
> My soul's a Moor, you know, salvation's white.
> What dare I not enact, then? Tush, he dies.[45]

That Faustus might be in such a condition is supported by Mephostophilis's claim:

> 'Twas I that, when thou were't i' the way to heaven,
> Damm'd up thy passage; when thou took'st the book
> To view the scriptures, then I turn'd the leaves
> And led thine eye.
>
> (5.2.86–89)

If Faustus was guided by Mephostophilis, the decision was God's. For protestant thought could not tolerate devils wandering round the world at whim: God does not just allow their activities, he contracts out tasks to them. They are "God's hang-men," King James wrote, "to execute such turns as he employs them in."[46] However, Calvin says, it is only the reprobate who are ultimately subject to them—God "does not allow Satan to have dominion over the souls of believers, but only gives over to his sway the impious and unbelieving, whom he deigns not to number among his flock" (*Institutes* 1.14.18). So Mephostophilis's intervention would be part of Faustus's punishment within the divine predetermination.

The issue is focused in Faustus's first speech when he juxtaposes two texts: "The reward of sin is death," and "If we say that we have no sin we deceive ourselves, and there is no truth in us." It appears that it has been arranged who shall sin and die; Faustus concludes:

> Why then, belike we must sin, and so consequently die.
> Ay, we must die an everlasting death.
> What doctrine call you this? *Che sera, sera.*
> What will be, shall be.
>
> (1.1.40–46)

Christians who wish usually manage to evade this discouraging thought. Douglas Cole says Faustus's texts are "glaring half-truths, for each of the propositions he cites from the Bible is drawn from contexts and passages which unite the helplessness of the sinner with the redeeming grace of God"; Cole's implication is that Faustus is so eager to damn himself that he disregards God's generous offers.[47] To be sure, "the wages of sin is death" continues: "but the gift of God is eternal life"; and the second quotation, about everyone sinning and dying, continues: "If we confess our sins, he is faithful and just to forgive us our sins, and to cleanse us from all unrighteousness." But Calvin uses the first text—all of it—to emphasize that salvation is entirely God's decision: the desert of all is death but some receive eternal life through "the gift of God" (*Institutes* 3.14.21). And Tyndale in his *Exposition of the First Epistle of St John* (1531) uses the second text to demonstrate that we have no say in the success of our confession: "our nature cannot but sin, if occasions be given, except that God of his especial grace keep us back: which pronity to sin is damnable sin in the law of God."[48] So God may indeed forgive us our sins if we repent, but some at least will be damned for sins to which they have, in their nature, a "pronity." Faustus's summary, "What will be, shall be," may be irreverent, but it is in the mainstream of Reformation thought. If he draws not comfort but blasphemy from his reading, that will perhaps be for the reason given by Tyndale in a rubric in the Prologue to the first edition of his *Exposition of . . . John*: "If God lighten not our hearts, we read the scripture in vain."[49]

If Faustus is damned from before the start (to pursue the hypothesis), what then of his efforts to repent? For modern readers and audiences who do not already know the story, there is a question: will he change or not? For Elizabethan orthodoxy the answer was the same again: repentance is not something for the individual to achieve, but a divine gift. "It is not in our powers to repent when we will. It is the Lord that giveth the gift, when, where, and to whom it pleaseth him," Phillip Stubbes declares.[50] So if Faustus does not have it, there is nothing he can do. Yet there are the injunctions of the Good Angel, which appear to represent, like the personifications in a morality play, a choice open to Faustus:

GOOD ANGEL: Faustus, repent; yet God will pity thee.

BAD ANGEL: Thou art a spirit [sc. devil]; God cannot pity thee.

FAUSTUS: Who buzzeth in mine ears I am a spirit?
Be I a devil, yet God may pity me;
Yea, God will pity me if I repent.

BAD ANGEL: Ay, but Faustus never shall repent.
Exeunt Angels.

FAUSTUS: My heart's so harden'd I cannot repent.
(2.2.12–18)

If Faustus's heart is hardened and he cannot repent, who has hardened it? This was a key question in the theology of election and reprobation. In Exodus (chapters 7–14) it is stated repeatedly that God hardens Pharoah's heart against the Israelites, so that he refuses to let them go despite divine smiting of the Egyptians with diverse plagues. This was taken as a paradigm of the way God treats the reprobate. Paul alludes to it when he confronts the question in the Epistle to the Romans: "Therefore hath he mercy on whom he will have mercy, and whom he will he hardeneth" (Rom. 9:18). Luther stressed this text, and Erasmus was obliged to admit that it appears to leave nothing to human choice.[51] For Calvin it was plain: "When God is said to visit in mercy or harden whom he will, men are reminded that they are not to seek for any cause beyond his will" (*Institutes* 3.22.11). Hence Donne's lines: "grace, if thou repent, thou canst not lack; / But who shall give thee that grace to begin?" (Holy Sonnet 4). And that is why Faustus can speak repentant words and it makes no difference. He actually calls upon Jesus: "Ah, Christ my saviour, my saviour, / Help to save distressed Faustus' soul." But the response is the entrance of Lucifer, Belzebub, and Mephostophilis: "Christ cannot save thy soul, for he is just," says Lucifer (2.2.83–85). Is this a devilish manipulation or a theological commonplace? It may be both—as Banquo says, instruments of darkness may tell us truths; it is the argument offered by Lawne's apologist for the *Institutes*.

Why then the appeals of the Good Angel? "What purpose, then, is served by exhortations?" Calvin asks himself. It is this: "As the wicked, with obstinate heart, despise them, they will be a testimony against them when they stand at the judgment-seat of God; nay, they even now strike and lash their consciences" (*Institutes* 2.5.5). On this argument, the role of the Good Angel is to tell Faustus what he ought to do but cannot, so that he will be unable to claim ignorance when God taxes him with his wickedness. This may well seem perverse to the modern reader, but is quite characteristic of the strategies by which the orthodox deity was said to maneuver himself into the right and humankind into the wrong. Perkins declares:

> Now the commandment of believing and applying the Gospel, is by God given to all within the Church; but not in the same manner to all. It is given to the Elect, that by believing they might indeed be saved; God inabling them to do that which he commands. To the rest, whom God in justice will refuse, the same commandment is given not for the same cause, but to another end, that they might see how they could not believe, and by this means be bereft of all excuse in the day of judgment.[52]

Such doctrine was preached from almost every pulpit.

Faustus is amenable at every point, I think, to a determined orthodox reading. Yet the play might do more to promote anxiety about such doctrine than to reinforce it. For although I have felt it necessary to argue for the Reformation reading, *Faustus* is in my view *entirely ambiguous*—altogether open to the more usual, modern, free-will reading. The theological implications of *Faustus* are radically and provocatively indeterminate.

A good deal might depend on which version is being used, for many of the exchanges added in the B text seem to sharpen the theological polarity. They include the lines where Lucifer, Belzebub, and Mephostophilis gloat over Faustus (5.2.1–19), and the speeches where Mephostophilis says he led Faustus's eye when he read the Bible and where the Good and Bad Angels vaunt over Faustus (5.2.80–125). These additions enhance the impression that the Reformation god is at work; William Empson argues that they were demanded by the censor, who wanted it clear that Faustus must suffer and be damned for his conjuring. Empson calls them "the sadistic additions," finding their "petty, spiteful, cosy and intensely self-righteous hatred" untypical of Marlowe.[53] Given the intermittent nature of the evidence, Empson's theory must be regarded as a stimulating indication of the awkward status of orthodoxy in the play, rather than as right or wrong. In any event, what Empson does not quite take on board is that the B text adds also two major passages that are *more* sympathetic to Faustus: the kind and gentle exhortation of the Old Man (5.1.36–52), and the scene after Faustus's removal to hell in which the Scholars resolve to mourn and give him due burial (5.3). These passages plant in the play a moral perspective alternative to God's. The Old Man and the Scholars pray for Faustus right up to the end, though theologians like Tyndale say we should not pray for apostates—except for their destruction, "as Paul prayed for Alexander the coppersmith (the ii Timothy, the last), 'that God would reward him according to his works.' "[54] The Old Man speaks

> not in wrath,
> Or envy of thee, but in tender love,
> And pity of thy future misery.
> (5.1.48–50)

Unlike in the A text at this point, the Old Man is far gentler than the Good Angel, who anyway has not visited Faustus for nine hundred lines and has only reproaches left to contribute (5.2.92–108; B text only). The Scholars, in the face of the horrific evidence of Faustus's destruction ("See, here are Faustus' limbs, / All torn asunder by the hand of death" [5.3.6–7]), agree to hold a noble funeral. It is rather like the endings of Euripides' *Hippolytus* and *Bacchae,* where the gods stand aside after their disastrous intrusions upon human affairs and the people draw together in sorrow and compassion.

This is why I say the B text sharpens the theological polarity, where-as Empson says it is only more sadistic: both the Reformation god and a more genial alternative are presented more vividly. This pro-duces the possibility, which would also fit the sense most readers have of Marlowe as an author, that at some stage at least the play was written to embarrass protestant doctrine. Richard Baines alleged that in order to persuade men to atheism, Marlowe "quoted a number of contrarieties out of the scripture,"[55] and the strenuous efforts of Chris-tian humanist critics to tame the play to their kind of order suffice to make it worth considering whether *Faustus* dwells provocatively upon such contrarieties. However, as I have argued in earlier chapters, there need not have been a precise intention in either direction, and no version of the play may represent, or ever have represented, a single coherent point of view. Substantial texts are in principle likely to be written across ideological faultlines because that is the most interest-ing kind of writing; they may well not be susceptible to any decisive reading. Their cultural power was partly in their indeterminacy—they spoke to and facilitated debate. But whoever rewrote parts of *Faustus,* and from whatever motive, the revisions indicate an unease with Ref-ormation theology and help to make plain the extent to which any extended treatment cannot but allow contradictions to be heard—by those situated to hear them.

A similar confusion appears in the text of Nathaniel Woodes's *The Conflict of Conscience* (1581), a play usually adduced to set off Mar-lowe's superior verse and humanity. It is based on the story of one Francesco Spiera, which was translated in 1550 and reissued in 1569–70 with a preface by Calvin. In Woodes's play, Philologus, despite good protestant beginnings, is tempted and indulges in worldly de-lights, and concludes that he is "reprobate" and cannot be saved: "I am secluded clean from grace, my heart is hardened quite."[56] But the play appeared in print in 1581 in two issues of the same quarto edi-tion, and with two contrasting endings. In the first Philologus kills himself and is indeed damned; in the second, a joyful messenger reports that he renounced his blasphemies at the last moment. (Both versions are headed on the title page "An excellent new Commedie.")

Evidently someone involved in the publication was worried. The two endings of *The Conflict of Conscience* correspond to the main alternatives in the Christian dilemma: either God must know who is to be damned and therefore, since he created everyone, must be responsible for people going to hell; or God has set the world going but has left it to myriad individual people to decide how it will all turn out. In the former version it is hard to discern his goodness; in the latter, he may be good but is disconcertingly impotent (perhaps rather than paring his fingernails, as James Joyce has it, he is gnawing them in suspense). Historically, each of these two theologies has fed on the inadequacy of the other. And so with the predestinarian and free-will readings of *Faustus*. In Marlowe's play they are, in effect, simultaneously present, but they cannot be read simultaneously; instead they obstruct, entangle, and choke each other. In performance, one or the other may be closed down, but the texts as we have them offer to nudge audiences first this way then that, not allowing interpretation to settle. *Faustus* exacerbates contrarieties in the protestant god so that divine purposes appear not just mysterious but incoherent.

Even critics who believe Faustus is able to choose freely do not thereby prevent the play from provoking embarrassment about God. They cannot settle the point at which Faustus is irrevocably committed, and this is related to God's goodness—the later the decision, the more chance Faustus seems to have. Many theologians have held apostasy to be irrevocable—the "sin against the Holy Ghost," the one that cannot be forgiven. The homily "Of Repentance" declares, "they that do utterly forsake the known truth do hate Christ and his word, they do crucify and mock him (but to their utter destruction), and therefore fall into desperation, and cannot repent." Richard Hooker said the same.[57] If this is so, Faustus's fate is settled very early, and most of the play shows God denying him further chance to repent; the effect is quite close to a predestinarian reading. No doubt this is why others have maintained that Faustus's situation becomes irretrievable when he conjures; or when he signs; or when he rejects the Good Angel; or when he visits hell; or when he despairs; or when he consorts with Helen; or not until the last hour. Such interpretive scope hardly makes for a persuasive theology. It may lead to the thought that there is no coherent or consistent answer because we are on an ideological fault-line where the churches have had to struggle to render their notions adequate. It may suggest not only that Faustus is caught in a cat-and-mouse game played by God at the expense of people, but also that God makes up the rules as he goes along.

Finally, *Faustus* disrupts any complacent view of orthodox theology through its very nature as a dramatic performance. Even for an audience that finds Faustus's blasphemy horrifying, an actor might very well establish a sufficient empathic human presence to make eternal damnation seem unfair. Faustus himself manifests at one point a morality provocatively superior to God's. Anticipating the terror of his last hour, he refuses the support of the Scholars: "Gentlemen, away, lest you perish with me" (there is no knowing what God might do)— "Talk not of me, but save yourselves and depart" (5.2.67–70). At this moment, when human companionship might be most desired, Faustus puts first his friends' safety. As with the Old Man and the Scholars, a generous concern for others is shown persisting in people beyond the point (whenever that is) where the Reformation god has decided that eternal punishment is the only proper outcome. It is one thing to argue in principle that the reprobate are destined for everlasting torment, but when Faustus is shown wriggling on the pin and panic-stricken in his last hour, members of an audience may think again. If this is what happened, for some at least, then there are two traps in the play. One is set by God for Dr. Faustus; the other is set by Marlowe, for God.

LEGITIMATING TAMBURLAINE

In *Tamburlaine* as in *Henry V* (see chapter 6), martial endeavor and legitimate succession depend on the production of gender difference and the subordination of the female and the feminine. Throughout, the men collude in using as a marker of their competing virilities violence against the women they claim as "theirs." At the start Mycetes' unfitness to rule is linked with unmanliness; Tamburlaine, meanwhile, is forcing Zenocrate. Like Henry V, he contrives to appear the irresistible wooer without sacrificing his martial stance: "Techelles, women must be flattered: / But this is she with whom I am in love" (1.2.107–8). In *Henry V,* banishment of the feminine and the female has to be repeated through the play; Tamburlaine, at the height of his achievement, seems to reclaim the feminine. He finds himself moved by Zenocrate's sympathy for her father, the Soldan, and attributes this in lofty "poetic" terms to her heavenly beauty. Such rapture is problematic:

> But how unseemly is it for my sex,
> My discipline of arms and chivalry,
> My nature, and the terror of my name,
> To harbour thoughts effeminate and faint!

However, it is all right, for beauty contributes to warrior culture:

> Save only that in beauty's just applause,
> With whose instinct the soul of man is touch'd,
> And every warrior that is rapt with love
> Of fame, of valour, and of victory,
> Must needs have beauty beat on his conceits.
> (1:5.1.174–82)

Actually, this appropriation occurs immediately after Tamburlaine has killed the innocent Virgins of Damascus and *during* the slaughter of the rest of the people of Damascus, so he is scarcely succumbing to thoughts effeminate and faint. In fact, the only beneficiary of Tamburlaine's change of heart is the Soldan. The latter declares himself "pleas'd with this my overthrow" (5.1.480)—the fate of his people does not weigh with him—and the play ends with him sponsoring the marriage of Tamburlaine and Zenocrate. Tamburlaine's sudden sympathy for Zenocrate's father was not disinterested, then: it is the Soldan alone who can regularize this union. As in *Henry V*, negotiation with the female and the conquered is necessary to secure a legitimate line.

Yet Zenocrate's grief at the continual indiscriminate killing is vividly expressed, and in part 2 the effeminate returns to trouble Tamburlaine in the person of their son Calyphas, whom he murders. He orders that Turkish concubines

> bury this effeminate brat;
> For not a common soldier shall defile
> His manly fingers with so faint a boy.
> (2:4.1.160–62)

Afterwards, Tamburlaine adds, he wants the concubines brought to his tent. The story ends with his death; what does he die of?—where is the pain that prevents him standing? I would show him clutching his groin.

Tamburlaine's claim that his campaigns are divinely ordained is specially provocative because he takes it as license not just to be violent, cruel, and oppressive, as many magnates were, but to rise against established authorities. He does not, like Henry V, adduce legal pretexts, but only military conquest. This indifference to orthodoxy renders his enterprise fraught with religious disturbance. Cosroe demands:

> What means this devilish shepherd to aspire
> With such a giantly presumption,

> To cast up hills against the face of heaven,
> And dare the force of angry Jupiter?
> (1:2.6.1–4)

But Tamburlaine says he is inspired by Jupiter's overthrow of his father: "What better precedent than mighty Jove?" he asks (1:2.7.17). The questions seem to invite audience speculation.

Many critics have felt that the plays work to ratify at least some of Tamburlaine's presumption at least some of the time. Roma Gill says in her edition that for most of part 1, Tamburlaine is "superhuman in his relentless ambition, and this sets him beyond considerations of ordinary morality."[58] Members of an Elizabethan audience would not necessarily have rejected this, despite the homilies and other exhortations to respect established authority. They might have been excited by Tamburlaine's indifference to the ideology of hierarchy and deference, and even by his disregard for ethical injunctions (which somehow always seem designed more for ordinary people than for rulers).

That some such response was conceivable is suggested by Machiavelli, who tells how Giovampagolo Baglioni of Perugia had in 1505 the opportunity to seize his enemy, Pope Julius II, together with all his cardinals, but shrank from such a bold deed. However, Machiavelli says, thoroughly "evil deeds have a certain grandeur and are openhanded in their way": Giovampagolo might have defied the whole church on earth, and thus "would have done a thing the greatness of which would have obliterated any infamy and any danger that might arise from it."[59] On this assumption, people might have been impressed by the panache with which Tamburlaine carries off his impertinent intrusions upon established power. His "giantly presumption" (Cosroe's phrase just quoted) suggests another Senecan model: the Herculean, godlike hero. Seneca's Hercules is sexually voracious and given to random violence, but he is a demigod and destined for heaven. In *Hercules furens,* Juno makes him mad, so that he kills his wife and children, but no criticism of him is ventured; he is "of mind unsound to see, / But yet full great." Finally Hercules kills himself, declaring:

> Forbear, forbear to moan for me, for virtue opened hath
> To me the passage to the stars, and set me in the path
> That guides to overlasting life.[60]

Such classical precedent might authorize Tamburlaine's amoral aspiration. His foreignness complicates the question, for it seems that early modern English people did not easily identify with Spaniards,

Italians, Turks, and Moors. However, Marlowe, here as elsewhere, throws into confusion such identifications, inhibiting any simple perception of the outsider. Tamburlaine, a Scythian shepherd, is not a notorious threat as the Turks were, is twice said to favor Christians, and behaves more honorably than the Christians of Hungary.

If members of an Elizabethan audience viewed Tamburlaine's audacity as somehow exhilarating, the political implications would be uncertain. It may be that respect for conventional pieties and authorities would be undermined. However, it is also feasible that Tamburlaine would be regarded principally as a more adventurous kind of magnate, in which case his bold stance might add credibility to the conspicuous violence and display customarily exercised by the nobility, and hence encourage deference. Simon Shepherd suggests that audiences might have associated Tamburlaine with contemporary hopes for a heroic "new man" who would defeat Spaniards, Turks, and the rest; such audiences would then have found themselves caught between the success and the cruelty of Tamburlaine, who turns out to be all too like the order he overthrows.[61] Probably there is no deciding between the exciting and the presumptuous readings of Tamburlaine's career (though this is the kind of issue upon which criticism has liked to exercise itself). Both responses may well have occurred; we should be investigating the way the text is set up to license such divergent possibilities.

From a Christian humanist point of view, the best move is to present Tamburlaine as vicious and disruptive of a divinely inspired order, but as ultimately involved in ratifying and restoring that order. In this vein, Roy W. Battenhouse argues that Elizabethans would see Tamburlaine as a divine agent ("scourge of God") but as acting nevertheless on his own responsibility.[62] By such an argument, God is exculpated yet remains somehow in control; the play seems to show the punishment of sinful passion within a providentially governed universe; and "order" wins out all round. However, I have maintained, that position is not coherent and was not orthodox. Protestant doctrine could not allow that Tamburlaine might be acting on his own initiative: it held that God does not merely permit violent and arbitrary magnates, he produces them to serve his purposes. "Vile monster, born of some infernal hag, / And sent from hell to tyrannize on earth," the governor of Babylon calls Tamburlaine (2:5.1.110–11), and in the protestant scheme of things the Scythian shepherd might well be that. But he would still be an instrument "of Divine Providence, being employed by the Lord himself to execute the judgments which he has resolved to inflict."[63]

Once again, we do not have to assume that orthodoxy was necessarily persuasive in stage performances of this text. Recent critics are surely right to say that the *Tamburlaine* plays systematically tease an audience with the prospect of ethical and political closure, thereby calling into question the patterns to which they allude.[64] An evident aspect of this, which has been well noticed, is the disorderly concatenation of classical, Christian, and Islamic religious terminology. Within and alongside that disturbance, Tamburlaine's god is strikingly like that of the protestants:

> There is a God, full of revenging wrath,
> From whom the thunder and the lightning breaks,
> Whose scourge I am, and him will I obey.
>   (2:5.1.181–83)

This is the god of Bishop Joseph Hall, for instance when the Philistines are destroyed: "Every man was either dead, or sick: those that were left living, through their extremity of pain envied the dead; and the cry of their whole cities went up to heaven. It is happy that God hath such store of plagues and thunderbolts for the wicked: if he had not a fire of judgment, wherewith the iron hearts of men might be made flexible, he would want obedience and the world peace."[65] This god was adduced continually to legitimize the violence of the ruling elite. Lancelot Andrewes explained, justifying Essex's attack on Ireland in 1599: "God stirreth up the spirit of princes abroad to take peace from the earth, thereby to chasten men by paring the growth of their wealth with his 'hired razor'; by wasting their strong men, the hand of the enemies eating them up; by making widows and fatherless children, by other like consequents of war."[66] (I illustrate from Andrewes because he is often presented as a Christian humanist—T. S. Eliot selected him for special approval.) Thus regarded, Tamburlaine and his consequents of war are not so excessive. Or, again, Cornwall putting out Gloucester's eyes and Regan killing his servant are not outrages of a kind that challenges any theodicy or any theory of obedience to rulers, but the kind of thing God arranged for rulers to do in order to pare the growth of our wealth. To a protestant, Gloucester's blinding may have served him right—Edgar, after all, says as much to Edmund:

> The Gods are just, and of our pleasant vices
> Make instruments to plague us.
> The dark and vicious place where thee he got
> Cost him his eyes.[67]

Notice the plague there: it was a common analogue for the activities of God and great magnates (plagues upon the Egyptian people accompanied the dispute between God and Pharaoh in which the latter's heart was hardened; and I have just quoted Hall rejoicing at God's "store of plagues" when the Philistines were defeated). This was because all three (plague, God, and magnates) worked through violent intrusions upon the lower orders and, concomitantly, all three both challenged and required the Reformation doctrine of providence. By stretching the idea of divine goodness, they provoked the typical Reformation response. Preaching during the epidemic of 1603, Andrewes felt obliged to insist that plague derives from God's care for people: "the plague is a thing causal, not casual; comes not merely by chance but hath somewhat, some cause that procureth it. Sure if a sparrow 'fall not to the ground' . . ."—the trope is familiar. As with today's AIDS "plague," the neatest technique of control and legitimation blames the victim: "So our inventions beget sin, sin provokes the wrath of God, the wrath of God sends the plague among us," Andrewes explained.[68] Plague actually did afflict mainly the people who usually lost out and who usually were blamed when things went wrong. By the early seventeenth century, Paul Slack has shown, "plague was concentrated in clearly distinguishable areas of each town, in the fringe parishes which were chiefly, though not wholly, inhabited by the labouring poor." "It is exceptional," F. P. Wilson observes, "to find a victim of mark and memory in a London plague."[69] This was because the poor suffered overcrowding, unsatisfactory hygiene, bad housing, and rapid turnover of population, and because the better-off left town (Andrewes did not resign everything to God—at the height of the epidemic, he fled his deanery). The correlation between poverty and plague was commonplace by 1603, to the point where the disease was apprehended as an aspect of the general threat posed by the "poorer sort"—and with some reason, for serious outbreaks were accompanied by a collapse of social discipline, with drunkenness, looting, and sexual license. Some commentators actually welcomed plague as a way of reducing the numbers of masterless men and cleansing the body politic.[70] Such intricate incorporation of plague into themes of divine and princely rule indicates once more an anxiously aggressive ideology of social control.

Tamburlaine says God wants him to "plague such peasants as resist in me / The power of heaven's eternal majesty." As elsewhere in the plays, and this is my point, his rhetoric of divine legitimation is basically like that of other rulers:

> Villains, these terrors and these tyrannies
> (If tyrannies war's justice ye repute)
> I execute, enjoin'd me from above,

To scourge the pride of such as Heaven abhors;
Nor am I made arch-monarch of the world,
Crown'd and invested by the hand of Jove,
For deeds of bounty or nobility;
But, since I exercise a greater name,
The scourge of God and terror of the world,
I must apply myself to fit those terms,
In war, in blood, in death, in cruelty,
And plague such peasants as resist in me
The power of heaven's eternal majesty.

(2:4.1.144–56)

These are the usual arguments, but with a provocative slant. Tamburlaine is explaining a specially nasty action (killing his "effeminate" son); he allows the word *tyranny* before repudiating it; explicitly disavows "deeds of bounty"; admits to "cruelty"; and acknowledges, virtually, that it is "peasants" who bear the brunt. Most notably, he implies that his divine mission obliges him to be more vicious than he otherwise might: "I must apply myself to fit those terms." It is "heaven's eternal majesty" that makes him thus. In *Richard III*, according to Tudor ideology, Richmond organizes an army so as to fight Richard III's army and thereby manifest God's marvelous providential care. When he claims to be God's minister in his prayer before the battle, Richmond's argument is very like Tamburlaine's:

O Thou, whose captain I account myself,
Look on my forces with a gracious eye;
Put in their hands Thy bruising irons of wrath
That they may crush down, with a heavy fall,
Th'usurping helmets of our adversaries;
Make us Thy ministers of chastisement,
That we may praise Thee in the victory![71]

The euphemisms here make Richmond's violence sound less immediate than Tamburlaine's—"bruising irons of wrath" seem epic rather than real weapons, "usurping helmets" seem scarcely to contain the heads of people. Where Tamburlaine's speech raises problems about God's chastising ministers, Richmond suppresses them.

Richard III works hard to convince us that the killing Richmond sponsors is in a good cause. But although the issue seems to be the diverse royal pedigrees of Tamburlaine, Cosroe, Richard, and Richmond, together with their respective hypocrisy and virtue, these texts cannot but allow the inference that the problem lies in political arrangements that place power in the hands of a few people who believe they justify their privilege by sending their subjects to war. Hamlet is not vicious like Cornwall and Tamburlaine (though he thinks he is heaven's "scourge and minister" [3.4.177]), but he gives his dying voice to Fortinbras, who already has organized the killing of vastly more people on his Polish expedition than the Danish royal family manages among itself. Hamlet's advice derives, not from his moral qualities, but from his position in the state. Edward Bond's play *Lear* first showed me that although Cordelia in *King Lear* may be good and loving, she is nonetheless acting on the customary assumptions of the governing elite when she raises an army and invades.[72] Her soldiers doubtless endure their going hence even as their coming hither, though prematurely and without remark. Good people may work a bad system.

Tamburlaine's rhetorical performance tends to foreground such dissident thoughts, for it throws into relief the claim of all magnates to divine legitimation. "Jove himself will stretch his hand from heaven / To ward the blow, and shield me safe from harm," he says. Theridamus is impressed: "Not Hermes, prolocutor to the gods, / Could use persuasions more pathetical" (1:1.2.180–81, 210–11). Tamburlaine's rhetoric works. But when others—established monarchs—use the same rhetoric it fails. Tamburlaine does not, as the Soldan threatens, rue the day he "wrought such ignominious wrong / Unto the hallow'd person of a prince" (1:4.3.39–40); the Hungarian Christians are not vindicated in their belief that God wants them to be the scourge of pagans (2:2.1.51–63); Callapine is not succoured by Mahomet, whom the king of Amasia sees "Marching about the air with armed men, / To join with you against this Tamburlaine" (2:5.2.34–35). The effect of these rival claims is to prise apart the language of legitimacy and its users. Anyone can allege divine endorsement—Tamburlaine's way of putting it suggests as much: "I . . . *am term'd* the scourge and wrath of god" and will "*write myself* great lord of Africa" (1:3.3.44, 245; my emphases). But whether the language sticks will depend on the balance of forces on the ground (Tamburlaine wins because his followers are more committed). In some circumstances plausible deployment of the rhetoric of divine legitimation may tip the balance, but it is still only rhetoric. That is why Tamburlaine gives Mycetes back his crown (1:2.4): what counts is who wins the battle.

Althusser's distinction between ideological and repressive state apparatuses may encourage the thought that the repressive agencies are resorted to when ideology has failed to produce acquiescent subjects. However, the two are linked from the start, for a key ideological maneuver is the legitimation of state violence. The contradictions inscribed in ideology produce very many confused or dissident subjects, and control of them depends upon convincing enough of the rest that such control is desirable and proper. Soldiers have to believe that they are different from terrorists, prison officers that they are different from kidnappers, judges that they are different from muggers; and most of us have to be persuaded to agree. Tamburlaine's assertions that his harsh regime is divinely required, and the mobility of such rhetoric of legitimation, expose the claims made generally by and on behalf of rulers.

The unstable relationship between ideology and military success in *Tamburlaine* lays bare the difficulty I identified in chapter 5, of maintaining the distinction between tyranny and lawful rule. Political theory and theodicy—necessarily both—are shot through with alarm that the distinction might be found inadequate, and have generated innumerable anxious attempts to stabilize it. No one in the governing elite was prepared to tolerate lower-class interference, but sometimes it was allowed that tyrannicide might be performed by lesser magistrates (this would include Hamlet, if Claudius is tyrannical enough).[73] Generally, such theories were endorsed by out-groups—by protestants in Catholic countries (the Dutch and Huguenots), and Catholics in protestant countries; it is a nice instance of the material basis of ideas. The distinction between tyranny and lawful rule occurred also, inevitably, in arguments about the reasonableness of the protestant deity: "To adjudge to destruction whom he will," says the objector to Calvin in Lawne's *Abridgement,* "is more agreeable to the lust of a tyrant, than to the lawful sentence of a judge" (p. 222). For Tamburlaine, "(If tyrannies war's justice ye repute)" is a parenthetical question whose validity he denies; he asserts that as God's agent he may kill whom he chooses. Lawne's orthodox response—"It is a point of bold wickedness even so much as to inquire the causes of God's will"— only restates the problem. Tamburlaine allows an audience to see this, and that the ultimate analogue for him is not the ruler but the god to whom all of them appeal—the monster who is said to legitimate it all.

Dramatists picked at the seam of the ill-fashioned garment of orthodoxy, and for a thoughtful audience it splits apart. To some commentators at least, the theaters seemed disruptive. Indeed, as Peter Womack has remarked, they were blamed, like the lower classes, for plague. "The cause of plagues is sin, if you look to it well: and the cause of sin are plays: therefore the cause of plagues are plays," one preacher declared.[74]

TRAGEDY AND THE WRITER

Fulke Greville had a third theory of tragedy, as well as the ancient and modern discussed earlier: his own—and it is at least incipiently materialist. His plays, he says, aim "to trace out the highways of ambitious governors, and to show in the practice of life that the more audacity, advantage and good success such sovereignties have, the more they hasten to their own desolation and ruin."[75] While there is a trace here of the protestant scheme whereby events are supposed to arrive at an ultimate, intricate, and mysterious rightness, Greville's orientation is distinctly towards social process and political critique. The reason for the ruin of princes is their behavior within the system of rule they operate. David Norbrook observes that Greville, like the French radical Etienne de la Boétie, "was concerned not so much with the specific differences between tyrants and good kings, the conventional matter of political theory, as with the general phenomenon of obedience by the majority to one man or to a small ruling elite."[76] Thus Greville approaches a structural understanding of politics like that of Machiavelli and Bacon. Some plays present this line of thought alongside providentialism. In Shakespeare's *Richard II,* for instance, the king claims the support of a typically interventionist, punitive deity (note the plague again):

> Yet know, my master, God omnipotent,
> Is mustering in the clouds on our behalf
> Armies of pestilence; and they shall strike
> Your children yet unborn and unbegot.

However, later on Richard offers a sheerly practical, almost structuralist analysis of the specific political difficulties that Northumberland's relationship with Bolingbroke will produce:

> thou shalt think,
> Though he divide the realm and give thee half,
> It is too little, helping him to all;
> And he shall think that thou, which know'st the way
> To plant unrightful kings, wilt know again,
> Being ne'er so little urg'd, another way
> To pluck him headlong from the usurped throne.[77]

Such empiricism is not necessarily at odds with the providential account of English history—God might be working through such political mechanisms. But in the light of Northumberland's analysis, Richard's armies of pestilence sound like a device to keep people in awe. As time passed many people would find the political, secular explanation the more effective, and providentialism faded—it was the same with plague.[78]

George Puttenham's account of tragedy reaches the protestant conclusion that it shows "the just punishment of God in revenge of a vicious and evil life," but offers first a materialist theory comparable to Greville's. The falls of princes occur, Puttenham says, because of their "lusts and licentiousness of life," and the writing of tragedy is a consequence:

> whereas before in their great prosperities they were both feared and reverenced in the highest degree, after their deaths when the posterity stood no more in dread of them, their infamous life and tyrannies were laid open to all the world, their wickedness reproached, their follies and extreme insolencies derided, and their miserable ends painted out in plays and pageants, to show the mutability of fortune, and the just punishment of God in revenge of a vicious and evil life.[79]

For Puttenham too, political critique is central to tragedies. And he adds a theory about the conditions in which they get written and take effect (which I take to be a distinctively cultural-materialist project). We cannot accept his argument on this literally—we have few plays evidently written after the deaths of princes to record their tyrannies. But the thought that tragedies make such reference as with impunity they can to actual political circumstances is to the point, and is sharpened by Puttenham's suggestion that monarchs may be "reverenced in the highest degree" only while people stand "in dread of them." In fact, comment on the fall of princes was never safe, for authorities tend to demand respect for authority in general and history was recognized as a powerful way of commenting on the present. Greville destroyed his *Antonie and Cleopatra*, he says, for fear that it be "construed or strained to a personating of vices in the present governors and government." And he wanted to write a history of the times of Queen Elizabeth but was prevented on the ground that "things done in that time . . . might perchance be construed to the prejudice of this."[80] This is what the writer Cremutius Corda is accused of in Ben Jonson's *Sejanus* (1603)—a play that, Dollimore observes, leaves unresolved a tension between secularist and providentialist worldviews.[81]

State intervention in writing was actually intermittent. I have argued that this volatile society produced "the writer" as a figure licensed and constrained in the task of confirming or changing the stories through which people conversed among themselves, and that writers, as a category, might well find themselves situated at a point of conflicting affiliation and hence relative autonomy. Of course, such an elaborate system could not be held to a single political line. Diverse writers were diversely situated—as nobility or gentry; in universities or the church; under patronage of the court or a large house; in the market, at the theater or through printing; they were highly visible at court or in the pulpit, virtually anonymous as pamphleteers; women as well as men. The boundaries of expression were differently set for different groups and at different political conjunctures—the penalties for commenting on the queen's proposed marriage were not the same for Philip Sidney and John Stubbe (see chapter 4). The stage and publishing history of *Sejanus* illustrate an intricate negotiation of changing contexts within and around such a text, and a sequence of revision and commentary, disavowal, and discreet assertion.[82]

Annabel Patterson's argument that early modern England evolved, quite consciously, "a joint project, a cultural bargain between writers and political leaders" seems right. There were "conventions that both sides accepted as to how far a writer could go in explicit address to the contentious issues of his day, how he could encode his opinions so that nobody would be *required* to make an example of him." Such a system explains our perception of veiled allusions, for instance in Spenser's *Shepheardes Calender*.[83] For such allusions to have any purpose at all, people in the know must have been likely to recognize them, in which case, we might think, how could Spenser's indirection protect him? The answer is that *manifest* discretion protects the system by indicating that the boundaries are respected. Patterson suggests that this permissive scope functioned as a safety valve and an early version of the opinion poll (pp. 13–14). That perhaps makes it sound too amiable; this was a dangerous game, with extreme penalties if you got the balance of comment and deference wrong. In fact, the element of give-and-take probably made it more menacing, for you have to be far more careful about overstepping a mark that is not visible. Cremutius Corda in *Sejanus* evidently believes he can comment on the contemporary suppression of liberties by writing history, but the rules are changing and he is obliged to disavow any such intention (and it does not protect him). Margot Heinemann has shown how control of the stage tightened under King James as relations between Crown, aristocracy, gentry, and city became more unsettled (she instances Samuel Daniel's *Philotas* [1605], which comes from a political position close to Greville's). Some writers were situated almost like attendant lords in tragedies: solicited by factional and dynastic rivals to enter the lists, then finding the stakes to be higher than they had imagined and their patrons all too ready to sacrifice them. Heinemann astutely suggests that prosecutions led "eventually to the Beaumont and Fletcher type of play, in which kings have wives, daughters and mistresses, favourites and rivals in love, but no subjects below the degree of nobility."[84]

Alongside the safety valve and opinion poll, we might discern an early version of the "open secret." The latter has been identified as the coercive mode imposed until recently upon most homosexuals in modern Western societies, whereby aberrant desire must not be allowed into the open, for that would grant it public status, yet must not become wholly invisible, for then it would no longer work as a stigmatizing mechanism controlling sexualities. The function of the secret, David A. Miller observes, "is not to conceal knowledge, so much as to conceal the knowledge of the knowledge."[85] The early modern political system held unspeakable political knowledge—of tyranny, corruption, hypocrisy, and incompetence—hovering on the boundary of visibility, so denying it the status of public utterance while keeping it within surveillance. It seems very like the situation in many tragedies. Hamlet's exile and death are arranged after his mousetrap play comments publicly, almost, on court scandal. Hippolito in Middleton's *Women Beware Women* says he would not mind Leantio having an affair with his sister if he observed "Art, silence, closeness, subtlety and darkness"; Leantio has to be killed because he is "An impudent daylight lecher!"[86] Disguise, madness, soliloquy, and aside are prominent formal devices in this drama because they are modes through which forbidden knowledge circulates without being allowed aloud. Everyone knows that the system is corrupt, but admitting to such knowledge may well be fatal.

Puttenham's idea of tragedy as the writer's opportunity at the fall of a repressive regime suggests a way of playing a little with the conclusion of *Hamlet*. For on Puttenham's theory, the likely tragic author after the reign of Claudius is Horatio. This is what Hamlet wants: "in this harsh world draw thy breath in pain / To tell my story" (5.2.353–54—rather as Greville tells Philip Sidney's story in the context of Elizabethan politics). Horatio is the obvious choice, for he is a scholar, an observer and given to poetic flourishes ("the morn in russet mantle clad / Walks o'er the dew of yon high eastward hill" [1.1.171–72]); Hamlet coopts him as special adviser for the mousetrap play. Even before our text is ended, Horatio is preparing to present a version of it:

> give order that these bodies
> High on a stage be placed to the view,
> And let me speak to th'yet unknowing world
> How these things came about.

His interpretation is carefully vague about who is responsible for it all, and allows the protestant-providential reading:

> So shall you hear
> Of carnal, bloody, and unnatural acts,
> Of accidental judgments, casual slaughters,
> Of deaths put on by cunning and forc'd cause,
> And, in the upshot, purposes mistook
> Fall'n on the inventors' heads.
>
> (5.2.382–90)

After all, Fortinbras may not welcome too precise a critique of his predecessor. But he does appreciate immediately the value to the new regime of a speedy representation of the circumstances that have brought him to power: "Let us haste to hear it, / And call the noblest to the audience" (5.2.391–92), he says. Horatio agrees that there are pressing political reasons to do so:

> But let this same be presently perform'd
> Even while men's minds are wild, lest more mischance
> On plots and errors happen.

Fortinbras adds his own stage directions: "Let four captains / Bear Hamlet like a soldier to the stage" (5.2.398–401). He thus recasts Hamlet as a soldier—like himself, of course—so that his own succession may seem to follow the better.

Perhaps Horatio will write it all up for the Players, who need some new material. If they survive, that is: audiences generally do not feel called upon to worry about what happens to the Players after Hamlet has used them (when Queen Anne's company upset King James, their royal protection was removed; on a further occasion "the King vowed they should never play more, but should first beg their bread").[87] But Horatio's will more likely be a closet drama, like Greville's, and the Players will develop their own version. Both will have to be discreet, for one oppressive system tends to be followed by another, and it never becomes altogether safe to discuss the contribution to human suffering of the ruling elite.

The displacement of such suffering onto supposed universal forces did not end with the decline of Calvinist providentialism. As Raymond Williams argued in *Modern Tragedy* (1966), it continued in the essentialist-humanist notion of "tragedy" as an allegedly universal form embodying the specially noble experience of elite individuals who create their own doom within an overarching framework of mysterious inevitability. In this notion, the scope for structural analysis and political change is still effaced. Brecht in *The Good Person of Szechwan* offers a materialist response to both branches of the tragic tradition. Wang suggests to the gods that floods occur in the province annually because the people are not god-fearing. "Rubbish," the Second God replies. "Because they didn't look after the dam properly."[88]

A Brief Photo-Essay
on Imperialism

Fig. 4. "Neptune Resigning the Empire of the Seas to Britannia," by William Dyce, 1847.

As Prospero knew, if you invade islands, it helps if you can tell the story of your triumphs prominently and in style.

William Dyce's fresco "Neptune Resigning His Empire of the Seas to Britannia" was commissioned by Queen Victoria and Prince Albert in 1846–47 for the staircase of their new Osborne House on the Isle of Wight. Albert was sponsoring artistic and national traditions in England, as he had in Germany, and fresco was revived as the prestigious mode of Renaissance painting (compare certain deployments of Shakespeare).[1] The seascape and swirl of bodies in Dyce's fresco plainly recall Raphael's "Galatea," in which the sea nymph rides in a chariot drawn by vigorous dolphins, surrounded by semi-human naked figures disporting themselves amorously. Such precedent sanctioned the "un-Victorian" frivolity in Dyce's fresco—Albert "thought it rather nude; the Queen however, said not at all"; but nurserymaids and French governesses were said to be scandalized.[2]

Fig. 5. Postcard on sale to tourists in Grenada, West Indies, 1984.

The juxtaposition of Dyce's exotic vision with a mural memorializing the intervention of the Airborne Division in Grenada in 1983 is, of course, unfair to the United States: there was ample self-righteousness in British imperial propaganda. The absence of humor should perhaps be credited to the immediacy of combat (the allusion to the fabled Greek valley of Tempe seems coincidence rather than witty juxtaposition). Dyce ventriloquizes Renaissance/classical myth; the interpretive question here is: Who speaks? The Airborne Division must have painted its own ensignia (there's more off to the left), and surely the fixation on the KGB is theirs. But who writes "thank you" to God and the USA?—the islanders may indeed have been thankful, but perhaps it seemed prudent, or just convenient, to speak for them.

The historical question that shines through Dyce's picture is whether we should deduce that camp undermined the British Empire, or that more unconventional humor and sexuality might have sustained it better. Even the lion, limp-pawed, looks unsure.

10 Cultural Imperialism and the Primal Scene of U.S. Man

This chapter is the product of working visits to the United States, visits marked especially by the generosity, intellectual and otherwise, of many friends. It is the fruit of my distinctive experience of the position of the Englit professor in North America. I discovered North Carolina; and being unwilling to have my horizons bounded by the question of who was next to be bought in by Duke University English Department, I got a map and set off for the Blue Ridge Mountains. There is a very beautiful parkway, though it is rather strange: it doesn't lead anywhere, in fact it carefully avoids all human purpose other than uninterrupted experience of the wilderness. I deduced that it was begun during the Depression to stimulate the local economy. Paths are interesting. It occurred to me only recently that the reason the Romans built straight roads is that they were an imperial power: they ignored the existing patterns of life, and with slave labor they did not have to take the easier route. British footpaths (trails) mostly derive from ancient rights-of-way, established perhaps as the route between the village church and a cottage long-disappeared; as these become tourist paths, one set of rural practices remains embedded within another. On the Blue Ridge, there are frequent places to pull off and look at the wilderness, without even getting out of the vehicle, with signs explaining what you're looking at. Or there should be signs: it being winter, many of them had been taken away for repair, and there was a tiny temporary notice apologizing politely for this. There were just the two upright posts and in between, instead of a sign about the landscape there was—the landscape. So I was in my individual

254

outpost of civilization, the automobile, staring out at the savage wilderness; and someone was trying to make it signify, but they were not getting through. It might seem that I was privileged with the revelation that Dean MacCannell says all tourists yearn for: a sudden vision of authentic America.[1] But, of course, I could make no sense of what I was looking at—the gap between the posts taunted me with the delusion of unmediated understanding. And I hadn't even read Stephen Greenblatt's essay "Towards a Poetics of Culture," where he notes how the boundaries of the natural are marked in Yosemite National Park.[2] In fact, at that time I thought Yosemite was pronounced like possum-fight, and might mean the fortunate practitioner of a perversion known to American Indians but denied to us by our depleted, civilized sensibilities.

I decided to intensify my engagement with the countryside. But in the wilderness you can't just *walk,* so I hiked a trail. It wasn't too organized—not too many signs telling you which birds to look at, to take your litter home, to brush your teeth twice a day, and always use a condom. But the trail was named—for Daniel Boone: again, my route was being given significance. So, being of scholarly disposition, I found out about Boone. I assume U.S. readers know all about him, because E. D. Hirsch in his *Cultural Literacy* says they should to be proper citizens.[3] At the time of the War of Independence, Boone was finding trails across the Alleghenies, into land where the Cherokee, Shawnee, Delaware, and Mingo tribes were living. In a series of fights with those Indians, Boone pioneered European settlement of what was to become Kentucky and became a national hero. Actually, Boone himself didn't do very well out of it all. He wasn't really an independent individual, as the myth has it; he was employed by a land speculator. He was cheated out of land he had been given, and owed large sums of money almost all his life. He illustrates the remark Brecht made about Mother Courage: that you need a large pair of scissors to take your cut from a war, or from capitalism generally. It seems, anyway, that Boone didn't want to extend civilization, but to get away from it; of course, he was the instrument of his own disappointment, for it was his forays that opened the trails for white settlement. He moved on to Tennessee, and at the age of sixty-five to Missouri, still questing for his own supersession.

Already in his lifetime, people began deploying Daniel Boone to render plausible ideas about distinctive U.S. virtues and the colonization of North America; he figures in the contest of stories through which ideology is produced.[4] This appropriation of Boone started with the "autobiography" ghosted by John Filson in 1784, in which "Boone" concludes:

> Many dark and sleepless nights have I spent, separated from the cheerful society of men, scorched by the summer's sun, and pinched by the winter's cold, an instrument ordained to settle the wilderness. But now the scene is changed: peace crowns the sylvan shade.[5]

The language attributed to "Boone" here is that of the eighteenth-century poet ("sylvan shade"). In part such speech effects the move from pioneer to cultivated gentleman that validates both Boone and his biographer; the U.S. citizen is now peacefully at home in the land he has settled in despite of nature. The wilderness becomes a country churchyard. Yet the disparity between language and context is there— William Carlos Williams complains of "the silly phrases and total disregard for what must have been the rude words of the old hunter."[6] There is a split between the virtues of pioneer and gentleman-poet— they represent my sense of an ideological faultline in U.S. Man. Also, in the passage quoted, we cannot but remark the idea that Boone is "an instrument ordained": he is credited with a belief in what came to be called "manifest destiny." The first book I found about Daniel Boone was by Edward Stewart White; published in 1922 to help establish the Boy Scouts of America, it tells us: "He spoke, feelingly and with solemnity, of being a creature of Providence, ordained by Heaven as a pioneer in the wilderness to advance the civilisation and the extension of his country."[7] European domination of North America is what God wants.

Quite diverse attitudes towards native peoples whom he was helping to displace are attributed to Boone. One time—not a time of particular strife—he sees a man fishing from a log, and just takes a shot at him and kills him. He is reported as saying: "We Virginians had for some time been waging a war of intrusion upon them, and I, amongst the rest, rambled through the woods in pursuit of their race, as I now would follow the tracks of any ravenous animal."[8] In other reports, Boone has a quite different attitude. He speaks admiringly of Indians and of their social and military customs; he says he could trust an Indian much more safely than a Yankee. The interviewer, disconcerted, felt Boone was "greatly prejudiced . . . in favour of the tawny inhabitants of the western wilderness."[9] The ideological convenience of the first of those attitudes is obvious: if the Indians are savage, like animals, then they can be killed and their land taken. "When dealing with savage men, as with savage beasts, no question of national honor can arise. Whether to fight, to run away, or to employ a ruse, is solely a question of expediency," the commissioner of Indian Affairs declared in 1871. White says "a deeply ingrained racial cruelty is one of the Indian characteristics; and it was a powerful factor, when the scales of Eternal Justice were poised, in bringing about his elimination from the land"; notice how providence slithers into Social Darwinism there.[10] Nevertheless, the second attitude, Boone's sense that the Indians were as human as himself, won't go away. White acknowledges repeatedly that both parties behaved violently. For instance, a man "might wantonly kill a perfectly friendly Indian on the very fringe of town; his action might be deplored or even frowned upon by his neighbours, but he would not be called to account" (p. 96). The distinction between civilization and savagery threatens to collapse.

Contradictory stories such as Boone was being made to tell appear also in other European colonies. As I have said (in chapter 2) the topics requiring most assiduous and continuous reworking are the awkward, unresolved ones: those are what people need to read and write about. Colonial Europeans spent a good part of their time producing self-justifying stories about the difference between the natives and themselves. In George Orwell's *Burmese Days* the club servant says: "I find it very difficult to keep ice cool now." Ponder for a moment: what is unacceptable about the servant's sentence?—"I find it very difficult to keep ice cool now." The colonist says:

> Don't talk like that, damn you—"I find it very difficult!" Have you swallowed a dictionary? "Please, master, can't keeping ice cool"—that's how you ought to talk. We shall have to sack this fellow if he gets to talk English too well. I can't stick servants who talk English.[11]

The settler wants the native to understand his commands, but fears that they may be understood all too well. The colonist must seek continually confirmation of superiority, because every time he or she looks at a native (and the Europeans' privilege is not to look, but always they must look), there is a risk of seeing more than he or she can cope with. And the native might return a look not of acquiescence but of knowledge, threatening authority. Almost all this analysis is in Doris Lessing's novel *The Grass Is Singing,* published in England in 1950, written out of Lessing's experience in Southern Rhodesia (Zimbabwe). Anything drawing attention to the constructedness of racial hierarchy causes anxiety—for instance "the growing army of poor whites," who are thought shocking (unlike millions of poor Blacks) because of "their betrayal of white standards."[12] I have written about this elsewhere, but invoke it here lest it appear that I am unaware that these ideological maneuvers were characteristic of the British Empire, and by no means special to North America.

Actually, the Indians and frontier whites were rather similar—because their culture was hugely influenced by the material conditions in which they were living. Apart from guns and experience of trying to assert imperial sway nearer to hand (for instance in Ireland), the Europeans brought with them little that was of much help in North America. They had to learn from the natives how to live. Daniel Boone didn't just walk into the wilderness (any more than I could). He picked up Indian trails; he depended on Indian techniques of living in that terrain, and on Indian trading practices—he moved in on their trade of supplying animal pelts.[13] When captured by the Shawnees, Boone was adopted into their tribe and managed perfectly well; they hoped he would stay, becoming a renegade like his contemporary Simon Girty—Boone lived for four months in their manner in their town of Chillicothe. Europeans had always a propensity to do this—already in 1610–11, the Jamestown Colony made it a capital offense to live with the Indians (Spenserians will notice the similarity to Calidore among the shepherds).[14] Because of his sojourn with the Shawnees, Boone was actually tried for treachery when he got back to his camp; so powerful was the anxiety about interchange between frontier and Indian lifestyles.

The emerging dominant ideology of the United States needed the renegade to be the anti-type of Daniel Boone (as, for instance, in Emerson Bennett's novel *The Renegade* [1848]) in order to demarcate the savage and the civilized. Indeed, since the Indians were not conceived of as fully human, it was possible to pretend that they were not really there: the places where they lived were spoken of as "free land"—meaning free for the whites to take (this was crucial to Frederick J. Turner's frontier thesis).[15] But the contradictions kept breaking through. When the government wanted to make treaties, it implied that the Indians were occupying their land in a recognizably human way, with a coherent social system and leaders who could sign away land rights; when the government wanted to break the treaties and seize more land, it said the opposite.[16] Yellow Wolf, of the Nez Percé people, understood how stories produce ideology; he said: "The whites told only one side. Told it to please themselves."[17] The Indians lost their lands and their lives partly because they lost out in the contest to establish plausible stories.

The Barbadian writer George Lamming made the same point in 1960 apropos of Shakespeare's *Tempest*. Caliban, Lamming says, is "an occasion, a state of existence which can be appropriated and exploited for the purposes of another's own development."[18] Caliban is a figure in Prospero's story, and the latter's humanity depends on the former's savagery. To justify imperial enterprise, European and U.S. Man have constituted themselves in contradistinction to identities they have foisted onto other races. This is cultural plunder: not just the material resources and labor of subjected peoples are taken, but their identity is constructed so as to attribute an essential humanity to the imperial power. "The European has only been able to become a man through creating slaves and monsters," Jean-Paul Sartre observed.[19] This imperial strategy, I'm suggesting, has enabled European expansion throughout the world, but it seems specially complex and compelling in the United States because the state was founded, explicitly, in Enlightenment, humanist ideas of Man and his freedom. The trouble is that to be free you must be Man, and the Indians were not; Chief Justice John Marshall, a most respected interpreter of the Constitution, pronounced in 1823 that, being savages, they were not entitled even to the protection that the conventions of warfare prescribe for the conquered.[20] Chief Joseph of the Nez Percés appealed:

> Let me be a free man—free to travel, free to stop, free to work, free to trade where I choose, free to choose my own teachers, free to follow the religion of my fathers, free to think and talk and act for myself—and I will obey every law, or submit to the penalty.[21]

In fact, the Indians represented to European peoples a subversive kind of freedom, reminiscent of that found so threatening in Elizabethan "masterless men," for, as against the settler ethos, they figured escape from political, social, and familial institutions. Partly for this reason, Michael Rogin suggests, they had to be displaced.[22] The Nez Percés welcomed the white people who crossed the Rockies in 1805 and lived peacefully alongside them for fifty years; but eventually, because of gold mining, they were killed, driven out, their villages burned. In the 1870s, they were moved from the Wallowa Valley, now on the borders of Washington, Idaho, and Oregon, where they had treaty rights. In violation of a truce, they were shipped like cattle to Fort Leavenworth, Kansas; after almost a hundred had perished in the swamp there, they were moved to a barren plain in the Indian Territory, where they sickened and died.

"Remember that whatever our ancestry of blood, in one sense we all have the same fathers—our Founding Fathers": so William Bennett, fearful that too many will distrust the paternal authority of the state.[23] Indians were encouraged to think of the U.S. president as the Great Father. The primal scene, according to Freud, is your parents having sexual intercourse. We call this love, but it may appear to the child "as something that the stronger participant is forcibly inflicting on the weaker . . . an act of violence."[24] The primal scene of European imperialism is the Europeans arriving, being welcomed by the local people, then driving them out, killing them and burning their village. Women were raped—as they were to be very often in slavery. Thus the Founding Fathers—they had to be fathers—conceived U.S. Man, in an act which they may have believed to be love (generously bestowing true religion and civilization) but which looks also like the rape of the inhabitants and the land. This scene has been by no means exclusive to the Americas, as I have said, and it is still being played out around the world.

I did find one sign still in place between its posts on the parkway: it said "Daniel Boone country." I had thought I was in a remote margin of European civilization, but ideologically I was in the center.

MAN AND HIS CULTURE

Literature, as a concept, evolved together with European Man. In a reciprocal movement, its possession attests his humanity, and the virtue often attributed to literature is that it instantiates that humanity. In British colonies, it was necessary to educate a proportion of indigenous peoples so that they should constitute a lower-middle class in the economy and a subaltern stratum in government and the military. Introducing them to literature helped to promote the idea that England had been blessed with a special genius, transcending commercial purposes; generously, this might be shared with subject peoples. Literature was particularly useful in India, because meddling with religion was thought too dangerous there. As Ania Loomba puts it, "English was not taught just as a foreign language but was the means of imposing a culture, a cluster of ideologies, a way of being and seeing, of which the literary text became the privileged signifier."[25] George Lamming describes how it worked in the Caribbean:

> The West Indian's education was imported in much the same way
> that flour and butter are imported from Canada. Since . . . England

had acquired, somehow, the divine right to organise the native's reading, it is to be expected that England's export of literature would be English. And the further back in time England went for these treasures, the safer was the English commodity. So the examinations, which would determine that Trinidadian's future in the Civil Service, imposed Shakespeare, and Wordsworth, and Jane Austen and George Eliot and the whole tabernacle of dead names, now come alive at the world's greatest summit of literary expression. How in the name of Heavens could a colonial native . . . ever get out from under this ancient mausoleum of historic achievement?[26]

The native was proffered a cultural allegiance that in actuality she or he was not allowed, fully, to adopt—not being white; and in the process was removed from the culture of her or his (mainly his) family and locality. Loomba observes: "The ideological effect of continuing reverence for the canon was to fix the Indian student, especially one not coming from an English-speaking background, in a position of disability, exclusion and awe."[27]

I would add two things. First, it should not be assumed (as does James Baldwin in *Notes of a Native Son*) that Europeans generally are in secure possession of Shakespeare, Bath, Chartres, and the like. The vast majority of Europeans, including most women, have no direct stake in official culture; those monuments act as instruments of domination within Europe also. Second, the process is not ineluctable: power still cannot control contradiction—Lamming and Baldwin got to write their critiques. For some individuals from subordinated groups, Shakespeare and other European authors have represented not just cultural privilege but an illuminating slant upon their own situation. Maya Angelou read "When in disgrace with fortune and men's eyes" and found it "a state with which I felt myself most familiar." Such instances do not, as some commentators would have it, constitute a general case for the political validity of Shakespearean texts. The effect depends on the specific conjuncture—for Richard Wright it was modern, politically conscious authors, Sinclair Lewis and Theodore Dreiser, that were illuminating; and Angelou does not record whether she identified with the "dark lady."[28] However, a British army general in India warned that in "native students who had obtained an insight into European literature and history . . . there seemed to be engendered a spirit of disaffection towards the British Government."[29]

I have suggested that U.S. and European imperialism are parts of the same movement. But U.S. Man had to handle also his own relation to Europe. In the United States, Shakespeare was initially an object of suspicion for a moralistic puritan tradition, but, correspondingly, admired by people who aspired to be "polite and cultivated," fashionably "European." The latter were "pathetically eager to acquire some part of the refinement which cast a glamor over life in countries beyond the Atlantic," said Joseph Quincy Adams.[30] Surely people of European derivation living in the Americas were Man as well? James Fenimore Cooper called Shakespeare "the great author of America, as he is of England," claiming that "Americans" had "just as good a right" to him as Britons. Ralph Waldo Emerson implied a relation through the Founding Fathers, declaring that Shakespeare "drew the man of England and Europe; the father of the man in America."[31] Shakespeare was even invoked to assert U.S. Man against English imperial pretensions. The Pennsylvania poet Peter Markoe wrote:

> Monopolising Britain! boast no more
> His genius to your narrow bounds confin'd;
> Shakespeare's bold spirit seeks our western shore,
> A gen'ral blessing for the world design'd,
> And, emulous to form the rising age,
> The noblest Bard demands the noblest Stage.[32]

Yet Ashley Thorndike, addressing the British Academy in 1927 on the theme "Shakespeare in America," pondered: "The United States has always had a frontier, has always been subduing wild land, establishing civilization anew. . . . Why should we care for the literature of yesterday?"[33] The problem that seemed to need attention, if Shakespeare was to be "American," was how the distinctively *cultivated* aura—which made him a desirable cultural token—might be reconciled with the more vigorous and practical domination of the land required in the Daniel Boone pioneer image, with its equally necessary contribution to U.S. ideology. This is the faultline that is apparent when Filson makes Boone speak like an English gentleman-poet. Fenimore Cooper was aware of it by 1823 when, in his novel *The Pioneers,* he conducted a particularly intricate negotiation between the virtues and interests of the pioneer, the settler, the English colonial, and the Indian, in which not only are pioneer and Indian qualities approved by those who are displacing them, but secret and mistaken identities actually allow qualities and persons to effect an imaginary interchange. Nevertheless, although the pioneer is in the last sentence saluted as "opening the way for the march of our nation across the continent," and the natural elements may at any time throw up difficulties that require his qualities, the settler gentry, with their Jane Austen lifestyle, have all the civil and most of the social power.[34] In his essay "Fenimore

Cooper's Literary Offences," Mark Twain complained that Cooper wrote stilted English and evidenced little familiarity with pioneer life. The issue came to be read as the East Coast versus the rest of the country; the historian Charles A. Beard complained that literary Easterners regarded people beyond the Alleghenies as "almost, if not quite, uncouth savages." The insistence of Frederick Jackson Turner on frontier virtues was designed to combat just this attitude; it was a "cultural revolt," says Richard Hofstadter, "a protest against the cultural dominance of the East and against its patronizing attitudes."[35] Turner was notably vague about how far literature and learning could be credited to the frontier. The humanist authority of literature was pulling against the pioneer virtues of U.S. Man.

The most appealing answer was that English letters, and Shakespeare especially, really *were* compatible with the frontier. Maurice Morgann took advantage of Voltaire's dismissal of Shakespeare as a barbarian to assert: "The *Apalachian* mountains, the banks of the *Ohio* . . . shall resound with the accents of this [alleged] Barbarian: In his native tongue he shall roll the genuine passions of nature."[36] Notice how Morgann retains the idea of barbarity for these western regions (even *they* will appreciate Shakespeare). He adds that the condition for such appreciation will be the emergence of the Shakespearean text from the commentary in which the British have smothered it: the natural Shakespeare will speak to these simple folk. The same appeal was made in the preface to the first U.S. edition of Shakespeare's plays and poems, published in Philadelphia in 1795, which was said not to include substantial annotations in the English manner because "the American reader is seldom disposed to wander through the wilderness of verbal criticism."[37] When you have a real wilderness of your own by no means yet under control, you don't need a wilderness of notes. To be sure, Shakespeare was the most popular playwright in the west. Touring companies followed the movement westward, traveling elocution teachers recited famous speeches, newspapers and politicians quoted them, amateurs performed them.[38] So, in Joseph Quincy Adams's account, "Shakespeare, bearing the sceptre of cultivation, moved in the dusty trail of the pioneers," among "people who in race were still essentially English": the "original virtue" of Shakespeare infused frontier life, and "from ocean to ocean it served to give to American civilisation something like homogeneity." However, Indians were sadly ambivalent: Cherokee chiefs are said to have been "honored" by plays performed in 1752 and 1767, but in the 1840s a roving Seminole band attacked a traveling company of players, killing two and taking the costumes for their own use.[39] Cultural plunder indeed.

Few commentators have resisted the temptation, at this point, to propose a mutual validation of Shakespeare and the frontier. Emerson managed this metaphorically by making Shakespeare himself into the pioneer—declaring that he has "planted the standard of humanity some furlongs forward into Chaos."[40] More prosaically, Louis B. Wright followed Esther Cloudman Dunn in the opinion that the element of melodrama that appealed in the plays to Shakespeare's groundlings would go down well on the frontier; but neither could resist having it both ways, claiming that there would also be some sophisticated people who properly honored and appreciated culture.[41] Actually, the popularity of Shakespeare in the United States, even more than in England during the nineteenth century, depended on the plays being wholly rewritten in ways that would now seem outrageous, and presented alongside unashamedly popular products.[42] Rather than celebrating the coincidence of the irrepressible spirits of Shakespeare and U.S. Man, we should be observing that Shakespeare was a site of cultural contest which, as usual, was also class contest. As is likely to happen with any powerful cultural token, conflicting groups in U.S. society conducted their struggle by attempting to establish alternative ideas of Shakespeare (as they were doing with Daniel Boone). The immediate occasion of the Astor Place "riot" in New York in 1849, where between twenty and thirty disorderly people were shot dead by soldiers, was rivalry between British (=upper-class) and U.S. (=lower-class) notions of how Shakespeare should be presented—whether, in the persons of William Charles Macready or Edwin Forrest respectively, the plays should be acted in a relatively gentrified or a populist manner. As with the "Old Price" "riots" at Covent Garden in 1809, the provocation was the establishment of exclusive, luxury theaters for the gentry; it was "a battle for the possession of Shakespeare."[43] This question correlated with popular hostility towards the upper classes and their Anglophile pretensions ("silk-gloved aristocrats," they were called), and upper-class determination to assert "law and order."[44]

Lawrence W. Levine has argued recently that Shakespeare was an essentially popular figure in the nineteenth century and that a split between lowbrow and highbrow conceptions occurred towards 1900. I think that is not quite right: both conceptions were present throughout, but in the end the latter came to dominate. Levine holds that in the nineteenth century, there was "a shared public culture" centered upon Shakespeare, and that "at the turn of the century . . . he was *transformed* from a playwright for the general public into one for a specific audience."[45] But Levine's own evidence indicates that "tensions and conflicts" and the segregation of popular and fashionable audiences ran through the century (pp. 56–60, 69–70). In the course of this contest, the East Coast gentry established a cultural hegemony, and this helped determine what kind of person U.S. Man was to be. As Robert Falk shows, from about 1800 "the recognition of Shakespeare by an emerging type of gentleman-scholar-writer [in the East] helped to establish a class of polite, belletristic *litterateurs* like Irving, Cooper, Poe, Lowell and Holmes."[46] Gradually, the highbrow idea of Shakespeare gained strength: the plays became noble texts to be read and reflected upon by ladies and gentlemen; stage productions became more restrained and thoughtful, and the "original" texts were "restored"; colleges put the plays onto syllabuses, expensive collections of research materials were established, productions aspired to correspond to notions of Shakespeare's Globe Theatre.[47] Today Shakespeare remains a figure in popular culture, but in England certainly his presence there is normally ironic—partly deferential, but more a way of resisting claims to class and educational superiority. Derek Longhurst has shown how radio and television comedy and advertisements appeal to working- or lower-middle-class identity by displacing Shakespearean tag-lines and images into grotesque, anarchic, often sexual contexts, or supplanting them with the alternative prestige of, for instance, football skills. The advertisement locates us in a theater:

> As Hamlet begins his "Alas, poor Yorick" the actor drops the skull, catching it like a football on his toe. A sequence follows, familiar from sports programmes demonstrating the skilfull ball-control of professional stars, with the skull bouncing from foot, head and shoulders to the excited "oohs" and "aahs" of the theatre audience. Another actor enters with "My noble Lord Hamlet—" but immediately reverts to "Over 'ere, son, on me 'ead." Finally "Hamlet" overhead kicks the skull into the crotch of the evening-suited drinker of Black Label seated in one of the boxes, who smiles at his companions in some painful embarrassment.[48]

The prestige of the Shakespearean audience is retained for the lager drinker, but other viewers are reassured by the recognition that there are other kinds of skill and enticed by being invited to share a joke at the expense of authority. As Longhurst remarks, transferring the big-match mode of enthusiasm to the normally sober theater audience effects the most telling juxtaposition.

By the end of the nineteenth century, U.S. cities and towns could no longer sustain several simultaneous productions of the same Shakespeare play. He had stopped being popular and become the province of the leisure class and the education system—the two were related, since it seemed natural that the former should set the criteria for the latter. Falk shows the leisure-class orientation of Richard Grant White and Howard Horace Furness, the principal nineteenth-century U.S. editors of Shakespeare, and of other key figures. These were very like the people who sponsored literary culture in Britain. Dunn derides most leisure-class use of Shakespeare as "an amateur's game. . . . One amassed a decent knowledge . . . and displayed it in correspondence, even printed correspondence, and in conversation. It was like stamp collector's lore, or golf, or racing, or book collecting."[49] But far more was at stake in this appropriation of Shakespeare, for he had become a place where ideas of the United States might be authorized.

Shakespeare, Englishness, and the humanities helped to make it plausible that class correlated with quality, indeed with civilization, so that the people who were in charge might seem rightly so. Irving Babbitt wanted education in the humanities to create "that aristocracy of character and intelligence that is needed in a community like ours to take the place of an aristocracy of birth, and to counteract the tendency towards an aristocracy of money"; this might be accomplished, he thought, by the "man of leisure."[50] It is the decline of such an arrangement that Allan Bloom laments. "Philosophers allied themselves with the gentlemen, making themselves useful to them, strengthening their gentleness and openness by reforming their education," he says. "Why are the gentlemen more open than the people? Because they have money and hence leisure and can appreciate the beautiful and useless."[51] On approximately this basis, the East Coast European-derived gentry sought a cultural hegemony within the United States, deploying Shakespeare especially to legitimate their claim; subordinate groups might aspire to share this powerful cultural token, but by so much they would acknowledge the priority and privilege of those who handled it with ease. "Not many communities in the west were too barbaric or remote to have a few citizens who treasured their editions of Shakespeare," Wright says.[52] In this view, being a proper U.S. community means knowing about Shakespeare. Centrality and civility are defined together against the alleged barbarity of regions not yet fully incorporated.

How this was contested may be observed in *She's Working Her Way through College* (1952), a film based on a stage play by James Thurber and Elliot Nugent and starring Ronald Reagan and Virginia Mayo. It is set in Midwest State University, where a professor of English and creative writing (Reagan) produces Shakespeare annually to small audiences. He hasn't had a raise in five years—it is the football team that brings in the money. "They don't seem to go for the classics," he says. But he gets a new idea from Angela, who has been working as a showgirl to earn the money to go to college. "Why don't you do something different?" she asks. The board of the college is too conservative, and wouldn't consider a modern work "cultural." But "is there anything cultural about a football team?" Angela asks. So the professor decides to make a musical of a play she has written and produce that. Angela says "the main thing is to get away from Shakespeare and give 'em what they want," so they make that the title: "Give Them What They Want." All seems well until it is revealed that Angela is a professional dancer (this gives Reagan, as the professor, opportunity to speak up for free access to education). However, the hypocritical chairman of the board of trustees has already tried to seduce Angela, and so proves vulnerable to blackmail. The show is a success and the professor gets his promotion; Shakespeare is forgotten. "Midwest" does better without the East Coast cultural tradition.

THE HEGEMONY OF U.S. MAN

By the turn of the century, after the closing of the frontier, the issue was not just class, but race and empire as well. British scholars have shown how Shakespeare's achievement was made to symbolize a supposed imperial English destiny to civilize the whole world. For Thomas Carlyle, for instance, Shakespeare was "the strongest of rallying-signs" for "a Saxondom covering great spaces of the Globe."[53] In claiming Shakespeare, North Americans claimed also validation for imperial destiny. Charles Mills Gayley, professor of English at Berkeley, set out to specify the line of transmission in his book *Shakespeare and the Founders of Liberty in America* (1917). He held that "the principles of liberty which America enjoys today" derive from Shakespeare via *The Tempest* and his association, which Gayley tries to demonstrate, with the Virginia Company.[54] Actually, the Virginia Company was a paradigm case of incipient capitalist-imperialist rapacity and dishonesty, but for Gayley this was not a problem, because for him "liberty" meant Anglo-Americans asserting themselves. Imperial Shakespeare seems to heal the split in concepts of U.S. Man: Daniel Boone was acting in the spirit of the Elizabethans, and Shakespeare's writing justifies Anglo-American dominance of diverse peoples and places. However, an important distinction was propounded: it was only the early pioneers—those who were now firmly established—who were in the true line.

By 1917, Gayley thought, people of other races had been allowed into the United States in dangerous numbers, and their pioneering was not to be endorsed; in fact, they seemed altogether too bold and independent, being inclined to socialism and anarchism. "We have with too light scrutiny admitted to our large freedom and easy fatness tens of thousands whose hands grasp our privileges, but whose hearts still cherish the superstitions of the political inhumanity from which we thought they had escaped," Gayley says (p. 223). However, all may yet be well, Gayley finds, for totting up the U.S. people who are "exclusively or predominantly British in blood," he makes the total come to "from fifty-five to sixty millions of our one hundred million." Further, "to these must be added the descendants of the Dutch, the Swedes, the Germans, who in the seventeenth century, and in the eighteenth before 1764, accepting British rule and law and speech, became one folk with the Britons in America and enriched the American spirit with strains of liberality and toleration" (pp. 222–23). It is not too hard to work out which peoples are excluded—even if they come from Europe and however long they have been in the country. In the reactionary mind, racial mixture often correlates with civil disturbance, but movements like the Wobblies (Industrial Workers of the World, founded in 1905) were indeed keen to recruit new immigrants from southern and eastern Europe—Italians and Jews—and Asian workers in California. However, such people could always be harassed, beaten, deported, imprisoned, framed, and judicially killed, like Joe Hill, Wesley Everest, Nicola Sacco, and Bartolomeo Vanzetti.[55] (According to Hirsch, none of these is "what literate Americans know"; nor are Emma Goldman and John Reed.) After raids ordered by Attorney General A. Mitchell Palmer in 1920, thousands of the foreign-born were imprisoned. And others could be kept out of the country through discriminatory measures like the Immigration Quota Law of 1921.[56] But it was altogether preferable if more recent immigrants could be persuaded to defer to the culture of U.S. Man.

As Ashley Thorndike put it in 1927, "In spite of the differences of climate, occupation, and race, in spite of the dividing and almost disruptive force of negro slavery, in spite of the constant clash between frontier and older communities . . . Shakespeare has been a symbol of unity, a moving force, almost a directing deity."[57] The success of this project was celebrated by Joseph Quincy Adams, dedicating the

Folger Shakespeare Library in Washington in 1932. To his mind, the late-nineteenth-century immigrants had entered "in floodgate fashion." The northern Europeans had been all right—"honest, thrifty, and altogether admirable as citizens," though they did "alter the solid Anglo-Saxon character of the people." But eastern and southern Europeans were another matter: "They swarmed into the land like the locust in Egypt; and everywhere, in an alarming way, they tended to keep to themselves." Worse, "they exhibited varied racial characteristics" (i.e., I suspect, some were Jewish).[58] However, and only just in time, compulsory education was installed and Shakespeare "made the corner-stone of cultural discipline" at the moment when "the forces of immigration became a menace to the preservation of our long-established English civilisation." So if "there has been evolved a homogeneous nation, with a culture that is still essentially English, we must acknowledge that in the process Shakespeare has played a major part."[59] Thorndike agreed: "We have a genius for compulsory legislation[!], and we decided to compel every child to get an education, and this soon included the study of Shakespeare. . . . There is no escaping him" (pp. 164–65). Lionel Trilling recognized the strategy with rather surprising explicitness, remarking that the English curriculum "has the political advantage, in a nation whose ethnic origins are so various, of seeming to suggest that one ethnic group, by reason of our special interest in the culture associated with it, is superior to all others."[60]

So alongside European Man and his imperial destiny, defined in England in relation to Shakespeare and literature (Beowulf to Virginia Woolf, or Plato to NATO, we say on the British left) appears U.S. Man: Daniel Boone to Allan Bloom. And why should the benefits be confined to North America? In *Shakespeare for Everyman*, Louis B. Wright updates imperial Shakespeare: the parallel to the Elizabethan spirit is none other than that of the United States in the 1960s. Wright sees three main similarities. First, the Virginia Company's efforts have now reached their proper culmination in "the business civilisation that came to its ultimate fruition in the United States" (pp. 3–9). Second, discovering America (discovering, of course, that it had been there all the time) is like space travel: "No little men from Mars," Wright says, "could create more excitement than the Indians whom ship captains occasionally kidnapped and brought to England" (pp. 14–15). And third, Elizabethan rivalry with Spain—partly over who was to grab the resources of the Americas—was in Wright's view like the Cold War (pp. 16–19). Behind the stunning complacency,

Wright's project is coherent enough. In proposing these continuities in imperialist enterprise, he is organizing the humanities and U.S. Man for world hegemony in the second half of the twentieth century.

World War II was fought partly to determine who would inherit the absurdly over-extended empires of the European nation-states. The new frontier was to be the Third World—the statue of Christopher Columbus on Telegraph Hill in San Francisco is looking out across the Pacific: he hasn't finished "discovering." It was suggested that the Pacific wouldn't really count as a frontier because those further lands are not contiguous. Albert J. Beveridge repudiated the thought: "Not contiguous! Our navy will make them contiguous."[61] With modern communications, this new imperial project could function largely through commercial domination, puppet governments, technical and military "advisers," loans, specific military interventions, "aid," and cultural hegemony, rather than an explicit imperial occupation in the old style. The major ideological formation was supplied by a highly convenient fusion of terms from the frontier and the Cold War. As I have said, nineteenth-century expansion of the United States often invoked freedom. Secretary of State James Buchanan wrote in 1847, while waging the war that led to the annexation of much of Mexico: "Our free institutions forbid that we should subject nations to our arbitrary sway. If they come within our power, we must bestow upon them the same blessings of liberty and law, which we ourselves enjoy."[62] One hundred years later, in 1947, President Truman decided to take over the task, which the British government could no longer afford, of imposing a right-wing military dictatorship in Greece, and freedom was again the watchword. The "Truman Doctrine" was announced, promising "to support free peoples who are resisting attempted subjugation by armed minorities or by outside pressures. . . . The free peoples of the world look to us for support in maintaining their freedoms." Thus reiterated, freedom became the banner for the new frontier. Well before President Kennedy used the phrase in 1960, Godfrey Hodgson points out, "the new frontier" meant that "American influence and American corporate business would spread around the world."[63] And the notion that this land was "free" was evident in the continuing readiness to override local ideas (hence the persistent perception of the wish for local self-determination as Moscow-inspired). "American energy will continually demand a wider field for its exercise. But never again will such gifts of free land offer themselves," Frederick Jackson Turner had observed.[64] The free world seemed to restore, metaphorically at least, the scope for "American energy." The aspiration remains with President Bush—in 1989 he quoted a British apostle of imperialism, Winston Churchill: "We Americans have only begun on our mission of goodness and greatness. And to those timid souls, I repeat the plea—give us the tools and we will do the job." It was Churchill who introduced the idea of aerial bombardment of Iraqi people as the way to subdue their unruly rulers. "So long as it acts as effective deterrent well and good," he wrote in 1921, "but we must beware of using it on too small a scale or so frequently that tribes learn to discount it, or in such a manner as to provoke retaliatory action with which we may not have adequate means of coping."[65]

U.S. people, Hirsch says, should know about the Truman Doctrine. What I want to add, is that along with the European empires, U.S. Man inherited literature and good culture as part of his justification. "America is from now on to be at the center of Western civilization rather than on the periphery," Walter Lippmann observed just after World War II. "The main premises of Western art have at last migrated to the United States, along with the center of gravity of industrial production and political power," Clement Greenberg wrote in 1948.[66] And since, especially during the Cold War, freedom has been identified as the leading characteristic of literature, it all fitted together. The writer was envisaged as a free mind, striking out beyond and above material affairs, untrammeled by history and the social order; and the reader was similarly free. The whole process was free from politics, because in the Free World there was little to be political about; yet by its very freedom literature manifested a critique of communism. A Harvard committee, with I. A. Richards a prominent member, reported on "General Education in a Free Society" and recommended the exposure of all students to the Great Texts of Literature; in an introduction, the president of Harvard, James Bryant Conant, saw as the goal "an appreciation of both the responsibilities and the benefits which come to [the students] because they are Americans and are free."[67] To make sure the rest of the world also appreciated this, the Central Intelligence Agency secretly financed the Congress for Cultural Freedom, which funded and supervised free literary-intellectual journals, edited by former leftists, in France, Italy, and Britain (*Preuves, Tempo Presente, Encounter*).[68]

A fear persisted that European culture might, through sheer longevity, still have the edge, but this could be reorganized as an advantage. Allan Bloom, in a chapter called "The Clean Slate," presents the U.S. reader's detachment from tradition as affording "free choice" and "equal access" to Great Books.[69] Hugh Kenner, writing on "the American Modernists," argues that in the United States the norms of language "are not imposed by history, they are elected, and if they turn out to be misleading us we can elect some new ones."[70] So language is like presidents: if you don't like the one you've got, you can elect another one: U.S. democracy is confirmed by cultural eclecticism. Kenner adds: "Two millennia's resources are simply available, for free election" (p. 218). This is the arrogance of empire: Kenner sees U.S. Man ranging (like the Virginia Company) through the "free land" of the universe, from Mexico to Mars, planting free democratic institutions and taking in return what he wants from the little green people. Above all, cultural plunder involved Shakespeare. Back in the 1840s P. T. Barnum wanted to buy the "birth-place" (supposing it was that) and transport it to the United States; in 1928 Henry Clay Folger, correspondingly, rejected the idea of establishing his great library in Stratford-on-Avon, his "ambition" being "to help make the United States a center for literary study and progress."[71] Along with the British Empire, though more slowly, the United States inherited dominance in the Shakespeare industry. The overwhelming power in the handling of Shakespeare is situated now in the United States (though the proportion of entries deriving from Japan in recent bibliographies perhaps points towards the next phase). As the United States was to define and maintain freedom, so it was to define and maintain the humanities; U.S. Man would become Man, and therefore by definition his culture would become worldwide. And why stop there?—Louis Marder in 1964 concluded his study of Shakespeare's reputation: "When life is discovered elsewhere in the universe and some interplanetary traveller brings to this new world the fruits of our terrestial culture, who can imagine anything but that among the first books carried to the curious strangers will be a Bible and the works of William Shakespeare?"[72] Now Columbus was looking through a radio telescope.

THE UNMANNING OF U.S. MAN

"Women's clubs particularly—and a good word ought to be said for these worthy women [says Louis B. Wright]—frequently devoted themselves to reading Shakespeare and teaching their children and husbands to love the dramatist."[73] Despite all the vigorous—indeed revealingly strenuous—attempts to link Shakespeare with pioneering, business and empire, the notion could not altogether be dispelled that the literary is associated with women and, worse, with "effeminacy."

This is the ultimate scandal, still almost unspeakable, founded in the haunting refusal of Shakespeare and Boone to cohere convincingly in other than fairly incidental ways. It is the furthest consequence of the ideological faultline in the constitution of U.S. Man.

The gendering of the pioneer image feeds into what Nina Baym has called the "melodramas of beset manhood" that have preponderated in "the American novel"; in the legend of Boone, the strength and resourcefulness of his wife was effaced, and she became passive and insignificant.[74] Anticipating my trope of the primal scene, the wilderness was imagined as female, "virgin land." Turner in his frontier thesis says the West opened her bosom and bestowed her treasures upon the pioneer who hacked his way through the virgin continent.[75] The same imagery appears in William Carlos Williams's account: Boone sought "with primal lust . . . the ecstasy of complete possession of the new country . . . there must be a new wedding."[76] The children's television series *Daniel Boone* (directed by William Wiard) has in its theme song the refrain: "Daniel Boone was a man, yes a BIG man, / And he fought for America, to make all Americans free." The corresponding construction of the feminine—by which I mean what our cultures perceive as the feminine—is contradictory (like the native, and other major cultural signifiers). Even as the woman is both whore and madonna, so she is both wilderness and cultivation. She is the dangerous other that must be conquered by masculinity, but she is also the special bearer of the finer feelings. Therefore, despite the nervous disavowals of many men of letters, she is central to the idea of literature. Despite the fearful attempts of Englit to efface them, there have been and are numerous female writers. Ann Douglas in her book *The Feminization of American Culture* has demonstrated the extent to which in the United States in the nineteenth century, women were recognized as dominating literary endeavor. The fashionable writer Nathaniel Willis observed: "It is the women who read. It is the women who are the tribunal of any question aside from politics or business. It is the women who give or withhold a literary reputation."[77]

And a hint of the feminine lurks around many male writers. In all but the most confident periods (and the confidence was usually founded in class—think of Bloomsbury) this has had to be disavowed. Often it was claimed that only false literature is feminine; in 1870 Alfred Austin lamented that whereas great art is "manly," those were "feminine, timorous, narrow, domesticated" times and productive of just such poetry. Douglas notes how Henry James "insisted to the reading public, and himself, that fiction, the traditional province of women, be accorded all the seriousness of history, the customary province of men"; Melville was misunderstood because he cultivated his own idea of masculinity.[78] The embarrassment could not easily be handled because it was not aberrant but fundamentally constitutive. For the force of literature in our cultures is supposed to reside in its resistance to workaday reality. It manifests a poetic, sensitive, and spiritual sensibility—and that correlates with the feminine. Consider Matthew Arnold's phraseology: sweetness and light versus barbarians and philistines. The latter sound like the real men.

Of course, this is not often directly acknowledged. Critics admire poetry for being concrete, for evincing tough reasonableness or a firm grasp of the actual; they call for their discipline to be scientific, precise, and systematic, a practice of rational elucidation. Behind such phrases stalks the anxiety that actually poetry is effeminate. One counterargument is to assert that this only *appears* to be so because women are allowed improper prominence. T. E. Hulme complained that "imitative poetry springs up like weeds, and women whimper and whine of you and I alas, and roses, roses all the way. It becomes the expression of sentimentality rather than of virile thought."[79] Frank Lentricchia quotes Wallace Stevens: "Poetry and Manhood: those who say poetry is now the peculiar province of women say so because ideas about poetry are effeminate. Homer, Dante, Shakespeare, Milton, Keats, Browning, much of Tennyson—they are your man-poets. Silly verse is always the work of silly men." Lentricchia argues that Stevens was actually in a complex negotiation with the idea of "Keats," which signified both resistance to "bourgeois economic contamination" and a culturally unacceptable loss of masculinity. Stevens recognized that the feminine aura of the literary in our cultures stood in opposition to the masculine ethos of capitalism, but also that this oppositional nexus was contained by the prevailing suggestion that the literary, by so much as it was feminine, was *trivial*. His task, therefore, was to deploy its critical capacity without sacrificing seriousness. He had to fashion a modernism that was not the same as "the effete modernity of his genteel contemporaries."[80]

This attempt to appropriate the radical aura of the feminine without the disabling stigma is profoundly typical of the difficulty that commonly besets dissident cultural formations. There was no way out, only a perpetual oscillation. The anxiety become plainest at the height of the Cold War. In 1951 Gilbert Seldes attributed the strength of "mass" culture to the gap between the "dandified" artist and the people, which derived, he said, from the gendering inscribed in the frontier mentality:

> The men left the arts to the women, and another American tradition took root—that the intellectual life of a community was women's affair. It was an unfortunate division of interest, reducing the area of sympathy between men and women, encouraging men to keep their active life away from their women and women to keep the life of the mind and the spirit away from their husbands; encouraging also the artist to address himself chiefly to women, to be precious and flattering and dandified.[81]

Adorno took the prevalence of the popular stereotype of the artist as "an 'aesthete', a weakling, and a 'sissy' " as one of the sinister and debilitating effects of "mass" culture. "Modern synthetic folklore," he believed, tends "to identify the artist with the homosexual and to respect only the 'man of action' as a real, strong man."[82] The very success of U.S. capitalism was producing embarrassment: just those entrepreneurial values that were supposed to secure freedom turned out to be devoted not, after all, to Shakespeare but to profit, and U.S. people were sliding back into savagery. Dwight Macdonald was moved to declare: "If one had no other data to go on, Masscult would expose capitalism as a class society rather than the harmonious commonwealth that, in election years, both parties tell us it is." However, Macdonald protected himself to some degree from the effects of this embarrassment by thinking of "mass" culture as the wilderness and himself as . . . well, you've guessed: "As an earlier settler in the wilderness of masscult who cleared his first tract thirty years ago . . . I have come to feel like the aging Daniel Boone when the plowed fields began to surround him in Kentucky."[83] Rather tidily, the imagery displaces the anxiety that the problem is constitutive of U.S. Man by making Macdonald the pioneer (and hence not, of course, feminine).

This topic links up with my earlier thoughts on the appropriation of Shakespeare by East Coast gentry, for there is also a class affiliation to effeminacy. I have argued elsewhere that literature may be located as a subculture of "middle-class dissidence"—as a form cultivated distinctively and most powerfully (though not exclusively) by a fraction of the bourgeoisie that has found itself, in diverse ways, hostile to the hegemony of the principal part of that class—the businessmen, industrialists, and empire builders. In E. M. Forster's *Howards End,* it is the Schlegels versus the Wilcoxes. This seems to have been as true in the United States as in England, and it is middle-class dissidence, uniquely, that has opposed the prevailing social order as excessively masculine. Together, literature and effeminacy contributed to the leisured ethos of the East Coast gentry—the men opposed by the populace at Astor Place as "silk-gloved aristocrats."[84] Ann Douglas points out that male authors took to travel writing because it seemed like aimless wandering: "They emphasized the casualness of their journeys, the haphazardness of their impressions, the uncollated quality of their notes. They escaped censure because they did not take themselves too seriously. They confessed to indolence." By acknowledging it, they anticipated the charge that they were not being masculine and purposeful. And notice the class implications: this was the stance of the dilettante, the leisured amateur. Travel-writing remained the mode of the effete gentleman through into the 1950s—hence the distrust of it then among lower-middle-class British "Movement" writers such as Kingsley Amis.[85] Of course, the dilettante stance was only a partial protection, but it represents the necessary maneuver of the literary and the leisured alike: to repudiate the masculine while trying not to fall too damagingly into the feminine. The commonest resolution in Britain is that a real man is big enough to admit to a feminine side in his nature—though of course he won't allow it to dominate. In the United States, I feel, this is more difficult, because pioneer masculinity is so central to the idea of the "American male," and the cultural authority of the leisure class (though not necessarily its economic and political power) has been correspondingly weaker.

The nexus of class, sex, and the humanities that I have been examining is apparent in *The Closing of the American Mind*. Allan Bloom yearns for a relationship between the university teacher and student such as he believes Socrates shared with the young male aristocrats of Athens. Surprisingly (it is the surprising part of the book), Bloom allows the sexual teasing in this relationship to become apparent. The young man who was "physically and spiritually virginal" would reveal "this literal lust for knowledge," and this "a teacher could see in the eyes of those who flattered him by giving such evidence of their need for him," Bloom says (pp. 135–36). Apparently this flirtatious relationship can work properly only with youths who "have not settled the sexual problem, who are still young, even look young for their age." Such an unformed young man may, as it were, be traveling to Florence in search of his Beatrice or, Bloom says, to Athens in search of his Socrates (p. 134)—so he may fall either for a nice young lady from Smith or for his male professor. Eve Sedgwick has also noticed this; she says Bloom has produced "an ingenuously faithful and candid representation of . . . the stimulation and glamorization of the energies of male-male desire" in humanities teaching.[86] However, the game has been spoilt, in Bloom's view, by the decline of the leisure class and by "Freudian" awareness of "sublimation," which encourages the inference that Socrates/Bloom "really" desires the youths sexually. A "naive and good-natured" freshman said as much to Bloom, who comments somewhat campily, "I was charmed by the lad's candor but could not regard him as a serious candidate for culture" (p. 234). The text he has to confront (it is the only one on which he offers more than brief comment) is Thomas Mann's *Death in Venice* (see pp. 230–38). In this story, Aschenbach's growing infatuation with Tadzio is accompanied by quotations from the *Phaedrus,* which keep coming into Aschenbach's head. Thus one of Bloom's most prized educational-erotic Platonic dialogues is made to speak, with what seems to Bloom "a rather heavy Freudian hand . . . the failure of sublimation" (pp. 230–31). As Sedgwick points out, there are two dangers for Bloom: that such desires will become petrified, and that they might be expressed. Mann blows the whistle on the discreet, passionate game that the upper-class youth, impressed with the European culture of his teacher, might be teased into playing.

Bloom's stance, poised with his hand on the latch of the closet, is both provocative and arrogant; he surely relies upon his new right supporters being discreet or preferring not to notice, and on his opponents declining to confront him in a way that might appear homophobic. Friends and enemies are coerced into a collusive hypocrisy. The usual project, in fact a persistent subtext in literary studies, has been to repudiate effeminacy even while leaving here and there the nuance required to indicate artistic sensitivity. Nina Baym has shown how the very idea of "the American novel" has been organized on the pioneer model, so that the kinds of books women chose to write do not count as instances.[87] Shakespeare has seemed a reassuringly manly writer—involved in the practical, business aspects of theater, with big tragic themes, heroes, plenty of fighting, a positive attitude to courtship and marriage, robust comedy, bawdy language; and just think of those codpieces. Note the traditional critical pleasure in Prince Hal's misspent youth in the stews (though of course we don't see him doing anything ignoble), and in Henry V's ready domination of his fiancée; and the need to place Macbeth's subordination to his wife (if he is too much influenced by her, he can't quite make it as a "tragic hero"). Shakespeare may be allowed a hint of the feminine, but not too much. Cross-dressing in the love comedies, for instance: the best strategy probably was to ignore it or declare it merely a convention. However, C. L. Barber risked recording his pleasure that "there is so little that is queazy in all Shakespeare's handling of boy actors playing women, and playing women pretending to be men."[88] Above all, there are the Sonnets. Henry Hallam, nervous about the "poetic" relationship between his son and Alfred Tennyson, observed: "it is impossible not to wish that Shakespeare had never written them. There is a weakness and folly in all excessive and mis-placed affection, which is not redeemed by the touches of nobler sentiments."[89] Eric Partridge, writing on "Shakespeare's bawdy," felt he could not quite ignore the topic. It is homosexuals, he says, who have claimed Shakespeare to be one of themselves, whereas "healthy-minded" commentators have repudiated the idea. Partridge quotes Hesketh Pearson's opinion that "most of the Sonnets may be read as literary exercises," remarking complacently that Shakespeare's attitude to homosexuality is shown by "much the same sort of kindly-contemptuous or un-mawkish-pitying remark as the averagely tolerant and understanding person of the present generation would make" (even in your pity you must be careful not to be mawkish). Nevertheless, Partridge quotes a "medical man" saying that "none of us can pride ourselves on being a hundred per cent. man or a hundred per cent. woman," thereby managing to leave the suggestion of Shakespeare as the complete human being, containing both genders.[90]

The further you advance in professional Englit, the more likely you are to be a man, and hence the embarrassment of many male professors at their predominantly female student enrollments. Charles Mills Gayley introduced the first Great Books course at Berkeley in 1901. His biographer, Benjamin Kurtz, tells of "some venturesome engineers who discarded jumpers and overalls, washed the laboratory grime from their hands, and sallied forth to a literary lecture room, only to find it so crowded with girls, women, coeds, pelicans, old maids, and females of every other sort and description, that they fled back to their hill fastnesses."[91] Gayley began to limit the number of women allowed to attend his classes so as to make room for men (an early instance of affirmative action). Irving Babbitt noted that "men of business" regard poetry as "a pretty enough thing for our wives and daughters" while men take science courses and women literary courses:

> The literary courses, indeed, are known in some of these institutions as "sissy" courses. The man who took literature too seriously would be suspected of effeminacy. The really virile thing to be is an electrical engineer. One already sees the time when the typical teacher of

literature will be some young dilettante who will interpret Keats and Shelley to a class of girls.[92]

Babbitt found that "the more vigorous and pushing teachers of language feel that they must assert their manhood by philological research"—though this was unnecessary, he believed, because the true humanist makes "a vigorous and virile application of ideas to life," his mind being "assimilative in the active and masculine sense" (pp. 119, 133, 135). This kind of thing runs all through F. R. Leavis; and Harold Bloom imagines literature passing from father to son in an Oedipal romance uncontaminated by female mediation. These days we have theory, which of course is really hunky.

MAN'S LAST STAND

I have tried elsewhere to trace aspects of the configuration through which Europeans seek to handle the collapse of their empires. Decolonization calls into question the superiority of European Man. During the Mau Mau resistance in Kenya in the mid 1950s, the Duchess of Manchester said: "The niggers—that is what we call them—have a list of Europeans they want to get rid of. But they can't manage without us, and they will have to see reason eventually. It is difficult to explain this to them because they have no brains, you know—only animal cunning."[93] But what if Africans, Asians, and Caribbean peoples were competent, did not need Europeans, did not respect their humanism? And what if the Europeans appeared violent, unjust, and, further, hypocritical? The ordeal of Kamau Kichina, a Kikuyu prisoner of the Kenyan imperial police, was described from court evidence:

> Throughout Kamau's captivity no effort was spared to force him to admit his guilt. He was flogged, kicked, handcuffed with his arms between his legs and fastened behind his neck, denied food for a period, and was left out at least two nights tied to a pole in a shed, not surrounded by walls, with only a roof overhead, and wearing merely a blanket to keep out the cold.[94]

Kamau Kichina died. This is the kind of news that disconcerted European humanists. There were ways of evading the implications—I found this instance quoted by the psychologist William Sargant as evidence of the subtle viciousness of the Kikuyu, his thought being that they had indoctrination techniques so devilish as to be proof against torture. Alternatively, you can cast around for plausible good whites; this is the tactic of the films *Cry Freedom* (Richard Attenborough) and *Mississippi Burning* (Alan Parker). But to many it was ev-ident that European Man was not as noble as he had believed himself to be. Lamming declared: "Now it is Prospero's turn to submit to the remorseless logic of his own past. . . . He cannot deny that past; nor can he abandon it without creating a total suicide of all those values which once sanctified his acts as coloniser." The point was taken explicitly by Sartre: "we must face that unexpected revelation, the strip-tease of our humanism. There you can see it, quite naked, and it's not a pretty sight. It was nothing but an ideology of lies, a perfect justification for pillage; its honeyed words, its affectation of sensibility were only alibis for our aggressions." Citing racial killings by the *colons* in Algiers, Sartre asked, "Now, which side are the savages on?"[95]

This crisis of European humanism provoked a specific reorgani-zation of Man: the savage is *relocated*. Though he is still stereotypically a former imperial subject, he is to be found also inside all of us. The notion of innate human depravity has, of course, a long history; but since the eighteenth century it has been challenged by beliefs that people are either innately good, or neither one nor the other and therefore improvable. In Conrad's *Heart of Darkness,* Kurtz, the classic renegade, succumbs to temptations to join the savages; however Mar-low, who constitutes the reading position offered to us, manages to maintain his equilibrium. One of Daniel Boone's biographers declares that the white hunter has "the instinct of the primitive man," but he has *also* "the advantage of a civilised mind, and thus provided seldom fails to outwit, under equal advantages, the cunning savage."[96] White men could afford to acknowledge some fraternity with the savages, so long as basic superiority was maintained. But after 1945 the most acclaimed writers were those who asserted *universal* savagery. The idea appears again and again during the period of decolonization and through into the present, especially in a potent compound of popular anthropology, psychology, and ethology, and in what has seemed to be England's profoundest literature (consider Harold Pinter, Ted Hughes, and the idea that humans must strive like animals for "territory").

The savage within is the final, desperate throw of a humiliated and exhausted European humanism. It manifests both an anxiety about and a continuing embroilment in imperialist ideology. It works like this: when it was just the natives who were brutal, the Europeans were enlightened and necessary rulers. But if the Europeans are (have been) brutal, that's human nature. There are three consolations for European Man in this move. First, the elaboration of the idea may, of itself, seem to witness to moral and philosophical profundity. Second, no analysis of classic colonialism or continuing capitalist imperialism need be conducted, since it is all human nature anyway. Third, Europeans may imagine themselves even now to possess at least "a veneer of civilisation," and hence retain the superior position.

With a rapidity that has surprised almost all observers, U.S. Man has followed a trajectory comparable in general form to that of European Man. The sense that U.S. power might be not a blessing to the world but a burden did not have to wait for Vietnam, still less for Gore Vidal's moment when "the American Empire died"—"September 16, 1985, when the Commerce Department announced that the United States had become a debtor nation."[97] The thought already haunted ex-left, Cold War intellectuals from the Hiroshima and Nagasaki bombs (why were two necessary?), through the Korean War and military operations in Iran, Lebanon, Dominica, Guatemala, and Cuba. As with the expulsion of the Europeans from their empires, it seems that the United States is not wanted, that its culture is not after all superior, that it behaves as badly as the people it wants to make free. Ray Bradbury's *Fahrenheit 451* broached the anxious question as early as 1954: "Is it because we're so rich and the rest of the world's so poor and we just don't care if they are? . . . Is that why we're hated so much?"[98] However, in this novel Great Books are still the answer. By the mid 1960s, Vietnam had cast further doubt on U.S. Man and his destiny, inviting renewed attention to the Indians—Dee Brown's *Bury My Heart at Wounded Knee* went through twenty-nine printings in hard and paper covers and three book-club editions in 1971–72. And, as Noam Chomsky conclusively demonstrated, intellectuals made a shocking contribution to the ideology that sustained the Vietnam War.[99]

I have not especially observed the "savage within" phenomenon in the United States (though it has certainly appealed to U.S. commentators on European writing), but the discrediting of U.S. Man surely informs the situation of Englit. Now, Allan Bloom complains, "we are used to hearing the Founders charged with being racists, murderers of Indians, representatives of class interests" (*Closing of the American Mind,* p. 29). He, Hirsch, and William Bennett, Ronald Reagan's secretary of education, believe that the answer is to reassert the humanities, since failure to promote them is undermining the ideological coherence of even the U.S. mainland empire. In fact, it is the other way about: the exposing of U.S. Man and his cultural claims as imperialist makes the established culture and its pretensions a source of

anxiety rather than pride, and helps to release the aspirations of subordinated groups. The humanist concept of U.S. Man, which proclaims his civilization, falls into question along with the pioneer concept that asserts his right to "free" land. Before going any further, it
needs to be said that Hirsch's "purely functional" case, that everyone
needs to know snatches of verse such as "Music hath charms to soothe
the savage breast" to get along in the United States today, is ridiculous
(pp. 106–7, 189), though in one sense at least that line from *Comus*
is apposite: it encapsulates Hirsch's fantasy that the feared savagery
of alien others may be magically soothed by a harmonious culture.
But beyond this, the reason of principle why new right fulminations
are unlikely to revivify even the humanities in academia, let alone the
wider culture, is that their demands cannot be separated from the
conditions that produce them. The peoples of non-Anglo-American
cultures, who are supposed to be socialized by Shakespeare and the
rest, are *reminders of the disgrace of empire.*

It is because U.S. imperial ideologies no longer carry spontaneous
conviction that the exhortations become panicky. We find new right
commentators attempting to assert, crudely and in the same breath,
the humanities and the destiny of the United States. Bloom, stating
that "there is no immediate, sensual experience of the nation's meaning or its project," thinks we should ask ourselves the traditional
humanist question, "What is man?" From his account it is hard to
see why there should be a problem, for he believes "America tells one
story: the unbroken, ineluctable progress of freedom and equality."
Hirsch even boasts that English was established as the national language in the United States without bloodshed—Blacks and Indians
are so remote from his thinking that he fails to notice how appallingly
they falsify his statement.[100] "Our society was founded upon such
principles as justice, liberty, government with the consent of the governed, and equality under the law," William Bennett declares (well,
homosexuality is indeed equally illegal in half of the states). These
ideas, Bennett says, "descended directly from great epochs of Western
civilization," and they "are the glue that binds together our pluralistic
nation."[101] There it is: Bennett says he is against the humanities being
"used as if they were the handmaiden of ideology, subordinated to
particular prejudices" (p. 10), but does not see his own slant as a
gross instance of just that.

Imperial ideology pretends that migrations towards the center of
power witness to a natural recognition of the superiority of the metropolitan economy, culture, and political arrangements. If this were

so, it would be reasonable to expect migrants to respect the metropolitan system. Actually, immigration is a by-product of the imperial structure—it is a consequence of trade, communications, poverty, repression, aid, warfare. Of course, people want to come to Europe and North America from countries impoverished by the loans their sometimes corrupt or puppet governments have been induced to accept. They are only following the resources that are being extracted from their countries. But they may not be grateful just to be here. They may not want to integrate in the ways expected. They may not be content to wait while some of their number get on and get out, leaving the rest behind to admire. They may take the "civil religion" at face value, asking for "rights." And they may feel that they can sustain a stronger dignity and cohesion by holding on to a version of their own culture. This is the great threat for Hirsch: "multilingualism enormously increases cultural fragmentation, civil antagonism, illiteracy, and economic-technological ineffectualness."[102] Bennett declares: "The fact that we as Americans—whether black or white, Asian or Hispanic, rich or poor—share these beliefs aligns us with other cultures of the Western tradition"; but he is contradicting himself, for his principal point has been that these knowledges are not currently "shared."[103] And this is what worries him: he observes widespread disaffection from U.S. institutions (such that only half those entitled to vote do so in presidential elections) and calls for more determined teaching of the "precious historical legacy" of the United States. He cannot afford to consider that people are disaffected from U.S. institutions, not because they have never heard about them, but because their everyday experience tells them that they have no real stake there. Hirsch and Bennett need to disqualify the cultures of subordinated peoples because they are bases from which political demands might be mounted—demands such as the "civil religion" was designed not to recognize but to restrain.

Once it becomes apparent that the most marked effect of U.S. Man and his humanism is to make other cultures appear inferior, tending thereby to justify the subordination of peoples who remain spectacularly impoverished in the midst of plenty, it is difficult to teach and study Shakespeare as if such study were neutral. It is not merely that the canon is questioned—that has happened before and could be accommodated. What is in doubt is the absolute and hence continuing wisdom of traditional, or indeed *any*, texts. Hirsch and Bloom are unwilling witnesses to this, for their attempts to present their Great Books as true guides to living today lead them into strenuous and absurdly simplified readings—actually threatening to undermine the seriousness of those books. Bloom is still deploying the old new critical maneuver of declaring that his central text, Plato's *Republic,* is to be read ironically—in order to prevent its apparent implications contradicting his whole theory.[104] Hirsch in *Cultural Literacy* claims that the value of Shakespeare is exemplified by the fact that his father used to exhort his employees to greater efforts with a phrase from *Julius Caesar:* "There is a tide . . ." (p. 9). This is, of course, the conjoining of Shakespeare, business culture, and the pioneer spirit proposed by Joseph Quincy Adams and Louis B. Wright (Hirsch acknowledges [p. ix] not just the finance but the inspiration of Exxon, the Great Polluter, in the person of the president of its education foundation). Yet one cannot help thinking that "Time is money" would have done as well or better, and that reading Shakespeare is a lot of bother just to pick up a few ideological tags. But then Hirsch thinks most people need only "a schematic conception of Shakespeare" (pp. 129–30). As with those "educators" who want history to be learning dates, critical thought is not the goal, and the separation of most people from students with some grasp of what these things might actually be about is to be maintained.

The fundamental point is that the position from which one reads can no longer be absolutized. The traditional quest for the true meaning assumed an essential humanity, informing both text and critic. If a lower-class person, woman, student, person of color, lesbian, or gay man did not "respond appropriately" to "the text," it was because they were reading partially, wrongly. But now we see that they were reading from outside or beneath the position of U.S. Man—white, adult, male, heterosexual, middle-class, "American." Almost anyone may learn to (re)produce an "appropriate" reading, but it will be at the expense of the person they thought they were.

New historicism recognizes the crisis of U.S. Man. Of course, there were historicists before, and good ones, but their work was situated within an overall confidence in literary humanism. New historicism collaborates in the relativizing of canonical texts by stressing their historical situations, and also through its use of anthropology; it places Great Books alongside other texts so that their authority seeps away, and often it acknowledges their roles in a contested drama of state power. These practices point either towards a poststructuralist sense of meaning as sliding always into a black hole of infinite textuality, or towards an awareness of ideology and politics. Specifically, new historicists are aware of what I have called the American primal scene, the moment of conception of U.S. Man. In chapter 5 of *Renaissance Self-Fashioning,* Stephen Greenblatt goes straight to the point and confronts the exuberant humanism that critics have found in the plays of Christopher Marlowe with an episode from Sierra Leone in 1586—an attack on a peaceful and orderly village.[105] This could as well have been Captain John Mason's massacre of Pequot Indians at Mystic River in 1637, or General Patrick E. Connor's attack on the Arapaho camp in 1865; it could have been My Lai. In *Apocalypse Now* the attack by helicopter gunships blaring out "The Ride of the Valkyries" improves on Conrad's *Heart of Darkness* by making the target a manifestly peaceful and civilized village. In Grenada "U.S. Army helicopter pilots, influenced by Francis Ford Coppola's *Apocalypse Now,* strung loudspeakers to their landing struts and invaded the island with Wagner's *Die Walküre* blasting from the amplifiers."[106]

Yet new historicism often hesitates to develop its political potential. It slides back into old historicism or takes the easy route into the new oblivious formalism of poststructuralist word games; it finds itself at odds with radical movements with which it should be allied. It is fascinated by a model of *ideological entrapment* whereby resistance is not just controlled, not just anticipated, but actually sponsored by the dominant to secure its own power. (Earlier chapters attempt to theorize an exit from the entrapment model of ideology and power.) This has led to major insights about how ideologies work, but has not helped much in figuring out how to develop into purposeful political action the dissidence that our societies do actually produce. At times it threatens to extend the line of nostrums, from original sin to existential absurdity and the savage within, through which intellectuals have relieved themselves of the burden of thinking about how the world might be improved. Like other commentators, I have been inclined to trace the sensitivity to entrapment in new historicism to the disappointments that followed the apparent empowering of dissident intellectuals in the 1960s, when the persistent replaying of the primal scene was protested by the Civil Rights movement and the Vietnam peace movement. More specifically, I relate it now to the professionalization of Englit.

IS THERE A CLASS IN THIS TEXT?

A Lyotardian might perceive the disqualifying of U.S. Man as one instance of the supposed disappearance of "grand narratives." However, it is a mistake to suppose that those are produced only by intellectuals; while the latter lament their confusion, narratives such as competitive individualism (Thatcherism) are peddled by politicians and the media. However, Lyotard is right to note, like Foucault, that intellectuals are valued now, not for their insight into Man, but for professional expertise.[107] My argument has been that the version of Man that appealed to literary intellectuals depended for its status upon its implication with an Anglo-American leisure elite. As that elite declined, theories of the universal relevance of literature *as such*—new criticism, Leavisism, "myth" criticism, the general education movement, even demands for equal access to higher education—were urgently propounded, though the leisured idea remained residually. But the actual outcome was that the base of Englit became entirely professional. The widespread anxiety today is that the humanities have, to use Steven Connor's term, become "operationalised"; they have become all too conveniently adapted to supplying "accreditation for all the traditionally privileged professions and social functions—which includes banking, commerce and industrial management alongside 'humane' occupations like teaching and social work."[108] And academia too is organized through "the dynamic of individualism, private ownership, and competition."[109] All this is discomforting for two reasons: first, it is specifically at odds with the humanistic concept of Man, which was supposed to transcend such matters (at this point Allan Bloom joins the left in complaining of the dominance of business [*Closing of the American Mind,* p. 260]). Second, operationalization is discomforting because it gives the humanities an embarrassing role in the perpetuation of an unjust system, as academics rank students according to criteria that would ideally be transcendent and at worst meritocratic, but actually are all too convenient to the requirements of corporate capitalism. In *Political Shakespeare* (chapter 8), I have discussed some of the mechanisms through which a facility for literature, against the wishes of many teachers, is used as a key educational criterion and hence as a ground of discrimination. The final twist is that when lower-class people do not take to good culture, it can be read as their fault, their failure to reach a full humanity.

In my view, the Englit profession is especially vulnerable to such appropriation because of the weakness of its rationale. This has perhaps three aspects. First, as T. S. Eliot warned in 1948, anticipating the decline of the leisure class, a profession is too narrow a base upon which to sustain the pretensions of good culture. Eliot held that such culture should be grounded in a class; otherwise the cultural elite "will consist solely of individuals whose only common bond will be their professional interest: with no social cohesion, with no social continuity."[110] Other subcultures, implicated in classes and class fractions, and around race, region, gender, and sexuality, have far more elaborate ramifications in the lives of individuals and in the social structure; they may involve neighborhood connections, work, and the home, and more than one generation in a family; whereas the humanities, almost by definition in their current meritocratic mode, have to be specially inculcated. The attenuated social location and allegiance of a profession is not sufficient to keep the idea of Man and literary culture relevant and persuasive to the rest of society. That is why the humanities have to be financed through public institutions, while popular subcultures sustain themselves in the face of official disapprobation.

Second, the tendency of a profession is to become self-referential—"colleague-oriented rather than client-oriented."[111] The profession establishes criteria of what you are supposed to do, and, in that process, questions about the purpose and meaning of the activity drop out of sight. Thus the activity seems to proceed out of its own resources, but in fact becomes progressively less necessary in the social formation. This effect may be gauged from the extent of the separation of Englit from the practice of other educated and/or thoughtful readers. This is far more pronounced in the United States than in Britain, for in the latter the leisure-class image of good culture remains as something of a bridge between the two through the mediation of "Oxbridge." Indeed, a notable proportion of general reviewing in publications such as the *New York Review of Books* is done by Oxbridge academics, who appear qualified for the task because of their wider role in Britain.[112]

Third, the replacement of the universal intellectual with the professional is distinctively problematic for Englit, for the expertise of this profession was supposed to consist in a profound intuition of—neither more nor less—the now-inconceivable universal. The collapse of Man has made the traditional project of Englit absurd; it has become an edifice built over a void. So the students drift away, for if professional attainment is the only reason for studying literature, why not choose a more useful major—law, for instance? New historicists, therefore, like their colleagues, are sustaining many of the old routines while knowing, really, that their validity has evaporated. That is why, very often, work is admired, not because it is right or useful (it may well be barely comprehensible), but because it is *smart*. Furthermore, new historicism is successful and itself entangled in institutional power. Michael Bristol relates the entrapment of new historicists to the changing status of Shakespeare: "That authority is still felt to be somehow binding, but it no longer contains any sense of openness to the future."[113] The sign has gone from between the posts, and we are gazing out at what used to be regarded as the savage other, realizing that behind the sign there is another sign and that the culture that was created in contradistinction is an ideological construction. But, by and large, we are still following the old institutional trails—out on the artificial parkway and not so far from Duke English Department as we thought.

Stanley Fish was one of the first to see that the readings of literary critics cannot be absolutized. *Is There a Text in This Class?* (1980) records how, by what now seem rather lengthy maneuverings (which show how difficult it was to kick the idea of Man as writer/reader), Fish reached the conclusion that it is the profession that determines which readings will pass as plausible. This is surely right: discourses are interactive, they make sense only because they are shared. However, Fish's position differs from that advanced in this book because he at once tries to totalize his argument, alleging that even apparently objective features like line endings "exist by virtue of perceptual strategies rather than the other way around."[114] This, he says, is because such features "will only be directions to those who already have the interpretive strategies in the first place" (p. 173). This is, of course, true, but it does not sustain Fish's case. Readers obviously have to know the relevant codes, but once the system is in motion, authors plant cues in their texts with such readers in mind. Reading is in fact collaborative: the text invites the application of decoding principles that the reader may or may not (1) recognize and (2) agree to put into operation. In other respects, Fish's argument obscures as much as it illuminates. He says that the reading of texts is governed by "interpretive communities" made up of "those who share interpretive strategies," and elaborates: "The only 'proof' of membership is fellowship, the nod of recognition from someone in the same community."[115] What is misleading here is the apparent geniality of the process: Fish's phrasing—sharing, community, fellowship, "nod of recognition"—effaces the hierarchy, competition, deference, and coercion in the profession.

The conservative bearing of his work is evident when, in a recent essay, Fish uses the idea of an interpretive community to disqualify the aspirations of some new historicists to exceed professional boundaries and give their work a more dissident political impetus.[116] Fish's tactic is to make absurd demands of a political criticism: he assumes that it must "grasp the political constructedness and relatedness of all things" (whereas just *some* things would be good going) and "not leave more in place than it disturbs" (even revolutions probably don't do that [pp. 313–14]). He mocks the idea that "the appearance on Monday of a new reading of *The Scarlet Letter* would be the occasion on Tuesday of discussion, debate, and proposed legislation on the floor of Congress" (p. 315). All this could be simple ignorance—there is no sign that Fish has encountered any one of the major theories of ideology. But that bullying tone is heard also when he insinuates that his colleagues' concerns are ad hominem (a shortage of "fellowship" here) and urges them to "sit back and enjoy the fruits of their professional success" (p. 315). Fish's main assertion is that academics are limited to the "particular game" and the "constitutive rules" established in the profession (p. 314). In other words, he is trying to insist that the profession not only does, but *must* limit the political scope of its members. Of course, this is not true: we can bend, stretch, violate, and extend the rules in all kinds of ways—the "game" analogy is misleading, for you can't do those things in most classic games. Fish cannot but grant that the rules are "provisional and revisable," but still wants to suggest that there is little scope for movement. Actually, there are all kinds of possibilities in interdisciplinary work still to be opened up, and salaried intellectuals have opportunities to enter general cultural commentary and to contribute to the specific concerns of subcultures. Fish's reply is that in attempting to focus on such enabling connections, "one would no longer be doing literary criticism" (pp. 314, 316). Here we see how coercive his "game" metaphor is: it allows him to suggest that there is something illegitimate about trying to develop alternative discourses.

What we may hope, Fish says, is that our work "will make a difference in the institutional setting that gives it a home" (p. 315). That is worth doing, but it may also be a rationalization for complacency. David Simpson quotes Paul de Man saying in 1986 that he preferred being in the United States because in Europe one is "much closer to ideological and political questions," whereas the U.S. university "has no cultural function at all." In the latter, therefore, de Man believed he could concentrate upon "the profession" where he could be "really and effectively subversive." We should ask, as Simpson does: "What might it mean to be 'subversive' in a subculture that has 'no cultural function'?"[117] The attitudes of Fish and de Man seem designed to head off such political potential as Englit may have, and to trap understanding within a closed system—one controlled by the senior professors with their nods of approval. It is all too close to the entrapment model of power favored by new historicists. But the trap, we may now see, is set by the profession—or, rather, by the ideas of its scope that we allow to prevail. So Fish may be right about the current dominance of merely professional structures, but not in his assertion that there is no alternative. Foucault, for instance, succeeded spectacularly in not being bounded by professional rules. He critiqued academic disciplines as "procedures for the subjection of discourses," ways of policing thought in the interest of the powerful.[118] Foucault took the intellectual's sphere to be discursive practices in general, and urged an erosion of professional boundaries with a view to detaching "the power of truth from the forms of hegemony (social, economic, and cultural) within which it operates at the present time." He wanted to "show up, transform and reverse the systems which quietly order us about" and to "show how one could escape."[119] Of course, that could never be easy, but if it were impossible nothing would ever change.

I conclude that the sense of entrapment that fascinates new historicism—in theory, in textual instances, and in its sense of its own political scope—is tellingly homologous with its own professional entrapment; and this derives ultimately from the discrediting of U.S. Man. However, new historicists generally are not complacent like Fish; they propound a wide range of attitudes, and, distinctively, they are *anxious about* entrapment. Freud suggests, in his analysis of Dora, that the discovery of the primal scene of parental intercourse may redirect the child's sexuality—away from masturbation and towards anxiety.[120] If we think of the naive humanist edifice of the nobility of U.S. Man, which Bloom and Hirsch would like to reerect, as a kind of masturbation fantasy (and I have nothing against masturbation as such), then we may understand new historicism as redirected *towards anxiety* by the recent and distressing discovery of the primal scene. New historicism has seen the violence and oppression at the conception of U.S. Man but, held within the family structure that generated the problem, it is paralyzed by anxiety about the dreadful knowledge it has helped to produce. However, whereas Freud's Dora became nervously short of breath, as her father had been from his primal exertions, Englit has become garrulous, overproducing frantically to reassure itself that it really exists.

SUBCULTURES

The culture of U.S. Man is not shared by everyone, and that is as it should be. A divided society should have a divided culture; anything else must be a mystifying pretense. An allegedly universal culture works to subordinate other cultures: it is defined as *not* special to a locality, gender, sexual orientation, race, nationality. It "rises above" such matters, and by just so much it pushes them down. Subcultural groups are, by definition, those whose claim to be Man is weaker. Herbert London, a dean at New York University, is reported as saying that the trouble with literature by women and nonwhites is that "it does not lead us towards our true humanity."[121] According to cultural materialism, our "humanity" is not an essential condition towards which we may aspire, but what people have as a consequence of being socialized into human communities; and it is damaging to human beings to persuade them that their language and culture are inferior. Bennett remarks of "students": "If their past is hidden from them, they will become aliens in their own culture, strangers in their own land."[122] This is a true and moving sentiment, but precisely misapplied, for it is supposed to justify insistence upon the one superior, homogenizing, hegemonic "past," requiring diverse peoples to repudiate their actual histories on pain of being stigmatized as "strangers in their own land." A project for cultural materialism is to discover ways taking the opposite direction: of working with subcultures to reinforce and extend the potential of people who inhabit them.

One reason why the profession of Englit exercises such power over its members is that in the process of joining it they, we, have been drawn away from alternative, subcultural allegiances that once were ours. The precise tendency of academia, in its current, meritocratic phase, is to detach individuals from other subcultural allegiances; one abandons subculture to become Man. As Fish amply shows, the profession requires you to read, not as a homosexual or a Black, but in accordance with its established criteria. Conversely, the professionalization of literature is facilitated by the deracination of many of its practitioners. The key group for this discussion has to be Jews—who were, of course, many of the immigrants that horrified Gayley and Adams. For many decades—the decades when literature was central to the culture of an Anglo-American leisured elite—they were excluded from English departments.[123] Aspirations to breach this barrier were not trivial; not, as we might imagine today, merely to do with income and status. For several generations, a priority for the immigrant family had to be attaining sufficient integration into "American" culture to feel relatively safe from the pogrom, exile, and the death camp; these remained powerful fears, reinforced by the John Birch Society, George Lincoln Rockwell, the Ku Klux Klan, and other North American racists.[124] The cultural significance of Englit made it obviously attractive. Richard Hofstadter observes: "In their search for new lives or new nationality, these immigrants have suffered much, and they have been rebuffed and made to feel inferior by the 'native stock' "; therefore "achieving a better type of job or better social status and becoming 'more American' have become practically synonymous."[125] A professor of English not only had better status and a better job but was installed in one of the places where U.S. Man was defined. There, surely, he would be sufficiently "American"? However, there were difficulties.

There might be an emotional cost. The disjunction between Orthodoxy and most canonical texts could be distressing, and might have to be handled through strategies not unlike those used by English puritans in the sixteenth century (see chapter 8 above; James Yaffe gives examples of how students at Yeshiva University in New York were doing this in the 1960s). *The Merchant of Venice* was an obvious test case, and a number of moves to drop it from syllabuses are recorded.[126] However, the student eager to join the dominant culture might tell herself, as did Lillian S. Robinson, that anti-Semitism in the *Merchant* could be set aside while one addressed "the real point of the work."[127] Lionel Trilling, the first Jew tenured in the English department at Columbia University, acknowledged no discomfort, then or later, when specifying the *Merchant* as one of the texts that was pressed upon him in high school. Though well aware of the political role of literature in maintaining the hegemony of the leisured elite, Trilling made it his project to reduce "cultural diversity to what appeared, from an intellectual standpoint, to be the highest common denominator, the English cultural tradition."[128] Such embracing of Englit was one facet of a far broader movement of incorporation and estrangement, as Jewish people colonized and were colonized by the U.S. intelligentsia. Irving Howe, Delmore Schwartz, Norman Podhoretz, and Daniel Bell have described the distress of their parents as their educational aspirations drew them away from their traditional language and culture. "Most of this generation, including myself, were ashamed of our parents," Bell records.[129] Probably a majority of teachers of Englit have had such experiences in respect of one or another subculture. Nevertheless, as Don Wayne observes, most U.S. academics give little indication in their work of "the factors in our respective genealogies and in our immediate social life that motivate the representations we construct"; Jonathan Culler has written tellingly of the reluctance of critics to criticize Christianity, despite its use as "a legitimation for many reactionary or repressive forces in the United

States."[130] Outside the Women's Movement, and often even there, nearly all criticism is written still from the traditional mandarin stance that once bespoke class confidence and now speaks professional competence.

There is also a question about the ultimate gains achieved by non-leisure-class people through the infiltration of academia. For the gaining of university posts by Jewish people, and other subordinated groups during the postwar and 1960s expansion, coincided with the slippage of U.S. Man into Englit professionalism and the ebbing away of precisely the cachet that had been valued. As Don Wayne remarks, it was the changing of literary study into "a work-discipline rather than genteel reflection by men of taste and proper breeding" that opened it to "scholars who didn't happen to come to school equipped with English surnames."[131] But this works both ways: terms like *taste* and *breeding* nominate just that overlap of class and cultural status that made Englit a significant place to be. The detachment of good culture from the leisure class was the condition upon which unleisured academics of diverse kinds were invited to join. Hence, I suggest, the preoccupation of new historicism with entrapment: the powerful readily let you share only what they no longer care too much about. However, I do not present this as an inevitable failure; rather as a warning against assuming that trying to join is necessarily the best strategy.

We tend to assess the gains and losses in abandoning subculture for Englit in respect of those individuals who make it through; that is what our cultures encourage us to do. We should consider also the effect on those who are left behind. Although they may well feel proud of those who moved up, on and out, they must often regret the distances such movement produces. They may well become convinced that the relative poverty of resource and experience of those who remain in the subordinate culture is justly theirs because they did not have what it takes (persuading people to internalize subordination as their due is one of the most insidious effects of ideology). Further, subcultures whose brightest youngsters leave will not themselves be unaffected. If the places from which we have come strike us now as unintellectual, uncritical, perhaps narrow and illiberal, may that not be partly because we left?

It is difficult to argue this case persuasively in the United States because the criterion is always whether individuals can achieve. Collectivity is rarely entertained as against individual striving, let alone preferred; and Englit in particular has been organized around the idea of free individuals striving to enhance their humanity (Babbitt defined the humanist as "interested in the perfecting of the individual rather than in schemes for the elevation of mankind as a whole").[132] But "individual rights" is very unsatisfactory as a political program (that is the understanding on which trades unionism is founded). First, it is virtually impossible for the individual to secure his or her "rights" without the resources to go to law, and only then if the "right" in question is recognized legally and culturally. Everyone knows this, but persists in regarding particular cases (such as homosexuality) as incidental malfunctions, rather than indicative of a flaw in the concept. Second, individual rights may undermine the rights of collectivities. One strategy through which Indian culture was destroyed was the insistence that tribal land be divided into individual lots: the lots were too small to sustain life, so the owners had to sell out to white businessmen.[133] Above all, the fact that some of us achieve individually and make it out (not very far out, normally, despite betraying the culture of family and neighborhood) is not the point, because it still leaves some *other* people to be lower class. So the deprived are always with us, and that offense is compounded by the ideology of individual attainment, which makes it more difficult for people to see what is happening. In his novel *Second Generation*, Raymond Williams's protagonist says, about education and social mobility: "It was really as if, oppressed by an enemy, a people had conceived its own liberation as training its sons for the enemy service. And they would even boast how well they were doing, how much the enemy thought of them."[134] In a collective ethos, a community would advance in wealth and dignity together, not clambering up on each other's shoulders, thrusting the others back down.

My preferred alternative is that academics should reverse the move away from subcultures of class, ethnicicity, gender, and sexuality. We should seek ways to break out of the professional subculture and work intellectually (not just live personally) in dissident subcultures. These are already active, denying the dominant a monopoly of plausibility, contributing to the solidarity and self-understanding of the groups that sponsor them. As well as the voice of the profession, we should cultivate ways of speaking and writing, and opportunities to do them, that might be appropriate for nonacademic subcultures where we can reasonably claim an affiliation.

Gay men in Britain have particular reason to ponder the wisdom of expecting their aspirations to be realized through an identification with Man. As my earlier argument on effeminacy implies, British and

North American cultures have long accorded gay men—though only rarely with candor—a special role in the circulation of good culture. This has been possible because (unlike some other subordinated groups) gay men can pass; they have been accepted as purveyors of culture on condition that they be discreet, thereby acknowledging their own unspeakableness. (I do not specify lesbians here, because although they have contributed at least proportionately to good culture, it is not part of the received stereotype that they have done so.) However, gay men in Britain have found that contributions to the dominant guarantee neither security nor respect. In 1988 the Thatcher government passed into law Section 28 of the Local Government Act, making it illegal for a municipality intentionally to spend money in ways that "promote homosexuality." This law—the more dangerously for its vagueness—seems to include classes in high school, plays in municipal theaters, pictures in galleries, books in libraries. (Ominously for North American lesbians and gay men, Section 28 was ignored by the *New York Times* in a Sunday magazine article purporting to describe censorship in Britain today; March 5, 1989.)

Major arts celebrities conducted a courageous, well-organized and much-publicized campaign against Section 28—pointing out particularly that gay men have produced a notable proportion of what is called art and literature. Astonishingly, at first sight, this carried precious little weight with the government and newspapers that support it; the votes in Parliament were the same at the end of the campaign as at the beginning. The reason, I believe, is that people in our cultures *already know* that the humanities are associated with male homosexuals. The stereotypes tell us that gay men may well be artistic—because good culture is "effeminate" anyway. This is the outcome of the organization of the humanities around the spiritual, the sensitive, the "feminine": because these are already positioned as subordinate terms (as against the practical, robust, and masculine), it is relatively easy, when push comes to shove, to set aside their pretensions. Good culture and homosexuality constitute together a potentially critical nexus—critical of the "normal" values of business and masculinity—and for some purposes the dominant credits this. But, in the last analysis, it can always be derogated in the interests of a stronger policing of sexuality and dissidence, and gains can be headed off. So artistic achievement does not make gay men respected and liked, but feeds into the pattern through which we may be despised.

It is a question, therefore, how far contributing to the dominant is likely to protect any subordinated group. Further, it is doubtful how much good culture ever did for gay men. Much more than nine to one, its representations assume that gay men and lesbians do not exist; if they do, they are usually bad and almost always stereotyped. One gay man recalls how he combed the literary canon, hoping to find among these respected stories a place for the feelings that were disturbing him. "I read of awful stereotyped 'queers', objects of derision, pathetic characters, bitchy, mentally unbalanced, sick, criminal almost by definition, at best to be pitied, sad and lonely." At Harvard the filmmaker Marlon T. Riggs dutifully "attended classes, in search of something more than knowledge or scholarship—in search of a history, a culture that spoke to my life," but found nothing of the kind. "I *served*, in rage, pain, and bitter, needless solitude, for three and a half of my undergraduate years, ignorant that there could be any other way."[135] Even writers, painters, and choreographers whom we have reason to think of as homosexual have very often adopted a heterosexual point of view in their work. It is because they would not have been published, shown, or performed otherwise; and/or were persuaded to believe that their work should be "universal"—that is, heterosexual. Decoding the work of closeted homosexual artists discovers not a ground for congratulation, but a record of oppression and humiliation. We hear all the time in the liberal media, as a term of praise, that an artwork coming from a subordinated group manages to "rise to the universal": this is said because representing the situation and aspirations of a subordinated group is not enough. "The writing of Charlotte Mew focusses on women but profoundly illuminates the complexities of all human experience"—so the back cover of the Virago edition of Mew's *Collected Poems and Prose* (1982). Humanism claims to celebrate both our individuality and our ultimate oneness, but in the process, and without malign intent, it effaces the differences that it finds inconvenient. Celia Kitzinger has criticized vividly humanist incorporations of lesbianism for their assumption "that the lesbian should not be segregated as an alien species, but accepted as part of humanity in all its rich variety." This depoliticizes lesbianism, heading off the danger it may constitute.[136] Adrienne Rich was right to be angry when friends said they found her lesbian poems "universal": she heard "a denial, a kind of resistance, a refusal to read and hear what I've actually written, to acknowledge what I am."[137]

The point of principle is that the dominant takes what it wants, and under pressure will abuse and abandon the subcultures it has plundered. The U.S. Constitution may well derive from the Iroquois Confederacy, but the Iroquois were not allowed to become citizens.[138]

"There is nowhere to turn for safety from physical and verbal attacks" in a homophobic culture, Suzanne Pharr has recently insisted. "No institutions, other than those created by lesbians and gays . . . affirm homosexuality and offer protection."[139] While AIDS was thought to affect only gay men, governments did almost nothing about it; but for gay subculture, thousands more would be dying now. There is no security in trying to join the mainstream. Subcultural groups gain more self-respect, more community feeling, and a better self-understanding by insisting on their own explicit subculture—history, fiction, music, cultural commentary. And intellectuals might contribute here, rather than cultivate always the voice of the center—which is actually only that of the profession.

Five clarifications, taking up points that have arisen in discussions about versions of this argument. I do not mean that working towards a subcultural affiliation is the only thing worth doing, that everything else is pointless or worse. Each of us needs to make a strategic evaluation of the opportunities open to himself or herself and work accordingly. At one time, one kind of activity will be possible and appropriate; at another, something else. I mainly want to challenge the assumption, so systematically and strategically produced in our societies, that the work that counts is in the mainstream. The central project of this chapter is to challenge the validity of the established voices that we might speak in—the voices of European Man, U.S. Man, the profession. Second, I certainly am committed to discovering and developing common ground between diverse subordinated groups. But here too, a determined commitment to subcultural distinctiveness is an important prerequisite, for when we attempt such interactions by going through the dominant, as a kind of central telephone exchange, looking as it might be for our "common humanity," we are in danger of contamination from the demeaning views of ourselves and other groups that are propagated there.

Third, I am not saying that we should all lock ourselves into subcultures and not venture out, for instance into traditional educational systems. To be sure, the oppressive identity is most often that which the hegemonic seeks to confer, and in subcultures this is at least negotiated, if not significantly repudiated. Nevertheless, in modern societies subcultures are usually highly permeable to the dominant and there is little chance of retreating into a ghetto. For, as I argued in chapter 2, partly following such theorists of lesbian identity as Judith Butler and Diana Fuss, identity should not be envisaged as unified or static. Rather, it is interactive and provisional, constructed inevitably in a process of circulation among various interlocking discourses. I am calling not for the discovery of an ineluctable selfhood, therefore, but for political allegiance. Furthermore, it is in the marginal regions of cultures, where they overlap or intersect—marginal regions that subordinated groups cannot avoid inhabiting for much of the time—that insight often arises. Richard Wright's spurning of black cultural traditions has been criticized, but there is also power in the case he makes in his essay "How 'Bigger' Was Born," where the development of black consciousness is attributed partly to living in proximity to white culture. However, the outcome of marginal interaction, by itself, is not always beneficial (Bigger becomes a murderer and rapist and is only belatedly influenced by political activists). A role for the intellectual might be to contribute to the discussion within a subculture about how it is to handle the disturbances that derive from contiguity with other cultures. Wright himself says that when he read white-authored novels, he "took these techniques, these ways of seeing and feeling, and twisted them, bent them, adapted them, until they became *my* ways of apprehending the locked-in life of the Black Belt areas."[140] The present chapter is oriented towards professional intellectuals and students, with the aim, not of dismissing the learning and skills we have attained, but of suggesting that we ponder how to take them back to the subordinated groups where we can claim an affiliation.

Fourth, it is not my thought that subcultures are specially authentic, or politically pure, or vital. (They may be producing better writing and a more vivid culture than the mainstream, but the object is not to rescue Englit with transfusions of novelty; whether placing Chicano women's writing on literature syllabuses is a good thing depends on how you talk about it.) Subcultures merit attention, not through an external evaluation of their quality, but through the fact of their subordination. They are important because of the people who inhabit them, who are having a bad time, not the other way around.[141] Subcultures may well exhibit racist, sexist, and homophobic features: this should not surprise us, given that they have arisen partly out of and partly in reaction to the dominant, such that for generations even their resistance has been constituted partly in terms set by the dominant. Features that we find unappealing, indeed unacceptable, are anxious strategies conceived by people casting around desperately for status in a humiliating social order. Part of my case is that this would not be so, or not in the same degree, if we had not left. *On the other hand,* there is Nicola Sacco's last message, before he was electrocuted in 1927, to his son, Dante: "Help the persecuted and the victim because they are your better friends."[142] Finally, I do not offer attention to subcultures as a strategy for winning—for introducing socialism, interracial harmony, or a genuine sexual liberation. My argument has been conceived defensively, in response to a disheartening historical conjuncture. The main goal is to help sustain the dignity and resistance of subordinated groups, and to be ready for the next propitious moment.

In the meantime, subcultures are places from which the dominant may yet be disconcerted and resisted. Tony Bennett proposes as a project for intellectual work that we seek to "interrupt, uncouple and disrupt the prevailing array of discourses through which subject identities are formed."[143] The dominant ideology strives to constitute subjectivities that will find "natural" its view of the world; to combat that, we need to develop and validate dissident subjectivities. Subcultural milieux are where that happens—where partly distinctive conditions of plausibility, alternative subject positions, are created. To be sure, subcultures cannot avoid some kind of implication with the dominant—often they are positioned as its defining others. But through this very mechanism, they may return to trouble the social order. They redeploy its most cherished values, downgrading, abusing, inverting or reapplying them; willy-nilly, they draw attention to its incoherences and contradictions, and to the economy of ideology and power that organizes them. As Barbara Babcock has written, "What is socially peripheral is often symbolically central."[144] Because subcultures are made to constitute the other, even because they are stigmatized and policed, they gain subversive leverage. Precisely their outlaw status may exert a fascination for the dominant, focusing subversive fantasies of freedom, vitality, even squalor. So they form points from which repression may be become apparent, silences audible. If focusing our work there is a withdrawal to base, it is a base from which the prevailing system may yet be discomposed, unsettled, obliged to acknowledge a larger conception of humanity.

WHAT *ABOUT* THE *MERCHANT*?

The standard liberal move with *The Merchant of Venice*, by critics and directors, is to try to soften it by making Shylock as human," as "sympathetic," as much "like the rest of us," as possible. The play, Leslie Fiedler observes, "in some sense celebrates, certainly releases ritually, the full horror of anti-Semitism." Modern readers and audiences are therefore especially "pleased to discover how much [Shakespeare] is like what we prefer to think ourselves, when for instance, he allows Shylock a sympathetic apology for himself: 'Hath not a Jew eyes?' "[145] In our cultures (though not for earlier generations), Shakespeare's claim on "man" is ratified if Shylock is permitted to join—if he is discovered to have traces of "humanity." That this move adds insult to injury has been noticed by Arnold Wesker. In an introduction to his rewrite, *Shylock* (initially titled *The Merchant*), Wesker says that however Shakespeare's Shylock is handled in the theater, "the image comes through inescapably: the Jew is mercenary and revengeful, sadistic, without pity." And "the so-called defence of Shylock," Wesker says (with Laurence Olivier's National Theatre production of 1973 in mind), "was so powerful that it dignified the anti-semitism. An audience, it seemed to me on that night, could come away with its prejudices about the Jew confirmed but held with an easy conscience because they thought they'd heard a noble plea for extenuating circumstances."[146] This need not mean that recognition of common humanity is always a false move, but that it affords no advantage where it is only a token. In Wesker's play, the normally kindly Shylock is enraged at just one point: when Lorenzo embarks complacently on the topic "After all, has not a Jew eyes?" Shylock says: "I do not want apologies for my humanity. Plead for me no special pleas. I will not have my humanity mocked and apologised for. If I am unexceptionally like any man then I need no exceptional portraiture. I merit no special pleas, no special cautions, no special gratitudes. My humanity is my right, not your bestowed and gracious privilege" (p. 255). The speech that humanists generally celebrate as redeeming Shakespeare's play is, by virtue of such a program of redemption, perceived as condescending. It is a powerful insight into how the invitation to join Man patronizes subordinated groups.

A different alternative to the liberal reading is to be found in a book on Shakespeare's politics published twenty-five years ago by Allan Bloom—yes, he who says your minds have been closing. In Bloom's view, Shylock asks for trouble, for he has "the soul of a man who has refused to assimilate. He is consequently distrusted and hated. He reciprocates, and his soul is poisoned."[147] Oppressors often feel better when they blame the victim. Accordingly, Bloom evaluates Portia's suitors on racist principles—of course Portia doesn't want to marry a foreigner, they are so lacking in humanity: "The South is barbaric; the North, cold and sententious. True civilisation implies a mixture of developed understanding and reflection with a full capacity to perceive; one must both see things as they are and react to them appropriately." To be a fully developed human being, in other words, you must not be foreign, or maintain any adherence to an ethnic culture. Bassanio, on the other hand, is "a true gentleman" (p. 26). The whole argument typifies the working of the concept *man*: it coincides, apparently fortuitously, with the indigenous leisure class and becomes ever more attenuated as one moves out from that center. Bloom's position is distinctively new right, in that he scarcely seeks to conceal this (few liberal evasions here): he justifies the victimization of Shylock not morally, but on grounds of personal prejudice and public convenience: "Venice is a Christian city, and Antonio her husband's friend. If the cancer of civil discord must be rooted out, then Shylock is the one to go" (p. 28). The moral is clear enough: abandon your subculture, or you deserve what you get. Actually, history shows, when they want a scapegoat you will get it anyway.

There is one further possibility. I saw Ian McDiarmid act Shylock at Stratford-upon-Avon in 1984, and he made him very stereotypically "Jewish," and determinedly hard and unyielding. In other words, Shylock was not being retrieved as ultimately "human." As in Bloom's reading, he was an outsider who despised the thought of appeasing his persecutors, and the other characters were appropriately horrid to him. But I did not find myself led to the conclusion that Bloom anticipates—doubtless because I have been socialized into a dissident reading formation. In the court scene, there was Shylock enduring the hostility of the Venetian upper class, and they did not seem quite like the usual version of Man: they were openly arrogant, scornful, snobbish, rich, and generally nasty. But, for once, it looked as though one of the underdogs was going to bite back. Just for once, the stigmatized other seemed to have the drop on the rest of them: their prized mercantile and legal system, which was designed to keep the Jews in servility, had allowed him a loophole (as sometimes it must), and he was going to turn the tables. Of course, the Venetians were all for the quality of mercy now, since one of them was under threat. But I thought: Right on, Shylock, now's your chance, don't take any notice of their tricks, stick on in there and get your pound of flesh . . .

I have to admit that this is a high-risk strategy, with the *Merchant* and in culture generally. Some people in the audience were manifestly, and unpleasantly, delighted when Shylock was defeated. Perhaps we cannot afford presentations that might be used to legitimize such attitudes; but then, on the other hand, we cannot afford to orient cultural work so as to accommodate hostile attitudes at every point, especially at the expense of opportunities to develop dissident insight and commitment. Of course, it was high-risk for Shylock as well. He, and we, should have known they wouldn't let him get away with it. The entire apparatus of the state lines up against him; the judge does not try to conceal his bias; they can afford to buy all the cleverest lawyers; they've even got a doubly transvestite lawyer!—and of course s/he is better. Well, there you are, that's how they get you; but he had a go.

Notes

PREFACE

1. Chapter 4 was first published in *English Literary History* 52 (1985): 259–77; chapter 5 in *Critical Quarterly* 28 (1986): 63–77. They are reprinted with thanks to the Johns Hopkins University Press and Manchester University Press respectively. Part of chapter 6 was first published in John Drakakis, ed., *Alternative Shakespeares* (Methuen, 1985): I am grateful to Routledge and to Jonathan Dollimore for agreeing that it should appear here.

2. Alan Sinfield, *Literature in Protestant England, 1560–1660* (London: Croom Helm, 1983; Totowa, N.J.: Barnes & Noble, 1983).

CHAPTER ONE

1. *Roland Barthes by Roland Barthes*, trans. Richard Howard (London: Macmillan, 1977), pp. 170–72.

2. It is a sentimental derivative of Claes Jansz Visscher's long view of London; see Irwin Smith, *Shakespeare's Globe Playhouse* (London: Peter Owen, 1963), pp. 20–23. I am indebted to Susan Schweik for showing me the advertisement.

3. Robert Fraser and Michael Wilson, *Privatisation: The UK Experience and International Trends* (London: Longman, 1988), pp. 81–82.

4. In this, Ordnance was only typical—like Bimec, Thorn EMI, Wickman Bennett, Racal, Churchill, and many continental European companies. See "How Minister Helped British Firms to Arm Saddam's Soldiers," *Sunday Times,* December 2, 1990, p. 5. John Drakakis drew this article to my attention.

5. *Financial Times,* February 27, 1991, pp. 22, 23.

6. "How Minister Helped British Firms," p. 5.

7. E. K. Chambers, *Sir Henry Lee: An Elizabethan Portrait* (Oxford: Clarendon Press, 1936), pp. 121, 119–27; and see H. C. Tomlinson, *Guns and*

Government: The Ordnance Office under the Later Stuarts (London: Royal Historical Society, 1979), pp. 1–6.

8. John Fekete, *The Critical Twilight* (London: Routledge, 1977), p. 195. See Jonathan Dollimore, *Radical Tragedy*, 2d ed. (Hemel Hempstead: Harvester Wheatsheaf, 1989), ch. 3.

9. *The Autobiography of Thomas Whythorne*, ed. James M. Osborn (Oxford: Clarendon Press, 1961), pp. xxviii–xxx, 83–86, 298–99.

10. Thomas Carlyle, *On Heroes, Hero-Worship and the Heroic in History* (London: James Frazer, 1841), p. 181; quoted by Malcolm Evans, *Signifying Nothing: Truth's True Contents in Shakespeare's Text*, 2d ed. (Hemel Hempstead: Harvester Wheatsheaf, 1989), p. 88; and see pp. 86–108. Wilson Knight is quoted by Terence Hawkes, *That Shakespeherean Rag: Essays on a Critical Process* (London: Methuen, 1986), p. 68. See also Peter Widdowson, ed., *ReReading English* (London: Methuen, 1982); Graham Holderness, ed., *The Shakespeare Myth* (Manchester Univ. Press, 1988); Chris Baldick, *The Social Mission of English Criticism, 1848–1932* (Oxford Univ. Press, 1983); Ania Loomba, *Gender, Race, Renaissance Drama* (Manchester Univ. Press, 1989).

11. *The Prose Works of Fulke Greville, Lord Brooke*, ed. John Gouws (Oxford: Clarendon Press, 1986), pp. 42, 45, 200.

12. J. Hillis Miller, "Presidential Address, 1986: The Triumph of Theory, the Resistance to Reading, and the Question of the Material Base," *PMLA* 102 (1987): 281–91, p. 287.

13. Letter from James Wood, *London Review of Books*, March 8, 1990; responding to a review article by Terence Hawkes in the issue of February 22.

14. Letter from Alan Sinfield, *London Review of Books*, April 19, 1990; see also the letter from John Drakakis in the issue of June 14.

15. See Raymond Williams, "Base and Superstructure in Marxist Cultural Theory," in Williams, *Problems in Materialism and Culture* (London: New Left Books, 1980).

16. Catherine Belsey, *The Subject of Tragedy* (London: Methuen, 1985), pp. 101–3; see also id., "Shakespeare and Film: A Question of Perspective," *Literature/Film Quarterly* 11 (1983): 152–58. For the case against "humanity," see, e.g., John Drakakis, ed., *Alternative Shakespeares* (London: Methuen, 1985), p. 4.

17. Quoted by Arthur Humphreys, ed., *Julius Caesar* (Oxford: Clarendon Press, 1984), p. 52.

18. John Ripley, *"Julius Caesar" on Stage in England and America, 1599–1973* (Cambridge Univ. Press, 1980), pp. 23–24, 28, 147.

19. Ibid., p. 100; Alfred Van Rensselaer Westfall, *American Shakespearean Criticism, 1607–1865* (New York: H. W. Wilson, 1939), p. 221.

20. Ripley, *"Julius Caesar,"* p. 317.

21. Raphael Samuel, Ewan MacColl, and Stuart Cosgrove, *Theatres of the Left, 1880–1935* (London: Routledge, 1985), pp. 8–9; see also E. P. Thompson, *The Making of the English Working Class*, rev. ed. (Harmondsworth: Penguin Books, 1968), p. 809. *Julius Caesar* is quoted from the New Arden edition, ed. T. S. Dorsch (London: Methuen, 1955), 1.2.94–95.

22. Ripley, *"Julius Caesar,"* pp. 140, 332. For further discussion of the history of Shakespearean stage productions in the United States, see chapter 10 below.

23. Ida M. Tarbell, *The Life of Abraham Lincoln* (New York: McClure, Phillips, 1908), 2:252–60. Tarbell's account is laced with implicit allusions to *Julius Caesar,* such as the tearing down of banners, speech-making, and crowd action against opponents; 3.2.135–39 is quoted (pp. 246–51).

24. David Donald, *Lincoln Reconsidered*, 2d ed. (New York: Knopf, 1965), p. 5; Michael Rogin, *"Ronald Reagan," The Movie* (Berkeley: Univ. of California Press, 1987), pp. 86–90, and illustrations 3.3, 3.4, 3.5. In 1939 *Julius Caesar* was found to have been the one most read in schools: see Esther Cloudman Dunn, *Shakespeare in America* (1939; New York: Benjamin Blom, 1968), pp. 219–20, 244.

25. Robert Justin Goldstein, *Political Repression in Modern America from 1870 to the Present* (Cambridge, Mass.: Schenkman, 1978), pp. 24–34.

26. Ripley, *"Julius Caesar,"* p. 223.

27. See Victor S. Navasky, *Naming Names* (New York: Viking Press, 1980), pp. 179–81. For the idea and the reference I am indebted to Vivian Sobchack, who placed Mankiewicz's *Caesar* in this context in a talk at Santa Cruz in 1988. On the liberalism of this film, see Belsey, "Shakespeare and Film."

28. See Ripley, *"Julius Caesar,"* p. 260. However, Glen Byam Shaw's 1957 Stratford production re-centred Caesar: see Roy Walker, "Unto Caesar: A Review of Recent Productions," *Shakespeare Survey* 11 (1958): 128–35.

29. Ralph Berry, *On Directing Shakespeare* (London: Croom Helm, 1977), pp. 75–81.

30. Interview with Trevor Nunn in Berry, *On Directing Shakespeare,* pp. 63–66; quotation from Nunn in Ripley, *"Julius Caesar,"* p. 270. For further comparable productions, see Humphreys, ed., *Julius Caesar,* pp. 66–71; Martin Spevack, ed., *Julius Caesar* (Cambridge Univ. Press, 1988), p. 40.

31. See Jonathan Goldberg, *James I and the Politics of Literature* (Baltimore: Johns Hopkins Univ. Press, 1983), pp. 163–76.

32. The time set for the inauguration of President Reagan had to be changed when astrologers said it was unfavorable for him. See Garry Wills, *Reagan's America* (New York: Doubleday, 1987), pp. 299, 196–97.

33. However, at the time of her removal from office, Mrs. Thatcher was widely compared to Julius Caesar, mainly in respect of the treachery of her colleagues: see the *Guardian*, November 26, 1990, p. 35.

34. Annabel Patterson, *Shakespeare and the Popular Voice* (Oxford: Blackwell, 1989), pp. 11, 129.

35. Richard Wilson, " 'Is this a holiday?': Shakespeare's Roman Carnival," *English Literary History* 54 (1987): 31–44, pp. 32–33. See Peter Stallybrass and Allon White, *The Politics and Poetics of Transgression* (London: Methuen, 1986), Introduction.

36. Here I disagree with David Margolies, "Teaching the Handsaw to Fly: Shakespeare as a Hegemonic Instrument," in Holderness, ed., *Shakespeare Myth,* p. 44.

37. S. A. Cook, F. E. Adcock, and M. P. Charlesworth, eds., *The Cambridge Ancient History* (Cambridge Univ. Press, 1932), 9:291–93, 334–36.

38. Niccolò Machiavelli, *The Discourses* 1.57–58, ed. Bernard Crick (Harmondsworth: Penguin Books, 1974), pp. 251, 255.

39. Dorsch, ed., *Julius Caesar,* pp. 138–39.

40. Thomas Kyd, *The First Part of Hieronimo and The Spanish Tragedy,* ed. Andrew S. Cairncross (London: Arnold, 1967), 1.1.90–91.

41. See Sinfield, "Royal Shakespeare," in Jonathan Dollimore and Alan Sinfield, eds., *Political Shakespeare* (Manchester: Manchester Univ. Press; Ithaca, N.Y.: Cornell Univ. Press, 1985), p. 160.

42. See Richard Wilson's powerful article, " 'A mingled yarn': Shakespeare and the Cloth Workers," *Literature and History* 12 (1986): 164–80, pp. 167–69; also my program note, "History and Power," for the Royal Shakespeare Company production of *The Plantagenets* (two reconstructed *Henry VI* plays plus *Richard III*), directed by Adrian Noble in 1988.

43. See Pierre Macherey, *A Theory of Literary Production,* trans. Geoffrey Wall (London: Routledge, 1978); also Jonathan Goldberg, "Speculations: *Macbeth* and Source," in Jean E. Howard and Marion F. O'Connor, eds., *Shakespeare Reproduced* (New York: Methuen, 1987), p. 247; and my chapter 2.

44. I rehearse here the argument in Sinfield, "Four Ways with a Reactionary Text," *LTP: Journal of Literature Teaching Politics* 2 (1983): 81–95.

45. Jonathan Dollimore, "Middleton and Barker: Creative Vandalism," in the program for the Royal Court production of *Women Beware Women,* published with a text of the play as Playscript 111 (London: Calder; New York: Riverrun, 1986). See also Dollimore's imagined camp production of *Antony and Cleopatra,* in Dollimore, "Shakespeare, Cultural Materialism, Feminism and Marxist Humanism," *New Literary History* 21 (1990): 471–93, pp. 484–90.

46. Marowitz's own account; in Charles Marowitz and Simon Trussler, eds., *Theatre at Work* (London: Methuen, 1967), p. 170.

47. Charles Marowitz, *The Marowitz Hamlet* (London: Allen Lane, 1968), pp. 16, 18. For discussion of this and Shakespearean plays by Tom Stoppard, Arnold Wesker, and Edward Bond, see Alan Sinfield, "Making Space: Appropriation and Confrontation in Recent British Plays," in Holderness, ed., *Shakespeare Myth.*

48. See the interviews with Bogdanov and Miller in Holderness, ed., *Shakespeare Myth,* pp. 89–91, 195, 200–202, and p. 182. On recent work by Bogdanov and the scope for radical productions, see Isobel Armstrong, "Thatcher's Shakespeare," *Textual Practice* 3 (1989): 1–14.

49. Raymond Williams, *Culture* (Glasgow: Fontana, 1981), p. 225; Humphreys, ed., *Julius Caesar,* p. 71.

50. Charles Marowitz, *The Marowitz Shakespeare* (London: Marion Boyars, 1978), p. 24. See Sinfield, "Making Space," and also, on Wesker's play, p. 300 below.

51. Robert S. Miola, *Shakespeare's Rome* (Cambridge Univ. Press, 1983), p. 96.

52. Richard Wilson points out that Jack Cade and his supporters are hostile to writing (" 'A mingled yarn,' " p. 168).

53. See Ann Thompson's New Cambridge edition of Shakespeare, *The Taming of the Shrew* (Cambridge Univ. Press, 1984), pp. 35–36, and the Bogdanov interview in Holderness, ed., *Shakespeare Myth*, p. 90.

54. A further clue: don't forget the spelling. This advertisement has been current for some months; it appeared in the *Daily Mirror* on February 25, 1991 (p. 13) immediately next to the following news report:

MPs Slam "Degree in Gays"

Students at a university are being offered a degree course in gay and lesbian studies. But the one year course at Sussex University in Brighton is under attack by Tory MPs. Terry Dicks said it was a waste of taxpayers' subsidy. "The place should be shut down and disinfected," he said.

It would be good if we could make Shakespeare comparably disconcerting.

55. Walter Benjamin, *Illuminations*, ed. Hannah Arendt, trans. Harry Zohn (Glasgow: Fontana/Collins, 1973), pp. 258–59.

CHAPTER TWO

1. *Othello* is quoted from the New Arden edition, ed. M. R. Ridley (London: Methuen, 1962). An earlier version of parts of this paper, entitled "Othello and the Politics of Character," was published in Manuel Barbeito, ed., *In Mortal Shakespeare: Radical Readings* (Santiago: Univ. de Santiago de Compostela, 1989).

2. Stephen Greenblatt, *Renaissance Self-Fashioning* (Chicago: Univ. of Chicago Press, 1980), p. 245; and also pp. 234–39, and Greenblatt, "Psychoanalysis and Renaissance Culture," in Patricia Parker and David Quint, eds., *Literary Theory / Renaissance Texts* (Baltimore: Johns Hopkins Univ. Press, 1986), p. 218. On stories in *Othello,* see further Jonathan Goldberg, "Shakespearean Inscriptions: The Voicing of Power," in Patricia Parker and Geoffrey Hartman, eds., *Shakespeare and the Question of Theory* (New York: Methuen, 1985), pp. 131–32.

3. Ania Loomba, *Gender, Race, Renaissance Drama* (Manchester Univ. Press, 1989), p. 48. See also Doris Adler, "The Rhetoric of *Black* and *White* in *Othello,*" *Shakespeare Quarterly* 25 (1974): 248–57.

4. Louis Althusser, "Ideological State Apparatuses," in Althusser, *Lenin and Philosophy and Other Essays,* trans. Ben Brewster (London: New Left Books, 1971), pp. 160–65.

5. Peter Stallybrass, "Patriarchal Territories: The Body Enclosed," in Margaret W. Ferguson, Maureen Quilligan, and Nancy J. Vickers, eds., *Rewriting the Renaissance* (Chicago: Univ. of Chicago Press, 1986), p. 139. Greenblatt makes a comparable point about Jews in Marlowe's *Jew of Malta,* though in *Othello* he stresses Iago's "ceaseless narrative invention": see *Renaissance Self-Fashioning,* pp. 208, 235. On Blacks in Shakespearean England, see Loomba, *Gender, Race, Renaissance Drama,* pp. 42–52; Ruth Cowhig, "Blacks in English Renaissance Drama and the Role of Shakespeare's *Othello,*" in David Dabydeen, ed., *The Black Presence in English Literature* (Manchester: Manchester Univ. Press, 1985).

6. Althusser, *Lenin and Philosophy*, pp. 123–28. For further elaboration of the theory presented here, see Alan Sinfield, *Literature, Politics and Culture in Postwar Britain* (Oxford: Basil Blackwell; Berkeley: Univ. of California Press, 1989), ch. 3.

7. Colin Sumner, *Reading Ideologies* (London and New York: Academic Press, 1979), p. 288.

8. Anthony Giddens, *Central Problems in Social Theory* (London: Macmillan, 1979), pp. 69–71, 77–78. Giddens's development of *langue* and *parole* is anticipated in Michel Foucault, *The Order of Things* (London: Tavistock, 1970), p. 380.

9. Stephen Orgel, "Nobody's Perfect: Or Why Did the English Stage Take Boys for Women?" *South Atlantic Quarterly* 88 (1989): 7–29, pp. 8–10. Jonathan Goldberg writes of the Duke's scripting in *Measure For Measure* in his *James I and the Politics of Literature* (Baltimore: Johns Hopkins Univ. Press, 1983), pp. 230–39. See also Steven Mullaney, *The Place of the Stage* (Chicago: Univ. of Chicago Press, 1988), pp. 107–10.

10. On attitudes to Turks, see Simon Shepherd, *Marlowe and the Politics of Elizabethan Theatre* (New York: St Martin's Press, 1986), pp. 142–49. The later part of Othello's career, in fact, has been devoted entirely to state violence—as Martin Orkin has suggested, he is sent to Cyprus to secure it for the colonial power: see Orkin, *Shakespeare against Apartheid* (Craighall, South Africa: Ad. Donker, 1987), pp. 88–96.

11. Karl Marx and Friedrich Engels, *The German Ideology* (London: Lawrence & Wishart, 1965), p. 61. See further Althusser, *Lenin and Philosophy*, pp. 139–42; Pierre Bourdieu, "Cultural Reproduction and Social Reproduction," in Richard Brown, ed., *Knowledge, Education and Cultural Change* (London: Tavistock, 1973).

12. See Lynda E. Boose, "The Family in Shakespearean Studies; or—Studies in the Family of Shakespeareans; or—the Politics of Politics," *Renaissance Quarterly* 40 (1987): 707–42; Carol Thomas Neely, "Constructing the Subject: Feminist Practice and the New Renaissance Discourses," *English Literary Renaissance* 18 (1988): 5–18.

13. Kathleen McLuskie, "The Patriarchal Bard: Feminist Criticism and Shakespeare," in Jonathan Dollimore and Alan Sinfield, eds., *Political Shakespeare* (Manchester: Manchester Univ. Press; Ithaca, N.Y.: Cornell Univ. Press, 1985), p. 97. For a reply to her critics by Kathleen McLuskie, see her *Renaissance Dramatists* (Hemel Hempstead: Harvester Wheatsheaf, 1989), pp. 224–29; and for further comment, Jonathan Dollimore, "Shakespeare, Cultural Materialism, Feminism and Marxist Humanism," *New Literary History* 21 (1990): 471–93.

14. Carolyn Ruth Swift Lenz, Gayle Greene, and Carol Thomas Neely, eds., *The Woman's Part* (Urbana: Univ. of Illinois Press, 1980), p. 5.

15. McLuskie, "Patriarchal Bard," p. 92.

16. Boose, "Family in Shakespearean Studies," pp. 734, 726, 724. See also Ann Thompson, "'The warrant of womanhood': Shakespeare and Feminist Criticism," in Graham Holderness, ed., *The Shakespeare Myth* (Manchester: Manchester Univ. Press, 1988); Judith Newton, "History as

Usual?: Feminism and the New Historicism," *Cultural Critique* 9 (1988): 87–121.

17. Richard Ohmann, *English in America* (New York: Oxford Univ. Press, 1976), p. 313. See V. N. Voloshinov, *Marxism and the Philosophy of Language*, trans. Ladislav Matejka and I. R. Titunik (New York and London: Seminar Press, 1973), pp. 17–24, 83–98.

18. Antonio Gramsci, *Selections from the Prison Notebooks*, ed. and trans. Quintin Hoare and Geoffrey Nowell-Smith (London: Lawrence & Wishart, 1971), p. 324.

19. Judith Butler, *Gender Trouble* (London: Routledge, 1990), p. 6. See Celia Kitzinger, *The Social Construction of Lesbianism* (London: Sage, 1987). Diana Fuss asks: "Is politics based on identity, or is identity based on politics?" (*Essentially Speaking* [London: Routledge, 1989], p. 100, and see ch. 6).

20. Neely, "Constructing the Subject," p. 7.

21. J. Hillis Miller, "Presidential Address, 1986: The Triumph of Theory, the Resistance to Reading, and the Question of the Material Base," *PMLA* 102 (1987): 281–91, pp. 290–91. Cf., e.g., Raymond Williams, "Base and Superstructure in Marxist Cultural Theory," *New Left Review* 82 (1973): 3–16; reprinted in Williams, *Problems in Materialism and Culture* (London: Verso, 1980; New York: Schocken Books, 1981). James Holstun, "Ranting at the New Historicism," *English Literary Renaissance* 19 (1989): 189–225, makes more effort than most to address European/Marxist work.)

22. Peter Nicholls, "State of the Art: Old Problems and the New Historicism," *Journal of American Studies* 23 (1989): 423–34, pp. 428, 429.

23. Don E. Wayne, "New Historicism," in Malcolm Kelsall, Martin Coyle, Peter Garside, and John Peck, eds., *Encyclopedia of Literature and Criticism* (London: Routledge, 1990), p. 795. I am grateful to Professor Wayne for showing this essay to me in typescript. Further on this topic, see Jean E. Howard and Marion F. O'Connor, "Introduction," Don E. Wayne, "Power, Politics and the Shakespearean Text: Recent Criticism in England and the United States," and Walter Cohen, "Political Criticism of Shakespeare," all in Jean E. Howard and Marion F. O'Connor, eds., *Shakespeare Reproduced* (London: Methuen, 1987); Louis Montrose, "Professing the Renaissance: The Poetics and Politics of Culture," in H. Aram Veeser, ed., *The New Historicism* (New York: Routledge, 1989), pp. 20–24; Alan Liu, "The Power of Formalism: The New Historicism," *English Literary History* 56 (1989): 721–77.

24. Greenblatt, *Renaissance Self-Fashioning*, pp. 120, 209–14. For further instantiation, see pp. 173–74.

25. Carolyn Porter, "Are We Being Historical Yet?" *South Atlantic Quarterly* 87 (1988): 743–86; see also Porter, "History and Literature: 'After the New Criticism,'" *New Literary History* 21 (1990): 253–72.

26. Stephen J. Greenblatt, *Learning to Course: Essays in Early Modern Culture* (London: Routledge, 1990), pp. 164–66.

27. Shakespeare, *Macbeth*, ed. Kenneth Muir, 9th ed. (London: Methuen, 1962), 1.4.12–13. See further chapter 5.

28. William Shakespeare, *King Henry V*, ed. J. H. Walter (London: Methuen, 1954), act 5, Chorus, 29–35. See further chapter 6.

29. Raymond Williams, *Culture* (Glasgow: Fontana, 1981), p. 201.

30. Porter, "Are We Being Historical Yet?" p. 774. For important recent discussions of the scope for movement in the early modern state, see Richard Cust and Ann Hughes, eds., *Conflict in Early Stuart England* (London: Longmans, 1989), esp. Johann Sommerville, "Ideology, Property and the Constitution."

31. I am not happy that race and sexuality tend to feature in distinct parts of this chapter; in this respect, my wish to clarify certain theoretical arguments has produced some simplification. Of course, race and sexuality are intertwined, in *Othello* as elsewhere. See Loomba, *Gender, Race, Renaissance Drama*, pp. 48-62; Karen Newman, " 'And wash the Ethiop white': Femininity and the Monstrous in *Othello*," in Howard and O'Connor, eds., *Shakespeare Reproduced*; Jonathan Dollimore, *Sexual Dissidence* (Oxford: Oxford Univ. Press, 1991), part 4.

32. I set out this argument in Alan Sinfield, *Literature in Protestant England, 1560-1660* (London: Croom Helm, 1983), ch. 4. See also Juliet Dusinberre, *Shakespeare and the Nature of Women* (London: Macmillan, 1976); Simon Shepherd, *Amazons and Warrior Women* (Brighton: Harvester, 1981), pp. 53-56, 107-18; Catherine Belsey, *The Subject of Tragedy* (London: Methuen, 1985), ch. 7; Dympna Callaghan, *Woman and Gender in Renaissance Tragedy* (Atlantic Highlands, N.J.: Humanities Press, 1989), ch. 2 et passim; McLuskie, *Renaissance Dramatists*, pp. 31-39, 50-55 et passim.

33. *Certain Sermons or Homilies* (London: Society for Promoting Religious Knowledge, 1899), p. 534.

34. Sir Philip Sidney, *Arcadia*, ed. Maurice Evans (Harmondsworth, Penguin Books, 1977), p. 501.

35. Robert Burton, *The Anatomy of Melancholy*, ed. Holbrook Jackson (London: Dent, 1932), 3:52-53.

36. *Certain Sermons*, p. 589.

37. Henry Smith, *Works*, with a memoir by Thomas Fuller (Edinburgh, 1886), 1: 32, 19.

38. Gerrard Winstanley, *Works*, ed. G. H. Sabine (Ithaca, N.Y.: Cornell Univ. Press, 1941), p. 599.

39. William Perkins, *Christian Economy* (1609), in *The Work of William Perkins*, ed. Ian Breward (Abingdon: Sutton Courtenay Press, 1970), pp. 418-19.

40. Lawrence Stone, *The Family, Sex and Marriage* (London: Weidenfeld & Nicolson, 1977), p. 137. See also ibid., pp. 151-59, 178-91, 195-302; Charles and Katherine George, *The Protestant Mind of the English Reformation* (Princeton: Princeton Univ. Press, 1961), pp. 257-94; Christopher Hill, *Society and Puritanism in Pre-Revolutionary England* (London: Panther, 1969), pp. 429-67; Louis Adrian Montrose, " 'Shaping Fantasies': Figurations of Gender and Power in Elizabethan Culture," in Stephen Greenblatt, ed., *Representing the English Renaissance* (Berkeley: Univ. of California Press, 1988), pp. 37-40; Lisa Jardine, *Still Harping on Daughters* (Brighton: Harvester, 1983), ch. 3; Leonard Tennenhouse, *Power on Display* (London: Methuen, 1986), pp. 17-30, 147-54; Patrick Collinson, *The Birthpangs of Protestant England* (London: Macmillan, 1988, ch. 3.

41. Callaghan, *Woman and Gender,* p. 21; also pp. 19–22, 101–5. On women's scope for negotiation, see also Ann Rosalind Jones, *The Currency of Eros: Women's Love Lyric in Europe, 1540–1620* (Bloomington: Indiana Univ. Press, 1990), pp. 1–10.

42. Montrose, " 'Shaping Fantasies,' " p. 37. For the thought that the men in *Othello* are preoccupied with their masculinity but ineffectual, see Carol Thomas Neely, *Broken Nuptials in Shakespeare's Plays* (New Haven: Yale Univ. Press, 1985), pp. 119–22.

43. John Clarke, Stuart Hall, Tony Jefferson, and Brian Roberts, "Subcultures, Cultures and Class," in Stuart Hall and Tony Jefferson, eds., *Resistance through Rituals* (London: Hutchinson; Birmingham: Centre for Contemporary Cultural Studies, 1976), p. 12. The final phrase is quoted from E. P. Thompson's essay "The Peculiarities of the English."

44. Giddens, *Central Problems,* p. 6. See further Raymond Williams, *Marxism and Literature* (Oxford: Oxford Univ. Press, 1977), pp. 108–27; Fredric Jameson, "Reification and Utopia in Mass Culture," *Social Text* 1 (1979): 144–48; Colin Gordon, "Afterword," in Michel Foucault, *Power/Knowledge* (Brighton: Harvester, 1980).

45. Michel Foucault, *The History of Sexuality: Volume 1,* trans. Robert Hurley (New York: Random House, Vintage Books, 1980), pp. 95–96. Also, as Jonathan Culler has remarked, Foucault's exposure of the ubiquity of regulatory practices may itself be experienced as liberatory: Culler, *Framing the Sign* (Oxford: Blackwell, 1988), pp. 66–67.

46. Foucault, *History of Sexuality,* p. 101. See Jonathan Dollimore and Alan Sinfield, "Culture and Textuality: Debating Cultural Materialism," *Textual Practice* 4, no. 1 (Spring 1990): 91–100, p. 95; and Jonathan Dollimore, "Sexuality, Subjectivity and Transgression: The Jacobean Connection," *Renaissance Drama,* n.s., 17 (1986): 53–82.

47. Jonathan Goldberg, "Speculations: *Macbeth* and Source," in Howard and O'Connor, *Shakespeare Reproduced,* pp. 244, 247. See also Jonathan Goldberg, *Writing Matter: From the Hands of the English Renaissance* (Stanford: Stanford Univ. Press, 1990), esp. pp. 41–55.

48. Williams, *Culture,* pp. 94, 110; Keith Thomas, "The Meaning of Literacy in Early Modern England," in Gerd Baumann, ed., *The Written Word: Literacy in Transition* (Oxford: Clarendon Press, 1986), pp. 116, 118.

49. Dollimore, "Shakespeare, Cultural Materialism, Feminism and Marxist Humanism," p. 482. See also Holstun, "Ranting at the New Historicism."

50. Dollimore and Sinfield, *Political Shakespeare,* p. 13; discussed in Dollimore and Sinfield, "Culture and Textuality." See also Alan Liu's argument that we need to consider not only subjects and representation, but action: Liu, "Power of Formalism," pp. 734–35.

51. Wayne, "New Historicism," in Kelsall, Coyle, Garside, and Peck, eds., *Encyclopedia,* pp. 801–2. See also Culler, *Framing,* p. 37; Porter, "History and Literature," pp. 253–56.

52. "The Political Function of the Intellectual," trans. Colin Gordon, *Radical Philosophy* 17 (1977): 12–15, p. 14; see Eve Tavor Bannet, *Structuralism and the Logic of Dissent* (London: Macmillan, 1989), pp. 170–83.

53. Raymond Williams, *Marxism and Literature* (Oxford: Oxford Univ. Press, 1977) p. 209.

CHAPTER THREE

Epigraphs: David Henry Hwang, *M. Butterfly* (New York: New American Library, 1989), p. 63; note Hwang's locution "supposed to act." Pope, *Moral Essays* 2.1–2.

1. The argument here formed part of a paper, "*Othello* and the Politics of Character," which I delivered at the University of Santiago de Compostella in 1987; it has been published in Manuel Barbeito, ed., *In Mortal Shakespeare: Radical Readings* (Santiago: Universidade de Santiago de Compostela, 1989). The problem I have in mind has been observed by Lena Cowen Orlin in a paper, "Desdemona's Disposition," which she has kindly allowed me to see; it was delivered to the Shakespeare Association of America in 1987. See also Peter Stallybrass, "Patriarchal Territories: The Body Enclosed," in Margaret W. Ferguson, Maureen Quilligan, and Nancy J. Vickers, eds., *Rewriting the Renaissance* (Chicago: Univ. of Chicago Press, 1986), p. 141; Kathleen McLuskie, *Renaissance Dramatists* (Hemel Hempstead: Harvester Wheatsheaf, 1989), pp. 149–52; Dympna Callaghan, *Woman and Gender in Renaissance Tragedy* (Atlantic Highlands, N.J.: Humanities Press International, 1989), pp. 91–93, pp. 116–17; and ch. 8.

2. *Othello* is quoted from the New Arden edition, ed. M. R. Ridley (London: Methuen, 1962).

3. Linda Woodbridge, *Women and the English Renaissance* (Brighton: Harvester, 1984), p. 195; cf. p. 327. Marvin Rosenberg says Desdemona has been seen as "a silly fool; an indelicate wanton; loving unnaturally; a sinful daughter; a deceiver; a moral coward; too gentle; a saint; a symbol" (*The Masks of Othello* [Berkeley: Univ. of California Press, 1971], p. 305).

4. Shakespeare, *Twelfth Night*, ed. J. M. Lothian and T. W. Craik (London: Methuen, 1975), 2.4.115; see Lisa Jardine, *Still Harping on Daughters*, 2d ed. (Hemel Hempstead: Harvester Wheatsheaf, 1989), pp. 181–93.

5. Catherine Belsey, *The Subject of Tragedy* (London: Methuen, 1985), p. 149.

6. Leonard Tennenhouse observes: "Shakespeare does not differ from Iago in terms of the basis upon which gender distinctions should be made" (*Power on Display* [London: Methuen, 1986], p. 126). See also Terry Eagleton, *William Shakespeare* (Oxford: Basil Blackwell, 1986), p. 68; McLuskie, *Renaissance Dramatists*, p. 150.

7. Janet Adelman, " 'This Is and Is Not Cressid': The Characterisation of Cressida," in Shirley Nelson Garner, Claire Kahane, and Madelon Sprengnether, eds., *The (M)other Tongue: Essays in Feminist Psychoanalytic Interpretation* (Ithaca, N.Y.: Cornell Univ. Press, 1985), p. 140. However, Adelman believes that Desdemona "remains a vigorous and independent character, larger than Othello's fantasies of her" (p. 140).

8. Sigmund Freud, "Some Character-Types Met within Psycho-Analytic Work" (1916), in *The Standard Edition of the Complete Psychological Works*, ed. James Strachey, vol. 14 (London: Hogarth Press, 1957), pp. 318–19;

reprinted in Alan Sinfield, ed., *"Macbeth": A New Casebook* (London: Macmillan, 1992).

9. E.g. A. W. Verity, ed., *Macbeth* (Cambridge: Cambridge Univ. Press, 1902, reprinted twenty-two times by 1952), pp. xxx–xxxiii. More recently, see Juliet Dusiberre, *Shakespeare and the Nature of Women* (London: Macmillan, 1975); Joan Larsen Klein, "Lady Macbeth: 'Infirm of purpose,' " in Carolyn Ruth Swift Lenz, Gayle Greene, and Carol Thomas Neely, eds., *The Woman's Part* (Urbana: Univ. of Illinois Press, 1980), pp. 241–44; David Norbrook, *"Macbeth* and the Politics of Historiography," in Kevin Sharpe and Steven N. Zwicker, eds., *Politics of Discourse: The Literature and History of Seventeenth-Century England* (Univ. of California Press, 1987), p. 104. However, Simon Shepherd turns the argument around, suggesting that Lady Macbeth mistakenly imagines that she must kill off the female in herself in order to be the partner Macbeth needs: her tragedy derives from this confusing of social and biological definitions of maleness (*Amazons and Warrior Women* [Brighton: Harvester, 1981], pp. 38–39). Tennenhouse avoids "ascribing a psychological cause" to the presentation of Lady Macbeth (*Power on Display,* p. 128), and Jardine regards her as frankly incredible, a "nightmare" (*Still Harping,* pp. 97–98).

10. G. Wilson Knight, *The Wheel of Fire* (1930; London: Methuen, 1949), p. 11. Cf. A. C. Bradley, *Shakespearean Tragedy* (1904; London: Macmillan, 1957).

11. L. C. Knights, "How Many Children Had Lady Macbeth?" (1933), in Knights, *Explorations* (London: Chatto, 1946).

12. Lily B. Campbell, *Shakespeare's Tragic Heroes* (1930; London, Methuen, 1961), p. vii; M. C. Bradbrook, *Themes and Conventions in Elizabethan Tragedy* (1935; Cambridge: Cambridge Univ. Press, 1960), pp. 50, 54. On these earlier critics, see pp. 109–10, and John Drakakis, ed., *Alternative Shakespeares* (London: Methuen, 1985), pp. 9–12, 18–22.

13. Barbara Everett, *Young Hamlet: Essays in Shakespeare's Tragedies* (Oxford: Clarendon Press, 1989), p. 103.

14. John Bayley, *Shakespeare and Tragedy* (London: Routledge, 1981), pp. 184, 164–66.

15. See Lenz, Greene, and Neely, *Woman's Part*; Irene G. Dash, *Wooing, Wedding and Power* (New York: Columbia Univ. Press, 1981). I have addressed aspects of this approach in chapter 2.

16. Woodbridge, *Women and the English Renaissance*, p. 327.

17. Jonathan Goldberg, "Shakespearean Inscriptions: The Voicing of Power," in Patricia Parker and Geoffrey Hartman, eds., *Shakespeare and the Question of Theory* (London: Methuen, 1985), pp. 118–19.

18. Catherine Belsey, "Disrupting Sexual Difference: Meaning and Gender in the Comedies," in Drakakis, ed., *Alternative Shakespeares*, pp. 187–88; Julia Kristeva, "Women's Time," *Signs* 7 (1981): 13–35.

19. Joel Fineman, *Shakespeare's Perjured Eye* (Berkeley: Univ. of California Press, 1986), pp. 25, 79–80, 82; see also pp. 42–43.

20. William Nigel Dodd, "Metalanguage and Character in Drama," *Lingua e Stile* 14 (1979): 135–50, pp. 136, 143–44; alluding to Peter Szondi, *Theorie des modernen Dramas* (Frankfurt am Main: Suhrkamp Verlag, 1956),

ch. 1. Dodd also discusses "out of character" speech to the audience, and ambiguous instances.

21. Belsey, *Subject of Tragedy*, p. 38 and ch. 2, with reference to Shakespeare, *3 Henry VI*, ed. Andrew S. Cairncross (London: Methuen, 1964), 5.6.80–91.

22. Francis Barker, *The Tremulous Private Body: Essays on Subjection* (London: Methuen, 1984), pp. 31, 35–38. I discuss *Hamlet* partly in this light in chapter 9 below.

23. Simon Shepherd, *Marlowe and the Politics of Elizabethan Theatre* (New York: St. Martin's Press, 1986), p. 81, and ch. 3.

24. Dollimore, *Radical Tragedy*, 2d ed., p. xxxii; and see ch. 10.

25. Bradley, *Shakespearean Tragedy*, p. 7.

26. Jacqueline Rose, "Sexuality in the Reading of Shakespeare: *Hamlet* and *Measure for Measure,*" in Drakakis, ed., *Alternative Shakespeares*, p. 102.

27. Cf. Belsey, *Subject of Tragedy*, pp. 47, 51; McLuskie, *Renaissance Dramatists*, p. 136 and ch. 6. For another argument about the realism of Shakespeare's characters, see A. D. Nuttall, *A New Mimesis* (London and New York: Methuen, 1983), pp. 80–100, 163–81. Nuttall allows my position when he acknowledges that Jack the Giant Killer is not real like Falstaff (p. 100), but I think he would disagree with me on how far Shakespearean characters are like Jack the Giant Killer.

28. *Twelfth Night*, New Arden ed., 2.1; 3.3; 3.4.356–79; 5.1.74–90, 216–26. Molly M. Mahood concludes her introduction to the New Penguin edition of the play (Harmondsworth, 1968) with the suggestion that Antonio's is "the true voice of feeling" and perhaps a "rare revelation" of Shakespeare's "personal experience" (p. 39).

29. Orgel, "Nobody's Perfect: Or, Why Did the English Stage Take Boys for Women?" *South Atlantic Quarterly* 88 (1989): 7–29; Louis Adrian Montrose, " 'Shaping Fantasies': Figurations of Gender and Power in Elizabethan Culture," in Stephen Greenblatt, ed., *Representing the English Renaissance"* (Berkeley: Univ. of California Press, 1988), p. 36.

30. Stephen Greenblatt, *Shakespearean Negotiations* (Oxford: Clarendon Press, 1988), pp. 67–68.

31. E.g., Coppélia Kahn, *Man's Estate* (Berkeley: Univ. of California Press, 1981), pp. 207–9. According to Kahn, the play ends with "men and women truly knowing themselves through choosing and loving the right mate" (p. 211). However, Olivia is appreciated as the principal threat to gender hierarchy in the play by Jean Howard, "Crossdressing, the Theater and Gender Struggle in Early Modern England," *Shakespeare Quarterly* 39 (1988): 418–40. For the view that Viola is no real challenge, see also Clara Clairborne Park, "As We Like It: How a Girl Can Be Smart and Still Popular," in Lenz, Greene, and Neely, *Woman's Part*, p. 108 et passim.

32. E.g., Juliet Dusinberre, *Shakespeare and the Nature of Women* (London: Macmillan, 1975), pp. 47–48.

33. See Jardine, *Still Harping*, pp. 78–80, 84–88, on some of the circumstances in which women might inherit and achieve some independence. I disagree with Stephen Greenblatt's expectation that courtship should be facilitated by the absence of males with whom Orsino would otherwise nego-

tiate; the play shows the opposite—that Orsino's courtship suffers from the absence of a sympathetic male to dominate Olivia on his behalf (*Shakespearean Negotiations*, pp. 68–69). Compare Portia in *The Merchant of Venice*, who is controlled by her father even after his death.

34. E.g. Richard P. Wheeler, *Shakespeare's Development and the Problem Comedies* (Berkeley: Univ. of California Press, 1981), p. 102; Howard, "Cross-dressing," p. 432.

35. Woodbridge, *Women and the English Renaissance*, p. 238. See also Tennenhouse, *Power on Display*, pp. 63–68.

36. Montrose, " 'Shaping Fantasies,' " p. 41.

37. John Webster, *The Duchess of Malfi*, in Jonathan Dollimore and Alan Sinfield, eds., *The Selected Plays of John Webster* (Cambridge: Cambridge Univ. Press, 1983), 1.1.7–9.

38. C. L. Barber, *Shakespeare's Festive Comedy* (Princeton: Princeton Univ. Press, 1959), pp. 244–45. Psychoanalytic criticism is likely to be reactionary here. For instance: "*Twelfth Night* traces the evolution of sexuality as related to identity, from the playful and unconscious toyings of youthful courtship, through a period of sexual confusion, to a final thriving in which swagger is left behind and men and women truly know themselves through choosing and loving the right mate"—so Kahn, *Man's Estate*, pp. 210–11.

39. Leslie Fiedler, *The Stranger in Shakespeare* (St Albans, Herts.: Paladin, 1974), pp. 76–79.

40. Callaghan, *Woman and Gender*, pp. 74–75 and ch. 5; see Pierre Macherey, *A Theory of Literary Production*, trans. Geoffrey Wall (London: Routledge, 1978); McLuskie, *Renaissance Dramatists*, p. 154.

41. See V. N. Volosinov, *Marxism and the Philosophy of Language*, trans. Ladislav Matejka and I. R. Titunik (New York and London: Seminar Press, 1973), pp. 17–24, 95–106.

42. Nicos Poulantzas, *Political Power and Social Classes*, trans. Timothy O'Hagan (London: New Left Books, 1973), p. 207.

43. See William Witherle Lawrence, *Shakespeare's Problem Comedies* (1931; New York: Ungar, 1960); E. M. W. Tillyard, *Shakespeare's Problem Plays* (London: Chatto, 1950); F. R. Leavis, *The Common Pursuit* (Harmondsworth: Penguin Books, 1962), p. 169. The ending, Leavis continues, is "marvellously adroit, with an adroitness that expresses, and derives from, the poet's sure human insight and his fineness of ethical and poetic sensibility."

44. On the interinvolvement of the elements in a binary stereotype, see Homi Bhabha, "The Other Question," *Screen* 24, no. 6 (1983): 18–36, p. 34; and Sinfield, *Literature, Politics and Culture*, pp. 116–21.

45. Jardine, *Still Harping*, pp. 75, 119–20, 184–85. See Orlin, "Desdemona's Disposition"; McLuskie, *Renaissance Dramatists*, pp. 150–51.

46. Wheeler, *Shakespeare's Development and the Problem Comedies*, pp. 128–30; see *Measure for Measure*, ed. J. W. Lever (London: Methuen, 1965), 5.1.95–104. Steven Mullaney argues that having to speak *as* Mariana helps Isabella internalize Angelo's view of her (*The Place of the Stage* [Chicago: Univ. of Chicago Press, 1988], pp. 108–11).

47. Callaghan, *Woman and Gender*, p. 67.

48. Edward A. Snow, "Sexual Anxiety and the Male Order of Things in *Othello*," *English Literary Renaissance* 10 (1980): 384–412.

49. Quoted by Karen Newman, "Femininity and Monstrosity in *Othello*," in Jean E. Howard and Marion F. O'Connor, eds., *Shakespeare Reproduced* (London: Methuen, 1987), p. 152.

50. On Adams, see Alfred Van Rensselaer Westfall, *American Shakespearean Criticism, 1607–1865* (New York: H. W. Wilson, 1939), pp. 224–26; and see Allan Bloom, *Shakespeare's Politics* (1964; Chicago: Univ. of Chicago Press, 1986), ch. 3. An alternative, of course, is to deny that Othello is really black: so Henry N. Hudson, replying to Adams (see Westfall, pp. 252–53), and M. R. Ridley in the introduction to the New Arden edition of *Othello*, pp. l–liv.

51. Peter Stallybrass, "*Macbeth* and Witchcraft," in John Russell Brown, ed., *Focus on "Macbeth"* (London: Routledge, 1982), p. 198. According to the historians Boece and Buchanan, Lady Macbeth and Macbeth did have a son and he was killed by Macduff, David Norbrook points out ("*Macbeth* and the Politics of Historiography," p. 89).

52. See Sinfield, *Literature, Politics and Culture*, pp. 116–21; and on Man, Jonathan Dollimore, *Radical Tragedy*, 2d ed. (Hemel Hempstead: Harvester Wheatsheaf, 1989), chs. 10, 16.

CHAPTER FOUR

1. *Dictionary of National Biography*, ed. Sidney Lee (London: Smith, Elder, 1909), 19: 118–19.

2. *Miscellaneous Prose of Sir Philip Sidney*, ed. Katherine Duncan-Jones and Jan van Dorsten (Oxford: Clarendon Press, 1973), p. 33.

3. Stephen Greenblatt, *Renaissance Self-Fashioning* (Chicago: Univ. of Chicago Press, 1980), p. 209.

4. Stephen Greenblatt, "Invisible Bullets: Renaissance Authority and Its Subversion," *Glyph* 8 (1981): 40–61, p. 53.

5. Jonathan Goldberg, *James I and the Politics of Literature* (Baltimore: Johns Hopkins Univ. Press, 1983), pp. 177, 116. The criticism of Greenblatt's "totalistic urge" is in Jonathan Goldberg, "The Politics of Renaissance Literature: A Review Essay," *English Literary History* 49 (1982): 514–42.

6. Greenblatt, "Invisible Bullets," p. 57; Goldberg, *James I*, p. 154.

7. Nicos Poulantzas, *Political Power and Social Classes*, trans. Timothy O'Hagan (London: New Left Books, 1975), pp. 161–62; see also pp. 168–72.

8. Perry Anderson, *Lineages of the Absolute State* (London: New Left Books, 1974), p. 142.

9. V. G. Kiernan, "State and Nation in Western Europe," *Past and Present* 31 (1965): 20–38, p. 33.

10. W. T. MacCaffrey, "England: The Crown and the New Aristocracy, 1540–1600," *Past and Present* 30 (1965): 52–64, p. 64.

11. Ernest William Talbert, *The Problem of Order* (Chapel Hill: Univ. of North Carolina Press, 1962), p. 28.

12. See Norbert Elias, *The Court Society*, trans. Edmund Jephcott (Oxford: Basil Blackwell, 1983).

13. W. T. MacCaffrey, "Elizabethan Politics: The First Decade, 1558–1568," *Past and Present* 24 (1963): 25–41, p. 41.

14. W. T. MacCaffrey, "Place and Patronage in Elizabethan Politics," in *Elizabethan Government and Society,* ed. S. T. Bindoff, J. Hurstfield, and C. H. Williams (London: Athlone Press, 1961), p. 97.

15. I owe this point to conversations with Philippa Berry. See also Elias, *Court Society,* p. 42: "Everything that came from the king's wider possessions, from the realm, had to pass through the filter of the court before it could reach him; through the same filter everything from the king had to pass before it reached the country"; et passim.

16. See Stephen Orgel, *The Illusion of Power* (Berkeley: Univ. of California Press, 1975), pp. 10–11, 14.

17. Louis Adrian Montrose, "Celebration and Insinuation: Sir Philip Sidney and the Motives of Elizabethan Courtship," *Renaissance Drama,* n.s., 8 (1977): 3–35, p. 15. For other evidence of the political scope of the masque, see Orgel, *Illusion of Power,* pp. 79–83; Marie Axton, "The Tudor Mask and Elizabethan Court Drama," in *English Drama: Forms and Development,* ed. Marie Axton and Raymond Williams (Cambridge: Cambridge Univ. Press, 1977), pp. 24–47; and Malcolm Smuts, "The Political Failure of Stuart Cultural Patronage," in *Patronage in the Renaissance,* ed. Guy Fitch Lytle and Stephen Orgel (Princeton: Princeton Univ. Press, 1981), pp. 165–87.

18. See MacCaffrey, "England: The Crown and the New Aristocracy," chapter 8.

19. *The Prose Works of Fulke Greville, Lord Brooke,* ed. John Gouws (Oxford: Clarendon Press, 1986), p. 32.

20. W. D. Briggs, "Political Ideas in Sidney's *Arcadia,*" *Studies in Philology* 28 (1931): 137–61; "Sidney's Political Ideas," *SP* 29 (1932): 534–42. See also James E. Phillips, "George Buchanan and the Sidney Circle," *Huntington Library Quarterly* 12 (1948–49): 23–55.

21. Sir Philip Sidney, *The Countess of Pembroke's Arcadia,* ed. Maurice Evans (Harmondsworth: Penguin Books, 1977), pp. 452–53.

22. Frances A. Yates, *Astraea: The Imperial Theme in the Sixteenth Century* (Harmondsworth: Penguin Books, 1977), pp. 88–94, 103–4; Roy Strong, *The Cult of Elizabeth* (London: Thames & Hudson, 1977), pp. 147–49.

23. See Anderson, *Lineages,* pp. 33–34; Poulantzas, *Political Power and Social Classes,* pp. 164–65; Michael Walzer, *The Revolution of the Saints* (New York: Atheneum, 1968), p. 241; MacCaffrey, "Elizabethan Politics: The First Decade," pp. 28–30.

24. *The Prose Works of Sir Philip Sidney,* ed. Albert Feuillerat (Cambridge: Cambridge Univ. Press, 1963), 3:166–67.

25. Ibid., p. 119; trans. Malcolm William Wallace, *The Life of Sir Philip Sidney* (Cambridge: Cambridge Univ. Press, 1915), p. 198.

26. Perez Zagorin, *The Court and the Country* (New York: Atheneum, 1970), pp. 54–55, 96–98.

27. Conyers Read, *Mr. Secretary Walsingham and the Policy of Queen Elizabeth* (Oxford: Clarendon Press, 1925), 1:416; see also 2:14–22. Between 1562 and 1584, Leicester, Warwick, and Sir Henry Sidney supported Christopher Goodman, who was often in trouble for his propagation of puritan

arguments for tyrannicide and the limitation of monarchical rule (Phillips, "George Buchanan and the Sidney Circle," pp. 28–30).

28. Lucien Goldmann, *The Hidden God,* trans. Philip Thody (London: Routledge, 1964), p. 120 et passim.

29. Pierre Bourdieu, "Symbolic Power," in *Identity and Structure: Issues in the Sociology of Education,* ed. Denis Gleeson (Driffield: Nafferton Books, 1977), p. 116. And see Poulantzas, *Political Power,* pp. 84, 113–16, 203.

30. See Raymond Williams, *Culture* (Glasgow: Fontana, 1981), pp. 38–46, 98–108; and in the present volume, pp. 171–73.

31. Leonard Tennenhouse, "Sir Walter Ralegh and the Literature of Clientage," in *Patronage in the Renaissance,* ed. Lytle and Orgel, pp. 247–58.

32. John Fiske and John Hartley, *Reading Television* (London: Methuen, 1978), p. 105. See also Manfred Naumann, "Literary Production and Reception," *New Literary History* 8 (1976): 107–26.

CHAPTER FIVE

1. *Macbeth* is quoted from the New Arden edition, ed. Kenneth Muir (London: Methuen, 1962). Since this chapter was written, I have become aware of two important essays that anticipate aspects of its argument. Harry Berger, Jr., "The Early Scenes of *Macbeth:* Preface to a New Interpretation," *English Literary History* 47 (1980): 1–31, shows how Duncan's Scotland is already subject to major structural political disturbance. David Norbrook, "*Macbeth* and the Politics of Historiography," in Kevin Sharpe and Steven N. Zwicker, eds., *Politics of Discourse: The Literature and History of Seventeenth-Century England* (Berkeley: Univ. of California Press, 1987), shows the significance of George Buchanan's account of Macbeth and Scottish history, and argues that Shakespeare follows neither Buchanan's hostility to unreasoning submission to hierarchy and tradition, nor King James's line.

2. See chapters 2 and 4.

3. Perry Anderson, *Lineages of the Absolute State* (London: New Left Books, 1974), p. 18. On attitudes to government and *Macbeth,* see Michael Hawkins, "History, Politics and *Macbeth,*" in John Russell Brown, ed., *Focus on "Macbeth"* (London: Routledge, 1982).

4. *King Richard II,* ed. Peter Ure (London: Methuen, 1956), 5.1.59–61.

5. See chapter 6.

6. John Gerard, *The Autobiography of an Elizabethan,* trans. Philip Caraman (London: Longman, 1951), pp. 52–53.

7. *The Political Works of James I,* ed. Charles Howard McIlwain (New York: Russell & Russell, 1965), p. 18.

8. James I, *Daemonologie (1597), Newes from Scotland (1591)* (London: Bodley Head, 1924), p. 55.

9. See James I, *The Trew Law of Free Monarchies,* in *Political Works,* ed. McIlwain, pp. 56–61, 66.

10. Henry Paul, *The Royal Play of "Macbeth"* (New York: Octagon Books, 1978), p. 373.

11. Francis Bacon, *Essays,* introduction by Michael J. Hawkins (London: Dent, 1972), p. 160. See further Jonathan Dollimore, *Radical Tragedy* (Brighton: Harvester, 1984), esp. ch. 5.

12. Paul, *Royal Play of "Macbeth,"* p. 196.

13. See W. D. Briggs, "Political Ideas in Sidney's *Arcadia,"* *Studies in Philology* 28 (1931): 137–61, and "Philip Sidney's Political Ideas," ibid. 29 (1932): 534–42.

14. See *The Tyrannous Reign of Mary Stewart, George Buchanan's Account,* trans. and ed. W. A. Gatherer (Edinburgh: Edinburgh Univ. Press, 1958), pp. 12–13; James E. Phillips, "George Buchanan and the Sidney Circle," *Huntington Library Quarterly* 12 (1948/49): 23–55; I. D. McFarlane, *Buchanan* (London: Duckworth, 1981), pp. 392–440.

15. *The Tyrannous Reign of Mary Stewart,* p. 49; see also p. 99.

16. Ibid., pp. 72, 86, 91, 111, 119, 145, 153; cf. *Macbeth* 3.1.48–56; 5.7.17–18; 3.5.130–31; 5.8.27–29.

17. See chapter 9.

18. However, as Jim McLaverty points out to me, the play has arranged that Macduff will not experience temptation from his wife. In the chronicles, Malcolm's son is overthrown by Donalbain; in Polanski's film of *Macbeth,* Donalbain is made to meet the Witches.

19. *The Trew Law of Free Monarchies,* in *Political Works,* ed. McIlwain, pp. 56–61; referring to 1 Sam. 8:9–20.

20. See Hunter, *Macbeth* (Penguin ed.), pp. 33–34; Dennis Bartholomeusz, *"Macbeth" and the Players* (Cambridge: Cambridge Univ. Press, 1969). On the Witches and the ideological roles of women in the play, see Peter Stallybrass, *"Macbeth* and Witchcraft," in Brown, ed., *Focus on "Macbeth."*

21. Muir in the New Arden *Macbeth,* p. xlix, quoting G. Wilson Knight, L. C. Knights, F. C. Kolbe, Derek Traversi. See also Irving Ribner, *Patterns in Shakespearean Tragedy* (London: Methuen, 1960), p. 153; Robert Ornstein, *The Moral Vision of Jacobean Tragedy* (Madison: Univ. of Wisconsin Press, 1965), p. 230; Hunter (Penguin ed.), p. 7.

22. Ribner, *Patterns in Shakespearean Tragedy,* p. 159.

23. Roger Scruton, *The Meaning of Conservatism* (Harmondsworth: Penguin Books, 1980), p. 21.

24. A. C. Bradley, *Shakespearean Tragedy,* 2d ed. (London: Macmillan, 1965), p. 305; Wayne Booth, "Macbeth as Tragic Hero," *Journal of General Education* 6 (1951): revised for *Shakespeare's Tragedies,* ed. Laurence Lerner (Harmondsworth: Penguin Books, 1963), p. 186. See also Hunter (Penguin ed.) pp. 26–29; Wilbur Sanders, *The Dramatist and the Received Idea* (Cambridge: Cambridge Univ. Press, 1968), pp. 282–307.

25. John Bayley, *Shakespeare and Tragedy* (London: Routledge, 1981), p. 199; see also p. 193. I am grateful for the stimulating comments of Russell Jackson, Tony Inglis, Peter Holland, and Jonathan Dollimore.

CHAPTER SIX

1. E. M. W. Tillyard, *Shakespeare's History Plays* (Harmondsworth: Penguin Books, 1962), p. 21.

2. Lily B. Campbell, *Shakespeare's Histories* (London: Methuen, 1964), pp. 3–4.

3. Tillyard, *Shakespeare's History Plays,* pp. 69, 237.

4. Campbell, *Shakespeare's Histories,* p. 6.

5. Jan Kott, *Shakespeare Our Contemporary,* 2d ed. (London: Methuen, 1967), pp. 14, 39.

6. See Jacques Derrida, *Writing and Difference,* trans. Alan Bass (London: Routledge, 1978), p. 19; and Jacques Derrida, *Of Grammatology,* trans. Gayatri Chakravorty Spivak (Baltimore: Johns Hopkins Univ. Press, 1976), p. 315.

7. See Alan Sinfield, ed., *Society and Literature, 1945–1970* (London: Methuen, 1983), pp. 94–105; Jonathan Dollimore and Alan Sinfield, eds., *Political Shakespeare* (Manchester: Manchester Univ. Press, 1985), pp. 131–33, 160–64.

8. Wilbur Sanders, *The Dramatist and the Received Idea* (Cambridge: Cambridge Univ. Press, 1968), pp. 157, 166, and also p. 190.

9. Cf. ibid., pp. 183–85.

10. G. K. Hunter, *Dramatic Identities and Cultural Tradition* (Liverpool: Liverpool Univ. Press, 1978), pp. 251–52.

11. A materialist criticism will be concerned with aspects of ideology additional to those dealt with here, and our emphasis on ideology as legitimation, though crucial, should not be taken as an exhaustive definition of the topic. For a fuller discussion of ideology and subjectivity, see Dollimore, *Radical Tragedy,* esp. chs. 1, 10, 16; Dollimore and Sinfield, eds., *Political Shakespeare*; and, more generally, Janet Wolff, *The Social Production of Art* (London: Macmillan, 1981), esp. ch. 3.

12. See Stephen Orgel, "Making Greatness Familiar," in Stephen Greenblatt, ed., *The Power of Forms in the English Renaissance* (Norman, Okla.: Pilgrim Books, 1982).

13. Ian Breward, ed., *The Work of William Perkins* (Abingdon: Sutton Courtenay Press, 1970), p. 150.

14. Ibid., p. 449.

15. Lancelot Andrewes, *Works* (Oxford: Clarendon Press, 1841), 1:325.

16. Shakespeare, *Henry V,* ed. John H. Walter (London: Methuen, 1954), 1.2.211–12.

17. See pp. 175–81, 199–200, and Alan Sinfield, *Literature in Protestant England, 1550–1660* (London: Croom Helm, 1983), ch. 7.

18. This distinction derives from (but also differs from) Anthony Giddens, *A Contemporary Critique of Historical Materialism* (London: Macmillan, 1981), 1:231–37.

19. See Raymond Williams, *Marxism and Literature* (Oxford: Oxford Univ. Press, 1977), pp. 121–27.

20. John Strype, *The Life and Acts of John Whitgift* (Oxford: Oxford Univ. Press, 1822), 1:524–26. See further Felicity Heal, *Of Prelates and Princes* (Cambridge: Cambridge Univ. Press, 1980).

21. J. E. Neale, *Elizabeth I and Her Parliaments, 1584–1601* (London: Cape, 1957), pp. 309–10; Lucy de Bruyn, *Mob-Rule and Riots* (London: Regency, 1981), p. 36.

22. William Hunt, *The Puritan Moment* (Cambridge, Mass.: Harvard Univ. Press, 1983), pp. 33, 60–61.

23. See Perry Anderson, *Lineages of the Absolute State* (London: New Left Books, 1974), pp. 16–59, 113–42; W. T. MacCaffrey, "England: The Crown and the New Aristocracy, 1540–1600," *Past and Present* 30 (1965): 52–64.

24. G. B. Harrison, *The Life and Death of Robert Devereux, Earl of Essex* (London: Cassell, 1937), p. 102 and chs. 9–12.

25. Ibid., pp. 214–15. See in the present volume pp. 40–41.

26. Geoffrey Bullough, *Narrative and Dramatic Sources of Shakespeare,* vol. 4, *Later English History Plays* (London: Routledge, 1966), p. 386.

27. Andrewes, *Works,* 1:326.

28. See Gary Taylor's note to these lines in his Oxford edition of *Henry V* (Oxford: Oxford Univ. Press, 1982).

29. Hunt, *Puritan Moment,* p. 60; de Bruyn, *Mob-Rule,* p. 62; for further instances see Hunt, p. 50; and de Bruyn, p. 26.

30. Philip Edwards, *Threshold of a Nation* (Cambridge: Cambridge Univ. Press, 1979), pp. 75–78, referring to *Henry V* 3.2.125–27. Edwards shows how an Irish captain who had been in Essex's army made a protest similar to that of Macmorris.

31. David Williams, *A History of Modern Wales,* 2d ed. (London: John Murray, 1977), ch. 3.

32. Paul L. Hughes and James F. Larkin, *Tudor Royal Proclamations* (New Haven: Yale Univ. Press, 1969), 3:134–35.

33. Edwards, *Threshold,* pp. 74–86. See David Beers Quinn, *The Eliza-bethans and the Irish* (Ithaca, N.Y.: Cornell Univ. Press, 1966), chs. 4, 5, and 7.

34. Richard Levin, "The Poetics and Politics of Bardicide," *PMLA* 105 (1990): 491–504.

35. Edmund Spenser, *A View of the Present State of Ireland,* ed. W. L. Renwick (Oxford: Clarendon Press, 1970), p. 104.

36. Hughes and Larkin, *Tudor Royal Proclamations,* 3:201.

37. George L. Geckle, "Politics and Sexuality in Shakespeare's Second Tetralogy," in H. W. Matalene, *Romanticism and Culture: A Tribute to Morse Peckham* (Columbia, S.C.: Camden House, 1984), pp. 130–31. The second half of the present chapter is new; Jonathan Dollimore and I have sometimes been asked why we did not address the sexual politics of *Henry V* in this essay as it appeared in *Alternative Shakespeares,* edited by John Drakakis. The answer is that other essays in *Alternative Shakespeares* were to do that (see the fine contributions of Jacqueline Rose and Catherine Belsey), and we had a strict word limit in which to attempt the complex topic of ideology.

38. Linda Bamber, *Comic Women, Tragic Men* (Stanford: Stanford Univ. Press, 1982), p. 152; Peter Erickson, *Patriarchal Structures in Shakespeare's Drama* (Berkeley: Univ. of California Press, 1985), p. 62. This is like Wilbur Sanders's centering of individuals in the history plays (see n. 8 above).

39. See Dollimore, in Dollimore and Sinfield, eds., *Political Shakespeare,* pp. 72–80.

40. Coppélia Kahn, *Man's Estate* (Berkeley: Univ. of California Press, 1981), p. 47; Bamber, *Comic Women,* pp. 135, 164–65; Erickson, *Patriarchal*

Structures, pp. 61–62. However, Phyllis Rackin argues that women are potentially subversive in Shakespearean history plays, that this subversion works only momentarily in *1 Henry VI,* and that it is effective in *King John* (Rackin, *Stages of History* [Ithaca, N.Y.: Cornell Univ. Press, 1990], ch. 4). See also Jean Howard, " 'Effeminately Dolent': Gender and Legitimacy in Ford's *Perkin Warbeck,"* in Michael Neill, ed., *John Ford: Critical Re-Visions* (Cambridge: Cambridge Univ. Press, 1988), pp. 263, 278, et passim.

41. 1.2.91–92. Here, no doubt significantly, but I am no Freudian, Coppélia Kahn slips, and says, "Henry bases his claim to the French crown on the Salic Law, which forbids inheritance through the female" (*Man's Estate,* p. 79). It is the other way round: Henry's title depends on denying that Salic law applies, he claims to inherit through the female line.

42. Rackin, *Stages of History,* p. 191; also pp. 167–68.

43. Shakespeare, *1 Henry IV,* ed. A. R. Humphreys (London: Methuen, 1960), 1.3.28–68.

44. Shakespeare, *Richard II,* ed. Peter Ure (London: Methuen, 1966), 5.3.7, 10–12.

45. *Richard III,* ed. Antony Hammond (London: Methuen, 1981), 3.7.210; *Romeo and Juliet,* ed. Brian Gibbons (London: Methuen, 1980), 3.1.116.

46. *1 Henry IV* 1.2.2–4, 3.3.150–52; *Richard II* 5.3.7. In an essay forthcoming in *Renaissance Drama* (1991), "Wales, Ireland, and *1 Henry IV,"* Christopher Highley shows how *1 Henry IV,* like other contemporary documents, imagines the threat from the Celtic fringe in terms of the overthrow of a masculine English identity through castration.

47. In Elaine Showalter, ed., *The New Feminist Criticism* (London: Virago, 1986), p. 278. Coppélia Kahn, partly following W. H. Auden in *The Dyer's Hand* (New York: Random House, 1963), p. 196, says Falstaff avoids "sexual maturity," desires food and drink more than women, and gives "his own deepest affections to a boy" (Kahn, *Man's Estate,* pp. 72–73). Of course, Auden and Kahn are hinting, darkly, at homosexuality.

48. Shakespeare, *2 Henry IV,* ed. A. R. Humphreys (London: Methuen, 1966), 4.4.31–33; 5.4.

49. Howard, " 'Effeminately Dolent,' " p. 275. Howard argues that Perkin Warbeck in John Ford's play of that name (c. 1632) is " 'contaminated' by traffic with the feminine," that his courtship is unlike that of Henry V, and that it all shows "the faltering, but hardly the collapse, of the machinery of patriarchal absolutism" (pp. 272, 276).

50. In the New Arden edition, John H. Walter says "the effeminate Dauphin is riding a lady's horse" (p. 84), but Gary Taylor in the Oxford edition says this need not be so, discerning no "signs of effeminacy in the Dauphin" (p. 197). Erickson says the Dauphin is "a travesty of masculinity" (*Patriarchal Structures,* p. 55).

51. Eve Kosofsky Sedgwick, *Between Men: English Literature and Male Homosocial Desire* (New York: Columbia Univ. Press, 1985), pp. 25, 5, and pp. 1–27, passim. See Stephen Orgel, "Nobody's Perfect: Or Why Did the English Stage Take Boys for Women?" *South Atlantic Quarterly* 88 (1989):

7–29; Alan Bray, *Homosexuality in Renaissance England* (London: Gay Men's Press, 1982); and Alan Bray's important new article: "Homosexuality and the Signs of Male Friendship in Elizabethan England," *History Workshop* 29 (1990): 1–19.

52. See Ian Maclean, *The Renaissance Notion of Women* (Cambridge: Cambridge Univ. Press, 1980); Thomas Laqueur, "Orgasm, Generation, and the Politics of Reproductive Biology," *Representations* 14 (1986): 1–41; Greenblatt, "Fiction and Friction," in Stephen Greenblatt, *Shakespearean Negotiations* (Oxford: Clarendon Press, 1988), pp. 73–86.

53. J. E. Neale, *Queen Elizabeth* (London: Cape, 1934), p. 279.

54. *Troilus and Cressida*, ed. Kenneth Palmer (London: Methuen, 1982), 3.3.216–19; Orgel, "Nobody's Perfect," pp. 14–15. Rebecca W. Bushnell observes that tyrants were said to be "effeminate"—subject to their lusts, mainly in respect of women (*Tragedies of Tyrants* [Ithaca, N.Y.: Cornell Univ. Press, 1990], pp. 63–69).

55. Spenser, *View*, ed. Renwick, pp. 69–70. Spenser says he is quoting Aristotle, but Renwick says it is an elaboration of Herodotus (p. 206).

56. For Erickson, this "set piece is a microcosm of the historical as well as psychological escapism implicit in Henry V's heroic impulse" (*Patriarchal Structures*, p. 54).

57. See Norman Rabkin, "Rabbits, Ducks and *Henry V*," *Shakespeare Quarterly* 28 (1977): 279–96; Kahn, *Man's Estate*, pp. 79–80; Colin MacCabe, "Towards a Modern Trivium—English Studies Today," *Critical Quarterly* 26 (1984): 69–82, p. 72; Leonard Tennenhouse, *Power on Display* (New York: Methuen, 1986), p. 71; Erickson, *Patriarchal Structures*, pp. 59–63; Lance Wilcox, "Katherine of France as Victim and Bride," *Shakespeare Studies* 17 (1985): 61–76.

58. Taylor, ed., *Henry V* (Oxford ed.), p. 270.

59. Kahn, *Man's Estate*, p. 79; Bamber, *Comic Women*, p. 146.

60. Wilcox, "Katherine of France," p. 66.

61. Shakespeare, *1 Henry VI*, ed. Andrew S. Cairncross (London: Methuen, 1962), 1.1.35, 5.4.107. Coppélia Kahn quotes the prophecy that there will be "none but women left to wail the dead" (*1 Henry VI* 1.1.51) and observes "the fear that without the masculine principle of succession the race will become impotent and feminized" (Kahn, *Man's Estate*, p. 62).

62. Spenser, *View*, ed. Renwick, pp. 66–68. See also the notes in Rudolf Gottfried, ed., *Spenser's Prose Works*, in Edwin Greenlaw, Charles Grosvenor Osgood, Frederick Morgan Padelford, and Ray Heffner, eds., *The Works of Edmund Spenser: A Variorum Edition* (Baltimore: Johns Hopkins Press, 1949), pp. 349–51.

CHAPTER SEVEN

1. See Roger Howell, *Sir Philip Sidney: The Shepherd Knight* (London: Hutchinson, 1968), chs. 1, 2, 5, 8, 10, et passim; James M. Osborn, *Young Philip Sidney, 1572–1577* (New Haven: Yale Univ. Press, 1972); Michael Walzer, *The Revolution of the Saints* (Cambridge, Mass.: Harvard Univ. Press,

1965), pp. 116 and 241, and also pp. 66–74, 236–47; Martin Bergbush, "Rebellion in the New Arcadia," Philological Quarterly 53 (1974): 29–41; David Norbrook, Poetry and Politics in the English Renaissance (London: Routledge, 1984), ch. 4 and chs. 3–6.

2. Patrick Collinson, The Elizabethan Puritan Movement (London: Cape, 1967); Christopher Hill, Society and Puritanism in Pre-Revolutionary England (London: Secker & Warburg, 1964; Panther, 1969), ch. 1; Peter Lake, Moderate Puritans and the Elizabethan Church (Cambridge: Cambridge Univ. Press, 1982).

3. The Thirty-nine Articles are printed at the end of the Church of England Book of Common Prayer. See Charles H. and Katherine George, The Protestant Mind of the English Reformation (Princeton: Princeton Univ. Press, 1961); J. F. New, Anglican and Puritan (London: Black, 1964); Andrew D. Weiner, Sir Philip Sidney and the Poetics of Protestantism (Minneapolis: Univ. of Minnesota Press, 1978), pp. 8–18.

4. Certain Sermons or Homilies (London: Society for Promoting Christian Knowledge, 1899), pp. 26–27 (cited hereafter as Homilies).

5. Theodore Spencer, Shakespeare and the Nature of Man, 2d ed. (London: Macmillan, 1958), p. 157.

6. However, from about 1970 literary studies began to engage with early modern protestantism. See Roland Mushat Frye, Shakespeare and Christian Doctrine (Princeton: Princeton Univ. Press, 1963); William R. Elton, "King Lear" and the Gods (San Marino, Calif.: Huntington Library, 1968); William G. Halewood, The Poetry of Grace (New Haven: Yale Univ. Press, 1970); Dominic Baker-Smith, "Religion and John Webster," in Brian Morris, ed., John Webster (London: Benn, 1970); H. A. Kelly, Divine Providence in the England of Shakespeare's Histories (Cambridge, Mass.: Harvard Univ. Press, 1970); Ivor Morris, Shakespeare's God (London: Allen & Unwin, 1972); Paul R. Sellin, "The Hidden God," in R. S. Kinsman, ed., The Darker Vision of the Renaissance (Berkeley: Univ. of California Press, 1974); Robert G. Hunter, Shakespeare and the Mystery of the Gods (Athens, Ga.: Univ. of Georgia Press, 1976); Stevie Davies, Renaissance Views of Man (Manchester: Manchester Univ. Press, 1978); Weiner, Sir Philip Sidney and the Poetics of Protestantism; Barbara Kiefer Lewalski, Protestant Poetics and the Seventeenth-Century Religious Lyric (Princeton: Princeton Univ. Press, 1979); Margot Heinemann, Puritanism and Theatre (Cambridge: Cambridge Univ. Press, 1980); Stephen Greenblatt, Renaissance Self-Fashioning (Chicago: Univ. of Chicago Press, 1980); A. D. Nuttall, Overheard by God (London: Methuen, 1980); John Carey, John Donne: Life, Mind and Art (London: Faber, 1981); John N. King, English Reformation Literature (Princeton: Princeton Univ. Press, 1982); Jonathan Dollimore, Radical Tragedy (1984), 2d ed. (Hemel Hempstead: Harvester Wheatsheaf, 1989); Anthea Hume, Edmund Spenser: Protestant Poet (Cambridge: Cambridge Univ. Press, 1984); Norbrook, Poetry and Politics; Gene Edward Veith, Jr., Reformation Spirituality: The Religion of George Herbert (London and Toronto: Associated Univ. Presses, 1985); Ernest B. Gilman, Iconoclasm and Poetry in the English Reformation (Chicago: Univ. of Chicago Press, 1986); David Morse, England's Time of Crisis: From Shakespeare to Milton (London: Macmillan, 1989).

7. Hugh Kearney, *Scholars and Gentlemen: Universities and Society in Pre-industrial Britain, 1500–1700* (London: Faber, 1970), pp. 22–35; see also Ronald A. Rebholz, *The Life of Fulke Greville* (Oxford: Clarendon Press, 1971), pp. 11–12.

8. Anthony Grafton and Lisa Jardine, *From Humanism to the Humanities* (London: Duckworth, 1986), pp. xii–xiv, also pp. 22–26 and ch. 7.

9. Jonathan Goldberg, *Writing Matter: From the Hands of the English Renaissance* (Stanford: Stanford Univ. Press, 1990), p. 3, quoting Claude Lévi-Strauss, *Tristes Tropiques*, trans. John and Doreen Weightman (New York: Atheneum, 1974), p. 300. See also Goldberg, pp. 2–7 and 41–55; and Brian V. Street, *Literacy in Theory and Practice* (Cambridge: Cambridge Univ. Press, 1984).

10. Goldberg, *Writing Matter*, p. 41, quoting Keith Thomas, "The Meaning of Literacy in Early Modern England," in Gerd Baumann, ed., *The Written Word: Literacy in Transition* (Oxford: Clarendon Press, 1986), p. 117.

11. Louis L. Martz, *The Poetry of Meditation*, rev. ed. (New Haven: Yale Univ. Press, 1962), pp. 15–20, also 43–56. Cf. Lewalski, *Protestant Poetics*, pp. 264–75, and chs. 5, 8.

12. Like Lewalski (*Protestant Poetics*, pp. 264–65), I follow the ordering of the Holy Sonnets in the 1635 manuscript, made conventional by Grierson; quoting from the modernized text edited by A. J. Smith: John Donne, *The Complete English Poems* (Harmondsworth: Penguin Books, 1971), pp. 309–17. See further Lewalski, *Protestant Poetics*, pp. 13–27 and ch. 8; Adrian James Pinnington, "Reformation Themes and Tensions in John Donne's 'Divine Poems'"(diss., University of Sussex, 1983); Thomas Docherty, *John Donne, Undone* (London: Methuen, 1986).

13. Sermon Preached at Whitehall, April 19, 1618: George R. Potter and Evelyn M. Simpson, *The Sermons of John Donne* (Berkeley: Univ. of California Press, 1953–62), 1:293. Donne makes other emphases at other points; my argument does not require that he be consistent: see Halewood, *Poetry of Grace*, pp. 58–65; John Carey, *John Donne*, pp. 241–45. Carey sees Donne's struggle with orthodoxy as a specially personal alarm consequent upon Donne's change from Catholicism. But most sixteenth-century protestants had been born into Catholic families. I disagree here also with the reading of Veith, *Reformation Spirituality*, ch. 5.

14. Herbert's poems are quoted from *The English Poems of George Herbert*, ed. C. A. Patrides (London: Dent, 1974); see also the poem "Grace." And see Halewood, *Poetry of Grace*, ch. 4; Lewalski, *Protestant Poetics*, pp. 285–87 and ch. 9; Veith, *Reformation Spirituality*.

15. See ch. 10 and Sinfield, *Literature, Politics and Culture*, ch. 4.

16. David Williams, *A History of Modern Wales*, 2d ed. (London: John Murray, 1977), pp. 150, 155–56, 246, 260–64; *Chronicle* (Newspaper for the Tanat and Cain Valleys), no. 119, July 1990, p. 2.

17. Howell, *Sir Philip Sidney*, pp. 128–29; Rebholz, *Life of Fulke Greville*, p. 10; *Exploring Shropshire* (Church Stretton: Scenesetters, 1990), p. 1.

18. Michael D. Bristol, *Shakespeare's America, America's Shakespeare* (London: Routledge, 1990), p. 154 (quoting Theodore Spencer, *Shakespeare and the Nature of Man*, p. 1), and see ch. 6.

19. Louis Montrose, "Professing the Renaissance," in H. Aram Veeser, ed., *The New Historicism* (London: Routledge, 1989), p. 24.

20. *The Norton Anthology of English Literature,* 5th ed. (New York: Norton, 1986), 1:1033–44.

21., Claire Cross, *Church and People, 1450–1660* (Glasgow: Fontana, 1976), p. 153; see H. C. Porter, *Reformation and Reaction in Tudor Cambridge* (Cambridge: Cambridge Univ. Press, 1958), p. 264.

22. Sinfield, "Against Appropriation," *Essays in Criticism* 31 (1981): 181–95.

23. "Four Ways with a Reactionary Text," *LTP: The Journal of Literature Teaching Politics* 2 (1983): 81–95; for an elaboration of the argument of this paper, see pp. 21–22 above. This issue of the journal has long been out of print; the last issue was no. 6, published at Bristol in 1987.

24. Jonathan Culler, *Framing the Sign* (Oxford: Blackwell, 1988), pp. 71, 78. Culler considers William Empson's work in this light.

25. John Calvin, *Calvin's Institutes* [trans. Henry Beveridge] (Florida: MacDonald Publishing, n.d.), 3.8.10, 3.7.10; cited hereafter in the text as *Institutes.*

26. E. Gordon Rupp and Philip S. Watson, eds., *Luther and Erasmus* (London: SCM, 1969), p. 228.

27. Thomas Aquinas, *Summa theologica,* pt. 1, quest. 23, art. 1.

28. Ian Breward, ed., *The Work of William Perkins* (Abingdon: Sutton Courtenay Press, 1970), pp. 142, 144. On widespread indifference to Christianity, see Keith Thomas, *Religion and the Decline of Magic* (Harmondsworth: Peregrine, 1978), pp. 183–88, 198–206; Keith Wrightson, *English Society, 1580–1680* (London: Hutchinson, 1982), pp. 199–214. On survivals of Catholicism, see J. J. Scarisbrick, *The Reformation and the English People* (Oxford: Basil Blackwell, 1984), chs. 7, 8.

29. Thomas Nashe, *The Unfortunate Traveller and Other Works,* ed. J. B. Steane (Harmondsworth: Penguin Books, 1972), p. 68. See G. T. Buckley, *Atheism in the English Renaissance* (New York: Russell, 1965); Herschel Baker, *The Wars of Truth* (London: Staples, 1952); Hiram Haydn, *The Counter-Renaissance* (New York: Scribner's, 1950); Elton, *"King Lear" and the Gods;* Dollimore, *Radical Tragedy,* chs. 1, 5.

30. Conrad Russell, *The Crisis of Parliaments* (Oxford: Oxford Univ. Press, 1971), p. 200; Michel de Montaigne, *Essays,* trans. John Florio (London: Dent, 1965), 2:126–27.

31. See C. M. Dent, *Protestant Reformers in Elizabethan Oxford* (Oxford: Oxford Univ. Press, 1983), pp. 93–102; Joan Simon, *Education and Society in Tudor England* (Cambridge: Cambridge Univ. Press, 1967), pp. 331–32.

32. Edmund Grindal, *Remains* (Cambridge: Cambridge Univ. Press, 1843), p. 339.

33. E.g., in 1563 we find the puritan Grindal suppressing the Dutch sponsor of the Family of Love, Justus Velsius, who held that Christ is "God in man" and that "all Christians are gods" (Grindal, *Remains,* pp. 439–40).

34. John Ayre, ed., *The Works of John Whitgift* (Cambridge: Cambridge Univ. Press, 1853), 3:612; see Powel Mills Dawley, *John Whitgift and the*

Reformation (London: Black, 1955), pp. 214–21. Even Lancelot Andrewes retained the substantial force of Reformation doctrine on human capacity and the priority of grace: see New, *Anglican and Puritan,* pp. 12–13. Andrewes was confident that most people will be damned: "The greatest part of the world by far are entered upon and held by the unholy spirit"(*Works* [Oxford: Clarendon Press, 1841], 6:191). See George and George, *Protestant Mind,* pp. 53–70; Lake, *Moderate Puritans,* ch. 9.

35. Dent, *Protestant Reformers,* pp. 220–31, 238–39; Kearney, *Scholars and Gentlemen,* pp. 44–45.

36. See Nicholas Tyacke, "Puritanism, Arminianism, and Counter-Revolution," in Conrad Russell, ed., *The Origins of the English Civil War* (London: Macmillan, 1973); A. G. Dickens, *The English Reformation* (London: Batsford, 1964), pp. 313–21; Russell, *Crisis of Parliaments,* pp. 209–17, 237–40, 313–17; Nicholas Tyacke, *Anti-Calvinists: The Rise of English Arminianism, c. 1590–1640* (Oxford: Oxford Univ. Press, 1987); Peter Lake, "Anti-Popery: The Structure of a Prejudice," in Richard Cust and Ann Hughes, eds., *Conflict in Early Stuart England* (London: Longman, 1989). On the Calvinism of James and his maintaining of this theology, see Cross, *Church and People,* pp. 162–74.

37. *Homilies,* p. 60. Greenblatt remarks that Catholics had been affirming the idea of the inner life of individuals, but the Reformation pushed Catholic apologists into asserting external authority (*Renaissance Self-Fashioning,* p. 99).

38. Rupp and Watson, eds., *Luther and Erasmus,* p. 137.

39. Richard Sibbes, *The Soul's Conflict,* 1635 (London: Religious Tract Society, 1837) p. 323; so, too, *Work of William Perkins,* ed. Breward, pp. 155–58. See Christopher Hill, *The World Turned Upside Down* (Harmondsworth: Penguin Books, 1975), pp. 152–55.

40. Andrewes, *Works,* 2:72; M. M. Knappen, ed., *Two Elizabethan Puritan Diaries* (Gloucester, Mass.: Peter Smith, 1966), p. 55.

41. George Herbert, *Works in Prose and Verse* (London: Frederick Warne, n.d.), p. 317.

42. Joseph Hall, *Works,* ed. Josiah Pratt (London: 1808), 1:344.

43. Rupp and Watson, eds., *Luther and Erasmus,* p. 88.

44. Ibid., p. 138.

45. Ibid., pp. 327–28. Calvin uses the image (*Institutes* 2.4.1), deriving it from Augustine.

46. Hugh Latimer, *Selected Sermons,* ed. A. R. Buckland (London: Religious Tract Society, 1904), p. 9.

47. *An Instruction touching Religious Worship* (1601), in *Work of William Perkins,* ed. Breward, p. 313.

48. William Tyndale, in *Writings of Tindal, Frith and Barnes* (London: Religious Tract Society, n.d.), p. 18; emphasis added. See Thomas F. Merrill, ed., *William Perkins* (Nieuwkoop: B. de Graaf, 1966), pp. 169–72.

49. Walzer, *Revolution of the Saints,* pp. 307–8. See also Hill, *World Turned Upside Down,* pp. 170–82. And cf. Knappen, ed., *Two Elizabethan Puritan Diaries,* pp. 14–16; Robert Burton, *The Anatomy of Melancholy,* ed. Holbrook Jackson (London: Dent, 1932), 3:392–432.

50. Carey, *John Donne,* p. 57.

51. Knappen, ed., *Two Elizabethan Puritan Diaries,* p. 62.

52. Ibid., pp. 119, 106. Daniel Dyke is typical: "The deceitfulness of our hearts must cause us daily to keep an audit in our own conscience, ever and anon calling them to their accounts" (*The Mystery of Selfe-Deceiving* [London: William Stansby, 1633], p. 367).

53. Halewood, *Poetry of Grace,* p. 80.

54. "Dialogue of the State of a Christian Man" (1588), in *Work of William Perkins,* ed. Breward, p. 368.

55. See Nuttall, *Overheard by God,* pp. 32–82.

56. Michel Foucault, *The History of Sexuality: Volume 1,* trans. Robert Hurley (New York: Random House, Vintage Books, 1980), pp. 61–62.

57. Merrill, ed., *William Perkins,* p. 9.

58. Tyndale, *Writings,* pp. 67–68. Greenblatt remarks: "To be left alone, unregarded and self-governing, is far worse than to be punished" (*Renaissance Self-Fashioning,* p. 125).

59. Louis Althusser, *Lenin and Philosophy and Other Essays,* trans. Ben Brewster (London: New Left Books, 1971), p. 167.

60. Greenblatt, *Renaissance Self-Fashioning,* p. 9.

61. Karl Marx, *Early Writings,* ed. and trans. T. B. Bottomore (New York: McGraw-Hill, 1964), p. 53. Marx adds that this did "pose the problem correctly": in terms of the struggle with one's *"own internal priest."*

62. E. G. Rupp and Benjamin Drewery, eds., *Martin Luther* (London: Arnold, 1970), p. 60.

63. Tyndale, *Writings,* pp. 159, 275, 50, 303.

64. Burton, *Anatomy of Melancholy,* 3:332; Althusser, *Lenin and Philosophy,* p. 169.

65. *The Psalmes of David and others. With M. John Calvins Commentaries,* trans. Arthur Golding (London: Tho. East and H. Middleton, 1571), vol. 1, "To the Reader"; Richard Sibbes takes the same approach in the opening section of *The Soul's Conflict* (1635). See Greenblatt, *Renaissance Self-Fashioning,* pp. 115–26; Lewalski, *Protestant Poetics and the Seventeenth-Century Religious Lyric,* pp. 131–34, 136–38.

66. Calvin, *Psalmes of David,* Preface.

67. Martin Luther, "Preface to the Psalms," trans. Bertram Lee Woolf, in *Martin Luther, Selections from his Writings,* ed. John Dillinger (New York: Doubleday, 1961), p. 41; Althusser says ideology is internalized in a process of double mirroring (*Lenin and Philosophy,* p. 168).

68. Patrick McGrath, *Papists and Puritans under Elizabeth I* (London: Blandford Press, 1967), pp. 311–12, 349.

69. Francis Bacon, *Essays,* intr. Oliphant Smeaton (London: Dent, 1906), p. 11.

70. Simon, *Education and Society,* p. 177.

71. McGrath, *Papists and Puritans,* pp. 116–21, 300–313; Cross, *Church and People,* pp. 143–46. On control of preaching, see Hill, *Society and Puritanism,* pp. 33–44. For instances of theater censorship, see E. K. Chambers, *The Elizabethan Stage* (Oxford: Clarendon Press, 1923), vol. 1, ch. 10; also Heinemann, *Puritanism and Theatre.*

72. Patrick Collinson, *The Religion of Protestants* (Oxford: Oxford Univ. Press, 1982), p. 150 and ch. 4; also Russell, *Crisis of Parliaments*, pp. 202–5, 210, 240, and Kearney, *Scholars and Gentlemen*, pp. 34–36.

73. John Morgan, *Godly Learning: Puritan Attitudes towards Reason, Learning, and Education, 1560–1640* (Cambridge: Cambridge Univ. Press, 1986), p. 86, and see p. 97.

74. Hill, *World Turned Upside Down*, p. 155; see Walzer, *Revolution of the Saints*, pp. 30–47.

75. Lawrence Stone, *The Family, Sex and Marriage in England, 1500–1800* (London: Weidenfeld, 1977).

76. Shakespeare, *1 Henry IV*, ed. A. R. Humphreys (London: Methuen, 1967), 3.2.4–11.

77. Hall, *Works*, 1:xxvi. See Thomas, *Religion and the Decline of Magic*, ch. 4.

78. Carey, *John Donne*, p. 123.

79. Thomas, *Religion and the Decline of Magic*, p. 194, and see p. 180.

80. Tyndale, *Writings*, pp. 61–62.

81. Ibid., p. 61. In Perkins's account of the body politic, "there be several members which are men walking in several callings and offices, the execution whereof must tend to the happy and good estate of the rest, yea, of all men everywhere, as much as possible is "(*Of the Vocations or Callings of Men*, in *Work of William Perkins*, ed. Breward, p. 449).

82. Hill, *World Turned Upside Down*, p. 153; Patrick Collinson, *The Birthpangs of Protestant England* (London: Macmillan, 1988), p. 148, also pp. 143–52 and chs. 1–2.

83. Hill, *Society and Puritanism*, p. 131, and ch. 4. Wrightson says Reformation doctrine was most influential among "a minority of the gentry, the yeomen and craftsmen of the villages, and the merchants, tradesmen and artisans of the towns "(*English Society*, pp. 213–14).

84. *The Prose Works of Sir Philip Sidney*, ed. Albert Feuillerat (Cambridge: Cambridge Univ. Press, 1963), 3:125. See Walzer, *Revolution of the Saints*, pp. 66–74, 116, 236–47; New, *Anglican and Puritan*, pp. 87–91; Claire Cross, *The Puritan Earl* (London: Macmillan, 1966), p. 4; Rebholz, *Life of Fulke Greville*, pp. 11–12.

85. See Knappen, ed., *Two Elizabethan Puritan Diaries*, pp. 29, 31–32; Eleanor Rosenberg, *Leicester, Patron of Letters* (New York: Columbia Univ. Press, 1955), ch. 6; Rosemary O'Day, *The English Clergy: The Emergence and Consolidation of a Profession, 1558–1642* (Leicester: Leicester Univ. Press, 1979), ch. 7; Cross, *Church and People*, p. 153, and ch. 7.

86. Latimer, *Selected Sermons*, ed. Buckland, pp. 90, 80.

87. O'Day, *English Clergy*, p. 27; O'Day shows in her chs. 4, 5, and 10 the extent to which this was changed. See also Simon, *Education and Society*, pp. 397–403; Dent, *Protestant Reformers*, chs. 7, 9; Hill, *Society and Puritanism*, chs. 2, 3; Collinson, *Birthpangs of Protestant England*, pp. 40–46; Morgan, *Godly Learning*.

88. John Brinsley the Younger, *The Preachers Charge and the People's Duty* (1631), pp. 4, 7, quoted in Morgan, *Godly Learning*, p. 81; see also Scarisbrick, *Reformation and the English People*, pp. 165–70.

89. O'Day, *English Clergy*, pp. 1–2, 126, 159–60, 189, 234, and chs. 10, 12, 16; see Morgan, *Godly Learning*, pp. 79–89.

90. See Sinfield, *Literature, Politics and Culture*, pp. 271–73; Wrightson, *English Society*, p. 209; Goldberg, *Writing Matter*, pp. 41–49.

91. Hill, *Society and Puritanism*, p. 98 and ch. 3, passim. See also Collinson, *Birthpangs of Protestant England*, pp. 56–58, 149–52; O'Day, *English Clergy*, ch. 14.

92. Hill, *Society and Puritanism*, pp. 135–40; Russell, *Crisis of Parliaments*, pp. 201, 204, 222–29, 237–40; Felicity Heal, *Of Prelates and Princes* (Cambridge: Cambridge Univ. Press, 1980).

93. Collinson, *Religion of Protestants*, p. 182.

94. William Haller, *The Rise of Puritanism* (New York: Columbia Univ. Press, 1938), p. 168. See Hill, *Society and Puritanism*, p. 241; Robert Weimann, "Discourse, Ideology and the Crisis of Authority in Post-Reformation England," *REAL: The Yearbook of Research in English and American Literature* 5 (1987): 109–40.

95. Dollimore, *Radical Tragedy*, p. 14.

96. See Greenblatt, *Renaissance Self-Fashioning*, pp. 57, 143, 151, 154, 161, 220. However, cf. p. 152, where "the conflicting cultural codes that fashion male identity in Tudor court lyrics" are invoked (though hardly specified).

97. Walzer, *Revolution of the Saints*, pp. 1–21, 95–98, 114–30, 310–20; Savonarola may be the exception (p. 9).

98. Hill, *Society and Puritanism*, pp. 476–77. At some points there was a specific organization—during the Marian persecution, and in the "classical movement" of the 1580s (see Collinson, *Elizabethan Puritan Movement*); at other times it was a looser association. See Natalie Zemon Davis, "The Sacred and the Body Social in Sixteenth-Century Lyon," *Past and Present* 90 (1981): 40–70, pp. 64–70; Simon Shepherd, *Marlowe and the Politics of Elizabethan Theatre* (New York: St. Martin's Press, 1986), p. 141.

99. Russell, *Crisis of Parliaments*, pp. 195–96. And see Wrightson, *English Society*, ch. 6 et passim; Hill, *World Turned Upside Down*, chs. 2, 3; Lucy de Bruyn, *Mob-Rule and Riots* (London: Regency Press, 1981); William Hunt, *The Puritan Moment* (Cambridge, Mass.: Harvard Univ. Press, 1983); Morse, *England's Time of Crisis*.

100. Thomas Hobbes, *Leviathan*, ed. C. B. Macpherson (Harmondsworth: Penguin Books, 1968), p. 179.

101. *The Journals of Søren Kierkegaard*, ed. and trans. Alexander Dru (London: Oxford Univ. Press, 1938), p. 1.

102. Wrightson, *English Society*, p. 217; see Hill, *Society and Puritanism*, pp. 242, 480, and *World Turned Upside Down*.

103. Gerrard Winstanley, *Works*, ed. G. H. Sabine (New York: Russell & Russell, 1965), p. 493; ensuing quotations are from this edition. Hill compares Winstanley and Hobbes: *World Turned Upside Down*, appendix 1; and see ch. 7.

104. Richard Verrall in *New Nation*, no. 1 (1980), quoted by Martin Barker, *The New Racism* (London: Junction Books, 1981), p. 100.

105. Richard Leakey and Roger Lewin, *People of the Lake* (London: Collins, 1979), p. 125; also p. 213. And see Robert David Sack, *Human Territoriality: Its Theory and History* (Cambridge: Cambridge Univ. Press, 1986), p. 217; Lionel Tiger, *Men in Groups* (London: Nelson, 1969), pp. 162–64; Richard Leakey, *The Making of Mankind* (London: Joseph, 1981), pp. 223–37; Sinfield, *Literature, Politics and Culture,* pp. 139–50.

106. Hill, *World Turned Upside Down,* chs. 2, 5, 6; Sabine, introduction to Winstanley, *Works,* pp. 21–35. See Janet E. Halley, "Heresy, Orthodoxy, and the Politics of Religious Discourse: The Case of the English Family of Love," in Stephen Greenblatt, ed., *Representing the English Renaissance* (Berkeley: Univ. of California Press, 1988).

107. Winstanley, *Works,* p. 523. On anticlericalism among sectarians, see O'Day, *English Clergy,* pp. 190–91 and ch. 15.

108. Carey, *John Donne,* pp. 239–40; Greenblatt, *Renaissance Self-Fashioning,* pp. 105–14.

109. Hill, *Society and Puritanism,* p. 480; Walzer, *Revolution of the Saints,* p. 42.

110. Walzer, *Revolution of the Saints,* p. 2, and pp. 310–15, 319–20.

111. Hill, *World Turned Upside Down,* p. 15. See also Malcolm Evans, *Signifying Nothing: Truth's True Contents in Shakespeare's Text,* 2d ed. (Hemel Hempstead: Harvester Wheatsheaf, 1989), pp. 254–64.

CHAPTER EIGHT

1. L. I. Brezhnev, *Report of the Central Committee of the CPSU to the XXVI Congress of the Communist Party of the Soviet Union* (Moscow: Novosti Press Agency, 1981), pp. 110–11. See Henri Arvon, *Marxist Esthetics,* trans. Henry R. Lane (Ithaca, N.Y.: Cornell Univ. Press, 1973), ch. 6; Jonathan Dollimore, *Radical Tragedy,* 2d ed. (Hemel Hempstead: Harvester Wheatsheaf, 1989), ch. 4.

2. Sir Philip Sidney, *Miscellaneous Prose,* ed. Katherine Duncan-Jones and Jan van Dorsten (Oxford: Clarendon Press, 1973), pp. 79, 88. The *Defence of Poetry* is quoted throughout from this edition.

3. Stephen Greenblatt, *Renaissance Self-Fashioning* (Chicago: Univ. of Chicago Press, 1980), p. 15; John N. King, *English Reformation Literature: The Tudor Origins of the Protestant Tradition* (Princeton: Princeton Univ. Press, 1982), pp. 233, 231–41.

4. C. Wright Mills, *Power, Politics and People,* ed. Irving Louis Horowitz (New York: Oxford Univ. Press, 1963), p. 406. See Malcolm Smuts, "The Political Failure of Stuart Cultural Patronage," in Guy Fitch Lytle and Stephen Orgel, eds., *Patronage in the Renaissance* (Princeton: Princeton Univ. Press, 1981), pp. 183–85; also Eleanor Rosenberg, *Leicester: Patron of Letters* (New York: Columbia Univ. Press, 1955), ch. 1; Kevin Sharpe and Steven N. Zwicker, eds., *Politics of Discourse: The Literature and History of Seventeenth-Century England* (Berkeley: Univ. of California Press, 1987), Introduction.

5. Sidney, *Defence of Poetry,* p. 90.

6. See Lawrence Stone, *The Crisis of the Aristocracy, 1558–1641* (Oxford: Clarendon Press, 1965), pp. 257–68.

7. King, *English Reformation Literature,* p. 20 et passim.

8. On Sidney's upbringing and activist circle, see Roger Howell, *Sir Philip Sidney: The Shepherd Knight* (London: Hutchinson, 1968), chs. 1, 2, 5, 8, 10, et passim; James M. Osborn, *Young Philip Sidney* (New Haven: Yale Univ. Press, 1972); Andrew D. Weiner, *Sir Philip Sidney and the Poetics of Protestantism* (Minneapolis: Univ. of Minnesota Press, 1978), pp. 3–8, 19–28.

9. On Leicester's contributions, see Rosenberg, *Leicester: Patron of Letters;* Golding's later translations were dedicated to Leicester, including *De la vérité de la religion chrestienne.* On Mary, countess of Pembroke, see John Buxton, *Sir Philip Sidney and the English Renaissance* (London: Macmillan, 1965), ch. 6, and Gary Waller, *Mary Sidney, Countess of Pembroke* (Salzburg: Institut für Anglistik und Amerikanistik, 1979), chs. 2, 3; on Huntingdon, see Claire Cross, *The Puritan Earl* (London: Macmillan, 1966), pp. 260–63. See Rosemary O'Day, *The English Clergy: The Emergence and Consolidation of a Profession, 1558–1642* (Leicester: Leicester Univ. Press, 1979), ch. 7; and Margaret Patterson Hannay, ed., *Silent but for the Word: Tudor Women as Patrons, Translators and Writers of Religious Works* (Kent, Ohio: Kent State Univ. Press, 1985).

10. Lawrence Humphrey, *The Nobles* (1563), sig. m.

11. On Goodman, see Howell, *Sir Philip Sidney,* p. 217; on Buste, see Osborn, *Young Philip Sidney,* pp. 313–17, and John Strype, *The Life and Acts of John Whitgift* (Oxford: Clarendon Press, 1822), 1:198–99; on Stiles, see Paul S. Seaver, *The Puritan Lecturerships* (Stanford: Stanford Univ. Press, 1970), pp. 150, 211.

12. On the Netherlands, see Jan van Dorsten, *Poets, Patrons and Professors* (Leiden: Leiden Univ. Press, 1962), pt. 2.

13. Languet is quoted from Osborn, *Young Philip Sidney,* p. 204; the bishop from John Strype, *Annals of the Reformation* (Oxford: Clarendon Press, 1824), 2, pt. 1, pp. 403–4. See also *The Prose Works of Fulke Greville, Lord Brooke,* ed. John Gouws (Oxford: Clarendon Press, 1986), pp. 21–22.

14. Trans. Malcolm Wallace, *The Life of Sir Philip Sidney* (Cambridge: Cambridge Univ. Press, 1915), p. 198.

15. See Louis A. Montrose, "Celebration and Insinuation: Sir Philip Sidney and the Motives of Elizabethan Courtship," *Renaissance Drama* 8 (1977): 3–35; Marie Axton, "The Tudor Mask and Elizabethan Court Drama," in Marie Axton and Raymond Williams, eds., *English Drama: Forms and Development* (Cambridge: Cambridge Univ. Press, 1977), pp. 38–42; Philippa Berry, *Of Chastity and Power: Elizabethan Literature and the Unmarried Queen* (London and New York: Routledge, 1989), ch. 4.

16. Anthony Grafton and Lisa Jardine, *From Humanism to the Humanities* (London: Duckworth, 1986), p. xiv; Jonathan Goldberg, *Writing Matter: From the Hands of the English Renaissance* (Stanford: Stanford Univ. Press, 1990), p. 45.

17. Grafton and Jardine, *From Humanism to the Humanities,* p. 144, and pp. 142–48.

18. King, *English Reformation Literature,* pp. 9–16, 42–56, 209–31. Conversely, King points out, More's *Utopia* flourishes on classical Greek authors only (p. 43).

19. Joan Simon, *Education and Society in Tudor England* (Cambridge: Cambridge Univ. Press, 1966), pp. 87, 89, 140.

20. *An Open Letter to the Christian Nobility* (1520), in Martin Luther, *Three Treatises* (Philadelphia: Lutheran Church in America, 1960), p. 93; Desiderius Erasmus, *Opus epistolarum*, ed. P. S. Allen and H. M. Allen (Oxford: Clarendon Press, 1906–58), 7:366. See also Stephen Orgel, "The Royal Theatre and the Role of the King," in Orgel and Lytle, eds., *Patronage in the Renaissance,* pp. 263–65.

21. Roger Ascham, *The Schoolmaster,* ed. Lawrence V. Ryan (Ithaca, N.Y.: Cornell Univ. Press, 1967), p. 70; see also Robert Burton, *The Anatomy of Melancholy,* ed. Holbrook Jackson (London: Dent, 1932), 3:387–88.

22. Sidney, *Defence of Poetry,* pp. 73, 75, 79, 86, 105–6, 109–10. On Sidney as champion of an Italianate style, see King, *English Reformation Literature,* pp. 11–12, 209–11.

23. Quoted by Simon, *Education and Society,* p. 324. By the late sixteenth century, the colloquies of Erasmus and Vives had been largely replaced in schools by the Genevan texts of Castellion and Corderius: John Morgan, *Godly Learning: Puritan Attitudes towards Reason, Learning and Education, 1560–1640* (Cambridge: Cambridge Univ. Press, 1986), p. 182; and chs. 3, 4, 6. See also M. M. Knappen, *Tudor Puritanism* (Chicago: Univ. of Chicago Press, 1939), ch. 26; Patrick Collinson, *The Birthpangs of Protestant England* (London: Macmillan, 1988), ch. 4; and Ernest B. Gilman, *Iconoclasm and Poetry in the English Reformation* (Chicago: Univ. of Chicago Press, 1986).

24. Thomas Starkey, *A Dialogue between Reginald Pole and Thomas Lupset,* ed. Kathleen M. Burton (London: Chatto, 1948), pp. 153, 35.

25. Lord Herbert of Cherbury, *Life,* ed. J. M. Shuttleworth (Oxford: Oxford Univ. Press, 1976), p. 24.

26. William Tyndale, *Doctrinal Treatises,* ed. Henry Walter (Cambridge: Cambridge Univ. Press, 1848), p. 107. So Calvin, *Institutes* 2.2.2.

27. John Donne, *Sermons,* ed. George R. Potter and Evelyn M. Simpson (Berkeley: Univ. of California Press, 1953–62), 2:308.

28. D. P. Walker, *The Ancient Theology* (London: Duckworth, 1972), p. 142 and ch. 4. Walker's mistaken account has often been followed—by Frances Yates in *Giordano Bruno and the Hermetic Tradition* (Chicago: Univ. of Chicago Press, 1964), pp. 176–79; William R. Elton, *"King Lear" and the Gods* (San Marino, Calif.: Huntington Library, 1968), pp. 38–42; and Roger Howell, Jr., "The Sidney Circle and the Protestant Cause in Elizabethan Foreign Policy," *Renaissance and Modern Studies* 19 (1975): 311–46. But see Weiner, *Sir Philip Sidney,* pp. 82–83; and, for a fuller refutation than here, see Sinfield, "Sidney, du Plessis-Mornay and the Pagans," *Philological Quarterly* 58 (1979): 26–39.

29. Philippe du Plessis-Mornay, *A Woorke concerning the Trewness of the Christian Religion,* trans. Arthur Golding, 2d ed. (London, 1592), p. 359; see also pp. 337, 356, 368–69, 373, 551. So Calvin, *Institutes* 1.15.8, 2.2.4.

John Reynolds took a similar line in his 1572 Oxford lecture on rhetoric, discussed in C. M. Dent, *Protestant Reformers in Elizabethan Oxford* (Oxford: Oxford Univ. Press, 1983), pp. 103–4. But cf. Marsilio Ficino, *The Philebus Commentary* (1469), trans. Michael J. B. Allen (Berkeley: Univ. of California Press, 1975), pp. 180, 246, 416.

30. Walker, *Ancient Theology*, p. 146; cf. Sinfield, "Sidney, du Plessis-Mornay," pp. 32–35; and R. B. Levinson, "The 'Godlesse Minde' in Sidney's *Arcadia*," *Modern Philology* 29 (1931): 21–26. Pamela's argument against Cecropia is in Sir Philip Sidney, *The Countess of Pembroke's Arcadia*, ed. Maurice Evans (Harmondsworth: Penguin Books, 1977), pp. 488–92; Cicero's Stoic arguments are in book 2 of *De natura deorum*. The issue comes up also in Sidney, *Defence of Poetry*, in *Miscellaneous Prose*, p. 108; and in Greville's account of Sidney's deathbed conversation (*Prose Works of Fulke Greville*, pp. 81–82).

31. John Calvin, *Commentaries on the First Book of Moses Called Genesis*, trans. John King (Edinburgh, 1847), 1:49.

32. Knappen, *Tudor Puritanism*, p. 474; Morgan, *Godly Learning*, pp. 199, 200, 241–43.

33. Stone, *Crisis of the Aristocrat*, pp. 740–41. See ch. 7; Morgan, *Godly Learning*, chs. 9–12; King, *English Reformation Literature*, passim; O'Day, *English Clergy*.

34. Quoted in Morgan, *Godly Learning*, p. 113; for further instances see pp. 157–59, 179, 187.

35. Thomas Becon, *The Catechism*, ed. John Ayre (Cambridge: Cambridge Univ. Press, 1844), p. 382.

36. Hugh Kearney, *Scholars and Gentlemen: Universities and Society in Pre-Industrial Britain, 1500–1700* (London: Faber, 1970), pp. 39–44.

37. Compare Jacopo Sannazaro's brief epic *The Virgin Birth* (1526), which invokes a classical pantheon to celebrate the birth of Jesus; and Pierre de Ronsard's *Hercule Chrestien* (1555) where the lives of Jesus and Hercules are paralleled (e.g., serpents were sent to kill the infant Hercules, and Herod tried to murder Jesus, and Hercules' self-immolation on Etna is like the crucifixion). Joseph Hall complains of such writing in *Virgidemiarum* (1598), 1.8.

38. Louis Thorn Golding, *An Elizabethan Puritan* (New York: Smith, 1937), chs. 4, 12, 13.

39. *Ovid's Metamorphoses*, trans. Arthur Golding, ed. John Frederick Nims (New York: Macmillan, 1965), Epistle, lines 111–16.

40. Torquato Tasso, *Discourses on the Heroic Poem*, trans. Mariella Cavalchini and Irene Samuel (Oxford: Clarendon Press, 1973), pp. 43–44; Marsilio Ficino, *Letters*, trans. Language Department of the School of Economic Science (London: Shepheard-Walwyn, 1975–88), 2:77–78. For an English version, see the Epistle to Henry, Prince of Wales, with which George Chapman prefaced his translation of Homer.

41. Niccolò Machiavelli, *The Discourses*, ed. Bernard Crick (Harmondsworth: Penguin Books, 1970), p. 278.

42. William Perkins, *The Cases of Conscience* (1600), in Thomas F. Merrill, ed., *William Perkins* (Nieukoop: B. de Graaf, 1966), p. 165. Mornay explained

the existence of suffering and error as God's way of discouraging godlike pretensions; otherwise "we would think at the length, that it was of our own steadiness, and not of God's upholding of us, not only that we tripped not, but also that we tumbled not down. For what made us fall but pride: and what manner of pride, but we thought we would be gods without God, yea even of ourselves" (Du Plessis-Mornay, *Woorke concerning the Trewness of the Christian Religion,* pp. 209–10).

43. Sidney, *The Countess of Pembroke's Arcadia,* ed. Evans, pp. 258, 275.

44. *Paradise Lost* 9.13–41, in John Milton, *Poetical Works,* ed. Douglas Bush (Oxford: Oxford Univ. Press, 1966). On heroism in Spenser and Milton, see further Alan Sinfield, *Literature in Protestant England, 1560–1660* (London: Croom Helm, 1983), pp. 37–48; on their attitudes to images, see Gilman, *Iconoclasm,* chs. 3, 6. On *standing,* see *Paradise Lost* 3.98–99, 178–79; 4.63–7; 6.911; 8.640–41; and Eph. 6:13–14.

45. James VI, *The Essayes of a Prentise,* ed. Edward Arber (London: Arber, 1869), p. 29; see Anne Lake Prescott, "The Reception of du Bartas in England," *Studies in the Renaissance* 15 (1968): 144–73; Alan Sinfield, "Sidney and du Bartas," *Comparative Literature* 27 (1975): 8–20. On divine poetry, see also King, *English Reformation Literature;* Lily B. Campbell, *Divine Poetry and Drama in Sixteenth-Century England* (Cambridge: Cambridge Univ. Press; Berkeley: Univ. of California Press, 1959); Barbara Kiefer Lewalski, *Protestant Poetics and the Seventeenth-Century Religious Lyric* (Princeton: Princeton Univ. Press, 1979).

46. *The English Poems of George Herbert,* ed. C. A. Patrides (London: Dent, 1974), p. 205.

47. Edmund Spenser, *Poetical Works,* ed. J. C. Smith and E. de Selincourt (London: Oxford Univ. Press, 1912), p. 593.

48. *The Poems of Sir Philip Sidney,* ed. William A. Ringler, Jr. (Oxford: Clarendon Press, 1962), p. 339; Ronald A. Rebholz, *The Life of Fulke Greville* (Oxford: Clarendon Press, 1971), p. 312 et passim.

49. Douglas Brooks-Davies, *Spenser's "Faerie Queene": A Critical Commentary on Books I and II* (Manchester: Manchester Univ. Press, 1977), p. 191.

50. Greenblatt, *Renaissance Self-Fashioning,* pp. 170–72.

51. Tasso, *Discourses on the Heroic Poem:* Armida's island is described in books 15 and 16, and Ariosto is criticized on pp. 11–12.

52. Sidney, *Defence of Poetry,* p. 77. Aspects of my theme are treated by G. F. Waller, " 'This Matching of Contraries': Bruno, Calvin and the Sidney Circle," *Neophilologus* 56 (1972): 331–43; and in Weiner, *Sir Philip Sidney,* pp. 28–50.

53. John Calvin, *Calvin's Institutes* [trans. Henry Beveridge] (MacDill, Fla.: MacDonald Publishing, n.d.), 2.2.22.

54. Printed by Osborn, *Young Philip Sidney,* p. 538. The moral philosophy Sidney recommends in the letter is Aristotle, Cicero, and Plutarch. The distinction had been drawn similarly by William Baldwin in his *Treatise of Morall Phylosophie* (1547–48): see King, *English Reformation Literature,* p. 361.

55. *The Whole Booke of Psalmes ... by T. Starnhold, J. Hopkins & Others* (London, 1562); Collinson, *Birthpangs of Protestant England,* p. 96. The present chapter is contrary to Collinson's argument that in 1580 protestants

ceased to take existing cultural forms and employ them for religious purposes (*Birthpangs,* pp. 98ff.). Rather, the relatively popular and amateur modes that Collinson mainly considers were overwhelmed by the developing sophistication of courtly and professional poetry and drama, such that the old questions took newly complex forms.

56. Francis Bacon, *Philosophical Works,* ed. John M. Robertson (London: Routledge, 1905), p. 335. See Sinfield, *Literature in Protestant England,* pp. 130–37; Keith Thomas, *Religion and the Decline of Magic* (Harmondsworth: Peregrine, 1978), ch. 4.

57. Calvin, *Institutes* 1.5.1, 1.14.21; *The Work of William Perkins,* ed. Ian Breward (Abingdon: Sutton Courtenay Press, 1970), p. 447. On special providence, see chapter 9.

58. Sir Thomas Elyot, *The Book named The Governor,* ed. S. E. Lehmberg (London: Dent, 1962), pp. 29–33, 47–50; George Puttenham, *The Arte of English Poesie,* ed. Gladys Doidge Willcock and Alice Walker (Cambridge: Cambridge Univ. Press, 1936), p. 227; the point about Sidney's wavering argument on love poetry is made by T. G. A. Nelson, "Sir John Harington as a Critic of Sir Philip Sidney," *Studies in Philology* 68 (1970): 41–56, pp. 45–49.

59. Stephen Gosson, *The Schoole of Abuse* (London: Shakespeare Society, 1841), p. 11.

60. Sidney, *Defence of Poetry,* pp. 90–91. Peter C. Herman points out that in letters to his brother Robert and to Edward Denny, Sidney does not encourage them to read poetry; in fact, he transfers to history and philosophy the qualities that in the *Defence* are supposed to assure poetry's superiority (Herman, " 'Do as I say, not as I do': The *Apology for Poetry* and Sir Philip Sidney's Letters to Edward Denny and Robert Sidney," *Sidney Newsletter,* 10, no. 1 [1989]: 13–24). I think this shows Sidney's sense of strategy—he makes the best case he can in each circumstance.

61. Marsilio Ficino, *Platonic Theology,* trans. Josephine L. Burroughs, *Journal of the History of Ideas* 5 (1944): 227–39, p. 233.

62. Weiner, *Sir Philip Sidney,* p. 35.

63. Ibid., p. 36; and see the commentary on the *Defence* by Katherine Duncan-Jones and Jan van Dorsten in Sidney, *Miscellaneous Prose,* p. 190. But cf. Waller, " 'This Matching of Contraries.' "

64. In Merrill, ed., *William Perkins,* p. 164.

65. Milton, *Paradise Lost* 7.505–16; see also 4.288–89, 8.258–61; and Davis P. Harding, *Milton and the Renaissance Ovid* (Urbana: Univ. of Illinois Press, 1946), pp. 77–78.

66. Richard Hooker, *Of the Laws of Ecclesiastical Polity,* ed. Christopher Morris (London: Dent, 1965), 1.7.3, in 1:170. Hooker does allow that the will, being free, may shrink from or decline a good object when it has "some difficulty or unpleasant quality annexed to it," but this and other reservations (1:171–73) are evidently designed to explain exceptional cases, not to admit a general recalcitrance. On Hooker's status in the period, see pp. 149–50 above.

67. For Calvin the question is "whether the will is so utterly vitiated and corrupted in every part as to produce nothing but evil, or whether it retains

some portion uninjured, and productive of good desires"; he concludes that since only divine grace can produce any good motions in fallen men, the will must be "bound with the closest chains" to sin (*Institutes* 2.2.26–27).

68. Erasmus, *Handbook of the Militant Christian,* trans. John P. Dolan (Notre Dame, Ind.: Fides, 1962), pp. 79, 82. Also, Erasmus totally fuses pagan reason and the regenerate spirit: "What the philosophers term 'reason' St Paul calls either 'the spirit' or 'the inner man' " (p. 85).

69. Anthony Giddens, *Central Problems in Social Theory* (London: Macmillan, 1979), pp. 193–95.

70. Terry Eagleton, *The Rape of Clarissa* (Oxford: Basil Blackwell, 1982), p. 4.

71. Stuart Hall, "Deviance, Politics, and the Media," in Paul Rock and Mary McIntosh, eds., *Deviance and Social Control* (London: Tavistock, 1974), p. 293.

72. Spenser, *Poetical Works,* p. 407.

73. Sir John Harington, in G. Gregory Smith, *Elizabethan Critical Essays* (London: Oxford Univ. Press, 1904), 2:197–99, 202–3.

74. Nelson, "Sir John Harington as a Critic of Sir Philip Sidney," pp. 49–50, 52.

75. Greville, *Prose Works,* p. 134. See also pp. 8–12; "A Treatie of Humane Learning," stanzas 111–15, in *Poems and Dramas of Fulke Greville,* ed. Geoffrey Bullough (Edinburgh: Oliver & Boyd, 1939); Rebholz, *Life of Fulke Greville,* p. 76; and Dollimore, *Radical Tragedy,* pp. 78–82.

76. Joseph Hall, *Collected Poems,* ed. A. Davenport (Liverpool: Liverpool Univ. Press, 1949), p. 97. Hall refers to Mary and Philip Sidney and Bartas in respect of his versification of the Psalms (p. 271). On the persistence of these topics in the seventeenth century, see Lewalski, *Protestant Poetics.*

77. Herbert, *English Poems,* ed. Patrides; Sidney, *Poems,* ed. Ringler.

78. John Milton, *Complete Prose Works* (New Haven: Yale Univ. Press, 1953–82), 1:817–18, 820–21.

79. Sidney was knighted in 1582 because prince John Casimir of the Palatinate nominated him as his proxy (Howell, *Sir Philip Sidney,* pp. 92–93).

80. Greville, *Prose Works,* p. 3. On Sidney's idealized reputation after death as a Protestant activist, see Howell, *Sir Philip Sidney,* pp. 5–11, 263–67.

81. *Poems of Ben Jonson,* ed. George Burke Johnston (London: Routledge, 1954).

82. *The Complete Works of Percy Bysshe Shelley,* ed. Thomas Hutchinson (Oxford: Oxford Univ. Press, 1943), p. 441; W. B. Yeats, "In Memory of Major Robert Gregory," in *Collected Poems* (London: Macmillan, 1933), p. 150.

83. Sir Arthur Quiller-Couch, *On the Art of Writing* (Cambridge: Cambridge Univ. Press, 1946), pp. 34–35.

84. Buxton, *Sir Philip Sidney,* pp. 54–55.

85. John Fekete, *The Critical Twilight* (London: Routledge, 1977), p. 195.

86. D. H. Craig, "The Hybrid Growth: Sidney's Theory of Poetry in *An Apology for Poetry,*" *English Literary Renaissance* 10 (1980): 183–201, pp. 183,

201; Martin N. Raitiere, "The Unity of Sidney's *Apology for Poetry*," *Studies in English Literature 1500–1900* 21 (1981): 37–58, p. 49.

CHAPTER NINE

1. M. M. Bakhtin and P. N. Medvedev, *The Formal Method in Literary Scholarship* (Baltimore: Johns Hopkins University Press, 1978), p. 121.

2. See Jonathan Dollimore, *Radical Tragedy,* 2d ed. (Hemel Hempstead: Harvester Wheatsheaf, 1989), pp. 22–28, et passim; Margot Heinemann, *Puritanism and Theatre* (Cambridge: Cambridge Univ. Press, 1980); David Morse, *England's Time of Crisis: from Shakespeare to Milton* (London: Macmillan, 1989), chs. 5, 8, 9, et passim.

3. G. K. Hunter, "Seneca and English Tragedy," in C. D. N. Costa, ed., *Seneca* (London: Routledge, 1974), p. 170.

4. T. S. Eliot, Introduction, in *Seneca, his Tenne Tragedies,* ed. Thomas Newton (1581; New York: AMS Press, 1967), 1:xliii. See also pp. xxxix and xlvii–xlviii, and John W. Cunliffe, *The Influence of Seneca on Elizabethan Tragedy* (Hamden, Conn.: Archon, 1965), especially pp. 9 and 54–55.

5. Quoted in Hunter, "Seneca and English Tragedy," pp. 171–72.

6. *Seneca, his Tenne Tragedies,* ed. Newton, 1:4–5; *The Seventh Tragedie of Seneca entitled Medea,* trans. John Studley (1566), prefatory letter (in Newton, vol. 2).

7. *The Miscellaneous Prose of Sir Philip Sidney,* ed. Katherine Duncan-Jones and Jan van Dorsten (Oxford: Clarendon Press, 1973), p. 96.

8. *The Prose Works of Fulke Greville, Lord Brooke,* ed. John Gouws (Oxford: Clarendon Press, 1986), p. 133.

9. Phillip Stubbes, *The Anatomie of Abuses,* ed. Frederick J. Furnivall (London: Trubner for the New Shakespeare Society, 1877–79), 1:143–44. On Bale and Protestant attitudes to theater, see John N. King, *English Reformation Literature* (Princeton: Princeton Univ. Press, 1982), pp. 275–78 and ch. 6. On the later period see Heinemann, *Puritanism and Theatre,* pp. 18–36.

10. See William R. Elton, *"King Lear" and the Gods* (San Marino, Calif.: Huntington Library, 1968); Dominic Baker-Smith, "Religion and John Webster," in Brian Morris, ed., *John Webster* (London: Benn, 1970); H. A. Kelly, *Divine Providence in the England of Shakespeare's Histories* (Cambridge, Mass.: Harvard Univ. Press, 1970); Paul R. Sellin, "The Hidden God," in R. S. Kinsman, ed., *The Darker Vision of the Renaissance* (Berkeley: Univ. of California Press, 1974); Robert G. Hunter, *Shakespeare and the Mystery of the Gods* (Athens, Ga.: Univ. of Georgia Press, 1976); Dollimore, *Radical Tragedy,* chs. 1, 5, 7.

11. *Jew of Malta* 5.5.125–26, in *The Plays of Christopher Marlowe,* ed. Roma Gill (Oxford: Oxford Univ. Press, 1971). Marlowe's plays are quoted hereafter from this edition.

12. Thomas Kyd, *The First Part of Hieronimo and The Spanish Tragedy,* ed. Andrew S. Cairncross (London: Arnold, 1967): *Spanish Tragedy* 4.1.31–33.

13. Sir Philip Sidney, *The Countess of Pembroke's Arcadia,* ed. Maurice Evans (Harmondsworth: Penguin Books, 1977), p. 817. Earlier in the *New*

Arcadia, Pamela says, in Stoic manner, that she and her friends are "balls to injurious fortune"; she is dissuaded, with a Stoic argument, from suicide (ed. Evans, pp. 584–85).

14. *Duchess of Malfi* 5.4.51–54; 5.5.100–103, in *The Selected Plays of John Webster,* ed. Jonathan Dollimore and Alan Sinfield (Cambridge: Cambridge Univ. Press, 1983).

15. E. Gordon Rupp and Philip S. Watson, eds., *Luther and Erasmus* (London: SCM, 1969), p. 41.

16. William Lawne, *An Abridgement of the Institution of Christian Religion, written by M. John Calvin,* trans. Christopher Fetherstone (Edinburgh, 1587), pp. 223–24. See Dollimore, *Radical Tragedy,* pp. xxix–xxxii and ch. 5.

17. Robert Burton, *The Anatomy of Melancholy,* ed. Holbrook Jackson (London: Dent, 1932), 3:419, quoting Matt. 20:16 and 22:14.

18. Ibid., p. 420, quoting 1 Tim. 2:4. Lawne's objector quotes this, but the reply is another text: "I will have mercy on whom I will have mercy" (Exod. 33:19, repeated by Paul, Rom. 9:15): Lawne, *Abridgement,* p. 230.

19. *Institutes* 1.3.2, 4.20.31; the opinion attributed to Marlowe is quoted from Paul Kocher, *Christopher Marlowe* (New York: Russell, 1962), p. 34.

20. Thomas Hobbes, *Leviathan,* ed. C. B. Macpherson (Harmondsworth: Penguin Books, 1968), p. 398, quoting Job 38:4.

21. *Hamlet* is quoted from the New Arden edn., ed. Harold Jenkins (London: Methuen, 1982).

22. Seneca, *Moral Essays,* trans. John W. Basore, Loeb ed. (Cambridge, Mass: Harvard Univ. Press, 1958), 1:36–39.

23. A. C. Bradley, *Shakespearean Tragedy* (London: Macmillan, 1960), p. 116. See also H. B. Charlton, *Shakespearian Tragedy* (Cambridge: Cambridge Univ. Press, 1949), pp. 103–4.

24. Roland Mushat Frye, *Shakespeare and Christian Doctrine* (Princeton: Princeton Univ. Press, 1963), p. 231. See also Ivor Morris, *Shakespeare's God* (London: Allen & Unwin, 1972), pp. 422–30.

25. Roy W. Battenhouse, *Shakespearean Tragedy, Its Art and Its Christian Premises* (Bloomington: Indiana Univ. Press, 1969), p. 250. See also Lily B. Campbell, *Shakespeare's Tragic Heroes* (Cambridge: Cambridge Univ. Press, 1930), pp. 141–47.

26. Kyd, *Spanish Tragedy,* ed. Cairncross, 3.13.1, 6–7; cf. Calvin, *Institutes* 2.2.24.

27. Seneca, *De ira* 1.12.2, in *Moral Essays,* trans. Basore, 1:136–37.

28. *Seneca, his Tenne Tragedies,* ed. Newton, 1:67.

29. Seneca, *Ad Lucilium epistulae morales* 24.25, trans. Richard M. Gunmere, Loeb ed. (Cambridge, Mass.: Harvard Univ. Press, 1961), 1:180–81. The secular manner in which Hamlet discusses suicide (3.1.56–88) recalls the disputes between Oedipus and Antigone in Seneca's *Phoenissae* (1–319), and Deianira, the Nurse and Hyllas in *Hercules Oetaeus* (842–1030).

30. Seneca, *De constantia* 8.2, in *Moral Essays,* trans. Basore, 1:72–73.

31. Henry Smith, *Works,* with introduction by Thomas Fuller (Edinburgh, 1866), 1:205.

32. Marsilio Ficino, *Platonic Theology,* trans. Josephine L. Burroughs, *Journal of the History of Ideas* 5 (1944): 227–39, p. 238. See Ernst Cassirer, Paul

Oskar Kristeller, and John Herman Randall, Jr., eds., *The Renaissance Philosophy of Man* (Chicago: Univ. of Chicago Press, 1948).

33. Joseph Hall, *Works,* ed. Josiah Pratt (London: 1808), 5:292. However, in *Heaven upon Earth* (1606), Hall made a typically "puritan humanist" attempt to reconcile Stoicism and protestantism.

34. John Marston, *Antonio and Mellida*, ed. G. K. Hunter (London: Arnold, 1965), 4.1.68–69. For the argument here, it does not matter whether *Hamlet* or the Antonio plays were produced first.

35. John Marston, *Antonio's Revenge*, ed. G. K. Hunter (London: Arnold, 1966), 4.3.69–75. See Dollimore, *Radical Tragedy,* pp. 30–39; and, on the interaction of Senecan and providential ideas of tragedy, see Willard Farnham, *The Medieval Heritage of Elizabethan Tragedy* (Oxford: Basil Blackwell, 1956), chs. 9–10 passim.

36. John Marston, *Poems,* ed. Arnold Davenport (Liverpool: Liverpool Univ. Press, 1961), p. 123.

37. Miriam T. Griffin, *Seneca, a Philosopher in Politics* (Oxford: Clarendon Press, 1976), p. 177.

38. Arthur Golding, *A Discourse upon the Earthquake* (1580), repr. in Louis Thorn Golding, *An Elizabethan Puritan* (New York: Richard H. Smith, 1937), p. 190. See also Henry Bullinger, *The Decades,* ed. Thomas Harding (Cambridge: Cambridge Univ. Press, 1849–52), 4:180, 194.

39. Rupp and Watson, eds., *Luther and Erasmus,* pp. 83–84.

40. Francis Barker, *The Tremulous Private Body* (London: Methuen, 1984), p. 39; see pp. 58–63 above.

41. Bullinger, *Decades,* 4:184.

42. Lawne, *Abridgement,* p. 49; Calvin, *Institutes* 1.17.4.

43. Perkins, "A Discourse of Conscience" (1596), in Thomas F. Merrill, ed., *William Perkins* (Nieuwkoop: B. de Graaf, 1966), p. 9.

44. On Christian humanists, see pp. 144–52 above. For a good selection, including James Smith, W. W. Greg, J. C. Maxwell, Helen Gardner, Cleanth Brooks, J. B. Steane, and L. C. Knights, see John Jump, ed., *Marlowe: "Dr Faustus": A Casebook* (London: Macmillan, 1969). However, Una Ellis Fermor found the God of *Faustus* to be "sadistic" and revolt against him only proper (Jump, ed., *Marlowe,* p. 43). For more recent attitudes, see Greenblatt, *Renaissance Self-Fashioning,* ch. 5; Dollimore, *Radical Tragedy,* ch. 6; Simon Shepherd, *Marlowe and the Politics of Elizabethan Theatre* (New York: St Martin's Press, 1986), pp. 100–108, 136–41. I come shortly to Empson.

45. Kyd, *First Part of Hieronimo and The Spanish Tragedy,* ed. Cairncross: *First Part of Hieronimo,* 3.59–62.

46. King James I, *Daemonologie (1597), Newes from Scotland (1591)* (London: Bodley Head, 1924), p. 20.

47. Douglas Cole, *Suffering and Evil in the Plays of Christopher Marlowe* (Princeton: Princeton Univ. Press, 1962), p. 198. Cole recognizes that Faustus's behavior is typical of the reprobate, but still believes he makes "his original choice by himself" (pp. 199–201). See also Helen Gardner and J. B. Steane, in Jump, ed., *Marlowe,* pp. 95, 181–82. Malcolm Kelsall says Faustus's tone and failure to complete his quotations show a superficial attitude and

"would be picked on by any school child" (*Christopher Marlowe* [Leiden: Brill, 1981], p. 163). The texts are 1 John 1:8–9 and Rom. 6:23.

48. T. H. L. Parker, *English Reformers* (London: SCM Press, 1966), p. 111.

49. G. E. Duffield, ed., *The Work of William Tyndale* (Appleford, Berks: Sutton Courtenay Press, 1964), p. 175.

50. Stubbes, *Anatomie of Abuses*, 1:190. However, Calvin seems uneasy at *Institutes* 3.3.24.

51. Rupp and Watson, eds., *Luther and Erasmus*, pp. 230–31, 64. Sidney's theory of poetry centers upon the claim that people are moved by it, but he accepts nevertheless that in Alexander Pheraeus, it "wrought no further good in him" beyond that he "withdrew himself from hearkening to that which might mollify his hardened heart" (Sidney, *Miscellaneous Prose*, pp. 96–97).

52. Perkins, "A Discourse of Conscience," in Merrill, ed., *William Perkins*, pp. 20–21; see Lawne, *Abridgement*, pp. 53, 72–73, 221. Apropos of the second commandment, where God promises to visit "the iniquity of the fathers upon the children unto the third and fourth generation" (Deut. 5:9), Lawne's objector is told that children are justly punished for the iniquity they themselves commit "when God taketh away grace and other helps of salvation from a family" (Lawne, *Abridgement*, pp. 86–87).

53. William Empson, *Faustus and the Censor* (Oxford: Basil Blackwell, 1987), p. 168 and ch. 6. Empson dismisses as insignificant Faustus's uncompleted biblical quotations (discussed above), on the ground that "to accept the promises of God requires a miracle" anyway, "and it had been vouchsafed to Luther but not to Faust" (p. 169).

54. In Parker, ed., *English Reformers*, p. 142.

55. Richard Baines's allegation, quoted from Kocher, *Christopher Marlowe*, p. 36.

56. Nathaniel Woodes, *The Conflict of Conscience* (Oxford: Malone Society, 1952), lines 2116, 2151. See Celesta Wine, "Nathaniel Wood's *Conflict of Conscience,*" *PMLA* 50 (1935): 661–78; Lily B. Campbell, "*Dr Faustus:* A Case of Conscience," *PMLA* 67 (1952): 219–39.

57. *Certain Sermons or Homilies* (London: Society for Promoting Christian Knowledge, 1899), p. 568; Hooker, *Of the Laws of Ecclesiastical Polity,* intro. C. Morris (London: Dent, 1969), 1:295. See also Calvin, *Institutes* 3.3.22; Ian Breward, ed., *The Work of William Perkins* (Abingdon: Sutton Courtenay Press, 1970), p. 254. And see *Plays of Christopher Marlowe,* ed. Gill, p. xxii.

58. *Plays of Christopher Marlowe,* ed. Gill, p. xiii.

59. Niccolò Machiavelli, *The Discourses,* ed. Bernard Crick (Harmondsworth: Penguin Books, 1970), p. 178.

60. *Seneca, his Tenne Tragedies,* ed. Newton, 1:40; 2:255. See Eugene M. Waith, *The Herculean Hero* (London: Chatto, 1962).

61. Shepherd, *Marlowe,* pp. 142–53.

62. Roy W. Battenhouse, *Marlowe's Tamburlaine* (Nashville, Tenn.: Vanderbilt Univ. Press, 1964), pp. 116–17, 86–92, 131–33, 169–74. Cf. C. J. Sisson's belief that Hamlet is "God's justiciar in Denmark" (*Shakespeare's Tragic Justice* [London: Methuen, 1963], p. 73 and ch. 3).

63. Calvin, *Institutes* 1.17.5; so *Homilies*, pp. 87–88, 595.

64. See Greenblatt, *Renaissance Self-Fashioning*, pp. 194, 202–3; Sinfield, *Literature in Protestant England*, pp. 82–83; Shepherd, *Marlowe*, pp. 18–22, 149–52.

65. Hall, *Works*, ed. Pratt, 1:274.

66. Lancelot Andrewes, *Works* (Oxford: Clarendon Press, 1841), 1:331. The hired razor is from Isa. 7:20.

67. Shakespeare, *King Lear*, ed. Kenneth Muir (London: Methuen, 1963), 5.3.170–73.

68. Andrewes, *Works*, 5:224, 234; so also Edmund Grindal, *Remains* (Cambridge: Cambridge Univ. Press, 1843), pp. 113–14.

69. Paul Slack, *The Impact of Plague in Tudor and Stuart England* (London: Routledge, 1985), p. 143 and chs. 5–7; F. P. Wilson, *The Plague in Shakespeare's London* (Oxford: Oxford Univ. Press, 1963), p. 172. On the behavior of Andrewes in the plague of 1603, see Slack, p. 234.

70. Wilson, *Plague in Shakespeare's London,* pp. 72, 153–54; Slack, *Impact of Plague,* pp. 239–40, 305–9.

71. Shakespeare, *Richard III*, ed. Antony Hammond (London: Methuen, 1981), 5.3.109–15.

72. See Alan Sinfield, *"King Lear* versus *Lear* at Stratford," *Critical Quarterly* 24 (1982): 5–14.

73. See W. D. Briggs, "Political Ideas in Sidney's *Arcadia," Studies in Philology* 28 (1931): 137–61, and "Sidney's Political Ideas," *Studies in Philology* 29 (1932): 534–42; Michael Walzer, *The Revolution of the Saints* (Cambridge, Mass.: Harvard Univ. Press, 1965), pp. 59–61, 78–87; Martin Bergbush, "Rebellion in the *New Arcadia," Philological Quarterly* 53 (1974): 29–41; Calvin, *Institutes* 4.20.31.

74. Peter Womack, *Ben Jonson* (Oxford: Basil Blackwell, 1986), pp. 135–37, quoting Wilson, *Plague in Shakespeare's London,* p. 52, quoting T. White preaching at Paul's Cross in 1577.

75. Greville, *Prose Works,* ed. Gouws, p. 133.

76. David Norbrook, *Poetry and Politics in the English Renaissance* (London: Routledge, 1984), p. 160, and ch. 6; see Dollimore, *Radical Tragedy,* pp. 78–82 and ch. 7.

77. Shakespeare, *Richard II,* ed. Peter Ure (London: Methuen, 1961), 3.3.85–88; 5.1.59–65.

78. Slack, *Impact of Plague,* pp. 228–44.

79. George Puttenham, *The Arte of English Poesie,* ed. Gladys Doidge Willcock and Alice Walker (Cambridge: Cambridge Univ. Press, 1936), p. 33.

80. Greville, *Prose Works,* pp. 93, 131. Greville very likely altered his *Alaham* for similar reasons: see Ronald A. Rebholz, *The Life of Fulke Greville* (Oxford: Clarendon Press, 1971), pp. 131–34.

81. Dollimore, *Radical Tragedy,* ch. 8.

82. See Annabel Patterson, *Censorship and Interpretation* (Madison: Univ. of Wisconsin Press, 1984), pp. 44–58; Heinemann, *Puritanism and Theatre,* pp. 36–47.

83. Patterson, *Censorship and Interpretation,* pp. 7, 11. On *The Shepheardes Calender,* see Norbrook, *Poetry and Politics,* ch. 3.

84. Heinemann, *Puritanism and Theatre,* pp. 36–47.

85. See David A. Miller, *The Novel and the Police* (Berkeley: Univ. of California Press, 1988), pp. 206–7; Eve Kosofsky Sedgwick, *Epistemology of the Closet* (Berkeley: Univ. of California Press, 1990), ch. 1; Alan Sinfield, "Private Lives / Public Theatre: Noel Coward and the Politics of Homosexual Representation," *Representations* 36 (1991): 43–63.

86. Thomas Middleton, *Women Beware Women,* ed. Roma Gill (London: Ernest Benn, 1968), 4.2.7–10.

87. Heinemann, *Puritanism and Theatre,* p. 45. See Peter Holland, "*Hamlet* and the Art of Acting," in *Drama and the Actor,* ed. James Redmond, *Themes in Drama* 6 (Cambridge: Cambridge Univ. Press, 1984): 39–61.

88. Bertolt Brecht, *Plays* (London: Methuen, 1962), 2:207. See Raymond Williams, *Modern Tragedy,* rev. ed. (London: Verso, 1979), pt. 1.

A BRIEF PHOTO-ESSAY

1. Marcia Pointon, *William Dyce, 1806–1864* (Oxford: Clarendon Press, 1979), pp. 93–95, 100. Prince Albert then commissioned Dyce to decorate the Queen's Robing Room in the rebuilt Palace of Westminster with frescoes of Malory's *Morte d'Arthur.* I'm grateful to Professor Pointon for discussing Dyce with me, and to Christine Barrow for showing me Grenada.

2. Pointon, *William Dyce,* p. 94. Raphael's *Galatea* (c. 1512), is in the Villa Farnesina, Rome; see Roger Jones and Nicholas Penny, *Raphael* (New Haven: Yale Univ. Press, 1983), pl. 106 and pp. 93–97.

CHAPTER TEN

1. Dean MacCannell, *The Tourist: A New Theory of the Leisure Class* (New York: Schocken Books, 1976).

2. Stephen Greenblatt, "Towards a Poetics of Culture," in H. Aram Veeser, ed., *The New Historicism* (New York: Routledge, 1989), pp. 8–10.

3. E. D. Hirsch, Jr., *Cultural Literacy* (Boston: Houghton Mifflin, 1987), p. 29.

4. Richard Slotkin, *Regeneration through Violence* (Middletown, Conn: Wesleyan Univ. Press, 1973), chs. 9–10; see Henry Nash Smith, *Virgin Land* (Cambridge, Mass.: Harvard Univ. Press, 1950), pp. 51–61. The theory implied here is set out in chapter 2 above.

5. [John Filson], *Life and Adventures of Colonel Daniel Boon . . . Written by Himself* (Brooklyn, N.Y.: C. Wilder, 1823), p. 25.

6. William Carlos Willliams, *In the American Grain* (New York: New Directions, 1956), p. 133.

7. Stewart Edward White, *Daniel Boone: Wilderness Scout* (New York: Garden City Publishing, 1922), p. 273.

8. Michael A. Lofaro, *The Life and Adventures of Daniel Boone* (Lexington: Univ. Press of Kentucky, 1986), p. 123.

9. [Filson], *Life and Adventures of Colonel Daniel Boon . . . Written by Himself,* pp. 33, 37.

10. John Collier, *Indians of the Americas* (New York: Mentor Books, 1963), p. 124; White, *Daniel Boone*, p. 82.

11. George Orwell, *Burmese Days* (1934; Harmondsworth: Penguin Books, 1967), p. 25.

12. Doris Lessing, *The Grass Is Singing* (Harmondsworth: Penguin Books, 1961), p. 192. See Sinfield, *Literature, Politics and Culture in Postwar Britain* (Oxford: Basil Blackwell; Berkeley: Univ. of California Press, 1989), pp. 119–22 and ch. 7.

13. Francis Jennings, *The Invasion of America* (New York: Norton, 1976), p. 90.

14. Bernard W. Sheehan, *Savagism and Civility* (Cambridge: Cambridge Univ. Press, 1980), pp. 110–15.

15. George Rogers Taylor, ed., *The Turner Thesis*, 3d ed. (Lexington, Mass.: D. C. Heath, 1972), pp. 27, 41–43; see Smith, *Virgin Land*. On *The Renegade*, see Roy Harvey Pearce, *The Savages of America*, rev. ed. (Baltimore: Johns Hopkins Press, 1965), p. 225 and ch. 7.

16. See Jennings, *Invasion*, chs. 7–8; and Michael Rogin, *"Ronald Reagan," The Movie* (Berkeley: Univ. of California Press, 1987), pp. 45–51.

17. Dee Brown, *Bury My Heart at Wounded Knee* (New York: Bantam Books, 1972), p. 300.

18. George Lamming, *The Pleasures of Exile* (London: Michael Joseph, 1960), p. 107.

19. Jean-Paul Sartre, Preface, in Frantz Fanon, *The Wretched of the Earth*, trans. Constance Farrington (Harmondsworth: Penguin Books, 1967), p. 22.

20. Jennings, *Invasion*, p. 60.

21. Brown, *Bury My Heart*, p. 313, and ch. 11.

22. Rogin, *"Ronald Reagan,"* pp. 45–51.

23. William Bennett, "Lost Generation: Why America's Children Are Strangers in Their Own Land," *Policy Review* 33 (1985): 43–45, p. 45.

24. Sigmund Freud, *On Sexuality: Three Essays on the Theory of Sexuality and Other Works*, ed. Angela Richards (Harmondsworth: Penguin Books, 1977), p. 198.

25. Ania Loomba, *Gender, Race, Renaissance Drama* (Manchester: Manchester Univ. Press, 1989), p. 16, and ch. 1. See also Lillian S. Robinson, *Sex, Class, and Culture* (New York: Methuen, 1986), pp. 22–46; Gauri Viswanathan, "Currying Favor: The Beginnings of English Literary Study in British India," *Social Text* 7, nos. 1–2 (Fall 1988): 85–104; Chris Baldick, *The Social Mission of English Criticism, 1848–1932* (Oxford: Oxford Univ. Press, 1983).

26. Lamming, *Pleasures*, p. 27. See also Lamming's novel *In the Castle of My Skin* (1953).

27. Loomba, *Gender, Race*, p. 22; see Sinfield, *Literature, Politics and Culture*, pp. 124–34.

28. Maya Angelou, *I Know Why the Caged Bird Sings* (New York: Bantam Books, 1971), p. 11; Richard Wright, *Black Boy* (New York: Harper & Row, 1966), pp. 273–74.

29. Viswanathan, "Currying Favor," p. 94.

30. Joseph Quincy Adams, "The Folger Shakespeare Memorial Dedicated: April 21, 1932: Shakespeare and American Culture," *Spinning Wheel* 12 (1932): 212–15 and 229–31, pp. 215, 229. See Stephen J. Brown, "The Uses of Shakespeare in America: A Study in Class Domination," in David Bevington and Jay L. Halio, eds., *Shakespeare, Pattern of Excelling Nature* (Newark: Univ. of Delaware Press, 1978); Esther Cloudman Dunn, *Shakespeare in America* (1939; New York: Benjamin Blom, 1968), chs. 3, 4, 8, 9; James G. McManaway, "Shakespeare in the United States," *PMLA* 79 (1964): 511–18, p. 514.

31. James Fenimore Cooper, *Notions of the Americans* (New York: Frederick Unger, 1962), 2:113, 100; *The Collected Works of Ralph Waldo Emerson*, vol. 4, *Representative Men*, ed. Wallace E. Williams and Douglas Emory Wilson (Cambridge, Mass.: Harvard Univ. Press, 1987), p. 121.

32. Alfred Van Rensselaer Westfall, *American Shakespearean Criticism, 1607–1865* (New York: H. W. Wilson, 1939), p. 202. See also Louis Marder, *His Entrances and Exits: The Story of Shakespeare's Reputation* (London: John Murray, 1964), 294–313; Lawrence L. Levine, *Highbrow/Lowbrow* (Cambridge, Mass.: Harvard Univ. Press, 1988), pp. 60–68; Adams, "Folger Shakespeare Memorial Dedicated," pp. 212–13.

33. Ashley Thorndike, "Shakespeare in America," *Proceedings of the British Academy* 13 (1927): 154.

34. James Fenimore Cooper, *The Pioneers* (New York: Holt, Rinehart & Winston, 1959), p. 476.

35. Richard Hofstadter, *The Progressive Historians* (New York: Knopf, 1968), p. 54, and Introduction to Hofstadter and Seymour Martin Lipset, eds., *Turner and the Sociology of the Frontier* (New York: Basic Books, 1968), p. 3.

36. *Sic*; Maurice Morgann, "An Essay on the Dramatic Character of Sir John Falstaff," in D. Nichol Smith, ed., *Eighteenth-Century Essays on Shakespeare* (Oxford: Clarendon Press, 1963), p. 233.

37. Quoted by Westfall, *American Shakespearean Criticism*, p. 80.

38. Thorndike, "Shakespeare in America," pp. 161–63; Dunn, *Shakespeare in America*, ch. 10; McManaway, "Shakespeare in the United States," p. 514; Louis B. Wright, *Shakespeare for Everyman* (New York: Washington Square Press, 1965), pp. 41–48; Levine, *Highbrow/Lowbrow*, pp. 16–21.

39. Adams, "Folger," p. 229; Wright, *Shakespeare for Everyman*, pp. 43–44.

40. Emerson, *Representative Men*, p. 125.

41. Dunn, *Shakespeare in America*, pp. 175–76; Wright, *Shakespeare for Everyman*, pp. 41–42. See Michael D. Bristol, *Shakespeare's America, America's Shakespeare* (New York: Routledge, 1990), p. 159 on Hardin Craig as pioneer.

42. Dunn, *Shakespeare in America*, chs. 5, 9; Marder, *His Entrances*, pp. 313–17; Levine, *Highbrow/Lowbrow*, pp. 13–16, 21–23, 42–45.

43. Jonathan Bate, *Shakespearean Constitutions* (Oxford: Clarendon Press, 1989), p. 43.

44. Marder, *His Entrances*, pp. 310–11; Levine, *Highbrow/Lowbrow*, pp. 63–68; Charles H. Shattuck, *Shakespeare on the American Stage* (Washington, D.C.: Folger Shakespeare Library, 1976), pp. 62–87.

45. Levine, *Highbrow/Lowbrow*, pp. 30, 56; Levine's emphasis.

46. Robert Falk, "Shakespeare in America: A Survey to 1900," *Shakespeare Survey* 18 (1965): 102–18, p. 103.

47. Dunn, *Shakespeare in America*, p. 129; Shattuck, *Shakespeare on the American Stage*, p. 97 and ch. 4; McManaway, "Shakespeare in the United States," pp. 516–18; Marder, *His Entrances*, pp. 317–18; Levine, *Highbrow/Lowbrow*, pp. 33–34, 45–56, 69–81.

48. Derek Longhurst, " 'You base football-player!': Shakespeare in Contemporary Popular Culture," in Graham Holderness, ed., *The Shakespeare Myth* (Manchester: Manchester Univ. Press, 1988), p. 67.

49. Falk, "Shakespeare in America," pp. 109–15; Sinfield, *Literature, Politics and Culture*, pp. 39–47; Dunn, *Shakespeare in America*, p. 278; she illustrates from Lincoln and John Quincy Adams.

50. Irving Babbitt, *Literature and the American College* (Boston: Houghton Mifflin, 1908), pp. 105, 151.

51. Allan Bloom, *The Closing of the American Mind* (New York: Simon & Schuster, 1987), p. 279, and pp. 251–54, 284.

52. Wright, *Shakespeare For Everyman*, p. 46.

53. Thomas Carlyle, *On Heroes, Hero-Worship and the Heroic in History* (London: James Frazer, 1841), pp. 184–85; quoted by Malcolm Evans, *Signifying Nothing*, 2d ed. (Hemel Hempstead: Harvester Wheatsheaf, 1989), p. 89; and see pp. 86–108.

54. Charles Mills Gayley, *Shakespeare and the Founders of Liberty in America* (New York: Macmillan, 1917), p. vi; see Bristol, *Shakespeare's America*, pp. 137–43. On the Virginia Company see Jennings, *Invasion*, pp. 53–56, 76–80.

55. Stewart Bird, Dan Georgakas and Deborah Shaffer, eds., *Solidarity Forever* (Chicago: Lake View Press, 1985), pp. 10–15, 140–41, and passim; Howard Zinn, *A People's History of the United States* (London: Longman, 1980), pp. 366–67.

56. James Yaffe, *The American Jews* (New York: Random House, 1968), p. 7.

57. Thorndike, "Shakespeare in America," pp. 159–60.

58. Adams, "Folger," p. 230.

59. Ibid., pp. 230–31. See Brown, "Uses of Shakespeare in America"; Louis A. Montrose, "Professing the Renaissance: The Poetics and Politics of Culture," in Veeser, ed., *New Historicism*, pp. 27–29; Bristol, *Shakespeare's America*, pp. 78–81; and on a similar attitude in the work of Hardin Craig, see Bristol, pp. 157–66.

60. Quoted by Don Wayne, "Power, Politics, and the Shakespearean Text: Recent Criticism in England and the United States," in Jean E. Howard and Marion F. O'Connor, eds., *Shakespeare Reproduced* (London: Methuen, 1987), p. 55.

61. Hofstadter, *Progressive Historians*, p. 85.

62. Frederick Merk, *Manifest Destiny and Mission in American History* (New York: Random House, Vintage Books, 1966), p. 119; and see p. 29.

63. Godfrey Hodgson, *America in Our Time* (New York: Random House, Vintage Books, 1978), pp. 468–70. Soviet unfreedom was branded, in imperialist terms, as "oriental": William Pietz, "The 'Post-Colonialism' of Cold

War Discourse," *Social Text* 7, nos. 1–2 (Fall 1988): 55–75, pp. 58–59. Diverse aspects of the argument in the remainder of this section are broached in Sinfield, *Literature, Politics and Culture:* see chs. 6 and 9.

64. Taylor, ed., *Turner Thesis,* p. 27.

65. *San Francisco Chronicle,* February 10, 1989; Martin Gilbert, *Winston Churchill,* vol. 4, *1916–22* (London: Heinemann, 1975), p. 797; also pp. 596, 610.

66. Serge Guilbaut, *How New York Stole the Idea of Modern Art,* trans. Arthur Goldhammer (Chicago: Univ. of Chicago Press, 1983), pp. 128, 172.

67. *General Education in a Free Society,* Report of the Harvard Committee (Cambridge, Mass.: Harvard Univ. Press., 1945), p. xv; see Richard Ohmann, *English in America* (New York: Oxford Univ. Press, 1976), pp. 70–80, 86–89; Gerald Graff, *Professing Literature* (Chicago: Univ. of Chicago Press, 1987), pp. 162–73; Elizabeth Bruss, *Beautiful Theories* (Baltimore: Johns Hopkins Univ. Press, 1982), pp. 10–13.

68. See Stephen Spender, *The Thirties and After* (New York: Random House, 1978), pp. 122–29.

69. Bloom, *Closing of the American Mind,* pp. 48, 54.

70. Hugh Kenner, *A Homemade World: The American Modernist Writers* (New York: Knopf, 1975), p. 213.

71. Westfall, *American Shakespearean Criticism,* pp. 203–4; Bristol, *Shakespeare's America,* p. 74.

72. Marder, *His Entrances,* p. 362.

73. Wright, *Shakespeare for Everyman,* p. 46.

74. Nina Baym, "Melodramas of Beset Manhood: How Theories of American Fiction Exclude Women Authors," in Elaine Showalter, ed., *Feminist Criticism* (London: Virago, 1986), pp. 71, 75; Slotkin, *Regeneration,* pp. 300–301.

75. Taylor, ed., *Turner Thesis,* pp. 14–56; see Smith, *Virgin Land;* Hofstadter, *Progressive Historians,* p. 151.

76. Williams, *In the American Grain,* pp. 136–37. Williams is full of respect for the Indians—they, in his view and, he says, Boone's, knew how to *possess* the land. But the native was "the prototype of it all," and as such necessarily overwhelmed by white men. See also Rupert Wilkinson, *American Tough* (Westport, Conn.: Greenwood, 1984), pp. 17–23, 47, 91–104.

77. Ann Douglas, *The Feminization of American Culture* (New York: Avon Books, 1978), p. 122; see also Nancy Armstrong, *Desire and Domestic Fiction* (Oxford: Oxford Univ. Press, 1987). For this situation in relation to England, see Sinfield, *Literature, Politics and Culture,* ch. 5.

78. Alfred Austin, *The Poetry of the Period,* in Joseph Bristow, ed., *The Victorian Poet: Poetics and Persona* (London: Croom Helm, 1987), pp. 120, 124; Douglas, *Feminization,* p. 314 and ch. 9. See Carol Christ, "The Feminine Subject in Victorian Poetry," *ELH* 54 (1987): 385–401.

79. Sandra M. Gilbert and Susan Gubar, *No Man's Land,* vol. 1: *The War of the Words* (New Haven: Yale Univ. Press, 1988), p. 154.

80. Quoted by Frank Lentricchia, *Ariel and the Police* (Brighton: Harvester, 1988), p. 161.

81. From Gilbert Seldes, *The Great Audience* (1951), repr. in Bernard Rosenberg and David Manning White, eds., *Mass Culture* (New York: Free Press, 1957), pp. 76–77.

82. Rosenberg and White, eds., *Mass Culture*, p. 486.

83. Dwight Macdonald, "Masscult & Midcult," in Macdonald, *Against the American Grain* (New York: Random House, 1962), pp. 14, ix. See Christopher Brookeman, *American Culture and Society since the 1930s* (London: Macmillan, 1984), chs. 5–6; Andrew Ross, *No Respect: Intellectuals and Popular Culture* (London: Routledge, 1989), ch. 2.

84. Marder, *His Entrances*, pp. 310–11. On the Schlegels and Wilcoxes, see Sinfield, *Literature, Politics and Culture*, pp. 39–43, 106–11, 238–45, 258–66.

85. Douglas, *Feminization*, p. 285; Blake Morrison, *The Movement* (London: Methuen, 1986), pp. 59–61.

86. Eve Kosofsky Sedgwick, *Epistemology of the Closet* (Berkeley: Univ. of California Press, 1990), p. 56.

87. Baym, "Melodramas of Beset Manhood," in Showalter, ed., *Feminist Criticism*.

88. C. L. Barber, *Shakespeare's Festive Comedy* (Princeton: Princeton Univ. Press, 1959), pp. 244–45; see pp. 70–71 above. For an investigation that addresses the anxiety and anticipates the current interest, see Leslie Fiedler, *The Stranger in Shakespeare* (St Albans: Paladin, 1974), pp. 15–40, 71–79.

89. Tennyson's vacillation between a transcendent and worldly role for poetry caused these anxieties to cluster around him: see Alan Sinfield, *Alfred Tennyson* (Oxford: Basil Blackwell, 1986), p. 128; also pp. 17–21 and ch. 5. Critical evasions are amusingly displayed by Simon Shepherd, "Shakespeare's Private Drawer: Shakespeare and Homosexuality," in Holderness, ed., *Shakespeare Myth*.

90. Eric Partridge, *Shakespeare's Bawdy* (New York: Dutton, 1948), pp. 13–18. "Lesbianism was an extremely rare deviation in Shakespearean England," Partridge says, but he doesn't share his evidence. I am grateful to Janet Adelman for drawing Partridge to my attention. Hesketh Pearson is quoted from his *Life of Shakespeare*.

91. Benjamin P. Kurtz, *Charles Mills Gayley* (Berkeley: Univ. of California Press, 1943), pp. 151–52.

92. Babbitt, *Literature and the American College*, pp. 118–19; see Gerald Graff, *Professing Literature* (Chicago: Univ. of Chicago Press, 1987), p. 107. From the 1890s on, there were attempts to reduce the proportions of women teachers and reverse the move towards co-education in colleges (Douglas, *Feminization*, p. 397).

93. John Montgomery, *The Fifties* (London: Allen & Unwin, 1965), p. 100; see Sinfield, *Literature, Politics and Culture*, pp. 134–39 and ch. 7.

94. *The Times,* September 1, 1955; quoted in William Sargant, *Battle for the Mind* (London: Heinemann, 1957), pp. 150–51.

95. Lamming, *Pleasures,* p. 85; Sartre, Preface, in Fanon, *Wretched of the Earth,* pp. 21, 24.

96. White, *Daniel Boone,* p. 263.

97. Gore Vidal, "The Day the American Empire Ran Out of Gas," in Vidal, *Armageddon?* (London: André Deutsch, 1987), p. 115.

98. Ray Bradbury, *Fahrenheit 451* (London: Corgi, 1969), p. 74.

99. Noam Chomsky, *American Power and the New Mandarins* (Harmondsworth: Penguin Books, 1969), pp. 23–61.

100. Bloom, *Closing of the American Mind,* pp. 56, 21, 55; Hirsch, *Cultural Literacy,* p. 91. In their book *Free to Choose* (London: Secker & Warburg, 1980, pp. 2–3), Milton and Rose Friedman assert that in the nineteenth century the United States experienced a "golden age," but begin their account by "omitting" Indians and "excepting" slavery!

101. William Bennett, "To Reclaim a Legacy," *American Education* 21 (1985): 4–15, pp. 14–15.

102. Hirsch, *Cultural Literacy,* p. 92.

103. Bennett, "To Reclaim a Legacy," p. 15. See Montrose, "Professing the Renaissance," pp. 27–28.

104. "In the *Republic* . . . the only possible solution is for philosophers to rule. . . . But this outline of a solution is ironic and impossible. It only serves to show what one must live with" (Bloom, *Closing of the American Mind,* p. 266; and see pp. 373–74).

105. By Greenblatt, see also *Renaissance Self-Fashioning,* pp. 180–88, 225–29; "Learning to Curse: Aspects of Linguistic Colonialism in the Sixteenth Century," in Fredi Chiapelli, ed., *First Images of America: The Impact of the New World on the Old* (Berkeley: Univ. of California Press, 1976), 2:568–76; and "Invisible Bullets: Renaissance Authority and Its Subversion," in Dollimore and Sinfield, eds., *Political Shakespeare.* Of course, others have addressed these issues; I cite Greenblatt to show their strong presence at the heart of new historicism.

106. C. D. B. Bryan, "Operation Desert Norm," *New Republic,* March 11, 1991, p. 26. I am grateful to Peter Dreyer for this reference. On the Pequote massacre, see Jennings, *Invasion,* pp. 220–25, and on the Arapaho, see Brown, *Bury My Heart,* pp. 108–9, also pp. 257–58, 278–79.

107. Michel Foucault, *Power/Knowledge,* ed. Colin Gordon (Brighton: Harvester, 1980), p. 126; "John K. Simon: A Conversation with Michel Foucault," *Partisan Review* 38 (1971): 192–201; Jean-François Lyotard, *The Postmodern Condition,* trans. Geoff Bennington and Brian Massumi (Manchester: Manchester Univ. Press, 1984), pp. 48–53. See Harold Perkin, *The Rise of Professional Society* (London: Routledge, 1969).

108. Steven Connor, *Postmodernist Culture* (Oxford: Basil Blackwell, 1989), pp. 17, 15; Connor argues that "the postmodern" may facilitate this tendency. See Wayne, "Power, Politics," pp. 59–62; Ross, *No Respect,* p. 211 and ch. 7.

109. Ohmann, *English in America,* pp. 86–89, 330.

110. T. S. Eliot, *Notes towards a Definition of Culture* (London: Faber & Faber, 1948), p. 42.

111. So Christopher Jencks and David Riesmann, quoted by Jonathan Culler, *Framing the Sign* (Oxford: Basil Blackwell, 1988), p. 29.

112. See Russell Jacoby, *The Last Intellectuals* (New York: Basic Books, 1987), pp. 219, 272.

113. Bristol, *Shakespeare's America,* p. 209. So Louis Montrose writes of "a nagging sense of professional, institutional, and political powerlessness or

irrelevance" ("Professing the Renaissance," p. 26). See also Walter Cohen, "Political Criticism of Shakespeare," in Howard and O'Connor, eds., *Shakespeare Reproduced*, pp. 35–38; Bloom, *Closing of the American Mind*, p. 353.

114. *Is There a Text in This Class?* (Cambridge, Mass.: Harvard Univ. Press, 1980), p. 165.

115. Ibid., pp. 171, 173. See Elizabeth A. Meese, "Sexual Politics and Critical Judgment," in Gregory S. Jay and David L. Miller, eds., *After Strange Texts* (University, Ala.: Univ. of Alabama Press, 1985).

116. Stanley Fish, "Commentary: The Young and the Restless," in Veeser, ed. *New Historicism*, pp. 312–15.

117. David Simpson, "Literary Criticism and the Return to 'History,' " *Critical Inquiry* 14 (1988): 721–47, p. 726. See also the powerful discussion in John Fekete, "Literature and Politics / Literary Politics," *Dalhousie Review* 66 (1986): 45–86.

118. Michel Foucault, *L'Ordre du discours* (Paris: Gallimard, 1971), p. 46; quoted by Eve Taylor Bannet, *Structuralism and the Logic of Dissent* (London: Macmillan, 1989), p. 177; and see pp. 170–83, 240–49.

119. Michel Foucault, "The Political Function of the Intellectual," trans. Colin Gordon, *Radical Philosophy* 17 (1977): 12–15, p. 14; "John K. Simon: A Conversation with Michel Foucault," p. 201. See Ross, *No Respect*, pp. 211–12.

120. Sigmund Freud, *Case Histories I: "Dora" and "Little Hans,"* ed. Angela Richards (Harmondsworth: Penguin Books, 1977), p. 117.

121. *The Nation*, December 12, 1988, p. 644; I am grateful to Richard Burt for this reference.

122. Bennett, "To Reclaim a Legacy," p. 15.

123. James Yaffe, *The American Jews* (New York: Random House, 1968), pp. 41, 51–52; Culler, *Framing the Sign*, pp. 31–32; Wayne, "Power, Politics," pp. 53–58; Bristol, *Shakespeare's America*, pp. 40–51.

124. Yaffe, *American Jews*, pp. 53–56 and ch. 4. Yaffe suggests that Jewish culture may have been readily adaptable to the professionalizing of culture—an old lullaby of the *shtetl* enjoins, "Study the Torah, darling. For Torah is the best merchandise": pp. 229–30. Russell Jacoby argues that in the 1950s, professionalization was a refuge from political visibility: Jacoby, *Last Intellectuals*, pp. 126–30, 135–39, 200–209.

125. Richard Hofstadter, "The Pseudo-Conservative Revolt," in Daniel Bell, ed., *The New American Right* (New York: Criterion Books, 1955), p. 46.

126. Yaffe, *American Jews*, pp. 126–27; Marder, *His Entrances*, pp. 292–93.

127. Robinson, *Sex, Class, and Culture*, p. 35.

128. Wayne, "Power, Politics," pp. 54–56; and see Jacoby, *Last Intellectuals*, ch. 4.

129. Alexander Bloom, *Prodigal Sons* (New York: Oxford Univ. Press, 1986), pp. 20–21.

130. Wayne, "Power, Politics," p. 58; Culler, *Framing the Sign*, p. 78 and ch. 4; see pp. 150–51 above.

131. Wayne, "Power, Politics," p. 53. Allan Bloom, of course, sees this as a loss for the education system: once Jews were admitted, he says, Harvard,

Yale, and Princeton ceased to be "the last resorts of aristocratic sentiment" (*Closing of the American Mind*, p. 89).

132. Babbitt, *Literature and the American College*, p. 8.

133. Collier, *Indians*, pp. 126–29.

134. Raymond Williams, *Second Generation* (London: Chatto & Windus, 1964), pp. 137–38.

135. John Banks and Martina Weitsch, eds., *Meeting Gay Friends* (Manchester: Friends Homosexual Fellowship, 1982), p. 18. Marlon T. Riggs, "What Time Is It?" *Out/Look*, Spring 1990, p. 135. I am grateful to Carrie Bramen for this reference.

136. Celia Kitzinger, "Liberal Humanism as an Ideology of Social Control: The Regulation of Lesbian Identities," in J. Shotter and K. Gergen, eds., *Texts of Identity* (London: Sage, 1989), pp. 85–86; see Kitzinger, *The Social Construction of Lesbianism* (London: Sage, 1987), chs. 2, 7.

137. Quoted in Lillian Faderman, *Surpassing the Love of Men* (London: Junction Books, 1985), p. 409. For a sequence of such responses, see Mandy Merck, " 'Liana' and the Lesbians of Art Cinema," in Charlotte Brunsdon, ed., *Films for Women* (London: British Film Institutte, 1986), p. 170.

138. See Collier, *Indians,* ch. 11.

139. Suzanne Pharr, *Homophobia: A Weapon of Sexism* (Inverness, Calif.: Chardon Press, 1988), p. 22.

140. Richard Wright, *Native Son* (1940; New York: Harper & Row, 1966), p. xvi. Cf. Henry Louis Gates, Jr., *The Signifying Monkey* (New York: Oxford Univ. Press, 1988), pp. 118–20, 181–83.

141. Cf. Barbara Herrnstein Smith, *Contingencies of Value* (Cambridge, Mass.: Harvard Univ. Press, 1988), pp. 166–79.

142. Zinn, *People's History*, p. 367.

143. Tony Bennett, "Texts in History: The Determinations of Readings and Their Texts," in Derek Attridge, Geoff Bennington and Robert Young, eds., *Post-Structuralism and the Question of History* (Cambridge: Cambridge Univ. Press, 1987), p. 68.

144. Quoted in Peter Stallybrass and Allon White, *The Politics and Poetics of Transgression* (London: Methuen, 1986), p. 20.

145. Fiedler, *Stranger,* pp. 82–83.

146. Arnold Wesker, *The Journalists / The Wedding Feast / Shylock* (Harmondsworth: Penguin Books, 1990), p. 178. Wesker's play is in effect close to Margaret Ferguson's suggestion that a historical study of productions of the *Merchant* might be mounted in a course perhaps entitled "Shakespeare and the American Ideology of the 'Melting Pot' " (Ferguson, "Afterword," in Howard and O'Connor, eds., *Shakespeare Reproduced,* p. 280).

147. Allan Bloom with Harry V. Jaffa, *Shakespeare's Politics* (New York: Basic Books, 1964; Univ. of Chicago Press, Midway Reprint, 1986), p. 21. It is amusing to note that the falling off of standards Bloom attributes to the 1960s and after in *Closing of the American Mind* (pp. 313–35) is already being lamented here in 1964 (pp. 1–2). It is typical of a conservative cultural critique to appeal to a supposed good past that always recedes as it is approached.

Index

Abbott, George, 154
Absolutism, 10, 40–42, 80–88, 95–104, 181–85, 206, 210. *See also* Tyranny
Adams, John Quincy, 76
Adams, Joseph Quincy, 262, 263, 268, 284, 291
Adelman, Janet, 54
Adorno, Theodore, 275
Albert, Prince, 252
Althusser, Louis, 9, 31, 32, 35, 39, 164–65, 244–45
Amis, Kingsley, 276
Anderson, Perry, 82, 96
Andrewes, Lancelot, 115, 122, 154, 156, 241–42, 327n34
Angelou, Maya, 261
Apocalypse Now, 285
Aquinas, Saint Thomas, 152, 205
Ariosto, Lodovico, 194–95
Aristotle, 134, 153, 186, 188, 189, 191, 196, 205
Arnold, Matthew, 274
Atheism, 152, 153, 168, 235. *See also* Pagans
Audiences, 59, 105, 229, 239–40, 251, 301
Augustine, Saint, 152

Babbitt, Irving, 266, 278–79, 293–94
Babcock, Barbara, 299
Bacon, Francis, 15, 61, 99, 117, 153, 166, 199, 246
Baines, Richard, 235
Bakhtin, Mikhail, 17, 128, 214
Baldwin, James, 261
Bale, John, 216
Bamber, Linda, 128
Barber, C. L., 70–71, 278
Barker, Francis, 60, 65, 227
Barker, Howard, 22
Barnes, Robert, 186
Barnum, P. T., 272
Bartas, Guillaume du, 192, 193, 198, 207
Barthes, Roland, 1
Barton, John, 20, 23
Base-superstructure, 38–39
Battenhouse, Roy W., 222, 240
Bayley, John, 57, 101
Baym, Nina, 273, 277
Beard, Charles A., 263
Beaumont, Francis, 249
Beckett, Samuel, 111
Becon, Thomas, 190
Bedford, Earl of, 171, 184
Bell, Daniel, 292

Belsey, Catherine, 53, 58, 60, 63
Benjamin, Walter, 26–27
Bennett, Emerson, 258
Bennett, Tony, 299
Bennett, William, 8, 260, 283, 291
Berger, Harry, Jr., 318n1
Beveridge, Albert J., 270
Beza, Theodore, 153, 191
Bible, the, 49, 104, 122, 147, 153, 164–66, 168, 171, 177, 186–87, 192–94, 198–99, 203, 219, 221, 223, 226, 231–33, 272
Blacks, 12, 29–36, 50–51, 76, 258, 260–61, 282, 283, 291, 298
Bloom, Allan, 76, 266, 269, 271, 276–77, 284, 286, 290, 300–301, 351n147
Bloom, Harold, 279
Blount, Sir Charles, 171
Boccaccio, 187
Bogdanov, Michael, 23
Bond, Edward, 22, 244
Boone, Daniel, 255–58, 260, 262, 264, 267, 269, 272–73, 275, 280
Boose, Lynda E., 35, 36–37
Bourdieu, Pierre, 92, 186
Bradbrook, Muriel C., 57
Bradbury, Ray, 281
Bradley, A. C., 56, 57, 62, 222, 226–28
Breaking points. *See* Faultlines
Brecht, Bertholt, 150, 251, 255
Brezhnev, Leonid, 181, 183, 213
Briggs, William Dinsmore, 85
Brinsley, John, 171
Bristol, Michael D., 7, 149, 287
British Empire, 4, 6–7, 11, 252–53, 257–58, 260–61, 267, 269–72, 279–81

Brooks-Davies, Douglas, 194
Brown, Dee, 281
Buchanan, George, 100–102, 104–5, 193, 198
Buchanan, James, 270
Bullinger, Henry, 153, 228
Bureaucracy, 89–92, 147, 172
Burghley, Lord, 91, 120
Burton, Robert, 43, 165, 219–20
Bush, George, 271
Buste, John, 184
Butler, Judith, 37–38, 297
Buxton, John, 212

Callaghan, Dympna, 45, 74, 75–76
Callings, 89, 114, 160, 169–70, 184–85
Calvin, John, and Calvinism, 143–44, 147–48, 151–57, 159, 166, 175–80, 189, 198, 200, 203–5, 212, 214, 216–21, 228–33, 235, 245–46. *See also* Election and reprobation; Protestantism; Puritans
Campbell, Lily B., 57, 109–10
Canon, literary. *See* Great Books
Carey, John, 159, 168, 180, 325n13
Caribbean, the, 253, 260–61, 281, 285
Carlyle, Thomas, 6, 267
Carnival, 17–18
Catholicism, Roman, 43, 97–98, 118, 125, 152, 154, 157, 158, 167, 171, 186, 245. *See also* Gunpowder Plot
Catullus, 201
Censorship, 154, 167, 177, 182, 236, 247–51, 295
Character, literary, 52–79, 111–13, 226–27
Charles I, 96, 154

Chomsky, Noam, 281
Christian humanism. *See* Humanism
Church, the, 117, 121–23, 129, 143–44, 153–55, 166–67, 176. *See also* Clergy
Churchill, Winston, 270–71
Cicero, 15, 186, 187–89
Class, 10, 13, 17–21, 41–42, 45–46, 47, 49, 85–94, 113, 116, 119–20, 124–25, 169–75, 264–67, 275–76, 284, 286–87, 292–94, 301
Clergy, 96, 122, 166–67, 170–75, 179–80, 208
Cold War, 13–14, 169, 181–83, 212–13, 253, 269–71, 274–75, 281
Cole, Douglas, 231
Collectivity, 13, 38, 177–80, 268, 288, 293–94, 297
Collinson, Patrick, 167, 170, 173, 199, 335–336n55
Columbus, Christopher, 270, 272
Communism. *See* Cold War; Marx, Karl, and Marxism
Conant, James Bryant, 271
Connor, Patrick E., 285
Connor, Steven, 286
Conrad, Joseph, 280, 285
Containment, 8–10, 19, 35–49, 64, 74–77, 80–85, 100–103, 126–27, 139–41, 164–80, 173–80, 285, 287–90, 293. *See also* Dissidence; Legitimation; Order and Disorder
Cooper, James Fenimore, 263, 265
Court, royal, 40, 81, 84–85, 89–93, 120–21, 130, 143, 146, 153, 170, 185, 187, 208, 248

Coverdale, Miles, 199
Craig, D. H., 212
Craig, Hardin, 149
Cross, Claire, 150
Cry Freedom, 279
Culler, Jonathan, 150–51, 292
Cultural materialism, 8–9, 22, 35–42, 46–51, 57, 79, 108, 110–11, 125–27, 177, 200, 213, 244, 246–48, 251, 291–99, 320n11. *See also* Subculture
Cultural production, 5–7, 21–51, 62, 92–94, 106, 170–72, 181–213, 235, 246–51, 264–67, 288–90. *See also* Censorship; Education; Ideology; Intellectuals; Patronage; Subculture; Writers

Daniel, Samuel, 248
Davenant, Sir William, 105
De Man, Paul, 289
deMille, Cecil B., 13
Derrida, Jacques, 111, 146
Descartes, Réné, 61
Disorder. *See* Order and disorder
Dissidence, 9, 18–19, 21–28, 35–51, 64, 80, 88–94, 104–8, 116–20, 164–80, 214, 217–21, 230, 245–51, 288–90, 294–99, 301–2. *See also* Containment; Order and Disorder
Divine poetry, 192–93, 197–99, 203–4, 209. *See also* Donne, John; Herbert, George; Psalms
Dodd, William Nigel, 59, 62, 65
Dollimore, Jonathan, 8–9, 10, 22, 49, 61, 97, 126, 173, 247

Donne, John, 147–48, 158–63, 165, 168, 173–74, 188, 221, 233
Douglas, Ann, 273, 276
Dunn, Esther Cloudman, 264, 266
Dyce, William, 252–53

Eagleton, Terry, 206
Education, 48–49, 92, 145–47, 152–53, 167, 171, 184–90, 265–67, 269, 271, 276–77, 283–84, 286
Edward VI, 184, 186
Edwards, Philip, 125
Effeminacy, 130–38, 140–43, 237–38, 243, 272–79, 295, 322n49, 323n54. *See also* Masculinity; Sexualities
Election and reprobation, 144, 147–48, 151–57, 161, 164, 175–80, 203–5, 218–20, 226, 228–37
Eliot, T. S., 57, 212, 215, 227, 241, 286
Elizabeth I, 4, 41, 55, 81, 83–86, 89, 91, 96, 117, 120, 135, 141, 143, 166, 168, 182, 185, 208, 247
Elyot, Sir Thomas, 146, 190, 198, 201
Emerson, Ralph Waldo, 263, 264
Empson, William, 234–35
Engels, Friedrich, 36
English literature. *See* Literary criticism
Entrapment. *See* Containment
Epicurus, 153
Erasmus, Desiderius, 151, 157, 186, 205, 215, 218, 220, 226
Erickson, Peter, 128
Essentialism, 35–38, 50, 56, 58–59, 61–63, 65–66, 78–79, 111–13, 181–85, 205–

13, 226, 251, 284–89, 291. *See also* Man
Essex, Earl of, 27, 40–41, 48, 115, 117, 118, 120–21, 208, 241
Ethnic minorities, 8, 10, 35, 38, 42, 50–51, 150, 267–69, 279–85, 291, 294. *See also* Blacks; Indians; Jews; Race and racism; Slavery; Turks
Euripides, 235
Evans, Malcolm, 8
Everest, Wesley, 268
Everett, Barbara, 57

Falk, Robert, 265–66
Faultlines, 9, 38–47, 73–77, 116, 138–41, 164–65, 169–70, 175–76, 200, 221, 227, 230, 235–37, 256, 262, 273. *See also* Containment; Dissidence; Ideology
Fekete, John, 6
Feminism, 8, 35–38, 52–54, 57–58, 127–28, 150, 282. *See also* Women
Ferguson, Margaret, 351n146
Ficino, Marsilio, 191, 202, 224
Fiedler, Leslie, 73, 299
Filson, John, 256, 262
Fineman, Joel, 58–59
Fish, Stanley, 288–91
Fiske, John, 94
Fletcher, John, 249
Folger Library, 268, 272
Ford, Boris, 16
Forrest, Edwin, 264
Forster, E. M., 275–76
Foucault, Michel, 9, 35, 47, 48, 50, 162–63, 286, 290
Foxe, John, 149
Freedom, 165, 176–80, 259, 270–73, 282

Freud, Sigmund, 53–57, 260, 277, 290. *See also* Psychoanalysis
Frye, Roland Mushat, 222
Furness, Howard Horace, 266
Fuss, Diana, 297, 309n19

Galen, 134
Garnier, Robert, 215
Gayley, Charles Mills, 267–68, 278, 291
Geckle, George L., 127
Gender. *See* Effeminacy; Feminism; Sexualities; Women
Gentry, 167, 169–70, 182, 187, 248, 256, 260–66, 275–76, 287, 293. *See also* Class
Giddens, Anthony, 33, 47, 206
Girty, Simon, 258
Globe Theater, xii, 1–5, 7, 25, 27
God, 44, 61, 63, 98, 111, 114, 116, 128, 144–93 passim, 216, 227, 231, 233, 236–37, 240–42. *See also* Providence
Goldberg, Jonathan, 48, 58, 63, 81, 146–47
Golding, Arthur, 184, 191, 210, 226
Goldman, Emma, 268
Goldmann, Lucien, 91
Goodman, Christopher, 184
Goody, Jack, 146
Gorboduc, 215
Gosson, Stephen, 202
Governing elite. *See* Class
Grafton, Anthony, 146–47, 185–86
Gramsci, Antonio, 37
Great Books, 21–22, 271, 281–84
Greenberg, Clement, 271

Greenblatt, Stephen, 29, 39, 67, 80–81, 92, 164, 173–74, 180, 182, 194, 255, 285
Greene, Gayle, 36
Greville, Sir Fulke, 85, 92, 148, 193, 208, 210, 216, 246–47, 248–50
Griffin, Miriam T., 225
Grindal, Edmund, 153
Gunpowder Plot, 97, 100, 101, 106

Halewood, William H., 160
Hall, Edward, 21
Hall, Joseph, 157, 168, 193, 209, 225, 241–42
Hall, Peter, 23
Hall, Stuart, 45, 206
Hallam, Henry, 278
Haller, William, 173
Harington, Sir John, 207–8
Hartley, John, 94
Hawkes, Terence, 8–9
Heinemann, Margot, 248
Henry VII, 141
Henry VIII, 96, 166, 182, 216
Henry of Navarre, 189, 192
Herbert, George, 147–48, 155–56, 162, 165, 169, 179, 193, 209
Herbert, Lord, 187
Heroes, 57, 191–92, 195, 201–2, 207, 211, 239–40
Highley, Christopher, 322n46
Hill, Christopher, 17, 167, 170, 173, 180
Hill, Joe, 268
Hirsch, E. D., Jr., 8, 255, 268, 271, 281–84, 290
Hitler, Adolf, 13
Hobbes, Thomas, 149, 175–78, 221
Hoby, Lady Margaret, 171

Hodgson, Godfrey, 270
Hofstadter, Richard, 263, 292
Holinshed, Raphael, 55, 103,
120
Homer, 190, 199, 202, 274
Homilies, 44, 110, 144, 154,
169
Homosexuality. *See* Sexualities
Hooker, Richard, 83, 149–50,
205, 236, 336n66
Horace, 190
Hotman, François, 85, 185
Howard, Jean, 132, 314n31
Howe, Irving, 292
Hughes, Ted, 280
Hulme, T. E., 274
Humanism: Christian, 112,
143–52, 204, 231–32, 235,
240–41; Puritan, 186–207;
"Renaissance," 92, 93, 145–
47, 184, 186–205, 224–25,
227. *See also* Essentialism;
Liberalism; Man;
Neoplatonism
Humanities. *See* Literary
criticism
Humphrey, Lawrence, 184,
190
Humphreys, Arthur, 19, 24
Hunt, William, 124
Hunter, G. K., 101, 112, 215
Hunter, Mark, 19
Huntingdon, Earl of, 91, 167,
171, 184
Hwang, David Henry, 52

Ideology, 10, 26, 31–35, 40–
42, 46–51, 74, 80–85, 92–
127, 139, 174, 177–82, 206,
207, 235, 243–46, 258, 260,
282, 285, 289, 299. *See also*
Cultural production;
Faultlines; Legitimation;
Plausibility

Imperialism. *See* British
Empire; United States of
America
Inchbald, Mrs. Elizabeth, 12
India, 257, 260–61
Indians (Native American),
255–59, 262, 263, 282, 285,
294, 296
Individuals. *See* Liberalism
Inheritance. *See* Property
Intellectuals, 14–15, 25–28,
90–94, 107–8, 151, 172,
175, 177, 179–80, 281,
286–90, 294–99. *See also*
Clergy; Cultural production;
Writers
Iraq, 4, 5, 271
Ireland, 41, 97, 106, 118, 120,
124–27, 141, 241, 258

Jaffer, Frances, 132
James VI and I (king of
Scotland and England), 55,
81, 96, 98–108, 141, 154,
166, 192, 231, 248, 250
James, Henry, 273
Jardine, Lisa, 75, 146–47,
185–86
Jefferson, Thomas, 11
Jews, 188, 268, 269, 291–93,
299–302
Jonson, Ben, 92, 210–11, 247,
248
Joyce, James, 236

Kahn, Coppélia, 314n31,
315n38, 322n41, 323n61
Kearney, Hugh, 145–46, 190
Keats, John, 274
Kennedy, John F., 270
Kenner, Hugh, 271–72
Kenya, 279
Kichina, Kamau, 279
Kierkegaard, Søren, 176

Kiernan, V. G., 82
King, John N., 182, 184
Kitzinger, Celia, 296
Knight, G. Wilson, 6, 25, 56–57
Knights, L. C., 57
Knollys, Sir Francis, 91
Kott, Jan, 23, 110–12
Kristeva, Julia, 58
Kyd, Thomas, 20, 215, 217, 223, 231

Lamming, George, 258–61, 280
Languet, Hubert, 85, 86, 184–85
Latimer, Hugh, 158, 171
Laud, John, 154, 209, 220
Lawne, William, 219, 221, 228–29, 233, 245–46
Lawrence, W. W., 74
Leakey, Richard, 178
Leavis, F. R., 75, 279
Legitimation, 6–7, 9–10, 15, 22, 32–35, 63–65, 95–102, 110, 113–27, 129–30, 132, 139–41, 150, 173, 220–21, 238–39, 244–46, 266, 281–83. *See also* Ideology; Order and Disorder; State, the
Leicester, Earl of, 88, 91, 120, 153, 184–85
Leisure class. *See* Class; Gentry
Lentricchia, Frank, 274
Lenz, Carolyn Ruth Swift, 36
Lessing, Doris, 257
Levin, Richard, 126
Levine, Lawrence W., 7, 264–65
Lévi-Strauss, Claude, 146, 206
Liberalism, 13–17, 26, 107–8, 111–12, 284, 293–94, 296, 299–301. *See also* Essentialism; Man
Lincoln, Abraham, 12–13

Lippmann, Walter, 271
Literary criticism, 7–8, 16, 21–22, 34, 36, 47, 49–51, 56–63, 74–75, 79, 104–8, 113, 131, 142–52, 159, 182, 205–13, 254, 273–79, 281, 285–99. *See also* Cultural materialism; Feminism; New Historicism; Psychoanalysis
Literature. *See* Literary criticism
Literature Teaching Politics, 150, 306n44
Locke, John, 149
London, Herbert, 291
London Review of Books, 8–9, 16
Longhurst, Derek, 265
Loomba, Ania, 31, 260–61
Lorentz, Konrad, 23
Lovejoy, A. O., 149
Lower classes. *See* Class
Lucian, 190, 201
Lucretius, 153
Luther, Martin, 143, 151, 155, 157, 158, 164–66, 179, 186, 226
Lyotard, Jean-François, 285–86

MacArthur, Douglas, 40
MacCaffrey, Wallace T., 83, 91
MacCannell, Dean, 255
McCarthy, Joseph, 13
McDiarmid, Ian, 301
Macdonald, Dwight, 275
Macherey, Pierre, 21, 74
Machiavelli, Niccolò, 18, 61, 153, 191, 239, 246
McLaverty, Jim, 319n18
McLuskie, Kathleen, 36–37
Macready, William Charles, 264
Mahood, Molly M., 314n28
Man, 61, 78–9, 111, 143, 178, 191–92, 202, 204–6, 224–25, 259–66, 279–81,

Man (*continued*), 286–88, 291, 294, 297, 300–301. *See also* Essentialism; Liberalism; U.S. Man
Mankiewicz, Joseph L., 13–14
Manliness. *See* Masculinity
Mann, Thomas, 277
Mann, Tom, 12
Marder, Louis, 272
Markoe, Peter, 262
Marlowe, Christopher, 80, 217, 220, 285; *Dr. Faustus*, 214, 230–37; *Tamburlaine*, 237–46
Marowitz, Charles, 22–23
Marriage, 42–47, 52–54, 71–74, 136–41
Marshall, John, 259
Marston, John, 225
Martial, 190, 201
Martyr, Peter, 153
Martz, Louis L., 147
Marx, Karl, and Marxism, 35, 38–39, 50, 164, 178, 180
Masculinity, 45, 47, 68–73, 127–42, 237–38, 273–79, 295, 322n50. *See also* Effeminacy
Mason, John, 285
Masque, 83–84, 92, 182, 208
Masterless men, 42, 124–25, 242–43, 259
Melville, Herman, 274
Mew, Charlotte, 296
Middleton, Thomas, 22, 249
Mildmay, Sir Walter, 91, 184
Miller, David A., 249
Miller, J. Hillis, 7, 39
Miller, Jonathan, 23
Mills, C. Wright, 182
Milton, John, 144, 192–94, 204, 209–10, 274, 282
Miola, Robert, 24
Miscegenation, 139–41

Misfortunes of Arthur, The, 215
Mississippi Burning, 280
Montaigne, Michel de, 61
Montrose, Louis A., 39, 66–67, 69, 84, 85, 149
More, Sir Thomas, 146
Morgan, John, 167
Morgann, Maurice, 263
Mornay, Philippe du Plessis, 61, 85, 185, 188, 191, 192, 334–35n42
Muir, Kenneth, 105, 106, 145

Nashe, Thomas, 153
National Endowment for the Humanities, 10
Native Americans. *See* Indians
Neely, Carol Thomas, 35–36, 38
Nelson, T. G. A., 208
Neoplatonism, 152, 191, 194, 224
New historicism, 7, 15, 19, 35, 39–42, 49–50, 80–82, 151, 177, 284–85, 287, 288, 290, 293, 309n23
New right, 178, 281–86. *See also* Social Darwinism
Newton, Thomas, 215
Nez Percés, 258–59
Nicholls, Peter, 39
Norbrook, David, 246, 316n51, 318n1
Nuttall, A. D., 314n27

Ocland, Christopher, 187
O'Day, Rosemary, 171–72
Ohmann, Richard, 33
Olivier, Sir Laurence, 300
Oppression. *See* Tyranny; War
Order and disorder, 5–7, 9, 23, 26, 32–35, 39–43, 45, 61, 63–65, 81–88, 95–101,

106–8, 110–31, 142, 145–49, 152–54, 164–80, 206, 215–28, 220–21, 224, 230, 235, 238–51, 259, 264, 282–83, 298, 300–301. *See also* Dissidence; Legitimation; State, the; Tyranny; War
Orgel, Stephen, 33, 66, 73, 135
Orwell, George, 257
Ovid, 190–91, 200, 204
Oxford, Earl of, 89

Pagans, 187–92, 198–207, 215–18, 228–30. *See also* Atheism
Painter, William, 6
Palmer, A. Mitchell, 268
Partridge, Eric, 278
Patronage, 84, 120, 168, 182, 184, 250–51
Patterson, Annabel, 17, 248
Paul, Henry, 100
Pemble, William, 169
Pembroke, Countess of, 171, 184, 215
Penry, John, 167
Perkins, William, 44, 150, 152, 153, 159, 161, 163, 191, 200, 203, 205, 229, 233
Petrarch, 69, 186, 187
Piers Plowman, 186
Pinter, Harold, 280
Plague, 186, 241–43, 246–47
Plato, 188, 189, 198, 201, 204, 269, 277, 284
Plausibility, 29–33, 37–38, 41–42, 47, 50–51, 53, 299
Pléiade, the, 198
Plutarch, 19, 21
Podhoretz, Norman, 292
Pomponazzi, Pietro, 153
Ponet, John, 83

Pope, Alexander, 52
Porter, Carolyn, 39, 42
Poststructuralism, 58–61, 63, 65–66, 285
Poulantzas, Nicos, 74, 82, 90–91
Predestination. *See* Election and reprobation
Prisca theologia, 188–89
Property, 43, 47, 103, 129–30, 139–41, 255–56, 258–60, 294
Protestantism, 43–44, 62, 84, 89, 91, 101, 143–80, 184–205, 216–21, 223–37, 240–42, 324n6. *See also* Calvin and Calvinism; Election and reprobation; Providence; Puritans
Providence, 99, 189, 217, 221–30, 240–44, 251, 256
Psalms, 165–66, 199, 203
Psychoanalysis, 70–71, 127–28, 315n38, 322n41. *See also* Barber, C. L.; Freud, Sigmund; Kahn, Coppélia
Puritans, 61, 143–44, 153–54, 167, 170–75, 180, 184, 186–207, 216, 262. *See also* Calvin and Calvinism; Protestantism
Puttenham, George, 198, 201, 247, 249–50

Quiller-Couch, Sir Arthur, 211

Race and racism, 30–31, 34, 50, 76, 139–41, 178, 256–60, 263, 267–69, 279–84, 291–92, 298, 300–302, 310n31. *See also* Ethnic minorities
Rackin, Phyllis, 130, 322n40
Rainolds, John, 190

Raitiere, Martin N., 212
Raleigh, Sir Walter, 92, 94
Raphael, 252
Reagan, Ronald, 16, 267, 281, 305n32
Reed, John, 268
Reformation. *See* Protestantism
Renaissance. *See* Humanism, "Renaissance"
Ribner, Irving, 106
Rich, Adrienne, 296
Richards, I. A., 271
Richardson, Samuel, 206
Ridley, M. R., 75
Riggs, Marlon T., 296
Robinson, Lillian S., 292
Rogers, Richard, 156, 159
Rogin, Michael, 16, 259
Roman Catholics. *See* Catholicism, Roman
Rose, Jacqueline, 63
Royal Ordnance, plc, 2–7, 10, 12, 27
Rymer, Thomas, 76

Sacco, Nicola, 268, 298
Saint Bartholomew's Day Massacre, 97
Sanders, Wilbur, 111–12
Sannazaro, Jacopo, 334n37
Sargant, William, 279
Sartre, Jean-Paul, 259, 280
Scaliger, Julius Caesar, 198
Schwartz, Delmore, 292
Scotland, 100–102, 118, 124, 192
Scruton, Roger, 106
Sedgwick, Eve Kosofsky, 134, 276–77
Seldes, Gilbert, 274
Seneca, 183, 214–17, 222–25, 227, 230, 239
Sexualities, 24, 35, 38, 47, 48, 51, 66–73, 127–36, 138–42,
249, 252–53, 275–78, 282, 284, 291, 294–98, 307n55, 310n31, 322n47, 348n89
Shakespeare, idea of, 9, 11, 15, 16, 21–24, 27–28, 149, 261–69, 272, 274, 277–78, 282; *Coriolanus*, 13, 17, 136; *Cymbeline*, 33; *Hamlet*, 22–24, 60, 65, 222–30, 244, 245, 249–51, 265; *1 Henry IV*, 168, 277; *2 Henry IV*, 119, 123, 131–32, 277; *Henry V*, 40–41, 97, 109–42, 237–38, 277; *1 Henry VI*, 20, 140–41; *2 Henry VI*, 20, 21; *3 Henry VI*, 20, 60; *Henry VIII*, 6, 10; *Julius Caesar*, 10–28, 44, 284; *King John*, 130; *King Lear*, 22, 33, 36, 42, 46, 112, 208, 217, 241–42, 244; *Macbeth*, 33, 40, 44, 53–57, 63–65, 77–78, 95–108, 145, 150, 233, 277; *Measure for Measure*, 22, 24, 33, 36, 46, 74–76; *Merchant of Venice*, 22, 24, 44, 46, 53, 58, 292, 299–302; *Midsummer Night's Dream*, 67–68, 208; *Othello*, 29–35, 38, 42, 44–47, 50–54, 63, 75–77, 79; *Richard II*, 97, 111, 131, 246–47; *Richard III*, 20, 55, 131, 243–44; *Romeo and Juliet*, 46, 131; *Sonnets*, 58–59, 261, 278; *Taming of the Shrew, The*, 23, 24, 26, 46; *Tempest, The*, 33, 46, 252, 258–59, 267, 280; *Troilus and Cressida*, 54, 135; *Twelfth Night*, 53, 58, 66–74
Shelley, Percy Bysshe, 211
Shepherd, Simon, 61, 240, 313n9

She's Working Her Way through College, 266–67
Sibbes, Richard, 155
Sidney, Sir Henry, 88–89, 148
Sidney, Sir Philip, 6, 7, 43, 80–94, 143, 148, 170, 172, 184–85, 191, 193, 228, 250; *Arcadia*, 85–94, 183, 188–89, 192, 208–9, 218; *Defence of Poetry*, 87, 181, 183, 187, 192, 197–210, 215; reputation of, 143, 206–12
Simpson, David, 289
Slack, Paul, 242
Slavery, 12, 260, 282
Smith, Henry, 44, 224
Smith, Sir John, 117–18
Smith, Sir Thomas, 83
Snow, Edward A., 76
Social control. *See* Order and disorder; Tyranny
Social Darwinism, 140, 177–78, 257, 280. *See also* New right
Spencer, Theodore, 145, 148
Spenser, Edmund, 193–97, 209, 248, 258; *Faerie Queene*, 84, 92, 101, 114, 194–97, 206, 207, 213, 230; on Ireland, 126, 135, 141
Stalin, Joseph, 182
Stallybrass, Peter, 31, 77
Starkey, Thomas, 187
State, the, 33–35, 40–42, 81–92, 95–108, 113–16, 120, 128, 130, 136, 139–41, 164–86, 228, 243–51, 259–60. *See also* Legitimation; Order and disorder
Stevens, Wallace, 274
Stiles, James, 184
Stoicism, 215, 222–26, 229–30
Stone, Lawrence, 44, 168, 189

Street, Brian, 146
Strong, Roy, 86
Stuart, Mary, 55, 96, 101, 102
Stubbe, John, 80, 84, 94
Stubbes, Philip, 216, 232
Studley, John, 215
Subculture, 37–38, 42, 175, 286–87, 290–99, 301. *See also* Ethnic minorities
Subjectivity, 9, 32, 35–38, 45, 56–66, 112–13, 154–71, 177–80, 226–27, 297–99
Subversion. *See* Dissidence
Sumner, Colin, 32
Szondi, Peter, 59

Talbert, Ernest William, 83, 85
Tancred and Gismund, 215
Tasso, Torquato, 191, 195
Taylor, Gary, 129, 136, 137
Tennenhouse, Leonard, 94
Tennyson, Alfred, 274, 278
Terence, 201
Thatcher, Margaret, 4, 16, 286, 295
Theater, 9–11, 13–17, 20–21, 23, 27, 59–60, 105, 111, 113, 129, 172, 214–16, 221–22, 237, 241, 246, 248, 250–51, 264–65, 300–302. *See also* Audiences
Thirty-nine Articles, 143–44, 149, 230
Thomas, Keith, 49, 146
Thorndike, Ashley, 262, 268–69
Tillyard, E. M. W., 23, 75, 109–10, 112
Tragedy, 46, 62, 106–8, 183, 192, 198, 214–51
Transgression. *See* Dissidence
Trilling, Lionel, 269, 292
Truman, Harry S, and Truman Doctrine, 40, 270, 271

Turks, 31, 34–35, 240
Turner, Frederick Jackson, 258, 263, 270, 273
Twain, Mark, 263
Tyndale, William, 159, 163, 165, 169–70, 188, 232, 234
Tyranny, 10, 11, 17–22, 86–87, 97–103, 143, 167–69, 178–80, 183, 215, 230, 238–39, 243–51. *See also* Absolutism; Order and disorder

United States of America, 4–5, 7–8, 13–16, 253, 149–51, 213, 254–85, 289–94
U.S. Man, 256, 259–85, 290–94, 297

Vanzetti, Bartolomeo, 268
Victoria, Queen, 252
Vidal, Gore, 281
Vietnam, 281, 285
Virgil, 181, 190, 198, 201, 208
Volanakis, Minos, 14

Wagner, Richard, 285
Wales, 118, 124–25, 148, 322n46
Walker, D. P., 188
Walsingham, Sir Francis, 91
Walzer, Michael, 159, 174, 180
War, 1–7, 10, 13, 40–41, 45, 114–20, 122, 130, 133–36, 237–39, 241, 243–44, 260, 270–71, 285, 303n4. *See also* Indians; Vietnam; World War II
Ward, Samuel, 160
Wars of the Roses, 20, 23
Warwick, Earl of, 5, 91, 153
Washington, George, 11

Wayne, Don E., 7, 39, 49, 292–93
Webster, John, 60, 70, 208–9, 217–18
Weiner, Andrew, 203
Welles, Orson, 13
Wesker, Arnold, 22, 24, 300
Wheeler, Richard P., 75
White, Edward Stuart, 256
Whitgift, John, 117, 154, 166
Wilcox, Lance, 139
Williams, Raymond, 9, 24, 41, 48, 49, 250, 294
Williams, William Carlos, 256, 273, 347n76
Willis, Nathaniel, 273
Wilson, F. P., 242
Wilson, Richard, 17
Wilson, Thomas, 190–91
Winstanley, Gerrard, 44, 177–80
Wiseman, Jane, 97, 99
Witches, 97, 100, 105, 138, 145
Wobblies, 268
Womack, Peter, 245
Women, 24, 33, 42–47, 50–51, 52–54, 66–77, 127–42, 237–38, 260, 261, 272–75, 291, 294, 298. *See also* Feminism
Wood, James, 8–9
Woodbridge, Linda, 53, 58, 69
Woodes, Nathaniel, 235–36
Wordsworth, William, 212
World War II, 110, 270
Wright, Louis B., 264, 266, 269–70, 272, 284
Wright, Richard, 261, 298
Wrightson, Keith, 176
Writers, 93–94, 172, 185–86, 246–51. *See also* Cultural production; Intellectuals; Humanism, Puritan
Wyatt, Sir Thomas, 174

Yaffe, James, 292
Yates, Frances, 86
Yeats, William Butler, 211

Zagorin, Perez, 91
Zhdanov, Andrei, 182